Scottish Presbyterian Worship

Scottish Presbyterian Worship

Proposals for Organic Change,
1843 to the Present Day

Bryan D. Spinks

Bishop F. Percy Goddard Professor of Liturgical Studies
and Pastoral Theology, Yale Institute of Sacred Music
and Yale Divinity School

SAINT ANDREW PRESS
Edinburgh

First published in 2020 by
SAINT ANDREW PRESS
121 George Street
Edinburgh EH2 4YN

ISBN 978 1 8008 3000 4

British Library Cataloguing in Publication Data

A catalogue record for this book is available from the British Library.

Typeset by Regent Typesetting Ltd

Printed and bound in the United Kingdom by
CPI Group (UK) Ltd

To
the Revd Dr Douglas Galbraith
and in memory of the Revd Tom Davidson Kelly,
my fellow Presbyters in the One Holy Catholic and
Apostolic Church
who contributed so much to this work.

Opponent and overseers of change;
from top right
James Veitch (see Introduction and Chapter 2)
Oswald Milligan (see Chapter 8)
Charles Robertson (see Chapter 10)
Main picture: High cross at Iona Abbey

Contents

Preface

On various occasions over the last five years I have been asked: 'Why should a priest of the Church of England who hails from East Anglia, and who now teaches liturgy at an American university, choose to write a book on Scottish Presbyterian worship?'

I am indebted to Scotland for my present family name. Until the birth of my grandfather, George Edward Spinks, the family surname was Spink. It is an Anglo-Saxon surname (fink/finch/small bird) and in the 1800s my ancestors were living in Aylsham, Norfolk. My great grandparents moved from East Anglia to Inverness, Scotland, and lived there for about two years before returning south to Wethersfield, Essex. My grandfather was born in Inverness in 1896, and the registrar added an 's' to his surname, and so my branch of the family became Spinks. Other than that, I can claim no Scottish family ancestry. It is my theological autobiography, though, that explains the connection.

During my undergraduate and initial graduate studies at Durham University, I read Karl Barth on Romans, and then much of his *Church Dogmatics*. From there I ventured into Calvin's *Institutes*. These brought me back from the extreme liberalism that I had embraced in rebellion against what I regarded as the intolerant Anglo-Catholicism of some of my fellow students at St Chad's College, Durham. A passion for liturgical study, inculcated and encouraged by A. H. Couratin, meshed with interest in Neo-Orthodoxy, and so my initial extended postgraduate research for the Durham University BD (at Cambridge, Oxford and Durham the BD ranked above PhD, but has been discontinued at Oxford and Durham), published as two books, was on English Reformed liturgy. This work entailed looking at the Genevan *Form of Prayers*, John Knox's liturgy for Berwick, and the Westminster *Directory*. In subsequent published work I have covered Scottish sacramental theology and liturgy from the sixteenth to the eighteenth centuries, and some aspects of nineteenth-century Scottish worship. I was also co-editor of the *Scottish Journal of Theology*, 1998–2015. My answer to the question is, therefore, 'Why not?'

In 1995–6, the Church Service Society of the Church of Scotland did me the honour of electing me as vice-president and then president of the Society – the first non-Presbyterian and the only Anglican until now to be elected to this post. 2015 was the 150th anniversary of the Society, and the Council once more honoured me with an invitation to deliver the lecture at New College, Edinburgh. As I worked on the lecture, 'The Nineteenth Century Liturgical Revival: Evolution and Devolution of Worship in the Kirk' (*The Record* 50 (2015), pp. 2–22), I realised that although aspects of nineteenth-century Scottish Presbyterian worship had been the subject of PhD theses, the nineteenth century to the present had hitherto been covered only in short summarising essays. In this book I hope to have told a deeper narrative.

As someone living outside Scotland and having no experiential knowledge of any of the Presbyterian Churches, this book could not have been written without the constant help and support of many institutions and individuals. A generous grant from the Conant Fund of the Episcopal Church of the USA allowed me to spend several weeks in Scotland, and to have access to the libraries of Edinburgh and the archives in the basement of the Church of Scotland at 121 George Street. I was given access to the library and archives of the Church Service Society, spending many hours with the latter at Canongate Church offices, as well as to the collection of service books held by St Giles's Cathedral. My wife Care and I were welcomed to services at Iona Abbey, and in the Free Church of Scotland and High Church of the Church of Scotland, Stornoway, Isle of Lewis, where Care was given permission to take photographs during the services. I thank them for those permissions given back in 2015, and my thanks to Care for her support in this venture and for some of the photographs in this book. Librarians and archivists of the Church of Scotland and Free Church of Scotland have generously provided me with official reports and other crucial documents. I would like to express my thanks to my research assistants over five years – Isaac Johnson, Patrick Keyser, Rosemary Williams and Mark Florig, who have checked my quotations and helped make some sentences more intelligible, and to Jenny Smith for Bulletins and the photo of Communion at the London City Presbyterian Church. I am grateful to the Revd James Stewart for drawing my attention to the worship services of William Logie, and for providing me with his collection of service bulletins from the 1970s. My thanks to the Revd John Bell, the Revd John Philip Newell, the Revd Dr Wayne Pearce, the Revd Charles Robertson, the Revd Dr Scott McKenna and the Very Revd Iain Torrance for conversations and suggestions, and to Iain for contributing the Appendix on the Chapel Royal. The work would have been totally impossible without the generous and constant assistance given to me by the former secretary of the Church Service Society, the Revd Dr Douglas Galbraith, and the late Revd Tom Davidson Kelly. Omissions, errors and misinterpretations are entirely my own.

I would like to thank the Alcuin Club and Saint Andrew Press for undertaking to publish the results of the study.

Bryan D. Spinks
Feast of the St Mark the Evangelist 2020

Biographical Note

Bryan D. Spinks, DD, FRHistS, is Bishop F. Percy Goddard Professor of Liturgical Studies and Pastoral Theology at the Yale Institute of Sacred Music, Yale Divinity School and Berkeley Divinity School at Yale. A priest of the Church of England, and author and editor of over twenty books, his most recent publications are *Do This in Remembrance of Me: The Eucharist from the Early Church to the Present Day* (SCM Press, 2013) and *The Rise and Fall of the Incomparable Liturgy: The Book of Common Prayer 1559-1906* (SPCK, 2017). He co-edited with Teresa Berger *The Spirit in Worship – Worship in the Spirit* (Liturgical Press, 2009) and *Liturgy's Imagined Past/s: Methodologies and Material in the Writing of Liturgical History Today* (Liturgical Press, 2016). Professor Spinks has previously served as chaplain at Churchill College, Cambridge, as president of the Society for Oriental Liturgy, co-editor of the *Scottish Journal of Theology*, a member of and consultant to the Church of England Liturgical Commission, and is president emeritus of the Church Service Society of the Church of Scotland.

List of Photographs

Introduction

It is the 18th of May, in the year 1843. What stirs the pulse of old Scotland, usually so healthful and so steady? Not since the day when the last of her martyrs stood beside the gallows that frowned in the Grass-market, high above the mute and awesome crowd, bidding farewell, for the sake of Christ, to sun, moon, and stars, and all earthly delights – not since that day has her life-blood throbbed so vehemently. The morning dawns over the city of Edinburgh, calm, close, sultry. The huge masses of building, irregular and picturesque, that bestride the back of that ridge which terminates abruptly in the Castle-rock, loom gloomily and silently against the early summer sky. Old St. Giles still rears his coronet above them – he has looked down on many a strange scene; but the HEART OF MID-LOTHIAN is not there to-day.[1]

These words begin chapter 23 of a novel that was published anonymously in London in 1847 under the title *Passages in the Life of an English Heiress*. The author was a young Scottish woman, Lydia Miller, and it is the subtitle of the novel that reveals its true focus, *Recollections of Disruption Times in Scotland*. The book was written to explain the Disruption of 1843 and the creation of the Free Church of Scotland. At the May 1843 General Assembly, after the official formalities, over a third of the Church of Scotland ministers walked out and left the established Church in protest over issues of patronage and appointment of ministers. This was not the first split within the Church of Scotland.[2] The Cameronian Church or Reformed Presbyterian Church of Scotland was a late-seventeenth-century secession. The United Secession Church and the Relief Church were notable eighteenth-century breakaways that were to unite in 1847 to form the United Presbyterian Church. However, these earlier splits lacked the magnitude of the event of 1843. As Professor Stewart J. Brown rightly noted, 'The Disruption of the Church of Scotland was the most important event in the history of

---

1 Lydia Miller, *Passages in the Life of an English Heiress or, Recollections of Disruption Times in Scotland*, reprinted with Introduction by Elizabeth Sutherland, Inverness: Right Reason Printers and Publishers, 2010, p. 261.

2 See Henry R. Sefton, 'Our Christian Heritage: The Story of the Scottish Churches', in Scottish Church Society: *Sharing the Past, Shaping the Future*, Tweedbank: William T. Hogg, 2009, pp. 1–23.

nineteenth-century Scotland.'[3] Given the shock waves that the Disruption caused not only within the national Church, but also in Scottish civic life, it would be difficult to dissent from this judgement.[4]

Though neither as dramatic nor as divisive as the event of May 1843, but perhaps of equal importance for the life of the Scottish Presbyterian churches then and continuing still, was what James Bulloch called 'Changing Worship' and A. C. Cheyne more aptly termed 'the Liturgical Revolution'.[5] Liturgical Disruption might be an equally apposite phrase, for as the *Report of the Committee on the Proper Conduct of Public Worship and the Sacraments* to the General Assembly of the Church of Scotland 1890 put it, 'if worshippers of the past generation were to enter some of our churches, they would find little to remind them of the traditional forms with which they and their fathers were familiar.'[6] The words 'some of our churches' are important here. Parish conservatism and the freedom of ministers meant that worship in many Scottish churches at the end of the nineteenth century was little changed from how it had been when the century began, and some were certain that there should be no change. In 1866, in the wake of what many felt were illegal innovations, Dr James Veitch, one of the ministers of St Cuthbert's, Edinburgh, published a statement against changes, citing Acts of 1690 (ratifying the Confession of Faith and settling Presbyterian Government), 1693 (settling the quiet and peace of the Church), and the Act of Union 1707, urging that the worship in place then was 'to continue to the people of this land in all succeeding generations'.[7] Veitch asserted that the Church of Scotland was 'not free to entertain any proposal for organic change'.[8] But some ministers and churches did entertain such proposals, and considerable changes did take place and have continued to do so, and hence the subtitle of this present work, *Proposals for Organic Change*. This study attempts to chart those 'organic changes' from the time around the Disruption and to trace this narrative of evolution and devolution through to the present.

---

3 Stewart J. Brown, 'The Ten Years' Conflict and the Disruption of 1843', in Stewart J. Brown and Michael Fry (eds), *Scotland in the Age of the Disruption*, Edinburgh: Edinburgh University Press, 1993, pp. 1–27, p. 2.

4 Iain Campbell, 'The Church in Scotland 1840–1940: An Overview', *Quodlibet Journal* 1 (1999) at www.quodlibet.net/articles/campbell-scotland.shtml, accessed 11.11.2015.

5 Andrew L. Drummond and James Bulloch, *The Church in Victorian Scotland 1843–1874*, Edinburgh: Saint Andrew Press, 1975, the title of chapter 7, p. 178; A. C. Cheyne, *The Transforming of the Kirk: Victorian Scotland's Religious Revolution*, Edinburgh: Saint Andrew Press, 1983, the title of chapter 4, p. 88.

6 'Report of the Committee on the proper Conduct of Public Worship and the Sacraments', in *Acts of the General Assembly of the Church of Scotland*, Edinburgh: Blackwood, 1890, pp. 989–1010, p. 1009.

7 James Veitch, *Statement Concerning Innovations as Now Attempted in the Church of Scotland*, Edinburgh: William Blackwood, 1866, p. 10. For the Act, see Joseph Chitty, *A Collection of Statutes of Practical Utility with Notes*, London: William Benning, 1829, Vol. 1 Part 2, p. 1069.

8 Veitch, *Statement Concerning Innovations*, p. 3.

It is perhaps providential that Veitch referred to changes in worship as 'organic', though apart from having a negative connotation, it is not obvious as to how he understood the term.[9] Fritz West has shown that the development of the so-called comparative liturgy method by the Roman Catholic lay liturgist, Anton Baumstark, took its inspiration from the comparative anatomy of Georges Cuvier and other nineteenth-century palaeontologists and biologists, as well as linguistics.[10] John Henry Newman wrote on the development of Christian doctrine, and in *The Descent of Man*, 1871, Charles Darwin had written that 'the formation of different languages and of distinct species and the proofs that both have been developed through a gradual process are curiously parallel.'[11] In his *Comparative Liturgy*, 1934, drawing on such parallels, Baumstark spoke of the laws of liturgical evolution. He posited two laws of liturgical development, the first of which he termed the 'Law of Organic Development'. He explained:

> ... ('Organic' and therefore 'Progressive'). In general, because the primitive elements are not immediately replaced by completely new ones, the newcomers at first take their place alongside the others. Before long they assume a more vigorous and resistant character, and when the tendency to abbreviation makes itself felt it is the more primitive elements which are the first to be affected; these disappear completely or leave only a few traces.[12]

Baumstark applied this to his observation that 'primitive' elements in the liturgy are joined by new elements and the latter act as a cuckoo in the nest, often eventually resulting in abbreviation or total replacement of earlier elements. The observation begged the question of whether the results were an improvement or retrograde. Some recent more conservative Roman Catholic writers have re-appropriated Baumstark's term, viewing the so-called Tridentine Mass in its 1962 form as a genuine 'organic development' of the Roman rite over against the 'genetically engineered' forms of Vatican II.[13] However, Baumstark himself felt that with the centralisation of the liturgy placed in the hands of the Pope at Trent, true organic development (local adaptation and variation – evolution!) ceased.[14] The medieval

---

9 The *Shorter Oxford English Dictionary* gives a range of meanings for 'organic': one from 1845 was in philology as 'belonging to the etymological structure of a word; not secondary or fortuitous', and another from 1850, 'Of pertaining to, or characterized by connection or co-ordination of parts in one whole; organized; systematic'. My thanks to Dr Gordon Jeanes for drawing my attention to this.

10 Fritz West, *The Comparative Liturgy of Anton Baumstark*, Bramcote: Alcuin/GROW Joint Liturgical Study 31, 1995.

11 John Henry Newman, *An Essay on the Development of Christian Doctrine*, London: James Toovey, 1845; Charles Darwin, *The Descent of Man*, London: Murray, 1871, p. 40.

12 West, *Comparative Liturgy* ET, p. 15.

13 For example, Alcuin Reid, *The Organic Development of the Liturgy*, Farnborough: St Michael's Abbey Press, 2004.

14 A. Baumstark, *On the Historical Development of the Liturgy*, trans. Fritz West, Collegeville, MN: Liturgical Press, 2011, pp. 230–43.

period – certainly in the West – could be claimed to exemplify organic development of the liturgy; as Susan Keefe remarked of the Carolingian baptismal rites, 'one can truly be amazed at the amount of liturgical diversity . . . diversity characterized public worship'.[15] Helen Gittos notes that it is precisely the degree to which medieval liturgy was diverse, informal and frequently revised and rewritten that makes it so valuable as historical evidence.[16] In the Western Catholic Church, this virtually came to an end with the Council of Trent.

'Organic' as an analogy for liturgical development is somewhat dated. More recently Nathan Mitchell has preferred to see liturgical development on analogy with the rhizome – a horizontal network of randomly connected roots, with maze-like, connective, crabgrass conditions.[17] Clare Johnson has suggested that changes in liturgy are better understood through the analogy of neuroplasticity than organic growth.[18] Just as the brain requires stimulus to continue growing and to ward off deterioration, so the liturgy needs to use its plasticity to interact with the outside stimuli of the real lives and cultures of those who celebrate it, if it is to continue to speak the Christian message.[19] In her view, 'Liturgico-plasticity provides an explanation of how the liturgy, as a complex divine–human ritual interaction, whereby faith in the paschal mystery is expressed and nourished, changed over time in relation to human cultural experience and expression.'[20] I appreciate the usefulness of these alternative analogies, but have preferred to stay with the older analogy of organic development (albeit not in quite the same manner as Baumstark had applied the term), since I believe that it is a more helpful lens for viewing the changes in Scottish Presbyterian worship from the time of the Disruption. Presbyterian ministers had, and continue to have, a certain autonomy regarding worship, and forms both 'evolve' and 'devolve' at a parish level. Evolution is a process of change, from a lower to a more complex state, or a gradual social, political and economic advance, and especially the development of a biological group, or phylogeny. Devolution, itself a nineteenth-century word in British politics, has had considerable recent currency in Scotland in the context of its political independence from Westminster.[21] The word can mean transfer

---

15 Susan A. Keefe, *Water and the Word: Baptism and the Education of the Clergy in the Carolingian Empire*, 2 vols, Notre Dame, IN: University of Notre Dame Press, 2002, vol. 1, p. 137.

16 Helen Gittos, 'Researching the History of Rites', in Helen Gittos and Sarah Hamilton (eds), *Understanding Medieval Liturgy: Essays in Interpretation*, Farnham: Ashgate Publishing, 2016, pp. 13–37, p. 14.

17 Nathan Mitchell, *Meeting Mystery: Liturgy, Worship, and Sacraments*, New York: Orbis, 2006, pp. 8 and 55.

18 Clare V. Johnson, 'From Organic Growth to Liturgico-Plasticity: Reconceptualizing the Process of Liturgical Reform', *Theological Studies* 76 (2015), pp. 87–111.

19 Johnson, 'From Organic Growth', p. 106.

20 Johnson, 'From Organic Growth', p. 108.

21 See Michael Keating, *European Devolution*, Oxford Handbooks Online, 2015, para. 23.1.

or delegation of power to a lower level, but it can mean descent, or even degeneration to a lower level, as well as in some contexts being almost synonymous with evolution. It would seem to me that these words, together with 'organic change', are helpful terms for looking at what Cheyne called a liturgical revolution in the Scottish Presbyterian Churches, and are also apropos churches that allow considerable freedom as to how ministers formulate public worship.

In modern evolutionary theory two basic elements are identified that give rise to mutation and change – internal and external. The internal changes seem triggered by hox genes, which have been described as being rather like a tool box and at times of drastic external change act as switches that can be triggered to make changes that allow a species to adapt and evolve.[22] At least as regards humans, more limited evolution has occurred through interbreeding. Recent studies have argued that non-African *homo Sapiens* is the result of cross-breeding with *homo Neanderthal*, giving Europeans between 2 per cent and 4 per cent of Neanderthal genomes.[23] The external circumstances that trigger evolution are not quite so easily pinpointed. Though there is evidence of asteroid impact, mass extinctions and major evolutionary changes seem to have been dictated mainly by climate change, high levels of hydrogen sulphide, either too much or too little oxygen and change in sea levels. All of these seem to be associated with oscillatory shifts in Earth's rotation axis, or polar wander.[24] As applied analogously to development or evolution of Scottish Presbyterian worship, this study will focus on the 'liturgical hox genes' and 'liturgical hybrids' that have resulted in changes. Internal shifts in biblical criticism and the understanding of the doctrine of the atonement also played their part. The external conditions that give rise to liturgical changes are also less easy to define and link, other than the general statement of changes in society and culture. At least for the nineteenth century, where this narrative begins, it seems closely related to Romanticism with its imagined pasts, especially the imagined medieval past, as well as urbanisation, industrialisation, better and wider education, changes in transportation and communication and scientific development, particularly Darwin and the theory of evolution.[25] This was of course not simply a Scottish Presbyterian phenomenon but a British, European and

---

22 Sean B. Carroll, *Endless Forms Most Beautiful*, New York: Norton & Company, 2005. I am acutely aware that evolutionary biologists disagree among themselves almost as much as liturgical scholars do.

23 Sriram Sankararaman et al., 'The genomic landscape of Neanderthal ancestry in present-day humans', *Nature* 507 (2014), pp. 354–7; Benjamin Vernot and Joshua M. Akey, 'Resurrecting Surviving Neandertal Lineages from Modern Human Genomes', *Science* 343 (2014), pp. 1017–21; Ewen Callaway, 'Neanderthals had outside effect on human biology', *Nature* 523 (2015) pp. 512–13.

24 Peter Ward and Joe Kirschvink, *A New History of Life*, New York: Bloomsbury Press, 2015.

25 Trevor Griffiths and Graeme Morton (eds), *A History of Everyday Life in Scotland, 1800 to 1900*, Edinburgh: Edinburgh University Press, 2011.

American one.[26] Just as the Royal Commission, which reported in 1906 on the liturgical turmoil and changes in the Church of England, stated that the law of public worship in the Church of England was too narrow for the religious life of that generation, so Dr Robert Lee of Greyfriars had noted as early as 1864 of the Church of Scotland, 'the National Church no longer satisfies the religious tastes and other demands of the population.'[27] This study will note the changes in society and culture that have and always will impact the worship of the churches, with the admission that it is not always possible to demonstrate a direct and obvious connection.

The main focus of Scottish Presbyterian worship was word-centred, not sacrament-centred, and in practice that is still the case. Part of the concern of the nineteenth-century liturgical revolution was to promote more regular celebrations of Holy Communion, and to have a fuller rite of baptism, as well as have responses and participation by the congregation. These two services will therefore also be the focus of this study, and with them, changing sacramental thought as expressed in selected doctrinal works, even though the communion service is, in some parishes, still only celebrated twice a year. Developments also took place in the design and furnishings of church buildings and in music, and these will also be touched upon where relevant.

The major focus will be the Church of Scotland. The majority of the Free Church of Scotland united with the United Presbyterian Church in 1900 to form the United Free Church. A small number of more conservative members of the Free Church of Scotland declined to enter the new Church and so a Free Church of Scotland continued to exist. The United Free Church and the Church of Scotland united in 1929 as the Church of Scotland, though a minority of the former felt unable to enter the union and continued under the name United Free Presbyterians. The Free Presbyterian Church of Scotland broke from the Free Church of Scotland in 1893, and in 2000 the Free Church of Scotland (Continuing) also broke from the Free Church. The Associated Presbyterian Church was formed in 1989, breaking from the Free Presbyterian Church. These smaller churches continue to be conservative towards their inherited traditions, and worship has tended to become frozen in time – the time of their breakaway. Where I have been able to discover or uncover information, the worship of these groups will be discussed, as well as any writings they have produced on worship and the sacraments.

---

26 Gerald Parsons (ed.), *Religion in Victorian Britain, vol. 1: Traditions*, Manchester: Manchester University Press, 1988, in association with the Open University, New York, 1988.

27 Robert Lee, *The Reform of the Church of Scotland in Worship, Government and Doctrine, Part 1: Worship*, Edinburgh: Edmonston & Douglas, 1864, p. 39. See also http://anglicanhistory.org/pwra/rced11.html, accessed 29.09.2015; Bryan D. Spinks, 'The Prayer Book in the Nineteenth Century', in Stephen Platten and Christopher Woods (eds), *Comfortable Words: Polity, Piety and the Book of Common Prayer*, London: SCM Press, 2012, pp. 98–120.

Inherited Patterns of Public Prayer and the 'Specimens of the Various Services of Presbyterian Worship'

In 1864, both the Church of Scotland and the Free Church of Scotland General Assemblies received reports on 'Innovations in Worship'. Both Churches grounded Scottish Presbyterian worship in the Westminster *Directory* of 1644, noting the General Assembly Act of 1705 recommending that all ministers observe the *Directory*, and in 1707 an Act was passed against innovations in worship.[1] The Church of Scotland report also noted that with the *Directory*, free prayer, which had formerly been permitted and encouraged, was made imperative, though the contents and scope were set forth in the *Directory*.[2] In addition, the Church of Scotland report gave a summary of what, in the light of questions to the presbyteries, was described as the 'uniformity in the mode of administering public worship'.[3] It noted that in many instances ministers exercised the discretion the *Directory* permitted on the precise sequence of the elements of worship. It reported:

> Slight changes in the order observed are to be found even in the same neighbourhood, and occasionally the service is shortened by the omission of one or more parts. But in general, almost universally, the order is as follows: Praise, Prayer, Reading of Scripture; Praise, Prayer, Lecture or Sermon; Prayer, Praise, Benediction.
>
> There is the same general uniformity in the order of service when the sacrament of the Lord's Supper is dispensed. After the action sermon, and prayer and praise, the Scriptural authority for administering the ordinance is exhibited, the tables are fenced, prayer is offered up before distributing the elements, and the communicants are successively addressed. At the

---

1 Free Church of Scotland, *Report of the Committee Appointed to Consider Generally the Legislation of the Church on the Subject of Innovations in Worship*, Edinburgh: Thomas Constable, 1864, pp. 7–8.

2 Church of Scotland, *Report of Committee Anent Innovations in Public Worship*, Edinburgh: William Blackwood, 1864, p. 9.

3 Church of Scotland, *Report of Committee*, p. 16

close praise is offered up, the presiding minister gives a concluding exhortation, and that is followed by prayer and praise, and the benediction.[4]

This reported variation within a uniformity may be illustrated from a number of nineteenth-century contemporary accounts of worship.

Contemporary accounts of traditional worship patterns

The immediate result of the Disruption of 1843 was that the ministers who had left the established Church had to leave their manse and church building, and make alternative arrangements for worship for their congregations. Some had to worship in the open air. The Revd R. Craig of Rothesay was able to take services in the Gaelic church and for 4 June 1843 *The Annals of the Disruption* record the following:

> A dense multitude crowds around the door of the Gaelic Church, vainly expecting admittance to what was already a packed house. The lobbies, the passages, the pulpit stairs, all are filled. Every inch of standing room is occupied. His former beadle, John Macdonald, is waiting to attend him *as usual*. The greater number of his attached elders surround him as *usual*. His congregation, too, is there *much as usual*. With great difficulty, from the density of the crowd, the pulpit is reached. After praise, prayer, and the reading of the Word, in all which exercises his own spirit was deeply moved, he discoursed with remarkable unction and power to the joy and edification of his people, from Psalm cxxvi.3: 'The Lord hath done great things for us, whereof we are glad.' This was a day never to be forgotten.[5]

The Disruption was *not* over forms of worship. Worship was *as usual*.

In the *Life and Letters of John Cairns*, Alexander Macewen described a similar Sabbath Morning service of the Church of Scotland at Berwick *c.*1850:

> As the town clock struck eleven, the beadle bustled up the steep pulpit stair with Bible and Psalm Book tucked under his arm, adjusted these with care on velvet cushions and then stood waiting at the foot of the stair. There was a hush – as seemly preparation for worship as any voluntary – amidst which the creaking of the minister's boots was heard, and all eyes were fixed on his solemn and stately approach, as he slowly mounted the stair and at once hid his face in his black-gloved hand. When he arose to give out the opening psalm, he showed a majestic presence . . . The psalm ended, there came the 'long prayer', so called to distinguish

---

4 Church of Scotland, *Report of Committee*, p. 16.
5 Thomas Brown, *Annals of the Disruption; with extracts from the Narratives of Ministers who left the Scottish Establishment in 1843*, Edinburgh: McNiven & Wallace, 1893, pp. 120–1; my italics.

it from the 'short prayer' which followed the sermon . . . it contained no argument, moving steadily and quietly along familiar lines of adoration, thanksgiving, confession, humiliation and supplication. Scriptural it was, not through quotation but by embodiment of Scripture truth; . . . Then came the reading of Scripture and another psalm as prelude to the sermon, which would last perhaps fifty minutes.[6]

Macewen omits to mention that a psalm followed the short prayer as a conclusion to the service with a Benediction. Similar patterns to this order of worship, which in the nineteenth century was regarded as traditional in Presbyterian Scotland, are attested to and supplemented by other contemporary or near-contemporary nineteenth-century writers. Elizabeth Grant described the same pattern of the worship service in the Highlands in 1809.[7] Anne Mary MacLeod attests the same in *Memories of the Manse*:

The perfect hush that pervades a Scottish congregation before service begins – the grave, expectant expression on every face – the reverend voice of the minister as he says, 'Let us begin the public worship of God by singing his praise,' – have been often remarked by strangers. . . . [Mr. Douglas] would have liked, years before, to do away with the habit of *lining* the psalms, . . . But the old people . . . never dreamed of finding the psalms for themselves, but depended solely on Alan MacDonald reading each line before he sang it . . . Lining was to them a regular part of the service, and singing without that preliminary was to be classed with reading sermons, kneeling at prayer, and other abominations of their arch enemies – popery and prelacy . . . At prayer, standing was, of course, the custom; . . . The prayers of Mr. Douglas were full of rugged eloquence and abounded in apt and forcible figures. The greatness and holiness of God, the insignificance and sinfulness of man, were set forth in strong contrast . . . As far as attention was concerned, Mr. Douglas's congregation was entirely satisfactory. When the minister announced the text, every one found it and followed the reading. Throughout the sermon a passage was never quoted or referred to without book, chapter and verse being named by the minister and instantly found by the people.[8]

It was the sermon text and content that seem to have been the main interest of laymen William Lamb and John Sturrock.[9] Robert Louis Stevenson

6 Alexander R. Macewen, *Life and Letters of John Cairns DD, LLD*, London: Hodder & Stoughton, 1895, pp. 321–2.

7 J. G. Fyfe (ed.) with J. D. Mackie, *Scottish Diaries and Memoirs 1746–1843*, Stirling: Eneas Mackay, 1942, pp. 492–4.

8 Anne Breadalbane (Anne Mary MacLeod), *Memories of the Manse*, Troy, NY: Nims, 1885, pp. 45–50.

9 Kirkwood Hewat, *M'Cheyne From the Pew: Being Extracts from the Diary of William Lamb*, Stirling: Drummond's Tract Depot (nd), pp. 41, 52, 53; Christopher A. Whatley (ed.), *The Diary of John Sturrock, Millwright, Dundee 1864–65*, East Linton: Tuckwell Press, 1996, pp. 90, 92, 96.

remarked of a service in 1883, that there was 'fifty minutes of solid sermon'.[10]

Communion was celebrated in most places only twice a year.[11] *The Record of the Free Church of Scotland* provides an interesting account of an annual Highlands Communion at Snizort, Skye in 1863, which again was regarded as preserving the older traditional Scottish communion service:

> Thursday, the 16th July, was the day specially set apart for prayer and humiliation before God. Four ministers had arrived at the manse to discharge the duties of the day; . . . Long before the usual hour of worship the people had assembled to ask a blessing on the word and ordinances. The public services of this day were held in the church, and were conducted in Gaelic and English. The Rev. Roderick M'Leod, who spoke in Gaelic, commenced in the usual way, by giving out the first seven verses of the fifty-first psalm, offering up prayer, and reading with a short comment on the fourteenth chapter of Jeremiah. The English services were then conducted by the Rev. Mr. Gualter, in the usual form of praise, prayer, and in the preaching of the word. Immediately following the English the Rev. Mr. Kippen ascended the pulpit, and conducted a similar form of service in Gaelic. Thus ended the public services, which lasted altogether about four hours and a half . . . But while the congregation at Snizort was engaged in these public devotions, two other congregations, in opposite districts of the parish, were also assembled for the same purpose . . . The special service of Friday forms a distinguishing feature of a Highland communion, and is therefore entirely conducted in Gaelic. This service is called 'a fellowship meeting', and is convened with the view of assisting intending communicants in the great duties of self-examination and preparation for the Lord's table. . . . The minister, Mr. Roderick M'Leod, presided, and opened the meeting with praise, prayer, and a short exposition; . . . He then called in turn upon six or eight elders, men of approved Christian character, to speak on the question; . . . On Saturday, Sabbath, and Monday, the numbers increased to such an extent that, as the church could not contain them, the Gaelic congregation had to be separated from the English, the former worshipping in the fields, the latter in the church. . . . These preliminary services were mainly intended to prepare the hearts of the people for the day of high communion; . . . The tent in which the minister stood was pitched at the foot of a sloping hill, gradually rising in an undulating form till it terminated in a heathery knoll. On a smooth sward, in front of the tent, the table, covered with clean white linen, was prepared. The whole face of the little hill was clothed with people . . . The Rev. Roderick Macleod preached to this large and interesting congregation from the appropriate words in Ps. xl. 6–8 . . . At the conclusion of

---

10 Sidney Colvin (ed.), *Letters and Miscellanies of Robert Louis Stevenson*, New York: Charles Scribner & Sons, 1900, p. 65.

11 Church of Scotland, *Report of Committee*, p. 17.

the service the English congregation left the church and joined the Gaelic congregation in the fields. Just as they approached, the invitation to come forward to the first Gaelic communion-table was being issued . . . The second table was served in English; and after this three other tables were administered in Gaelic. The whole services, which lasted about seven hours and a half, were brought to a close by an earnest and impressive address by the Rev. Dr. Mackay. . . . On Monday the attendance both in the Gaelic and English was quite as large as on the preceding Sabbath.[12]

Dr Norman Macleod gave a very similar description of a Church of Scotland communion celebration of the mid-century in the Highlands:

The previous Friday had been, as usual, set apart for a day of fasting and prayer. Then the officiating clergy preached specially upon the Communion, and on the character required in those who intended to partake of it; and young persons, after instruction and examination, were for the first time formally admitted (as at confirmation in the Episcopal Church) into full membership . . .

The service in the church to-day was in English, and a wooden pulpit, or 'tent', as it is called, (I remember when it was made of boat sails,) was, according to custom, erected near the old arch in the churchyard, where service was conducted in Gaelic.

. . . The Communion service of the Church of Scotland is a very simple one, and may be briefly described. It is celebrated in the church, of course, after the service and prayers are ended. In most cases a long, narrow table, like a bench, covered with white cloth, occupies the whole length of the church, and the communicants are seated on each side of it. . . . The presiding minister, after reading an account of the institution from the Gospels and Epistles, and giving a few words of suitable instruction, offers up what is called the consecration prayer, thus setting apart the bread and wine before him as symbols of the body and blood of Jesus. After this he takes the bread, and, breaking it, gives it to the communicants near him, saying 'This is my body broken for you, eat ye all of it'. He afterwards hands to them the cup, saying, 'This cup is the new testament in my blood, shed for the remission of the sins of many, drink ye all of it; for as oft as ye eat this bread and drink this cup, ye do show forth the Lord's death until He come again.' The bread and wine are then passed from the communicants to each other, assisted by the elders who are in attendance. In solemn silence the Lord is remembered, and by every true communicant is received as the living bread, the life of their souls, even as they receive into their bodies the bread and wine. During the silence of communion every head is bowed down, and many an eye and heart are filled, as the thoughts of Jesus at such a time mingle with those departed ones, with whom they enjoy, in and through Him, the communion of

12 *The Record of the Free Church of Scotland*, 1 October 1863, pp. 350–3.

saints. Then follows an exhortation by the minister to faith and love and renewed obedience; and then the 103d Psalm is generally sung, and while singing it the worshippers retire from the table, which is soon filled with other communicants; and this is repeated several times, until the whole service is ended with prayer and praise.[13]

Macleod explained that because of the unreliability of the weather, Communion in the Highlands was once a year in the summer. According to Kirkwood Hewat, the practice of Robert Murray M'Cheyne, minister of St Peter's Church Dundee (1838–43), was to have two preparatory services on the Thursday, one on the Friday, and one on the Saturday before the Communion Sabbath, and a thanksgiving service on the Monday.[14] Hewat noted:

In the celebration of the ordinance there were many table services, as only a comparatively small number could come forward at the same time, and the membership was large. At each table service fresh devotional exercises were engaged in, and fresh addresses delivered, involving a large expenditure of thought and labour, but these were cheerfully rendered by ministers from all parts of the country. Sunday was 'the great day of the feast.' On that day immense crowds assembled, with a large muster of ministers. Those who chiefly assisted M'Cheyne at these Communion seasons were the Rev. Andrew Bonar, and his brother, the Rev. Horatius Bonar, the Rev. Robert Macdonald of Blairgowrie, and the Rev. James Grierson of Errol.[15]

M'Cheyne increased the number of celebrations from twice a year to four times, an innovation that pleased one of his elders, John Lamb.[16] However, there is no hint that M'Cheyne's communion services were huge outdoor events. This seems to be the case also of the summary by Andrew Carstairs in 1829:

The Thursday immediately preceding the Communion Sabbath, is accordingly held as a solemn fast, on which there is public worship; and all ordinary business is suspended. The afternoon of Saturday is also set apart for public worship; and upon these days, after divine service, tokens

---

13 Dr Norman Macleod, in his *Reminiscences of a Highland Parish*, third edition, London: Strahan & Co., 1871, written in mid-century, recorded a typical communion service at that time.

14 Hewat, *M'Cheyne From the Pew*, p. 68. Compare also the descriptions of MacLeod, *Memories of the Manse*, pp. 97–102, and James Russell, *Reminiscences of Yarrow*, Selkirk: George Lewis & Son, 1894, pp. 148–52 and 303. M'Cheyne died just prior to the Disruption, and both the Church of Scotland and Free Church of Scotland have claimed him as their own.

15 Hewat, *M'Cheyne From the Pew*, pp. 68–9.

16 Hewat, *M'Cheyne From the Pew*, pp. 69–71.

of admission are distributed to intending communicants, by the minister and elders of the parish.

The parish churches of Scotland are generally constructed, as to admit of a table of considerable length being placed in front of the pulpit on sacramental occasions; and the communicants receive the sacrament seated at this table. After the more ordinary service of the Lord's day is performed, the sacramental elements are placed by the elders upon the communion table. The minister then reads from Scripture his warrant for dispensing the Sacrament of the Lord's Supper; and in an address, (commonly called Fencing the Tables), he warns his hearers of the danger of pertaking (*sic*) in it unworthily, and describes the qualifications of those who ought, and of those who ought not, to 'eat of that bread and drink of that cup' now placed before them. He then descends from the pulpit, and places himself at the head of the table, where, after offering up prayer and thanksgiving to God, he delivers a short address to those who are to communicate; and, repeating the words of the institution, he breaks the bread, and presents it to those of them seated nearest him, by whom it its passed to the rest in succession. The cup is presented and passed in the same manner; the elders attending upon the communicants, and receiving the elements at the foot of the table. The act of communion is commonly performed in solemn silence; after which the clergyman again shortly addressed those who have communicated; and, while some verses of a Psalm are sung, they depart from the table, at which other intending communicants place themselves. All the tables, except the first, are generally served by the ministers from neighbouring parishes, invited to assist upon the occasion.

After all who wished to partake of the Holy Sacrament have in this manner communicated, the solemn service is concluded by another address from the pulpit, and by prayers and praise to God.

The forenoon of the following day is generally set apart for public worship and thanksgiving.[17]

Yet already in a number of churches, Communion was not by tables, but was served to the communicants in the pews. The change is attributed to Dr Thomas Chalmers sometime after 1819 when he found the difficulties of serving large congregations at the long table in St John's Glasgow insufferable.[18]

The 1864 reports on innovations in worship of both the Church of Scotland and the Free Church anchored the liturgical practices in the *Directory* of 1644, and in *The Worship, Rites, and Ceremonies of the*

17 Andrew Carstairs, *The Scottish Communion Service: with the Public Services for the Fast Day, Saturday and Monday before and after Communion*, Edinburgh: John Anderson, 1829, pp. ix–xi.

18 George B. Burnet, *The Holy Communion in the Reformed Church of Scotland 1560–1960*, Edinburgh: Oliver & Boyd, 1960, p. 269.

Church of Scotland, 1863, G. W. Sprott did the same.[19] The Sabbath Service of the Word was certainly in continuity with much of that recommended by the *Directory*, but as George Burnet and Leigh Eric Schmidt have shown, the communion practices had a more complex background. The Communion Seasons, or Holy Fairs, originated prior to the *Directory*, and devolved from the revival associated with Robert Bruce and that of Shotts, 1630, and later as developed by the Covenanters.[20] The compilers of the communion service in the *Directory*, other than perhaps Samuel Rutherford and George Gillespie, had in mind on the one hand the Communion as contained in the *Book of Common Order*, and on the other, via Thomas Goodwin and Philip Nye, the form celebrated monthly by the Independents, best outlined by John Cotton.[21] The Communion Season services that became the norm in Scotland were different from the older Scottish and Independent models. The early traditional nineteenth-century communion celebrations, with preparatory services and post-communion thanksgiving services, might best be characterised as the result of devolution from the hybrid produced by a fusing of the seventeenth-century *Directory* and the revival Communions at Shotts.

One of the complaints made by some nineteenth-century critics was the poor quality of the traditional worship, and poor extemporary prayer, as well as the omission by some ministers of Bible readings, the Lord's Prayer and Creed, though the *Directory* had only enjoined the Lord's Prayer.[22] In his magisterial prose, Dr Robert Lee wrote of the large number of ministers who prayed extempore, that they plunged 'into the great wilderness of thought and language – like Abraham who went forth not knowing whither he went, but who was safe under the promised guidance from above, which these men shew, by their dreary wanderings, that they do not enjoy'.[23] G. W. Sprott referred to 'well-known scraps of bad taste and nonsensical misquotations of Scripture which second-rate men rhyme over'.[24] John Cumming felt that many ministers lacked both spiritual mindedness and the gifts with utterance, resulting in mediocrity and painful harangues.[25]

---

19 G. W. Sprott, *The Worship, Rites, and Ceremonies of the Church of Scotland*, Edinburgh: Blackwood, 1863.

20 Burnet, *The Holy Communion*; Leigh Eric Schmidt, *Holy Fairs, Scotland and the Making of American Revivalism*, second edition, Grand Rapids, MI: Eerdmans, 2001.

21 Bryan D. Spinks, 'The Origins of the Antipathy to set Liturgical Forms in the English-Speaking Reformed Tradition', in Lukas Vischer (ed.), *Christian Worship in Reformed Churches Past and Present*, Grand Rapids, MI: Eerdmans, 2003, pp. 66–82. For John Cotton, see *The Way of the Churches of Christ in New England*, London 1645, reprint Weston Rhyn: Quinta Press, 2006.

22 Text in Richard A. Muller and Ronald S. Ward, *Scripture and Worship*, Phillipsburg, NJ: P&R Publishing Company, 2007.

23 Robert Lee, *The Reform of the Church of Scotland, Part 1, Worship*, Edinburgh: Edmonston & Douglas, 1864, pp. 15–16.

24 Sprott, *The Worship, Rites, and Ceremonies*, pp. 4–5

25 John Cumming, *The Liturgy of the Church of Scotland, or John Knox's Book of Common Order*, London: J. Leslie, 1840, pp. ix and xxiv.

The Episcopal Dean of Edinburgh, who claimed that the reports were true, gave examples of minuteness of detail and a quaintness of language, such as in a Sabbath service: 'O Lord, we pray thee to send us wind, no a rantin' tearin' wind, but a soughin' winnin' wind', and at the Fencing of the Table, 'I debar all those who use such minced oaths as faith! troth! losh! gosh! and loveanendie!'[26]

'Specimens' for services

A need for ministerial guidance is evidenced by the appearance of printed ministerial aids for good practice for the traditional forms, or 'specimens of the various services of Presbyterian worship', as James Grierson called them.[27] The first of these was *The Scotch Minister's Assistant*, 1802, which was reissued in 1822 under the title *The Presbyterian Minister's Assistant*, the author being Harry Robertson of Kiltearn. It contained orders of service and prayers for marriage, baptism, for Fencing the Table, Table Addresses and post-communion exhortations, prayers at Communion and blessing the elements, as well as prayers before and after the sermon, and prayers for particular pastoral occasions. Robertson explained his rationale:

> It has often been complained of as a considerable disadvantage, that there are no Forms prescribed by the Church of Scotland for celebrating Marriage, Baptism and the Lord's Supper. Every Clergyman is left to exercise his own talents upon such occasions, with no other assistance than a few general instructions laid down in the Directory annexed to the Confession of Faith.
>
> As no attempt has hitherto been made by any Minister of the Church of Scotland to remedy this obvious inconvenience, the Author flatters himself that the following work, with all its imperfections, will be favourably received by his younger Brethren, for whose use it is chiefly intended.[28]

Other important exemplars included Andrew Carstairs, minister of Anstruther West, *The Scottish Communion Service: with the Public Services for the*

---

26 E. B. Ramsay, *Reminiscences of Scottish Life and Character*, twentieth edition, Edinburgh: Edmonston & Douglas, 1871, pp. 22–3. Although it is tempting to regard this as episcopal bias and exaggeration, many amusing anecdotes are also told by Nicholas Dickson in *The Kirk and Its Worthies*, Edinburgh: T. N. Foulis, 1914, though unfortunately these are not differentiated across the centuries. One of the problems with extemporary prayer is that it is open to faux pas statements.

27 James Grierson, *A Doctrinal and Practical Treatise on the Lord's Supper*, Edinburgh: John Johnston, 1839, pp. 6–7.

28 Harry Robertson, *The Scotch Minister's Assistant, or a Collection of Forms, for Celebrating the Ordinances of Marriage, Baptism, and the LORD'S SUPPER, according to the Usage of the Church of Scotland, with Suitable Devotions for Church and Family Worship*, Edinburgh: Young & Imray, 1802, pp. iii–iv

Fast Day, Saturday and Monday before and after Communion, Edinburgh 1829; William Liston of Redgorton, *The Service of the House of God, according to the Practice of the Church of Scotland*, Glasgow 1843; Alexander Brunton of New Greyfriars, Edinburgh, *Forms for Public Worship in the Church of Scotland*, Edinburgh 1848; and James Anderson, of Cults, *The Minister's Directory*, Edinburgh 1856 and 1862. Thanks to a rediscovery by James C. Stewart, to these may now be added William Logie, *Sermons and Services of the Church*, Edinburgh, 1857. Logie was minister of St Magnus, Kirkwall, Orkney. He died in 1856 and his sermons and services, with a memorial, were published by his son. In 1859, Dr Daniel Dewar of Marischal College, Aberdeen, published some sermons preached at Communion and included a number of prayers that he had used after the sermon and at the communion table.[29] Some Communion Addresses by Robert Murray M'Cheyne, who had died in 1843, were also published by Andrew Bonar of the Free Church of Scotland in 1878, and are an additional source for practice in the first decades of the century.[30]

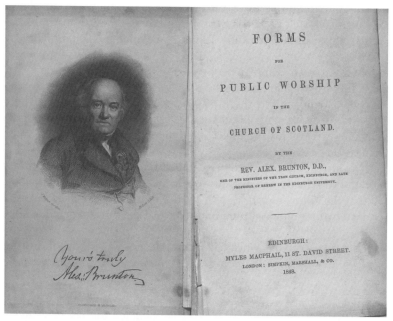

1.1 The Revd Alex Brunton and title page of *Forms for Public Worship*, 1848

29 Daniel Dewar, *The Communion Services of the Church of Scotland*, Glasgow: W. R. M'Phun, and London, 1859.

30 Andrew A. Bonar, *Memoir and Remains of the Rev. Robert Murray M'Cheyne, Minister of St. Peter's Church, Dundee*, Edinburgh: William Oliphant & Co., 1878, pp. 419–31.

Some of these, such as those of Carstairs and Logie, did not provide for the regular Sabbath worship, but only services for the less frequently celebrated liturgical occasions such as baptism, marriage and the communion days. The thought may have been that it was in the less oft-repeated occasions that ministers needed most guidance. Although there is far from complete uniformity, these do mostly follow a generic pattern, giving some idea of the diversity within an accepted traditional form. In this they are all excellent examples of liturgical devolution as well as witnessing to the type of services typical of the first half of the nineteenth century.

In *The Scotch Minister's Assistant*, Robertson provided some lengthy prayers for before and after the sermon of the Sabbath Service. Liston provided three Sabbath Morning services, each with a Prayer, Lecture (a short reading with a mini-sermon), Intermediate Prayer, Sermon (unrelated to the short reading) and 'Public' or Concluding Prayer. In an 'Advertisement' at the beginning of his collection, Brunton referred to his friend Liston, whose work had escaped him until his book was sent to the publisher. Brunton in fact gives much more material, since he provided services for four Sundays, both morning and evening. In addition, he gave appropriate psalmody. Thus, in the first Forenoon service, there are verses from the metrical psalms, Prayer, Lecture (short reading and explanation), Prayer, Paraphrase and Benediction. The Afternoon service took a similar format, though only a sentence of Scripture was read and it, with the discourse that followed, was called the 'Sermon'. Anderson gave a single service for the Forenoon and Afternoon, with metrical psalmody, Prayer, provision for reading a portion of the Old and New Testaments, a verse of a psalm, Prayer, Lecture or Sermon, psalm verse, Prayer, psalm verse and Blessing. Together they provide an interesting spread of the variations within a Sunday service. Something of the styles may be illustrated from the first prayers of Robertson, Liston and Brunton.

The *Directory* had advised beginning worship with acknowledging the incomprehensible greatness and majesty of the Lord, and to confess human sin and seek pardon. Intercessory prayer was in the prayer after the sermon. Robertson's first prayer before the sermon generally reflects the themes of the *Directory*'s opening recommendations, although it spends considerable time on the majesty of God:

O Most glorious, and highly exalted Lord our God! Thou art greatly to be feared in the assembly of thy saints, and to be had in reverence of all that would draw nigh unto thee. We thy dependent creatures, would present ourselves before thee at this time, with sentiments of humility and profound veneration; adoring thee as the only living and true God, the only proper object of our religious homage and worship.[31]

---

31 Robertson, *The Scotch Minister's Assistant*, p. 17.

Sin is mentioned, but in the context of petition for us to avoid sin, offer true worship and, 'May gospel ordinances be dispensed in purity, and accompanied with power in the several corners of thy vineyard, that sinners may be converted, and turn to the Lord, and saints be edified and comforted.'[32]

Liston's First Sabbath Morning Prayer is of eight paragraphs over four pages, and begins:

> O Lord, thou art the most high God – the only Holy One – the Almighty Sovereign of heaven and earth. Thou, O Lord, art from everlasting. All the gods of the nations are but idols; but the Lord has made the heavens, even the heaven of heavens, and all their hosts.
>
> And as, by thy great power, thou hast created all things and brought them out of nothing into being, so, by thine infinite wisdom, hast thou preserved them in existence; and they all continue this day according to thine appointment. The day is thine; the night also is thine. For thou hast made the light and the sun.[33]

Towards the bottom of the second page, sin is acknowledged 'with shame and sorrow', and on the third page:

> To us belong shame and confusion of face, because we have sinned against thee. O that thou wouldest awaken in us that godly sorrow which worketh repentance not to be repented of. Smite, Lord our hard hearts, and grant us that contrition of spirit which is a sacrifice thou wilt not despise; touch our consciences with a sense of our sins before it be too late; convince us of those sins that most easily beset us, before they have obtained dominion over us, and we find no place of repentance.[34]

Brunton provided a psalm from *The Scottish Psalter*, Psalm 139:7–13. The prayer is ten paragraphs and comparable in length to Liston's. It began:

> Whither can we go from thy presence, O God? Whither can we flee from thy Spirit, O Thou the Most High? In the heaven of heavens thy glory dwells. There the angels behold its brightness; and the spirits of the just made perfect rejoice before Thee![35]

It extols the work of the Creator – 'The herb of the field grows by a power which is not its own. The animals awaken into life, and are supported in being by thine interposition only.'[36] This prayer sees sin as forgetting the

---

32 Robertson, *The Scotch Minister's Assistant*, p. 175.

33 William Liston, *The Service of the House of God, according to the Practice of the Church of Scotland*, Glasgow: Robert Forrester, 1843, p. 1.

34 Liston, *The Service of the House of God*, p. 3.

35 Alexander Brunton, *Forms for Public Worship in the Church of Scotland*, Edinburgh: Myles Macphail, 1848, p. 25.

36 Brunton, *Forms for Public Worship*, p. 25.

presence of God, both in nature and in ourselves. It asks for grace to confess transgressions and to lament and forsake them.[37] The prayer after the sermon in all three of these books have intercessions as suggested by the *Directory*.

Theologies of baptism and the Lord's Supper: Hill, Dick, Dewar and Grierson

What of the provisions for the two ordinances or sacraments, Baptism and Communion? The foundational and binding documents for the Scottish Presbyterian Churches in the nineteenth century remained the Westminster Confession and the Catechisms.

Chapter XXVII of the Westminster Confession defined sacraments as 'holy signs and seals of the covenant of grace', instituted by God, representing Christ and his benefits, and to confirm our interest in him. The grace that is exhibited in or by sacraments is not conferred by any power in them but 'upon the work of the Spirit and the word of institution, which contains, together with a precept authorizing the use thereof, a promise of benefit to worthy receivers'.[38] Chapter XXVIII expounded baptism. It is a sacrament of the New Testament, ordained by Christ, and is a sign and seal of the covenant of grace. The outward element is water, with the trinitarian formula. Dipping is not necessary; pouring and sprinkling water suffices. Believers and the infants of one or both believing parents are to be baptised. Grace and salvation are, however, not tied to the sacrament, nor is its efficacy tied to the moment of administration. Chapter XXIX expounded the Lord's Supper, noting that Christ in this ordinance has appointed ministers 'to declare his word of institution to the people, to pray, and bless the elements of bread and wine, and thereby to set them apart from a common to an holy use; and to take and break the bread'. Worthy receivers in partaking of the visible elements receive Christ, not carnally in, with, or under the bread and wine, but spiritually and really.[39] 'Spiritually' here is regarded as being far superior to, and much more real than 'in, with, or under'.

Some idea of how sacraments were considered at the beginning of the nineteenth century may be gleaned from the *Lectures in Divinity* given by Dr George Hill (1750–1819), Principal of St Mary's College, St Andrew's; *Lectures on Theology* by Dr John Dick (1764–1833) minister of the United Associate Congregation, Greyfriars, and Professor of Theology to the United Secession Church; and the work on the Lord's Supper by Daniel

---

37 Brunton, *Forms for Public Worship*, p. 27.

38 Text in Philip Schaff, revised by David S. Schaff, *The Creeds of Christendom with a History and Critical Notes*, Grand Rapids, MI: Baker Books, 1998 reprint, vol. 3, p. 661.

39 Schaff, *The Creeds of Christendom*, vol. 3, pp. 665–6.

Dewar in his *Elements of Systematic Divinity*, 1866, and by Dr James Grierson (1791–1875), who joined the Free Church at the Disruption.[40]

George Hill treated sacraments under a discussion of the covenant of grace. One of the results of the covenant of grace is the obligation to prayer in general, and the propriety of its several parts.[41] In section IV he observed that covenants are confirmed by certain solemnities that in the Christian world are called sacraments, and are twofold: baptism and the Lord's Supper. He wrote:

> In each there is matter, an external visible substance; and there is also a positive institution authorizing that substance to be used with certain words in a religious rite. And we think that both from the nature of the institution, and from the manner in which each sacrament is mentioned in other places of the New Testament, the two are not barely signs of invisible grace, or badges of the Christian profession, but were intended by him who appointed them to be pledges of that grace, and seals of the covenant by which it is conveyed.[42]

Baptism is distinguished as a rite by the threefold trinitarian baptismal formula, and has taken the place of circumcision.

> The immersion in water of the bodies of those who were baptized is an emblem of that death unto sin, by which the conversion of Christians is generally expressed: the rising out of the water, the breathing the air again after having been for some time in another element, is an emblem of that new life, which Christians by their profession are bound, and by the power of their religion are enabled to lead.[43]

Baptism as a mere act of washing does not save unless it is accompanied with 'the answer of a good conscience towards God'. Since it is a federal act, it might suggest that it be delayed until the party concerned understands it. However, it takes the place of circumcision and parents make the promises, not for the child, but for themselves, and with the understanding that they will engage the child to undertake the obligations in the future.

> We believe that, as they have enjoyed the advantages of infant baptism, and are thereby prepared for making 'the answer of a good conscience towards God,' all the inward grace which that sacrament exhibits will be

---

40 Alexander Hill (ed.), *Lectures in Divinity by the late George Hill, D.D.*, New York: Robert Carter, 1847; John Dick, *Lectures on Theology*, published under the superintendence of his son, Cincinnati: Applegate & Co., 1858; Daniel Dewar, *Elements of Systematic Divinity*, vol. 3, Glasgow: Thomas Murray & Son, 1866; Grierson, *A Doctrinal and Practical Treatise*.

41 Hill, *Lectures on Divinity*, p. 649.

42 Hill, *Lectures on Divinity*, p. 655.

43 Hill, *Lectures on Divinity*, p. 660.

conveyed to their souls, when they partake worthily of the other: for then the covenant with God is upon their part confirmed; and as certainly as they know that they fulfil what he requires of them, so certainly may they be assured that he will fulfil what he has promised.[44]

When treating the Lord's Supper in section VII, Hill wrote:

The Lord's Supper exhibits by a significant action, the characteristical doctrine of the Christian faith, that the death of its author, which seemed to be the completion of the rage of enemies, was a voluntary sacrifice, so efficacious as to supersede the necessity of every other; and that his blood was shed for the remission of sins.[45]

He treated at length the Roman and Lutheran views, rejecting these along with Zwingli and the Cambridge Platonists' idea of a feast of a sacrifice, and espoused what he described as Calvin's view, that 'to all who remember the death of Christ in a proper manner, Christ, by the use of these signs, is spiritually present, – present to their minds.'[46] He wrote:

For while they engage, at a time when every sentiment of piety and gratitude may be supposed to be strong and warm in their breasts, that they will fulfil their part of their covenant, they behold in the actions which they perform a striking representation of that event, by which the covenant was confirmed; and they receive, in the grace and strength then conveyed to their souls, a seal of that forgiveness of sins, which, through the blood of the covenant, is granted to all that repent, and a pledge of the future blessings promised to those who are 'faithful unto death'.[47]

The *Lectures* by John Dick are much more detailed than Hill's, and Lecture LXXXVI treated the background of the term sacrament and includes the definitions from the Westminster Standards.[48] After discussion of the term 'mystery', Dick noted that in a sacrament two things are considered – the sign, and the thing signified.[49] They are divine institutions, appointed by God to ratify his covenant, and these signs or seals are assurances that the blessings promised will be enjoyed.[50] When turning to the two dominical sacraments recognised by the Westminster Standards, he defended different modes of application of the water of baptism, and argued that baptism had replaced circumcision.[51] The trinitarian formula was essential. The

---

44 Hill, *Lectures in Divinity*, p. 667.
45 Hill, *Lectures in Divinity*, p. 669.
46 Hill, *Lectures in Divinity*, p. 677.
47 Hill, *Lectures in Divinity*, p. 679.
48 Dick, *Lectures on Theology*, p. 458.
49 Dick, *Lectures on Theology*, p. 459.
50 Dick, *Lectures on Theology*, p. 461.
51 Dick, *Lectures on Theology*, pp. 471–4.

blessings it bestows are regeneration, forgiveness of sins and admission to the family of God, and the promise of resurrection.[52] It implies an engagement to believe all the truths that Christ has revealed and to observe his ordinances.[53] Dick believed that the baptism of children is calculated to produce the best effects upon parents and places their children in a new relationship with them.

Much of his treatment of the Lord's Supper was taken up with repudiating the Roman and Lutheran views on presence. He discussed the views of Zwingli and Calvin, and suggested that Zwingli had been misunderstood. On the other hand, Dick says that he did understand Calvin's need to assert a presence through the Holy Spirit, and thought that Calvin's view was little different from the papists' and Lutherans'![54] Dick expressed his view thus:

> Stript of all metaphorical terms, the action must mean that, in the believing and grateful commemoration of [Christ's] death, we enjoy the blessings which were purchased by it, in the same manner in which we enjoy them when we exercise faith in hearing the Gospel.[55]

Many would see this as reflecting Zwingli's view. Indeed, Dick continued: 'There is an absurdity in the notion, that there is any communion with the body and blood of Christ considered in themselves; that he intended any such thing; or that it would be of any advantage to us.'[56] This accounts for Dick's interpretation of the words of the Westminster Confession chapter XXIX concerning the body and blood being really but spiritually present to the communicants: 'it can mean only, that our incarnate suffering saviour is apprehended by their minds, through the instituted signs; and that by faith they enjoy peace and hope; or it means something unintelligible and unscriptural.'[57] A sign, he noted, is very far from implying that the thing signified is present. He summarised:

> [The bread and wine] signify that believers enjoy fellowship with their Saviour in the holy supper. His death is exhibited as the meritorious cause of their reconciliation to God; and it is exhibited in so impressive a manner, as to strengthen their faith, and to fill them with joy and peace in believing.[58]

Worthiness and therefore self-examination is important, and 'to assist Christians in this inquiry, is the design of that part of the service of our

---

52 Dick, *Lectures on Theology*, pp. 475 and 477–8.
53 Dick, *Lectures on Theology*, pp. 478–9.
54 Dick, *Lectures on Theology*, p. 490.
55 Dick, *Lectures on Theology*, p. 490.
56 Dick, *Lectures on Theology*, p. 490.
57 Dick, *Lectures on Theology*, p. 491.
58 Dick, *Lectures on Theology*, p. 493.

Church which is commonly called Fencing the Tables.'[59] On the question of frequency, he opined that since Scripture didn't mandate a frequency, but on analogy with Jewish festivals, he thought the early Church celebrated it but once a year.[60]

In *Elements of Systematic Divinity*, Daniel Dewar described the bread and wine of the Lord's Supper as 'appropriate emblems' of the ordinance of the memorial of the substitution and atoning death of Christ.[61] The ordinance exhibits in characters calculated to affect the heart deeply. The broken bread is a figure of Christ's body and it exhibits to us by an appropriate figure the suffering that the Lord endured for sins.[62] When the communicants receive the emblems, their hearts are affected with penitential sorrow, and filled with holy love. In a discussion of Calvin and Zwingli, Dewar presented Calvin as stressing incorporation into Christ, and Dewar argued that the union of Christ and believer 'is impressively exhibited at this holy ordinance'.[63] Arguing that at the Last Supper Christ sat (!), he defended sitting at the table for Communion, concluding that, 'to every believer at the communion-table the Lord's Supper is a sealing ordinance, inasmuch as god, in putting the emblems of Christ's body and blood into his hands, conveys to him the assurance of pardon, and peace, and everlasting life.'[64] He argued the need for careful self-examination, and discussed the views of 'the Romish Church', particularly transubstantiation. He concluded by outlining three theories of the Supper – transubstantiation, consubstantiation and the symbolical and spiritual view held by most Protestants. 'The true interpretation of our Lord's words is to be found in the emblematic service He was observing with His disciples when he instituted the Eucharist. It was emblematical as well as commemorative.'[65] Although Dewar used Calvin's term 'exhibit', Dewar himself seemed to suggest that the elements were emblematic representations, and not 'instruments' as Calvin had designated them.

Grierson's work of 270 pages was solely concerned with the Lord's Supper, and much of it is about preparation for the Supper and its spiritual benefits. However, he did refer to baptism in the introduction as a sacrament and to the importance of the trinitarian formula.[66] The doctrinal basis for the Lord's Supper was discussed in the first chapter. The Supper is an ordinance in which the gospel is preached by means of sensible signs in which the most affecting pledges are exhibited of the blessings of the covenant of grace. Grierson wrote:

59 Dick, *Lectures on Theology*, p. 495.
60 Dick, *Lectures on Theology*, p. 495.
61 Dewar, *Elements*, p. 276.
62 Dewar, *Elements*, p. 284.
63 Dewar, *Elements*, p. 286.
64 Dewar, *Elements*, p. 291.
65 Dewar, *Elements*, p. 322.
66 Grierson, *A Doctrinal and Practical Treatise*, pp. 13 and 15.

Not only is there, in this ordinance, a *representation* of Christ's body and blood – nay, of his body *broken* and of his blood *shed* in behalf of sinners, and of his actually and *freely giving himself* 'for the life of the world,' – but to the worthy partakers there is, through faith, a real, although, of course, a spiritual *participation* of his body and blood, with all the benefits and blessings which they have purchased, and of which, they are declared to be emblems or the means.[67]

In this ordinance, said Grierson, Christ is set forth as symbolically crucified before our eyes, and thus:

We have then, at the outset, his own authority for regarding the *bread* used in the Supper as an *emblem* or representation of his *body*, and the *wine* as a representation of his *blood*. We cannot, therefore, even for a moment, behold these sacred elements on a communion table, without calling to remembrance the amazing fact, that our adorable Redeemer, although in the highest sense the Son of God, condescended to become a *partaker of flesh and blood*.[68]

The breaking of the bread represents the wounding of his body and the pouring out of the wine represents the shedding of his blood.[69] In receiving the elements, the communicants show their acceptance of Christ and his benefits.[70] The Supper assures us of the love of Christ and that he will come again.[71] It also reminds us of our brotherly union one with another, which ought to subsist among those who partake.[72] It thus requires self-examination.[73] Though outwardly we simply receive bread and wine, those who receive worthily spiritually receive and feed upon Christ crucified, and all his benefits.[74] The elements are not only signs but also seals of the blessings of the covenant.[75]

These four theologians span several of the Scottish Presbyterian Churches, and reflect a wide spectrum of belief.

Baptism and the Lord's Supper in the 'specimens'

How then were any of these very varied beliefs, as well as other beliefs, reflected in the liturgical celebrations of baptism and the Lord's Supper suggested by the 'specimens'?

---

67 Grierson, *A Doctrinal and Practical Treatise*, p. 26–7.
68 Grierson, *A Doctrinal and Practical Treatise*, p. 30.
69 Grierson, *A Doctrinal and Practical Treatise*, p. 31.
70 Grierson, *A Doctrinal and Practical Treatise*, p. 35.
71 Grierson, *A Doctrinal and Practical Treatise*, p. 50.
72 Grierson, *A Doctrinal and Practical Treatise*, p. 105.
73 Grierson, *A Doctrinal and Practical Treatise*, p. 103.
74 Grierson, *A Doctrinal and Practical Treatise*, p. 168.
75 Grierson, *A Doctrinal and Practical Treatise*, p. 169.

The *Directory* provisions for the baptismal rite began by ruling out private baptism and lay administration of baptism. The initial exhortation, or 'Instruction', described baptism as a 'Seale of the Covenant of Grace, of our Ingrafting into Christ, and of our Union with him'. It is the seal of remission of sins, regeneration, adoption and life eternal. Appeal was made to the covenant of grace for infant baptism, because children are 'federally holy before Baptisme'. The 'Instruction' also noted that the inward grace and virtue of baptism is not tied to the moment of baptism. In many ways, the 'Instruction' is a quasi-liturgical rehearsal of the section found in the Westminster Confession.[76]

Once the 'teaching' was complete, the minister was to pray that God would bless and sanctify the ordinance, and join the outward to the inward. After the child was named, it was baptised with the triune formula. Afterwards the minister was to give thanks 'to this or the like purpose':

Acknowledging with all thankfulnesse, that the Lord is true and faithfull in keeping Covenant and Mercy; That hee is good and gracious, not onely in that he numbreth us among his Saints, but is pleased also to bestow upon our children this singular token and badge of his love in Christ: That in his truth and speciall providence, hee daily bringeth some into the bosome of his Church, to be partakers of his inestimable benefits, purchased by the blood of his dear Son, for the continuance and increase of his Church.[77]

Entirely omitted were the recitation of the Lord's Prayer and the Apostles' Creed.

Robertson (1802) presented six forms of baptism, though in reality there was one form with five alternative 'discourses' or explications of the meaning for baptism. The service he suggested began with a prayer, thanking God for 'our baptism' and dedicating the infant to God's service. It also asked for God to pour down the Spirit upon 'our seed' and his blessing upon 'our offspring, that they may spring up as Willows by the water courses, that they may become trees of righteousness, the planting of the Lord, in whom he will be glorified'. The Minister asks the parent or sponsor to present the child, and then follows a discourse. Then follow creedal vow, framed around belief in the Scripture, the Westminster Confession and catechisms, and an undertaking to bring up the child in the Christian religion. Prayer follows, including a petition for God's presence and grace, and: 'Sanctify the element of water which is now exhibited and applied as a sign and symbol of thy grace. Let the outward Baptism with water be accompanied with the inward Baptism of the Holy Spirit.'[78] It also asked God to remove the pollution of the first Adam. A 'little water' was sprinkled on the face

---

76 Muller and Ward, *Scripture and Worship*, pp. 156–9.
77 Muller and Ward, *Scripture and Worship*, pp. 158–9.
78 Robertson, *The Scotch Minister's Assistant*, p. 36.

of the child with the trinitarian formula, and a concluding prayer for the child and for the family and their duties. This last prayer, which asks God to ratify in heaven what has been done on earth, and asks that the family has 'a living mother', was used as a model for the post-baptismal prayer in some of the other books. W. D. Bailie commented:

> This service shows obvious affinities with the Westminster Directory for Public Worship. It only deviates from the earlier work by having a Prayer at the commencement of the service, and by adding petitions to the Post-baptismal prayer for the parents of the child.[79]

The discourses outline the various dimensions of baptismal theology – the covenant, purification, the need for a good conscience towards God, parental duties, and justification of infant baptism.

Subsequent 'specimens' seem to have drawn on or have been inspired by Robertson's prose, though it is difficult in some cases to know whether there is direct textual dependence or simply common stock phrases taken from Scripture and the Westminster standards.

Liston provided only one baptismal service, prefaced with a general morning prayer and a lengthy sermon on baptism. The service itself began with the presentation, and then an explication on baptism, based upon the statement that it is a sacrament in which we are united to Christ, made partakers of the Covenant of Grace, and brought under the obligations of the Christian life, and recounting the duties of parents. A short prayer asked that the outward act of baptism be matched with inward baptism. After the trinitarian formula, a prayer asked for blessings on the child, the mother, and for all present that they remember that we all share the same spiritual engagements or obligations, and Liston seems to have been aware of Robertson's text. Brunton also provided one short formula, with the same sequence – presentation, explication on the obligations and duties of the patents and a short prayer, which included the petition: 'Sanctify so much of the element of water as is used in this solemnity. Seal, by thy grace, its meaning on our souls.'[80] After the baptism (sprinkling water on the face and Trinitarian formula), the concluding prayer asked God to ratify in heaven what has been done on earth, with prayers for the child and mother, and seems to have been modelled on Robertson's prayer, using identical phraseology. Anderson gave two baptismal rites in the 1856 edition, the second of which seems incomplete. The 1862 edition had three full forms, and it is this edition used here. Each rite began with a rubric concerning registration of the birth, and noting that baptism is administered on Sunday immediately after the sermon, though it acknow-

---

79 W. D. Bailie, 'The Rites of Baptism and Admission of Catechumens ('Confirmation') according to the Liturgy and History of the Church of the Church of Scotland', PhD thesis, Queen's University, Belfast, 1959, chapter 8, p. 5.

80 Brunton, *Forms for Public Worship*, p. 191.

ledged (the more common) private baptism. There was an introductory prayer, presentation, explication ('Address'), prayer, baptism and post-baptismal prayer. Forms 2 and 3 provide alternatives from the presentation to the end. It is clear that Anderson has drawn on the work of Robertson, Liston and Brunton. In Form 1 the prayer asks God to sanctify and bless his own ordinance (*Directory*), and uses words from Brunton, and the post-baptismal prayer adapts that of Liston. The post-baptismal prayer in Form 2 is Brunton's, which in turn was from Robertson. Form 3 is a completion of the incomplete Form 2 of the 1856 edition. Logie provided an Address after the presentation of the child, declaring that Baptism is to be regarded as an external sign of spiritual and internal operations, and as a seal of the covenant of grace.[81] The parent/sponsor is reminded of their obligations. Logie then provided a 'Consecration Prayer', giving thanks for the ordinance, which echoes Brunton's prayer:

> Consecrate, and set apart from a common to a holy use, so much of the element of water as is now to be used. While we sprinkle pure water on this child, do Thou baptize with the Holy Ghost as with purifying fire; and may baptism become to this infant the laver of regeneration, in which the guilt of hereditary sin may be washed away.[82]

The trinitarian baptismal formula was followed by the Aaronic blessing, and the post-baptismal prayer was mainly focused on the child, with only brief prayer for the mother and family at the end of the prayer.[83]

The recommended order for the Lord's Supper in the *Directory* followed on from the usual Sunday service. It outlined an exhortation on the benefit of the sacrament, excommunication of the unworthy, and encouragement to repentance; the recital of the words of institution; optional explanation of the words of institution; prayer of thanksgiving or blessing of the elements; fraction and delivery; exhortation; solemn thanksgiving. A rubric directed the minister 'to begin the action of sanctifying and blessing the elements of bread and wine', and in the prayer after the Institution narrative to pray God 'to vouchsafe his gracious presence, and the effectual working of his Spirit in us; and so to sanctify these elements both of bread and wine, and to bless his own ordinance, that we may receive by faith the body and blood of Jesus Christ, crucified for us'.[84] Communion could be at the table or around it. However, as we have noted, the Scottish communion service had been heavily influenced by the Shotts revival and the Covenanters, and was surrounded by preparation days and a post-communion thanksgiving day.

---

81 William Logie, *Sermons and Services of the Church*, William Oliphant & Sons, Edinburgh, 1862, p. 299.
82 Logie, *Sermons and Services*, p. 302.
83 Logie, *Sermons and Services*, p. 303.
84 Muller and Ward, *Scripture and Worship*, pp. 159–62.

With regard to the provisions of the nineteenth-century guides or 'specimens' for Communion, Kenneth Hughes observed that more noticeable than their differences is the common ground they shared with respect to the details of service.[85] Robertson, for example, provided six forms for Fencing the Table and Table Services, and two forms of concluding exhortations. The communion prayers were in a separate section of his book, with two consecration prayers and two concluding prayers. Carstairs provided material for the Fast Day morning and evening, a Saturday service, the main Sabbath forenoon service with Communion, post-communion Sabbath evening service and Monday service. The Sabbath forenoon service provided Psalm 95:1–6, a long prayer, a sample sermon, the Lord's Prayer, Paraphrase 26:1–3, an Address from the pulpit commonly called 'The Fencing of the Table', which included the Ten Commandments and the Beatitudes, Paraphrase 35:1–4, the consecration prayer, five table services addressed to the communicants and each ending with a paraphrase, a concluding Address, prayer, Psalm 72:17–19 and a blessing. Liston offered a vast amount of material: a preparation Sabbath service with morning prayer, sermon, concluding prayer, and Address; a Fast Day service with prayers, two sermons and Address; and Communion Sabbath service, with morning prayer, sermon intermediate prayer, Fencing the Tables, First Table service with consecration prayer, four more Table services, exhortation or concluding Address, Prayer after the Communion, sermon and public or concluding prayer. William Logie provided for Morning Prayer, Action Sermon, Fencing of the Tables, Consecration Prayer, and four Table Addresses, a concluding exhortation and prayer, an evening sermon and an Address to new communicants. Dewar published only a selection of prayers after the sermon, and at the Communion Table.

Robertson's forms for Fencing the Tables vary from an appeal to self-examination (Form I) to debarring various categories of sinners and outsiders (Form V) to a diatribe against popery (Form VI). All have some explicit instruction on doctrine within them. The Table Addresses give further instruction and exhortation to devotion. The first consecration prayer opens with words of adoration from Revelation 4:11 and subsequent verses, blesses God for the seals of the covenant and asks: 'Grant, O Lord, we beseech thee, that while we partake of the outward elements of bread and wine, we may by a lively faith, behold Christ crucified evidently set before us, and feed on him to our spiritual nourishment and growth in grace.'[86]

The second requests that the communicants, who have been called and invited to the marriage-supper of the Lamb, would clothe themselves with the wedding garment, that they may find Christ's flesh to be meat indeed,

---

85 Kenneth Grant Hughes, 'Holy Communion in the Church of Scotland in the Nineteenth Century', PhD thesis, University of Glasgow, 1987, p. 74. For Logan, see Robin Leaver, *A Communion Sunday in Scotland ca.1780*, Lanham, MD: Scarecrow Press, 2010.

86 Robertson, *The Scotch Minister's Assistant*, pp. 231–2.

and his blood to be drink indeed, and that God will grace his own ordinance. Later it prayed:

> Bow the heavens and come down; shine forth thou that dwelleth between the cherubims, stir up thy strength, and come and save us. May we hear thy voice, and taste thy goodness; may we feel the powerful influence of thy Spirit upon our hearts, communicating life and light and joy in our souls.[87]

Carstairs in his consecration prayer invoked a presence, but is more concerned with our part in renewing the covenant:

> Be with us, O Lord, we humbly entreat thee, in the celebration of this ordinance. O thou who dwellest on high! Bend thy heavens and come down; – graciously accept this tribute of our gratitude to him who died that we might live. May the great Master of the feast be present; may he be made known to us in the breaking of bread. May we sit down under his shadow with great delight, and find his fruit sweet unto our taste.
> Over these symbols of his death, we solemnly devote ourselves to his service – we solemnly renounce the pleasures of sin, etc.[88]

Liston's consecration prayer was followed by the Institution narrative, and seems more reflective of the *Directory* suggestions than were Robertson's prayers. The prayer opened with words from elsewhere in Revelation, and has a more substantial petition for presence/blessing:

> Bend, O God, the heavens, and come down, and let this be a solemnity acceptable to the Saviour, and solacing to the souls of thy people. Sanctify with thy blessing so much of the elements as shall be used on this occasion, that, as the symbols of the Saviour's broken body and shed blood, they may prove refreshing, comfortable, and strengthening to every serious and devout receiver. And while we beg thy blessing on the elements to be used, we would implore thy presence with those who are to receive them.[89]

Brunton provided what he entitles a Consecration Prayer, which is mainly a prayer blessing God for his goodness and benefits. The prayer announced to God that, 'Upon this table are the pledges of salvation', and that God is in the midst of us, and requested:

> O, may thy blessing here rest upon us abundantly. Give that blessing on the symbols of bread and wine; which, by thy command, we employ

87 Robertson, *The Scotch Minister's Assistant*, p. 237.
88 Carstairs, *The Scottish Communion Service*, p. 152.
89 Liston, *The Service of the House of God*, p. 235.

to represent the body and blood of our Lord. Give that blessing on the hearts of the worshippers. These hearts are open before Thee. They are ever in thy hand, and 'Thou turnest them, as Thou turnest the rivers of water.' Inspire them now with the dispositions which Thou approves; that our communion-service may be accepted and useful.[90]

Earlier in his Sabbath service, the opening long prayer has requested, 'May we see, in the emblems of the Saviour's broken body and shed blood, those mysteries of godliness which they are ordained to typify. Make Thyself known in the breaking of bread.'[91]

William Lamb, who attended Robert Murray M'Cheyne's services, welcomed the more frequent celebration of Communion, but remarked in his diary that there is too much said about the Sacrament, so that the uneducated or more ignorant failed to see that 'it is merely a *commemoration service*' and were apt to think that there was some innate virtue in the ordinance.[92] It would be hard to conclude from Brunton's prose that the service was anything more than merely a commemoration service.

James Anderson provided a wealth of material for the preparation and dispensing of the Communion, with suitable Fencings of the Table, Addresses, sermons, prayers and appropriate psalmody or paraphrases, covering some 150 pages. Like Brunton, the Consecration Prayer is a thanksgiving to God for his benefits and asks for worthy reception. Anderson prayed:

Grant, O gracious Father, that by partaking of these outward and visible signs, the symbols of the body and blood of Christ, we may receive that inward and spiritual grace which will sanctify our souls, and strengthen our feeble resolutions, and enable us to triumph over the world, the flesh, and the devil. . . . In the emblems of Christ's body and blood, which are here set before us, and which we pray thee to sanctify for our use, may we see that life of the soul which he purchased for us by his death, and henceforth live as he has commanded us.[93]

Daniel Dewar's prayers are for the most part so general that they could have been prayed at any service. In at least two prayers he drew on Psalm 132:15, praying, 'do thou, O Lord, bless the provision of Zion, and satisfy her poor with bread.' He also drew on 1 Corinthians 10:16, as in his third set of prayers:

May the bread which we break be unto us the communion of the body of Christ, and may the cup of blessing which we bless, be to us the communion of the blood of Christ. And as we receive these memorials of the

---

90 Brunton, *Forms for Public Worship*, p. 283.
91 Brunton, *Forms for Public Worship*, p. 255.
92 Hewat, *M'Cheyne From the Pew*, p. 74.
93 James Anderson, *The Ministers' Directory*, Edinburgh: William P. Nimmo, pp. 150–1.

Saviour's broken body and shed blood, oh may we receive the blessings that are signified thereby. May we receive Christ himself into our hearts, as all our salvation, – as our life and righteousness, our hope and glory![94]

Prayer set five asked, 'Blessed Jesus! Be graciously present with us in this solemn ordinance', and set eight asked the Redeemer, 'be pleased to make thyself known to us in the breaking of bread and in prayer.'[95] The prayers dwelt mostly on the saving work of Christ and the atonement, and seem to have been designed to convey a strong mental image of the suffering Christ.

Finally, in the forms authored by William Logie, there are all the ingredients for the Communion-Sabbath Service – Morning Prayer, Action Sermon, Fencing of the Tables, Consecration Prayer, four Table Addresses, a concluding exhortation and prayer, as well as an evening sermon.

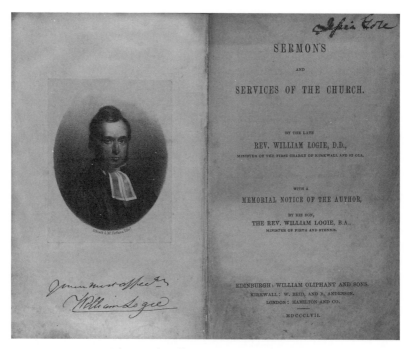

1.2 The Revd William Logie and title page of
Sermons and Services of the Church, 1857

Logie's consecration prayer commenced with an explicit trinitarian Address with each member of the Trinity being referenced, and then a thanksgiving for the work of salvation. It requested both God's presence and communion:

---

94 Dewar, *The Communion Services of the Church of Scotland*, p. 344.
95 Dewar, *The Communion Services of the Church of Scotland*, pp. 351 and 363.

We rejoice that we are this day invited to contemplate in the glass of an ordinance, all the wonders of His love, and partake of the symbols of his body broken, and His blood shed for our redemption.

In obedience, blessed Jesus, to Thy command, we come to show forth Thy death, and muse on all Thy marvelous, thy matchless, Thy mysterious love to us – love which many waters could not quench, nor the floods drown. God of our salvation, bow the heavens and come down. Come, Thou risen and exalted Saviour – stand in the midst of us, and make Thyself known unto us in the breaking of bread.

Sanctify those symbols of bread and wine for the sacred use to which they are to be applied. May the bread which we break be unto us the communion of the body of Christ; and the cup of blessing which we bless, the communion of His blood.[96]

It is perhaps the most elegant of the consecration prayers.

The provision for a number of tables in these services witnessed to the fact that this was still the prevailing custom. However, where Communion was served in the pews, the multiple Addresses were rendered unnecessary at a stroke and the length of the service was reduced considerably. Kenneth Hughes has noted that in the Fencing of the Tables there is a gradual shift from exclusion, 'I debar', to invitation.[97] The different terminologies in the consecration prayers also confirm Hughes' observation that there was no common mind with respect to the nature and purpose of consecration.[98]

Conclusion

Comparing the services in these collections, some common DNA is identifiable as well as significant variations, reflecting both ministerial and parochial preferences, and they are good examples of liturgical devolution. John Lamb aptly commented that the appearance of these liturgical aids shows a growing interest in public worship in many quarters in Scotland, together with a dissatisfaction with the general manner of its performance and a hope to bring it to a higher level of order and decency.[99] Lamb also noted the verbose and didactic nature of much of the material. The forms were, of course, traditional, but what was traditional would come to be regarded by some leading churchman of the established Church as being a liturgical species that needed to adapt or else would become extinct.

---

96 Logie, *Sermons and Services*, p. 234.

97 Hughes, 'Holy Communion in the Church of Scotland in the Nineteenth Century', p. 94.

98 Hughes, 'Holy Communion in the Church of Scotland in the Nineteenth Century', p. 94.

99 John Lamb, 'Aids to Public Worship in Scotland 1800–1850', *Records of the Scottish Church History Society* 13 (1959), pp. 171–85, p. 184.

2

Liturgical Disruption: Dr Robert Lee of Greyfriars Edinburgh

In a sketch of the life of the late Dr Robert Lee of Edinburgh published in June 1870, it was stated:

> No one acquainted with Scotland needs to be told that public worship is now conducted in a far more becoming and reverent fashion. Kneeling at prayer is becoming general; carefully written prayers are used by many of the most distinguished clergymen; the organ has been introduced into not a few of the largest churches; the music, instrumental and vocal, is generally well executed and carefully chosen. An air of solemnity and impressiveness has been cast around the bald and uninviting service of the Puritans, and Scotsmen have at last consented to behave with decency in the sanctuary. To the resolute efforts of Dr. Lee, to his keen perception of what was indecorous and unbecoming, as well as to his fine taste, and cultivated feeling for the beautiful, the improvement is mainly to be attributed.[1]

Whether all the changes in worship listed here can in fact be attributed to Lee is questionable, but that does not detract from the fact that it was he who initiated what might be termed a liturgical disruption in the Church of Scotland, which in turn led to what Cheyne called a liturgical revolution.

Robert Lee and the first innovations at Greyfriars

Robert Lee (1804–67) was born south of the border, at Tweedmouth, County Durham, and was sent to school at Berwick-on-Tweed.[2] However, his university education was at St Andrews and he went through the eight-year curriculum required of candidates seeking ordination, and distinguished himself academically. In 1833 he was elected minister of Inverbrothock Church, which was a chapel of ease at Arbroath. He was

---

1 'Dr. Robert Lee of Edinburgh. A Sketch by Shirley', in *Fraser's Magazine*, New Series vol. 1, London: Longmans, Green & Co., 1870, pp. 86–106, pp. 101–2.

2 Robert H. Story, *Life and Remains of Robert Lee, DD*, in 2 volumes, London: Hurst & Blackett, 1870, vol. 1, pp. 2–3.

2.1 The Revd Dr Robert Lee

already regarded as a fine preacher, and his biographer, R. H. Story, recorded that among Lee's papers were some communion services, including Table Addresses and Fencings of the Table 'in the style common in those days, but now found chiefly among the older clergy, of considerable length, and somewhat sermonic in their tone'.[3] In 1836 he was called to the parish of Campsie in the Presbytery of Glasgow, and in 1843, four months after the Disruption, he was appointed to Old Greyfriars, Edinburgh. He was awarded the degree of DD in 1844, and in 1847 was appointed Professor of Biblical Criticism at Edinburgh University. However, on 19 January 1846, a fire had destroyed Old Greyfriars. It reopened in 1857, and its restoration and decoration included some stained-glass windows. Lee took the opportunity to begin to make changes in worship. This included standing to sing and kneeling for prayer, and conforming more faithfully to the order of service outlined in the Westminster *Directory*, which was not the general custom. He also drew up and printed a liturgy, *Prayers for Public Worship*, 1857, and so introduced read prayers from a printed book. Story noted:

> For a time all went well. The church was crowded – the congregation was unanimous. The service, with all its adjuncts, was felt to be invested with a solemnity and beauty rarely to be witnessed, in a like measure, within a Presbyterian temple.
>
> But opposition and trouble, before a year was over, began to darken the horizon.[4]

In the General Assembly of 1858 overtures from the Synod of Dumfries and the Presbytery of Aberdeen were presented, asking the Assembly to prevent innovations in worship. Lee was not named directly, though it was clear beyond doubt that the overtures were aimed at him. Lee's response was to bring out a second edition of his book of public prayers, and much expanded by including forms for the sacraments, marriage and burial, as well as meditations, songs of praise and prayers.

The Presbytery of Edinburgh then stepped into the growing debate, and called Lee to answer the accusation of innovation in worship. His speech in defence was reprinted by Story, and Lee, appealing to the Westminster *Directory*, asserted that 'I myself, my kirk-session, and the members of my

---

3 Story, *Life and Remains*, vol. 1, p. 13.
4 Story, *Life and Remains*, vol. 1, p. 337.

congregation, observe the only rule for determining the order of worship known to this Church, or consistent with its laws.'[5] Lee insisted that he was following the law whereas many of his brethren followed custom as though it were law:

> I know another church in which the minister begins with an exposition of the psalm that is to be sung – that is, with a lecture. Some ministers sing two psalms during the worship – some sing three – others sing four. Which is the custom? Which is the law?[6]

Although Lee gave a powerful defence, a majority of the Presbytery voted to refer the matter to a committee, which after reviewing the controversy, requested that innovations unknown and unauthorised by the Church should be discontinued. The case went from there to the Synod and then to the General Assembly. The Assembly found only that the reading of prayers from a book was contrary to the laws and usage of the Church, and Lee undertook to refrain from this practice.

It was during the Lee controversy that the General Assembly published *Prayers for Social and Family Worship*, 1859. This was the work of a committee that had been appointed in 1849 to prepare forms of service, not for the use of ministers but 'as aids to the exercise of Social Worship, according to the manner of the Church of Scotland, by Soldiers, Sailors, Colonists, Sojourners in India or in foreign countries, who are deprived of the regular services of a Christian Ministry'.[7] The Preface claimed that the morning and evening services had been compiled from the devotional writings of Calvin, Knox and other Reformers, as well as the Westminster *Directory*. The recommended order as represented by the first morning service was prayer ending in the Lord's Prayer, a prose psalm, scripture readings from the old and New testaments with a psalm sung between them, prayer with special petitions and thanksgivings, sung psalm, sermon or reading that would edify the worshippers, prayer, psalm or paraphrase and blessing. What is significant is that this is set forth as 'according to the manner of the Church of Scotland' and was indirectly a recommendation of a particular order of public worship. It can only be speculated whether ministers were guided by the order, and whether some used some of the prayers as the basis for their own. The ad hoc committee that had prepared this was transformed into the Aids to Devotion Committee under the convenorship of Professor Crawford.[8]

---

5 Story, *Life and Remains*, vol. 1, p. 340.

6 Story, *Life and Remains*, vol. 1, p. 347.

7 *Prayers for Social and Family Worship*, Edinburgh: William Blackwood & Sons, 1859, p. v.

8 Foster Franklin, 'Phases of Order in Church of Scotland Worship', *Church Service Society Annual* 31 (1961), pp. 3–12, p. 10.

May 1864: Lee's *Reform of the Church of Scotland* and the *Report of Committee Anent Innovations in Public Worship*

Charles McCrie commented on the 1859 General Assembly ruling, 'Dr Lee and his sympathisers regarded the first decision of that Court as substantially in his favour, virtually sanctioning the changes he had then introduced, with the exception of reading prayers from a printed book or from manuscript.'[9] Music had not been an item of controversy and in the Spring of 1863 Lee introduced another innovation, namely a harmonium to accompany singing. It may have been this together with dissatisfaction with the mild condemnation made of Lee at the 1859 Assembly that prompted further agitation, with the result that in 1863 a committee was appointed by the General Assembly to investigate innovations in public worship. Meanwhile, Lee was engaged in writing an apologia and forceful justification of his liturgical programme, and May 1864 saw the publication both of his book, *The Reform of the Church of Scotland*, and the report of the General Assembly's committee on innovations in Public worship.

A. K. H. Boyd wrote of Lee that:

His marvelous cleverness and smartness, and his capacity as a hard hitter, seemed not quite the characteristics of the man who was to mend the devotions of the Church. He was as alert and bright a debater as ever I listened to; but even a great Lord President dismissed these qualities with the single word 'flippant'.[10]

All of these qualities are displayed in his *The Reform of the Church of Scotland*. It was Part 1, Worship, but no Part 2 was ever completed. The book gave in extended form Lee's attack on the state of worship in the Church of Scotland, and his defence and advocacy of the changes he wished to make. Against those who argued that worship was settled in the seventeenth century and in subsequent Acts of the General Assembly, Lee asserted:

We cannot make *yesterday to-day*, however we may cherish its memory or value its lessons. It is gone, dead and buried, and we inherit only the legacy it has bequeathed to us . . . Change is the order of the universe, the normal condition of all things mundane and human. Man may modify, he cannot prevent or arrest it; he may use it for his own benefit, but he can no more abrogate this than any other of the laws of nature. The chariot of Divine Providence still moves on in its glorious course, but it crushes those who stand in its way.[11]

---

9 Charles Greig McCrie, *The Public Worship of the Church of Scotland Historically Treated*, Edinburgh, 1892, pp. 327–8; Story, *Life and Remains*, vol. 1, p. 365: 'The Assembly decided for me, substantially, by a majority of 140 to 110.'

10 A. K. H. Boyd, *St. Andrews and Elsewhere*, London: Longmans, Green & Co., 1894, p. 208.

11 Robert Lee, *The Reform of the Church of Scotland in Worship, Government and Doctrine*, Part 1: Worship, Edinburgh: Edmonston & Douglas, 1864, p. 3.

Lee was an intellectual and on the liberal side of nineteenth-century the-ology, and it may well be that he was aware of the debate on evolution, which had accelerated after Darwin's *On the Origin of Species*, 1859. Lee ended his first chapter with the words,

> If the world continually go forward, and the Church stand still or go backward, what can happen but an eternal separation between science and religion; they who study God's works, and they who preach his Word regarding each other not as allies and friends, but rivals and enemies, and the multitude gradually imbibing the notion that He who inspired the Bible is not the same God who governs all things and made the worlds.[12]

Lee then proceeded to give a historical narrative clearly demonstrating that worship in the Church of Scotland had never been static as his opponents liked to believe. In his witty manner he was critical of the realities of extemporary prayer:

> Many ministers pray always the same prayers in public worship, without change or variety, from month to month and year to year, during their whole lives. Others have two, three, or four prayers, which they repeat in succession; and probably a much larger number pray extempore in the most absolute sense – plunging, on each occasion, into the great wilder-ness of thought and language – like Abraham who went forth not know-ing whither he went, but who was safe under the promised guidance from above, which these men shew, by their dreary wanderings, that they do not enjoy.[13]

Lee questioned whether the reading of prayers was a departure from Pres-byterian practice and a betrayal of ordination vows to maintain 'the purity of worship *authorized* and *practised*'.[14] He quoted from Cunningham's *Church History of Scotland*, which opined that although the State had fixed the faith of the Church, it had not fixed its worship.[15] Lee wrote:

> I have often been told, both in public and in private, that such novelties as standing to sing, kneeling to pray, reading of prayers, or the use of an organ, would be quite in order, *if the sanction of the Church Courts was first obtained*. But these things are either forbidden by the constitution and laws of the Church, or they are not.[16]

Lee argued that these had not been forbidden, and cited the use of Para-phrases in worship, which had never been either sanctioned or forbidden.

---

12 Lee, *The Reform of the Church of Scotland*, p. 8.
13 Lee, *The Reform of the Church of Scotland*, pp. 15–16.
14 Lee, *The Reform of the Church of Scotland*, p. 20.
15 Lee, *The Reform of the Church of Scotland*, p. 27.
16 Lee, *The Reform of the Church of Scotland*, p. 28.

He listed other 'innovations' that had been simply accepted, such as chanting prose psalms, and the introduction of stained-glass windows (the latter, of course, he had himself introduced!). His justification for any of his 'alleged' innovations was that none of them had ever been forbidden by the Church Courts. The need for improvement in public worship was illustrated by the losses to the Episcopal Church because of disgust and offence at Church of Scotland worship.[17] Whatever the problems with a set liturgical text, the result of extemporary prayer was in fact that every minister has 'a fixed unvarying liturgy of their own, put together by chance, stereotyped by custom – wanting both the care, finish, completeness of a systematically formed service, and also the warmth and freshness of really earnest, unpremeditated speech – uniting the faults of both methods with the virtues of neither'.[18]

Lee wrote lengthy defences of his encouragement of kneeling for prayer, and the use of instrumental music, urging the use of the harmonium, if not 'that most noble and perfect of instruments – the organ'.[19] He also urged the use of hymns in worship in addition to the metrical psalms, and referred to Mr Geikie's 'Songs of the Sanctuary', which was employed in Greyfriars.[20] After reviewing the Westminster *Directory*, *Book of Common Order* and Book of Common Prayer, Lee then presented what he regarded as the ideal or appropriate order for Church of Scotland worship:

> [A] good Church Service is a work of art – as a good sermon is – and they who imagine they can produce either without thought, labour, and skill, have either a very exalted idea of their own abilities, or a very mean conception of what they are called to do. No doubt 'it is the Spirit that quickeneth'; but the Spirit quickens and blesses those who use and improve His gifts, and leaves those who are negligent and slothful to unfruitfulness and reproof.[21]

Lee firmly urged that the service should flow and not appear disjointed, and after a solemn call to worship and prayer and praise, there should be a reading from the Old Testament. This should be followed by more prayer and praise, a New Testament reading, with prayer and praise, and after the sermon, a further prayer and a concluding doxology.[22] He also called for the immediate preparation of services for the Sacraments, marriage and burial.[23] In conclusion Lee observed, 'We are not always surely to continue the slaves of our forefathers' superstitions, prejudices, or other peculiarities.

---

17 Lee, *The Reform of the Church of Scotland*, p. 48.

18 Lee, *The Reform of the Church of Scotland*, p. 80.

19 Lee, *The Reform of the Church of Scotland*, p. 134.

20 Lee, *The Reform of the Church of Scotland*, pp. 154–5. James Stewart Geikie's collection was published in 1863.

21 Lee, *The Reform of the Church of Scotland*, pp. 180–1.

22 Lee, *The Reform of the Church of Scotland*, pp. 181–2.

23 Lee, *The Reform of the Church of Scotland*, p. 189.

Our circumstances are different; our experience is incomparably wider, and our lights are far greater than theirs.'[24] But perhaps his most important assertion was that the decline in numbers at worship 'indicates that the National Church no longer satisfies the religious tastes' of the population, which was a recognition of a shift in nineteenth-century Scottish society and culture.[25]

In the same month there appeared the *Report of Committee Anent Innovations in Public Worship* requested by the General Assembly of 1863 and which focused on 'the laws and usages of the church in regard to the administration of Public Worship'.[26] As might be expected, the report was an examination of what the legal situation was and was not, and began with a historical review from the 1550s onwards. The report felt that it would be straining the Acts of the Assembly to represent them as making the *Book of Common* Order more than a general Directory, or as intended to restrict ordained ministers at least to the rigid observance of minute regulations or the use of the *ipsissima verba* of its forms of prayer.[27] It rejected the argument that the *Book of Common Order* curtailed free prayer in contrast to the *Directory*, which encouraged it, though conceded that the *Directory* required much more effort on the part of ministers to adapt it for use.[28] It argued that the proposal for a *Directory* was initiated by the Church of Scotland, which had been requested such guidance in an Act of Assembly in 1643 (though the Act suggests it was for uniformity to avoid schism).[29] It further argued that by adopting the Westminster *Directory*, free prayer, which had formerly been permitted and encouraged, was now made imperative.[30] It noted that after the events of 1689 and the Act of 1693, the *Directory* was not specifically sanctioned but only the forms of worship in use 'at present'.[31] In Act X of the 1705 Assembly the use of the *Directory* was only recommended. In surveying the Presbyteries on current use, the report found a considerable uniformity in Sabbath Public worship: Praise, Prayer, Reading of Scripture; Praise, Prayer, lecture or Sermon; Prayer, Praise, Benediction.[32] A similar uniformity was found for Communion:

> After the action sermon, and prayer and praise, the Scriptural authority for administering the ordinance is exhibited, the tables are fenced, prayer is offered up before distributing the elements, and the communicants are successively addressed. At the close praise is offered up, the presiding

---

24 Lee, *The Reform of the Church of Scotland*, p. 195.

25 Lee, *The Reform of the Church of Scotland*, p. 39.

26 *Report of Committee Anent Innovations in Public Worship*, Edinburgh: William Blackwood & Sons, 1864, p. 3.

27 *Report of Committee*, p. 5.

28 *Report of Committee*, p. 7.

29 *Report of Committee*, p. 8, which quoted part of the Act.

30 *Report of Committee*, p. 9.

31 *Report of Committee*, p. 11.

32 *Report of Committee*, p. 16.

minister gives a concluding exhortation, and that is followed by prayer and praise, and the Benediction.[33]

The report noted:

In Old Greyfriars' the prayers are printed. A harmonium is used, and has been in use for nearly a twelvemonth.

In one church in the Presbytery of Glasgow, which has lately been erected into a parish church, the minister reports that manuscript forms are used for certain portions of the prayers.

In the Presbytery of Kelso it is in like manner reported that in one church manuscript is partially used.[34]

It additionally reported that some churches said the Lord's Prayer regularly, some occasionally, and some ministers never used it. Some 200–300 churches had choirs or bands, and in a few, chanting had been recently introduced. The Lord's Supper was celebrated at least once a year, in most twice a year, and in some, three or four times a year. In about fifty churches and chapels, Communion was administered simultaneously, but most still administered it by successive tables.[35] There were different customs for standing or sitting for prayer and vice versa for singing, and also new hymns were being used in one church. The report referred to Dr Lee's appeal to the General Assembly against the judgement of the Synod of Lothian and Tweeddale of 1859, and noted that the General Assembly had sustained the appeal, finding only that the reading from a printed book was an innovation contrary to the laws and usage of the Church. The report itself left open whether the 1864 Assembly needed to take measures or not with regard to the reported use (at Greyfriars) of reading from a printed book, and two other churches that used a manuscript.[36] It did, however, press on ministers the need to prepare public worship properly. The Committee felt there was no need to take any legislative measures concerning public worship, and noted that there was a high degree of uniformity in practice, and changes that had been made regarding the Lord's Supper should be regarded less as innovations and more the result of need for convenience and edification of members of the Church.[37]

Lee and the Committee had different interpretations of the status of the *Book of Common Order* and the normativity of the Westminster *Directory*. The Committee seemed not to want to pursue any matters with Lee or other possible innovations beyond what the Assembly had already ruled on regarding the practices at Greyfriars. The remit of the Committee

---

33 *Report of Committee*, p. 16.
34 *Report of Committee*, p. 17.
35 *Report of Committee*, p. 18.
36 *Report of Committee*, p. 21.
37 *Report of Committee*, pp. 22–3.

was limited and hence the report was focused on law and custom. Lee, by contrast, had the freedom of an author to probe more widely, and to note the changes in society that demanded change from what may have been appropriate for the eighteenth century. Lee's intellect allowed him to express this prophetical voice, which was to resonate with many other churchmen, regardless of the legal question.

Innovations resumed and unresolved

The 1864 report on innovations recorded the response from Greyfriars Edinburgh reporting that prayers were being read from a printed book. Robert Lee had laid aside the book for a period of time, though he continued to revise and publish it. However, in 1863 he resumed use of a printed liturgy. Lee could rightly claim that it was not the printed book condemned in 1859 – it was one of the new expanded editions! The congregation were quite satisfied, but once more Lee found himself charged with innovation and disobedience against the General Assembly.

At the General Assembly of 1865 the former Moderator, Dr Pirie, made plain his hostility to Lee's liturgical innovations, and put forward a motion that worship should be regulated by the Presbytery. After much debate as to whether this was actually legal, the motion was passed and became known as the Pirie Act. The Act noted that certain ministers had introduced changes in the form of worship, and so:

> The General Assembly, while recommending the utmost tenderness to the feelings of unanimous congregations as to the matters of form, do hereby Declare and Enact, that arrangements with regard to Public Worship and other religious services and ecclesiastical arrangements of any kind in Parishes or Congregations, are to be regulated by the Presbyteries of the bounds, subject always to the ordinary right of appeal, even though no express law should exist with reference to such particulars, the decisions of Presbyteries in each case being absolute and obligatory until such decisions have been finally reverses by the competent courts of review. And the General Assembly strictly prohibit all Ministers and office-bearers from assuming independent jurisdiction in such matters, as inconsistent with the vows of submission, pledged by them at ordination, to the superior Courts, under pain of the highest censure; and in the event of disobedience, the General Assembly further authorize and enjoin Presbyteries to proceed with and prosecute such censures to such conclusion as may seem essential for restoring the peace and asserting the Constitution of the Church.[38]

---

38 *Acts of the Assembly 1865*, Edinburgh: Blackwood, 1865, p. 28.

Dr Lee regarded this as legally flawed, and subverted the legal process in the church courts. Thus R. H. Story observed:

> The Decision of the Assembly on Dr Pirie's motion did not induce Dr Lee to make any change in his order of service. On the 30th May, a meeting of his congregation was held, at which resolutions were passed expressing confidence in him, and thorough sympathy with his reforms.[39]

Although the 1865 General Assembly had dismissed the complaints against Lee that had come via the Synod of Lothian and Tweeddale, the Revd John Stewart, minister of Liberton, reopened the complaint against read prayers in a motion to the Presbytery of Edinburgh in December 1865. Stewart's motion was lost, but he with Dr Muir, Dr Veitch and others, appealed to the Synod.[40] In the meantime yet another 'innovation' was widely reported, namely that Lee had officiated with his printed liturgy at a wedding in church. The *Courant* newspaper reported:

> Dr Lee, who was arrayed in his robe, with purple hood, having taken his seat in front of the table, began by the organ playing a 'voluntary'. The 128th psalm was sung by the choir, with organ accompaniment, after which Dr Lee read the service, the Lord's Prayer being repeated by the choir after the minister, and the 'Amens' given by the choir and organ. The *Te Deum* was beautifully sung to a Gregorian chant, and as the party left the church Mendelssohn's 'Wedding March' was played. The ceremony lasted half an hour.[41]

In fact a wedding in church, which had ceased to be the custom, was a restoration, but those unaware of their tradition did not perceive it as such. Dr James Veitch of St Cuthbert's, Edinburgh published, 'at the request of certain members of the Presbytery of Edinburgh', a statement on the question of innovations, and expressed the view that 'we are not free to entertain any proposal for organic change, but are bound to "assert, maintain, and defend (the Church of Scotland's) doctrine, worship, and discipline, and never to endeavour, either directly or indirectly, the prejudice or subversion of it".'[42] This statement added nothing new to the debate, and discussed the historical background in much the same manner as the General Assembly Committee report of 1864. It noted that 'innovators seem especially anxious to escape the suspicion of aiming at the introduction of a liturgy, by fastidiously rejecting the term as applied to the service-book

---

39 Story, *Life and Remains*, vol. 2, p. 181.

40 Story, *Life and Remains*, vol. 2, p. 237.

41 *Edinburgh Evening Courant*, 28 December 1865, quoted in Story, *Life and Remains*, vol. 2, pp. 237–8.

42 James Veitch, *Statement Concerning Innovations as now attempted in the Church of Scotland*, Edinburgh: Blackwood, 1866, title page and p. 3.

which a minister himself prepares and uses at his own discretion.'[43] Among innovations the statement listed posture, prayers and instrumental music, and Veitch presented them as an escalation.[44] In the view of Veitch and the 'certain ministers', these novelties were but old things revived again.[45]

The Synod met in May, and reversed the decision of the Presbytery.[46] The Presbytery of Edinburgh and a number of Synods and Presbyteries had sent overtures questioning the Pirie Act, on the grounds that it has transferred powers to Presbyteries that hitherto had been the concern of the Kirk Session. However, attempts to repeal the Act were unsuccessful. The complaint against Lee and his innovations was renewed in the Presbytery, and appealed to the Synod in November 1866, which found in favour of those alleging innovation. A committee was appointed to confer with Dr Lee. It met on 13 February 1867, and Lee presented a document with full explanation and defence of his actions. It was in this document that Lee admitted that he had resumed the use of a book of prayers in the winter of 1863, but it was not the same book as had been forbidden in 1859. The Presbytery found against Lee, and Lee and his supporters appealed the decision and Lee himself continued conducting services in his usual manner.[47] The result was that Lee's non-compliance was reported to the General Assembly. He issued a 'Letter to the members of the ensuing General Assembly', published on 18 May, once more setting out his case, and his belief that the ruling of 1859 had been abrogated by the 1864 Assembly.[48] The whole ordeal was taking its toll on Lee's health. On 22 May, the day before the Assembly was due to meet, he suffered a stroke and fell from his horse, never fully recovered, and died from a second stroke on 12 March 1868. On account of his illness, the matter could not be discussed by the General Assembly, and his death meant that it could never be resumed. Writing in 1870, R. H. Story commented:

> The protracted discussions upon Innovations thus came to a vague and undefined close. The 'Greyfriars' case' remains still unfinished – ending only in a postponement. Dr Lee's friends were not sorry that it should end thus, as they knew that, if the appeal had been heard, the decision of the Assembly would have been adverse. They knew that his long contest had produced results sufficiently substantial, even although his right to use a printed book of prayers had not been vindicated.[49]

In some respects, this tragic conclusion may have been, after all, part of the path of that chariot of divine providence that Lee spoke of. Lee himself

---

43 Veitch, *Statement*, p. 9.
44 Veitch, *Statement*, p. 11.
45 Veitch, *Statement*, p. 15.
46 See reports in the Edinburgh *Daily Review*, 1 March 1866 and 2 May 1866.
47 For a report on the Presbytery of Edinburgh, see *The Scotsman*, 15 March 1867.
48 Story, *Life and Remains*, vol. 2, pp. 337–49.
49 Story, *Life and Remains*, vol. 2, p. 353.

might not have benefited, but his 'liturgical disruptions' appealed to a good many ministers and the fruits would be reaped by his friends and successors. Dr Lee had rightly discerned that organic change, rather like evolution, might be delayed but could not be halted.

Lee's liturgies: from *Prayers for Public Worship* to the *Order of Public Worship*

The original form of *Prayers for Public Worship* was published in 1857, and contained services for three Sundays of the month. A revised second edition appeared the following year, containing a fourth Sunday service, as well as services for baptism, the Lord's Supper, marriage and burial, and a prose psalter and canticles. A third edition followed in 1863 under the title *A Presbyterian Prayer Book*, and a fourth was published in 1864 under the title *The Order of Public Worship and Administration of the Sacraments as used in the Church of Greyfriars, Edinburgh*. Lee's executors issued a fifth edition under the same title in 1873. These were in the hands of the congregation of Greyfriars, but the number of editions suggest that there was a wider market or audience for Lee's 'innovations'.

Writing in 1890, A. K. H. Boyd wrote of Lee's liturgical compilations:

He had little ear for the melody of liturgical prayer. . . . The genuine liturgical flow was quite lacking in most of Dr Lee's prayers, which were to a considerable degree original. They were likewise, very naturally flavoured with Dr Lee's theology; which was more advanced than was in those days common.[50]

Lee was regarded by many as a liberal in theology. He had been appointed Professor of Biblical Criticism at Edinburgh, and in his inaugural lecture had questioned the apparent Christian adoption of the Rabbinic view on the inerrancy of the Scriptural text.[51] John O'Neill summarised:

He insisted in his inaugural lecture on the need to ask whether statements in the Bible on physics, astronomy, natural history of theology were to be understood as 'the dictates of the Spirit of God, or only as made in accommodation to the popular opinions prevailing in the times of the writers, whether those opinions were true or false'. He noticed that textual criticism of the New Testament had removed two readings in support of the doctrine of the Trinity (in 1 Timothy 3:16; 1 John 5:7–8), and looked for the 'reconcilement' of Christians when the New Testa-

---

50 A. K. H. Boyd, 'The New Liturgies of the Scottish Kirk', *Blackwood's Edinburgh Magazine* 148 (1890), pp. 665, 670.

51 Story, *Life and Remains*, vol. 1. pp. 122–3.

ment should become the text-book from which all parties were content *immediately* to draw their theology.[52]

Lee was certainly acquainted with the classical Eastern and Western liturgies but he had no particular antiquarian interests in them. R. Stuart Louden (one of Lee's twentieth-century successors at Greyfriars) rightly commented that Lee's worship reforms had aesthetic rather than technically liturgical origins.[53] Louden observed that a critical examination of the Greyfriars service book reveals the temptation to indulge in 'purple passages'; to employ extravagances of language or irrelevant archaisms; and to be pompous, vague and repetitious.[54] Lee's liberalism, for example, is illustrated in his very free emendation of the text of the *Te Deum*.

In the preface of the first edition Lee claimed that he had done his best to ensure that the prayers should not be declamatory, oratorical, or fine – familiar, tedious or particular – didactic or sermonizing; and he had laboured to make them, as far as he could, simple, dignified and devotional; suggesting as much as possible, without running into detail.[55] It was in this preface that he mentioned his acquaintance with the Latin and Greek liturgies collected by Renaudot, as well as the older Presbyterian liturgies, but wisdom dictated against seeking to revive them, and instead to make compositions more directly from Scripture.

The provisions for public worship in this first edition[56] consists of three morning and afternoon services, plus psalms. The first Forenoon service began with two sentences of Scripture, an exhortation to pray and an opening prayer, 'O God, whom heaven and the heaven of heavens cannot contain', followed by further scripture sentences (from Psalm 61), and a prayer of confession, sentences from Psalm 130, a thanksgiving prayer and then an Old Testament lesson. Sentences from Psalm 93 followed, and then three prayers leading up to the New Testament reading and optional singing of a Psalm. A whole series of prayers and intercessions followed, leading to saying a Psalm of praise (Psalm 9) and then the Lord's Prayer, a sung psalm and the Benediction (Grace). All the services followed a similar format. A prose text of extracts from the psalter was also included. Something of Lee's style is illustrated in the prayer for grace in the Forenoon service for the second Sunday:

---

52 John O'Neill, 'New Testament', in David F. Wright and Gary D. Badcock (eds), *Disruption to Diversity: Edinburgh Divinity 1846–1996*, Edinburgh: T & T Clark, 1996, pp. 73–97, p. 74.

53 R. Stuart Louden, 'The Lee Lecture for 1968', *Church Service Society Annual* 39 (1969) pp. 27–37, p. 32.

54 Louden, 'The Lee Lecture', pp. 32–3.

55 As reprinted in the second edition, *Prayers for Public Worship*, Edinburgh: John Menzies, 1858 (Facsimile reprint, Delhi, 2015), pp. v–vi.

56 *Prayers for Public Worship, with extracts from the Psalms*, Edinburgh: John Greenhill, 1857. I am grateful to Douglas Galbraith for providing me with photographs of the copy of this liturgy in the library of the University of St Andrews.

Almighty God, Father of our Lord Jesus Christ, who hast, in thy Gospel, proclaimed remission of sins to all them that believe in the name of thy Son, and repent of their transgressions against thee; confirm us, we beseech thee, O Lord, in the faith and hope of this thy promise. And, for this end, so work in us, by thy Holy Spirit, that we may embrace and hold fast thy truth, in a pure conscience, unto the end; and also may bring forth fruits meet for repentance: that being justified freely by thy grace, and walking continually in the way of thy commandments, we may glorify thy holy name; and may know that we are thy children, and heirs of that kingdom which thou hast promised to them that love thee.[57]

Although laced with biblical phrases, it illustrates Boyd's criticism of lacking a liturgical flow.

The preface to the second edition explained that 'the approbation with which these Prayers have been received has induced me to revise them with care; in consequence, some slight alterations, chiefly in arrangement, have been made.'[58] Services for Forenoon and Afternoon were now provided for four Sundays of the month. The structure was uniform, and his short prayers were interspersed with scripture sentences. For the Forenoon Service Lee provided opening sentences of Scripture, invitation, introductory prayer, scripture sentences, confession, comfortable words of Scripture, prayer for grace, Old Testament reading, optional Psalm sung, prayer with Scripture, New Testament, optional Psalm sung, sermon, (or these may come after the Lord's Prayer), intercessions, Psalm of praise, Benediction. The Afternoon Service had sentences of Scripture, invitation, introductory prayer, further scripture sentences, scripture reading, optional Psalm sung, prayer interspersed with scripture sentences, optional sermon and optional Psalm sung, prayers, intercessions, an evening prayer, a Psalm of praise, Lord's Prayer, Psalm sung and Benediction.

Much of the material of the services for the first three Sundays was carried over from the first edition, but with minor changes, some omissions, and rewording and altered punctuation. For example, in the first Forenoon service, more scripture sentences have been added at the beginning of the service, and the exhortation to prayer was altered, that of 1857 appearing in expanded version in the first Afternoon service.

The rite for the Lord's Supper followed what Lee termed 'the preliminary Services', which would seem to refer to preparation services rather than a Forenoon service. It commenced with scripture sentences from 1 Corinthians 10, and then an introductory prayer of confession with a prayer for grace, which was a version of the 'Prayer of the Veil' probably suggested by the Catholic Apostolic Liturgy. A 'Eucharistic Prayer' followed, which was simply that – a prayer of thanksgiving for creation and salvation history. A

---

57 *Prayers for Public Worship*, 1857, p. 33.
58 *Prayers for Public Worship*, 1858, p. iii.

paraphrase was then sung, 'O Thou my soul, bless God the Lord'. A short 'Consecration Prayer' followed:

Almighty God, we, thy servants, calling to mind the most blessed sacrifice of thy Son, rejoicing in that salvation which he hath accomplished for us, do in this manner, eating this bread and drinking of this cup, according to his command, show forth the Lord's death till he come again:

Wherefore, we entreat thee to grant thy heavenly benediction, that these creatures of bread and wine may be set apart and consecrated to this holy use and mystery: that we, by faith, may look upon Christ our Lord, set forth under these symbols, and may receive the bread of everlasting life, and the cup of eternal salvation, so that the hunger and thirst of our souls may be satisfied, that the power of sin and death may be destroyed, both in the flesh and in the spirit, and we may be preserved in soul and body unto eternal life. Amen.[59]

The division between a 'Eucharistic Prayer' and 'Consecration Prayer' may possibly be the influence of the Catholic Apostolic Liturgy.[60] Lee's consecration prayer has echoes of the classical anamnesis, but also the Westminster *Directory* recommendations for setting apart the elements, as well as the Book of Common Prayer. A Psalm of praise followed, during which it seems that Communion was administered. A rubric from the Westminster *Directory* is placed after the Psalm, and then a post-communion prayer almost word for word from the Book of Common Prayer. Intercessions followed, which made mention of the saints and the patriarchs and prophets, apostle, evangelists, martyrs and confessors. A concluding prayer – again borrowed from the Catholic Apostolic Liturgy – with the Lord's Prayer followed, a hymn and a Benediction.

The provision for baptism began with scripture sentences, and then inserted a rubric from the Westminster *Directory*, and the prayer before the baptism was mainly that of the *Directory* turned into a prayer. Two post-baptismal prayers and the Lord's Prayer, Psalm and Benediction concluded this short rite.

Services for marriage and for burial were also provided. After scripture sentences, two introductory prayers were given, and after enquiring about impediments, formulae for the vows were given. After the declaration of marriage came the Aaronic Benediction, a reading from Ephesians 5:22–33 or a selection from 1 Peter 3:1–7, 1 Corinthians 6 and 7. This was followed by three prayers, the Lord's Prayer and Psalm 128, said or sung, and the service concluded with the Grace. Burial of the Dead had scripture sentences (cf. Book of Common Prayer) a choice of psalmody, a choice of scripture readings, two prayers, the committal, two further prayers and

---

59 *Prayers for Public Worship*, 1858, p. 122.

60 See Kenneth W. Stevenson, 'The Catholic Apostolic Eucharist', PhD thesis, University of Southampton, 1973.

the Lord's Prayer and the Grace. Two prayers from the Dutch Reformed liturgy were given as alternatives. The body of psalms is virtually the same, but, again, there have been a small handful of alterations – for example, a curtailment of the extract from Psalm 119 but with a slight addition.

The edition of 1863 was entitled *A Presbyterian Prayer Book and Psalm Book.*[61] In the 'Advertisement', Lee explained that the services contained in the first part of the volume were those of 1858, but 'with some changes, and many additions, derived chiefly from the author's "Prayers for Family Worship", 1861'. Services for a fifth Sunday had been added, and although it contained a service for the Lord's Supper, Lee took the decision not to include services for baptism, marriage and burial, and this edition also omitted the prose psalms.

The Sunday services were arranged as three acts of Word, Prayer and Praise, with the sermon, prayer and praise being a fourth segment. Although Lee could honestly claim that the liturgy of 1863 was not that of 1858, which that the Assembly had requested him to lay aside, the fact remains that it was closely modelled on it. For example, the first Sunday Forenoon service of 1863 dropped one scripture sentence of 1858 but retained the rest, and the opening prayers are exactly the same, save for altered punctuation. The psalm verses and responses were altered and some scripture sentences reversed in order of sequence. The position of the Lord's Prayer was altered and selected psalms were given prior to an Old Testament reading. Lee's method, therefore, was to rearrange the sequence of prayers and lightly alter the phraseology. The same is true for the Lord's Supper. Prayers now were provided for the Fast Day preceding Communion. The service itself now commenced with reading 1 Corinthians 11:23–29, followed by a section from Hebrews 12, and then the sentences provided in 1858. The Apostles' Creed and a Psalm have now been inserted before the prayers before the communion prayers as in 1858. The metrical psalm between the 'Eucharistic Prayer and 'Consecration Prayer' was moved to during the administration, and the title of the two prayers were removed. The remainder of the service was as that of 1858.

The definitive form of Lee's liturgical endeavours was published in 1864, with the title *The Order of Public Worship*, and this was the book that was the subject of the complaint and appeal before the General Assembly in 1867. An Advertisement in the 1864 book explained that it was a reprint of *A Presbyterian Prayer Book* but with some slight corrections and additions. The additions included a restoration of the other services as in 1858. The posthumously published 1873 version was simply a reprint of 1864.

Lee claimed that his prayers were taken from Scripture rather than being modelled on classic liturgical sources, and that they asserted or implied 'Christian doctrines in a catholic spirit, avoiding all sectarian vehemence

---

61 Robert Lee, *A Presbyterian Prayer-Book and Psalm-Book*, Edinburgh: John Greenhill, 1863, copy in Lambeth Palace Library.

and controversial exaggeration'.[62] Lee also claimed – with some exaggeration – that numerous works 'of the same class' had appeared within recent years from Presbyterian and independent churches, and were a pleasing sign that prejudices against composed prayers were 'rapidly dying away'.[63] In the Lord's Supper, the taking of the bread and the cup are made explicit, and words of administration were provided. The baptismal service underwent a more considerable revision. The opening sentences remained but provision was made to ask the father or sponsor if baptism was desired, followed by an explication of the 'holy signs and badges', together with the duties of sponsors. The Apostle's Creed was then recited, followed by a prayer for the infant and then the Lord's Prayer, and then the baptism with the triune formula. The post-baptismal prayers were new compositions. In the marriage service a formula for asking about impediments was given and the vows were rewritten. The burial service was largely left intact.

For Lee this may have been a *different book*, but for his opponents the problem was that it was still *a book*.

A. K. Robertson observed that Lee's persistence in practice left the way open for others to prepare and use books of prayers in church.[64] In the year of Lee's stroke and fall from his horse, another book appeared on the market, the *Euchologion*, prepared by the Church Service Society. Lee was persuaded to become a member of this Society, founded in 1865. He contributed a paper for the Society on 'The Arrangement of the several Parts of Public Worship', and his baptismal liturgy was incorporated into the first edition of the *Euchologion*. Without the 'liturgical disruption' of Lee, the Society might have met with far more resistance to its aims and work than was actually the case. In a sense, Lee's work provided the DNA from which a better adapted species of liturgy could evolve.

---

62 *The Order of public Worship*, 1864/1873; 1873 edition, Edinburgh: Thomas & Archibald Constable, p. v.

63 *The Order of Public Worship*, p. v.

64 A. K. Robertson, 'The Place of Dr Robert Lee in the Development in the Public Worship of the Church of Scotland 1840–1940', in *Church Service Society Annual* 28 (1958), pp. 31–46, p. 33.

3

The Church Service Society
and the *Euchologion*

In his *A Handbook of the Church of Scotland* of 1888, Dr James Rankin listed some of the recent improvements made in 'Taste, Tolerance, and Literature' in the Kirk. In addition to restoration of certain church buildings, improvements in church music, and the publication by the General Assembly of certain forms of private devotional prayers, he also noted that:

> there is a special Church Service Society, at present consisting of 566 members (of whom 466 are clergymen), whose efforts have been directed towards a compilation of prayers from sources ancient and modern, with a view towards the improvement of the public prayers of the Church.[1]

Whether or not Professor Malcolm Campbell Taylor, who had become a member of the Church Service Society in 1875 when minister of Morningside, Edinburgh, and who chaired the Annual Church Service Society meeting in 1885, had been inspired by the Society's first *Euchologion* when published in 1867 will probably remain unknown. However, at least when minister of Crathie (1867–73), his ministrations of both the sacraments were appreciated by Queen Victoria, and also witness to the trend towards improvement in decency and order that was already afoot in the Church. The Queen described a baptism that took place in the home of John Thomson on 24 October 1868:

> Dr. Taylor (who wore his gown) then began with an address and prayer, giving thanks 'for a living mother and a living child' after which followed another prayer; he then read a few passages from Scripture, after which came the usual questions which he addressed to the father, and to which he bowed assent. Then the minister told him – 'Present your child for baptism'. After this the father took the child and held it while the minister baptised it, sprinkling it with water, but not making the sign of the cross, saying first to those present: 'The child's name is Victoria'; and then to the child:

1 James Rankin, *A Handbook of the Church of Scotland*, Edinburgh: William Blackwood & Sons, 1888, p. 293. He gave the year of founding as 1864, which in fact is not correct.

Victoria, I baptise thee in the name of the Father, and of the Son, and of the Holy Ghost, One God blessed for ever, – Amen.

The Lord bless thee and keep thee! The Lord make His face to shine upon thee and be gracious unto thee! The Lord lift up His countenance upon thee and give thee peace!

The service was concluded with another short prayer and the usual blessing. . . . It was all so nicely done, so simply, and yet with such dignity.[2]

On Sunday 13 November 1871, the Queen attended a communion service at Crathie Parish Church, and described it thus:

At the end of the sermon began the service of the Communion, which is most touching and beautiful, and impressed and moved me more than I can express. I shall never forget it.

The appearance of the kirk was very striking, with the tables in the cross seats, on either side facing the pulpit, covered with a white cloth. Neither Brown, though he came with us, nor any of our Scotch servants sat behind us, as usual, but all below, as every one does who intends taking the sacrament at the 'first table'. A table, also covered with a white cloth, was placed in front of the middle pew, directly facing the pulpit.

The service was the same as that on ordinary Sundays until after the sermon, excepting that every psalm and prayer had reference to the Lord's Supper, and the sermon was on the *perfect obedience of the Son* (Hebrews ii.10).

The prayer after the sermon was very short, after which Dr. Taylor delivered an address from the pulpit, in which he very beautifully invited all true penitents to receive the communion, the hardened sinner alone to abstain. It was done in a very kind and encouraging tone. Dr. Taylor adopted part of one of the English prayers, only shortened and simplified . . . After this address – 'the Fencing of the Tables' as it is called – the minister came down to the small table in front of the pulpit, where he stood with the assistant minister, and the elders on either side, and while the 35th Paraphrase was being sung the elders brought in the Elements and placed them on the table, viz. the bread cut into small pieces, and two large plates lined with napkins, and the wine in four large silver cups. The minister then read the words of the institution of the Lord's Supper, from 1 Corinthians xi.23, and this was followed by a short but very impressive prayer of consecration.

This done, he handed the bread first, and then the wine, right and left to the elders, Francis Leys (Brown's uncle), Symon 'the merchant', Hunter, and Dr. Robertson, to dispense; himself giving both to one or two people nearest to him, who were in the middle pew, where the Thomsons all sit generally, and in which, on this occasion, were old Donald Stewart and

---

2 Queen Victoria, *More Leaves from the Journal of a life in the Highlands: From 1862 to 1882*, London: Smith, Elder & Co., 1884, pp. 111–12.

his wife (eighty-six and eighty-one, looking so nice and venerable), the young Donald Stewarts, The Thomsons, old Mr. and Mrs. Brown (he eighty-one and very much bent, and she seventy-one). Old John Brown and old Donald Stewart wore large plaids; old Smith of *Kintore* was likewise in this pew. The bread was then reverently eaten, and the wine drunk, sitting, each person passing it on one to the other; the cup being replaced by each on the table before them after they had partaken of the wine, and then the elder carried it on to the next pews, in which there were tables, until all those in that portion of the church prepared for the Lord's Supper, had communicated. After which the elders replaced the Elements on the table before the minister, who delivered a short address of thankfulness and exhortation. He then gave out the 103rd Psalm, which was sung while the communicants were leaving the tables, to be occupied in turn by others.

We left after this. It would indeed be impossible to say how deeply we were impressed by the grand simplicity of the service. It was all so truly earnest, and no description can do justice to the perfect devotion of the whole assemblage.[3]

Taylor's care and concern for devout and moving services made him an obvious prospective member of that 'special Church Service Society'.

The founding of the Society

The Church Service Society was officially founded, not in 1864 as Rankin stated but on 31 January 1865, at a meeting held at the Religious Institution Rooms in Glasgow. The first page of the Minute Book 1865–1899, reads:

Mr. Wilson was called to the chair, and opened the meeting with prayer.
Mr. Campbell was appointed Clerk to the meeting.
The Chairman having stated the object of the meeting to be the formation of a Society for the study of the ancient and reformed liturgies, and the preparation of prayers and other services adapted for the worship of the Church of Scotland.[4]

The founding of the Society was planned by R. H. Story, Cameron Lees and George Campbell. In a letter of 1904, George Campbell, who served for many years as the secretary of the Society, explained:

I think, the month of November 1864, I was assisting at the Communion in a country parish in the neighbourhood, where I spent several days with Dr. Cameron Lees, then of Paisley, and a co-Presbyter of my own. Our

---

3 Queen Victoria, *More Leaves*, pp. 152–5.
4 Church Service Society Minutes 1865–1899, p. 1. This is a manuscript transcription of the original Minutes.

minds were full, as were those of many others at that time, of improvements in Church services. I had been taken with the idea of a Society for the purpose first propounded by Dr Sprott in a pamphlet shortly before published by him, bearing the title of 'The Worship, Rites, and Ceremonies of the Church of Scotland', or such like . . . Dr. Cameron Lees took it up eagerly, and he often dwells in conversation with me on a winter morning walk which we took together, and he identifies the very spot on the Eaglesham Road where we came to the resolution to proceed actively in the matter. It was agreed that I was to write to Dr. Story and inform him of what we had concluded, asking his co-operation . . . We three conspirators then met in Glasgow and agreed to sound the views of various like-minded ministers, and to invite them to attend a meeting for the purpose.[5]

As Campbell acknowledged in this letter, a major catalyst that led to the founding of the Church Service Society was a publication of 1863 by George Washington Sprott.

3.1
The Revd George Campbell,
The Revd Dr Cameron Lees,
The Revd Dr R. H. Story,
The Revd Dr G. W. Sprott

---

5 The letter was reproduced in John Kerr, *The Renascence of Worship: The Origin, Aims, and Achievements of the Church Service Society*, Edinburgh: J. Gardner Hitt, 1910, pp. 6–9.

George Sprott was born in Nova Scotia in 1829, the son of a Presbyterian minister, and decided to train for the ministry, studying at the University of Glasgow.[6] He was licensed by the Presbytery of Dunoon in 1852 for work overseas, and returned to Nova Scotia. After brief pastorates back in Scotland at Greenock and Dumfries, he went as chaplain of the Scots Kirk in Kandy, Ceylon (Sri Lanka) from 1857 to 1864. He returned to the United Kingdom and spent a year as acting chaplain at Portsmouth, and in 1866 became minister at Garioch and later at North Berwick. He was thus able to play a leading role in the society, which had been founded on the inspiration of his 1863 publication, *The Worship, Rites and Ceremonies of the Church of Scotland*. This was both a review of the history of worship in the Church of Scotland and a guide for better and more reverent worship. He discussed the *Directory* but did not regard this as the sole ancestor of Scottish worship. He suggested a wider liturgical gene pool, including not only the *The Book of Common Order* but also other Reformed rites, the Catholic Apostolic Church's rite or 'Irvingite' as he termed it, and the Greek liturgies. In order to make sure any changes in worship were 'informed changes', Sprott recommended that the clergy of the Church of Scotland should acquaint themselves with the Reformed and early liturgies, since a 'man should know what he is about before he interferes with what has been consecrated by time and ancestral associations'.[7] While not particularly enamoured of the *Directory*, he believed that the practice of clergymen was considerably below even the standard of the *Directory*.[8] He believed that the study of liturgy would assist clergy to 'prepare prayers of a simpler and purer type than those long addresses to the Deity which are not unfrequent – prayers purged of their well-known scraps of bad taste and nonsensical misquotations of Scripture which second-rate men rhyme over'.[9]

This short pamphlet of fifty-four pages included discussion on improvements of Public Worship (the morning service), Baptism, Confirmation, The Lord's Supper, Marriage and Burial of the Dead. In his discussion of the Lord's Supper, Sprott (who had probably read the Mercersburg theologian, John William Nevin's *The Mystical Presence*, 1846) urged that Calvin's view on presence be restored to the Church:

> According to this view, the Lord's Supper is a feast on the memorials of the great sacrifice; to them who received aright, though the elements are in their substance unchanged, Christ is really present, and there is a mysterious participation of His glorified nature by the faithful; though

---

6 Details from J. Clark Saunders, 'George Sprott and the Revival of Worship in Scotland, Part I: Sprott's Theological Principles', *Liturgical Review* 7 (1977), pp. 45–54; 'Part II: Sprott's Liturgical Work', *Liturgical Review* 8 (1978), pp. 11–22.

7 G. W. Sprott, *The Worship, Rites, and Ceremonies of the Church of Scotland*, Edinburgh: Blackwoods, 1863, p. 1.

8 Sprott, *The Worship*, p. 4.

9 Sprott, *The Worship*, pp. 4–5.

this participation is not peculiar to this ordinance there is in it a receiving of Christ which surpasseth comprehension.[10]

Sprott questioned the necessity of the number of days over which Communion was celebrated, as well as the length of the Communion Addresses given at the tables.[11] However, it was in the Introduction that he suggested that:

> there should be a self-constituted Society of the liturgical scholars in the Church, who would, after due time and full consideration of the whole subject, draw up a book of prayers for public worship and of forms for the administration of the sacraments and other special services, as a guide to the clergy.[12]

It was this suggestion that the 'three conspirators' made an official reality in January 1865.

The aims and intentions of the Society

The main aim and purpose of the Church Service Society would be stated in Article V:

> That the object of the Society shall be the study of the liturgies – ancient and modern – of the Christian Church, with a view to the preparation and publication of forms of Prayer for Public Worship, and services for the Administration of the Sacraments, the Celebration of Marriage, the Burial of the Dead, etc.[13]

This Article of the Constitution would allow the Society to widen the liturgical gene pool by publishing liturgies of the past and present, as well as preparing liturgical forms itself.

The formation of the Society did not go unnoticed or without comment. John Kerr observed:

> But no sooner was the Church Service Society formed than showers of polysyllabic denunciation and abuse descended upon its founders.
> They were 'a set of beardless youths', a crime of which their accusers would gladly have been guilty; they were Romanists, Ritualists, Prelatists, Jesuits, traitors, conspirators, and what not, the ecclesiastical vocabulary, which is not at any time meagre, being insufficient for their full description.[14]

---

10 Sprott, *The Worship*, p. 38.
11 Sprott, *The Worship*, p. 40.
12 Sprott, *The Worship*, p. 5.
13 Kerr, *The Renascence*, p. 72.
14 Kerr, *The Renascence*, p. 15.

3.2 First page of the copied minutes of the Church Service Society, 1865

A report prepared by a sub-committee under the convenorship of R. H. Story was read and adopted by the Society at its 31 March 1865 meeting at Glasgow, and this attempted to dispel accusations that the purpose of the Society was to introduce a liturgy into the Church of Scotland. The report insisted:

That the introduction of a Liturgy into any Church whose worship has not been hitherto liturgical, must be a measure long considered, slowly matured, and ultimately carried, not by any private association of clergy-men, but by the public, official, and constitutional action of the Church herself. It is hoped that no Member of the Society will require further assurance that the Society's aim is not (as has been insinuated) to intro-duce a Liturgy.[15]

The report defended the aims of the society to prepare (not impose) forms of worship:

In considering the subject remitted to them, it has appeared to the Sub-Committee that there are at present two somewhat powerful currents of feeling in the Church which are generally supposed to run counter to each other, but which in reality do not, or at least need not, do so. The one feeling is that of sincere attachment to the simplicity of our non-liturgical worship. The other is an earnest desire for a worship more solemn, uni-form, and devout, than (in tone and aspect at least) our non-liturgical service generally is.[16]

A distinction was drawn in the report between simplicity and lifelessness, and much worship in the Church, according to the Sub-Committee, was lifeless. It argued that the work of the Society should be divided into two main branches, called the Constructive and the Eclectic. The former would entail compilations of special services such as for baptism and the Lord's Supper. In the Lord's Supper, it noted that it was important that the com-municant was being addressed by the Church and not the individual ideas of the minister. The 'Eclectic' would entail a compilation of classic prayers from the whole Christian tradition. At a meeting of the committee on 14 August 1865, reference was made to a paper on public prayer by C. J. Brown of Edinburgh, which it was thought might be circulated among ministers. A paper 'On Public Prayer' was indeed printed and circulated. It must be assumed it was Brown's paper, though the curiosity is that Brown was a minister of the Free Church of Scotland, and initially membership of the Society was limited to members of the Church of Scotland. The paper argued that worship forms were capable of improvement, and should be improved. Problems with current modes of worship included confused and confusing repetitions, misquotations of Scripture and the intrusion of personal opinion or bias in intercessions. Questions that needed to be asked included: who is the object of worship and by whom is worship offered? Brown's paper suggested some guides, such as that public prayer should be simple, reverent, have a certain uniformity of expression, a certain uniformity or catholicity of language and of plan. It concluded:

15 Report, p. 1. This is reprinted in Kerr, *The Renascence*, pp. 53–60.
16 Report, p. 3; Kerr, *The Renascence*, p. 55.

Prayers may become 'common' not because they are prescribed and we dare not use any others, but because their own saintly, grave, and solemn music has passed into the common heart and memory – has become dear and familiar from its own surpassing beauty to pastors and people alike – and rises to their lips as the most apt expression of their deepest wants and holiest aspirations.[17]

This paper referred to Dr Robert Lee's 'valuable Books of Devotion'.[18] Lee was consulted about the formation of the Society, and did become a member, but seems to have had a somewhat ambivalent relationship to it. R. H. Story explained:

[Lee] would have liked that his book should be adopted by the Society, and that the members should use it as far as they found it practicable to do so. It was impossible, however, that there could be any general, or even a partial, agreement to this effect.[19]

Lee considered resigning from the Society but in the event was persuaded to remain, and contributed to the *Euchologion* – its first baptismal service was based on that in his 1864 book. He also wrote for the Society one of its key papers, 'Arrangement of the Several Parts of Public Worship', in which he urged the Society to adopt an order or sequence that he used in his own book.[20] In the event it did not meet with cordial reception.[21]

Resistance to any changes in worship, though, was strong, and even something as simple as change of posture in worship was a delicate issue for many. In 1866, J. H. Tait, minister of Aberlady, addressed a seven-page letter to his parishioners arguing for kneeling for prayer and standing to sing. The letter was passed to the Church Service Society, which discussed it at a committee meeting.[22] However, from the start the concern of the 'three conspirators' and their supporters was to prepare a volume of church services. The Minutes record that at the meeting in Glasgow on 14 August 1865: 'The Committee next took into consideration the preparation of a volume of public prayers etc., and agreed that the special services should be first drawn up by different members of Committee.'[23]

This was the conception of the *Euchologion*.

---

17 'On Public Prayer'. Issued by Church Service Society (1865), p. 11; Kerr, *The Renascence*, p. 83.

18 'On Public Prayer', p. 5; Kerr, *The Renascence*, p. 80.

19 R. H. Story, *The Life and Remains of Robert Lee, DD*, in 2 volumes, London: Hurst & Blackett, 1870, vol. 2, p. 140.

20 Church Service Society Minutes (Editorial Committee), 4 June 1866, p. 25. Lee's lengthy proposal is recorded in Story, *The Life and Remains*, vol. 2, pp. 142–8.

21 William McMillan, 'Euchologion: The Book of Common Order', *Church Service Society Annual* 9 (1936–7), pp. 24–33, p. 25.

22 J. H. Tait, Letter to the Parishioners of Aberlady, November 1866, copy in the Church Service Society archives. Tait was a member of the Society, though is not listed by Kerr until 1870.

23 Church Service Society, Minutes I, p. 15.

The *Euchologion*: its birth, evolution and influence

The Society Minutes record the distribution of the services intended for the volume that became the *Euchologion* as follows: The Communion, G. W. Sprott; Baptism, J. H. Tait and R. H. Story; Marriage, Dr John Cunningham; Burial, J. Dodds; Ordination, W. Tait; Morning and Evening Worship, Principal Campbell, Dr McCulloch, Dr Watson, Dr Boyd, Cameron Lees and George Campbell; and Principal Tulloch, a collection of prayers and thanksgivings, though William McMillan was of the opinion that the bulk of the work was done by Sprott, Tulloch and Story.[24] The work seems to have proceeded apace, and at the Editorial Committee meeting at Glasgow on 15 January 1866, it was reported that drafts of two baptismal services, one communion service, three services for Morning worship and one for evening worship had been prepared for circulation among the members of the editorial committee.[25] On 9 May 1867 the proofs were available and the publication of the volume was sanctioned.[26]

The Preface of the 1867 *Euchologion* explained that it was not the intention of a private group of clergymen to introduce a liturgy into the Church and that since the Kirk is a National branch of the Church Catholic, each clergyman has the liberty to use whatever in the recorded devotions of that Church he finds most suitable to his congregation's needs.[27]

This first edition provided information about the wider gene pool that the compilers had used. Thus the first baptismal rite is inspired by the *Book of Common Order*. Outlines of the Eucharist from Justin Martyr, *Apostolic Constitutions*, J. M. Neale's Eastern Orthodox rite, the Roman Mass, some continental Reformed rites, the Church of England rite, as well as the Irvingites' (Catholic Apostolic Church) and Mercersburg (American German Reformed Church) were given. A lectionary was offered providing for a Psalm, Old Testament and New Testament readings, and in the last pages of the book there was a collection of materials for the Sabbath service from which selections could be made. This latter consisted of fourteen sections: Sentences of Scripture, Introductory Prayers, Confession of Sin, Thanksgiving, Supplications, A General Pleading, Prayers, Prayers before the Sermon, Ascriptions of Praise (after the Sermon), Intercession, Collects, Suggested Canticles and Paraphrases, and Benedictions. Footnotes gave the sources. Of the two baptismal rites, the first purported to be based on Knox's *Book of Common Order*, and in fact was that of Lee's 1864 book. The second was constructed from the recommendations of the Westminster *Directory* and included a long explication on baptism.

---

24 Minutes I, pp. 15–16; McMillan, 'Euchologion: The Book of Common Order', p. 24.
25 Minutes I, p. 20.
26 Minutes I, pp. 30–1.
27 *Euchologion or Book of Prayers, Being Forms of Worship Issued by the Church Service Society*, Edinburgh: Blackwood, 1867, Preface, p. iv.

The Church Service Society wanted to promote more frequent celebration of the Communion and so, regardless of the reality of Church of Scotland worship, which was infrequent celebration, this rite may be regarded as the centrepiece. Probably the greatest inspiration for the Communion rite was the liturgy of the Catholic Apostolic Church and that of the American German Reformed Church, its provisional liturgy itself being heavily inspired by the Catholic Apostolic Liturgy. The *Euchologion* listed what it deemed 'Material for a Service Having General Sanction':

1. The Offertory. Originally offerings were made from which the elements were provided; and from the first, alms have been given by common Christian consent at the Communion.
2. Bringing forward the elements at the commencement of the service, when the alms are collected.
3. The Creed. Given in substance in the earliest forms, it became common after A.D.500, and has since been retained either in the service proper, or preparatory.
4. Prayer of confession and for worthiness. This is universal either in the Communion Office proper, or in the preparatory service.
5. The Eucharistic Prayer or Preface, with Salutation, Sursum Corda, and Seraphic Hymn. The use of this has been universal from the beginning, except in some of the Reformed Services, and even in them the Sursum Corda occurs in the Address.
6. Words of Institution, and Invocation of the Spirit. The latter is not given distinctly in the Roman Office, nor in the Anglican, nor in some of the Foreign Reformed; but it was universal of old, was considered essential, and is prescribed in our Directory.
7. Intercession for the Church Militant and thanksgiving for the righteous departed, – the communion of saints being a prominent thought connected with the Lord's Supper. The intercession either forms part of the Communion Services, or of the prayers after the sermon preparatory to the Communion.
8. The Lord's Prayer. Anciently this was said at the end of the prayers before the Communion, and the use of it in this way was probably apostolic.
9. Prayer, &c., and Sancta Sanctis.
10. Singing of psalms at intervals during the Communion, if there be more than one 'Table'.
11. Prayer of thanksgiving for the Sacrament, and of self-dedication.
12. Praise.
13. Benediction.[28]

It noted that the Decalogue is not part of the service except in the Anglican rite, that there were no exhortations in ancient forms, and 'Table Addresses'

---

28 *Euchologion*, 1867, pp. 40–1.

were unknown beyond the optional use 'of a few words'. The order ultimately adopted – prefaced by an exhortation – was:

Introductory:
Offertory
Elements brought forward
Places taken
35th Paraphrase being sung meanwhile.

Institution:
Minister's Salutation
Words of Institution
Address.

Eucharistic Invocation &c:
Profession of Faith
Prayer of Access
Eucharistic Prayer, with Seraphic Hymn
Invocation of the Holy Spirit
Lord's Prayer.

COMMUNION

Post-Communion:
Exhortation to Thankfulness
Prayer of Thanks, and Self-Dedication
Great Intercession for the Living, and thanks for
the Righteous Departed
Praise – Song of Simeon
Benediction.[29]

After the sermon of the morning service there was provision for an examination before Communion with a Benediction and a hymn. A rubric directed that the minister and elders bring in the elements for Communion, and after the grace and words of institution came a Communion Address. This latter was based on that of Lee's liturgy but presented Calvin's teaching on union and the signs exhibiting what they signify:

And as the Lord hath ordained that we are to eat of this bread, and drink of this cup, to assure us of our union with Him, and that He giveth us His body and His blood to be our meat and our drink unto life eternal, we are not to doubt His goodness, but to be firmly persuaded that He accomplisheth spiritually in us all that He outwardly exhibits.[30]

---

29 *Euchologion*, 1867, pp. 44–5.
30 *Euchologion*, 1867, p. 50.

The Profession of Faith was the Apostles' Creed, not Nicene, and the prayer immediately before the Eucharistic Prayer was the Prayer of the Veil derived most from the Catholic Apostolic Liturgy or the Mercersburg Provisional Liturgy. As in Lee's Communion, the Society compilers made a distinction (strange to modern liturgical scholarship) between The Eucharistic Prayer (a long preface culminating with the Sanctus) and a (short) Invocation or epiclesis. The Preface echoes the anaphora of *Apostolic Constitutions* 8 and that of *St. James*, and also the Catholic Apostolic rite. The second paragraph, with words from *Apostolic Constitutions*, 'Not as we ought, but as we are able, we bless Thee for His holy incarnation', would become a hallmark in subsequent editions of the *Euchologion* and its many official offspring of the Church of Scotland. The section marked 'Communion' entailed the recitation of the words of Institution. An Exhortation to Thankfulness was taken from the Dutch Reformed rite. Thanksgiving and intercession for living and departed came after the act of Communion. The service concluded with the Nunc Dimittis and a blessing.

The first Marriage rite was claimed to be based on the provisions of the *Directory*, though one of the prayers was acknowledged to be from 'an American revision of Forms in the Directory'.[31] Other acknowledged sources were the Book of Common Prayer, the *Book of Common Order*, Lee's liturgy, the Dutch Reformed rite and an Eastern source. The second order was 'that prepared by the Revd Dr Bethune of Brooklyn, N.Y., for the revised liturgy of the Reformed Dutch Church'.[32]

The forms for Burial of the Dead were preceded by 'Manual for the Burial of the Dead', which was in fact a long apologetic for the contrast between the *Directory* provisions for the dead and the growing practice in Victorian Scotland of a public funeral. To cover all bases, material was provided for in the home and a second section provided for public burial.

Probably in the light of the opposition to Lee's read prayers, the Editorial Committee issued a guide to members on the 'Use of "Euchologion"'. The guide reminded members that by the law of the Church, they were perfectly free to use materials from any source, so long as that did not violate any legal rule of the Church. A form might be permissible or acceptable in one jurisdiction but not be so in another, and the practical support and sympathy of a congregation was necessary. The object of the Society, said the guide, 'is to secure, as far as is possible, a general agreement in the plan, order, and style of all public religious services throughout the Church, so that the obvious weakness of a non-liturgical service, – its entire dependence on the individual minister, – shall less obtrude itself than has hitherto been common'.[33] The guide dealt with the ordinary service first because that

---

31 *Euchologion*, 1867, p. 64.
32 *Euchologion*, 1867, p. 75.
33 'Use of "Euchologion"', nd, Church Service Society archives p. 2; Kerr, *The Renascence*, p. 85.

was the most common, and because they are the most difficult to change. It added in respect to Baptism, the Lord's Supper, Marriage and Burial:

> So various are the forms at present in use among the clergy generally, and so little do the people know what precisely to expect in these special Services, that the adoption of a settled form would at first attract little notice; but gradually, as it was persevered in, it would secure interest and approval, and would be recognized by the people no less than by the ministers, as a relief from the ordinary incertitude and diversity.[34]

The guide urged members to persuade others of the value of the holy and reverent character of common prayer.

At the Society's annual meeting in Edinburgh May 1868 it was recorded: 'That the Society regards with satisfaction, the universally favourable reception which has been accorded to its published volume and resolves to persevere in exclusive adherence to the objects for which it was instituted, as expressed in its constitution.'[35]

Although the term 'universally' was an exaggeration, the publication of the *Euchologion* clearly met a deep need in many quarters of the Church of Scotland. William McMillan commented:

> The volume, as can easily be imagined, had a somewhat mixed reception. Those who had most need of it were probably the loudest in their condemnation; but it must have had a considerable sale and, as we learn from the Convener of the Editorial Committee, 'The book met with much approbation from those whose approbation is valuable.' Sufficient success was obtained to justify the Society in proceeding to the preparation of some additional services, to be issued in a second edition as soon as the supplies of the first were exhausted.[36]

At the annual May meeting of 1869, G. W. Sprott moved to record the satisfaction of the Society that a new and enlarged edition of the *Euchologion* had been called for, and indeed a second edition appeared in 1869.[37] In this edition, which had the subtitle *Book of Common Order*, the background information disappeared and the material for constructing Sunday morning and evening services, together with actual forms for these services, were placed at the beginning of the volume. The actual services were taken from the writings of Jeremy Taylor and from the Catholic Apostolic Liturgy. Given that Morning and Evening worship with rare celebrations of Communion was the reality of Scottish Presbyterian worship, this placing made better sense. Yet it still remained the theological conviction and pastoral

---

34 'Use of "Euchologion"', p. 3; Kerr, *The Renascence*, p. 86.
35 Church Service Society, Minutes I, p. 36.
36 McMillan, 'Euchologion: The Book of Common Order', p. 26.
37 Church Service Society, Minutes I, p. 40.

dream of the Society that there would be more frequent celebration of the Lord's Supper, and this rite continued to be the theological core of the book. In the *Euchologion* of 1869 the Examination before Communion was expanded with alternatives and new material. The rubric regarding the bringing of the elements was shortened. The Communion Address was rewritten. For example, whereas 1867 read 'Connecting these elements with the body of our Lord, we must be fully persuaded in our hearts of the mystery of His holy incarnation', 1869 has 'Setting apart these elements by the Word and prayer to be sacramentally the body and blood of Christ, we must be fully persuaded . . .' In the invocation or epiclesis, the phraseology had been slightly modified to that found in one of the English Nonjuring rites. This latter had been given in footnote in 1867, but now, without further acknowledgement, replaced the 1867 wording. Only one form for Baptism and one for Marriage were provided, but a new addition was a service for the Admission of Catechumens.

It seems that as soon as 1869 had established itself, plans were underway for a further edition – agreed upon in October 1871 and well underway through 1872.[38] The third edition appeared in 1874, with five orders for Morning Service and five for Evening Service, arranged according to the Sundays of the month. This edition was published in two volumes. McMillan noted:

> In the Communion Service a new rubric is introduced, indicating that at the 'setting apart' of the Elements before the Consecration Prayer 'the Minister may take the paten and cup into his hand.' This was the old Scots custom, and its partial cessation among the followers of the Erskines gave rise to the 'Lifter' controversy, which added another to the many splits among the Seceders.[39]

The fourth edition appeared in 1877, and in a copy that had belonged to one of the members, McMillan found initials attached to the Sunday services indicating the author of each: Sprott, First Sunday; Cameron Lees, Second Sunday; G. Campbell, Third Sunday; and R.H. Story, the Fourth.[40] By October 1880 it was resolved to commence work on a fifth edition,[41] and in October 1881 it was reported that the second Morning Service be remitted to Dr Cameron Lees for revision and improvement, and:

> The Intercessions of the Evening Service of the Second Sunday was in like manner remitted to Dr. Sprott, that the third Morning Service to Mr. Duke, that of the third Evening service to Mr. Cooper, and that of the

---

38 Church Service Society, Minutes I, pp. 48, 51, 52 and 53.
39 McMillan, 'Euchologion: The Book of Common Order', p. 27.
40 McMillan, 'Euchologion: The Book of Common Order', p. 28.
41 Church Service Society, Minutes I, p. 87.

fourth Evening Service to Dr. Story. The Fourth Morning Service was revised and approved.[42]

This new addition, which contained some new services such as Admission of Elders, was published in 1884. In 1885 it was agreed to prepare children's services, and these, together with suitable hymns, were published in 1886.[43] At the May meeting of 1886, Dr William Milligan proposed that a further edition of *Euchologion* be prepared.[44] However, this sixth edition of 1890 would prove controversial.

As might be expected, the membership of the Society embraced a variety of churchmanships. In 1888 a manifesto, signed by Professor Allan Menzies and some 145 members who described themselves as 'Broad Church', suggested changes in the next edition to cater for their interests.[45] It suggested that the forms of morning and evening worship were in general 'too doctrinal in tone and expression'; that many of the confessions of sin were of an unreal character, being statements of doctrine rather than experience; that use of the Apostles' Creed should be more occasional; that the services should make more appeal to a wider society, and 'that the intellectual virtues of love of truth, openness of mind, and courage in upholding conscientious convictions, merit direct encouragement in the worship of the Church'; that in the services of baptism and the Lord's Supper the benefits of Christianity are connected too directly, in a mechanical way, to the ordinances; and that the use of extemporary prayer be recognised. It requested that a new service for morning and evening prayer be included in the new edition that would express their desires and concerns. The result was that Allan Menzies was given the task of drawing up morning and evening prayer for the Fifth Sunday of the month.

At the same time, a change was made in the orders of morning and evening prayer which, in the words of Robertson, showed the full extent of the 'Anglicanising spirit which was at work in the Society'.[46] The usual order of Scottish Morning and Evening worship was altered to the format found in Morning and Evening Prayer of the Church of England. McMillan comprehensively explained:

Up till then the traditional Scottish order had been followed and the first prayer had included Invocation, Confession, Prayer for Pardon, Supplication; the second prayer embraced Thanksgiving, Prayer for Illumination, and the Lord's Prayer; while the third prayer consisted of Prayer after

---

42 Church Service Society, Minutes I, p. 99.

43 Church Service Society, Minutes I, p. 134. *An Order of Divine Service for Children, issued by the Church Service Society*, Edinburgh: Blackwood, 1886.

44 Church Service Society, Minutes I, p. 138.

45 Kerr, *The Renascence*, pp. 95–7.

46 Alastair Kenneth Robertson, 'The Revival of Church Worship in the Church of Scotland from Dr Robert Lee (1804–67) to Dr H. J. Wotherspoon (1850–1930)', PhD thesis, University of Edinburgh, 1956, p. 229.

Sermon, Intercession, Thanksgiving for Faithful Departed. In the new edition the order was the same for the first prayer except that the Lord's Prayer was now appended thereto, the second prayer consisted of Intercessions and Thanksgivings, the third prayer was for Illumination, while the Sermon was followed by a Collect.

This change was largely due to what may fairly be called an 'Anglicanising' party in the Society, whose aim seemed to be the making of Scottish services like the Anglican Orders for Morning and Evening Prayer. In addition to the alterations in the orders of the prayers, it was further recommended that the *Te Deum* should be sung between the lessons in the morning, and the *Benedictus* after them; while the *Magnificat* and the *Nunc Dimittis* should have similar places in the evening. This procedure, it need hardly be said, is based entirely on the Anglican forms.[47]

Sprott and Leishman protested the changes, but they were out-voted. Additionally in this edition, the prayer of humble access of the Church of England was included, together with the Agnus Dei, before the Eucharistic Prayer. This latter was now introduced with 'lift up your hearts', with congregational response. The final words of the epiclesis were changed to 'with all His benefits, to our spiritual nourishment and growth in grace', suggesting that sacraments did give grace. In the final edition this paragraph would be further expanded.

In 1895 revision of the sixth edition was discussed; the process was completed by March 1896, and it had been published by the time of the annual meeting in May.[48] It was reported in 1898 that like previous editions, it was enjoying satisfactory sales.[49] Although later editions appeared – the ninth in 1913 – these were really impressions rather than revisions, and later still the cost of printing was such that publication ceased, although the Society continues. The 1903 edition contained a lengthy introduction by Sprott giving a brief history of the liturgical revival up to his day.

The many editions of the *Euchologion* testify both to the refining element at work in the Society and also to the huge popularity of its liturgy. The lectures of G. W. Sprott, published in 1882 as *The Worship and Offices of the Church of Scotland*, represented the historically based scholarly apologia for the *Euchologion*, and in his 'Concluding Observations' Sprott suggested that the promoters of the Society 'have checked the tendency of individuals to introduce inventions of their own, and have kept the Church from drifting into ill-considered changes which rest on no principle, and contribute nothing to heart and devout worship'.[50] In 1890, A. K. H. Boyd

---

47 McMillan, 'Euchologion: The Book of Common Order', pp. 28–9. He also was critical of the rubric requiring kneeling not only for the confession of sin, but other prayers too – even though sitting or kneeling was becoming more common and preferable to standing.
48 Church Service Society, Minutes I, pp. 209 and 214.
49 Church Service Society, Minutes I, p. 228.
50 Sprott, *The Worship*, p. 269.

reported that there were 506 clerical and 130 lay members of the Society, and claimed of the influence of the *Euchologion* that: 'You can enter few Scottish parish-churches now in which you will not recognise the beautiful and familiar sentences pervading all the prayers.'[51] Over 10,000 copies were sold, and it is estimated that by the turn of the century a third of the clergy were members of the Society.[52] Robertson is correct when he says:

> . . . some, at least, within the Society, saw themselves to be preparing the way for something in the nature of a new BOOK OF COMMON ORDER, but providing the Church with material which could be used experimentally. To some extent this is what happened. The order for the Holy Communion from EUCHOLOGION was used at the General Assembly from 1890 to 1926, and PRAYERS FOR DIVINE SERVICE owes a debt to the same book.[53]

The forms of the *Euchologion* became the basis for devolution in the parishes, as testified by the *Report of the Committee on Proper Conduct of Public Worship and Sacraments to the General Assembly* in 1890, and the Committee's recommendations of 1891 and 1892, and it was also the pro-genitor of the *Recommendations for the Proper Conduct of Public Worship and the Celebration of the Sacraments*, 1894. The 1890 report summarised returns from parishes about the orders of service that were observed, and a good number of parishes simply reported, 'as in the *Euchologion*'. The 1894 Recommendations were published as a result of the earlier reports, and the recommended outlines of services are clearly influenced by those in the *Euchologion*. There was an inevitability about self-promotion. The prominent members of the Society were also prominent members of the General Assembly Committees, and believed that what they had produced through the Society was the best practice for the Church. The benefits of the *Euchologion* were admirably testified to by Dr R. H. Fisher, minister of St Cuthbert's, Edinburgh, in his 'Reminiscences' published in 1919. Fisher wrote, 'Even when the words of Euchologion are not heard in public worship, its influence has settled the lines on which the prayers of the modern Church of Scotland are composed. It also should be revised, abbreviated, simplified. But, such as it is, it has rendered very valuable service.'[54] Fisher listed several beneficent results of the book. The first was that a younger generation of ministers have learned that prayer should never be rhetorical, and so hopefully would avoid monstrosities such as closing a prayer with

51 A. K. H. Boyd, 'The New Liturgies of the Scottish Kirk', *Blackwood's Edinburgh Magazine* 148 (1890), pp. 659–75, p. 659.

52 Douglas Murray, 'From Disruption to Union', in Duncan B. Forrester and Douglas M. Murray, *Studies in the History of Worship in the Church of Scotland*, Edinburgh: T&T Clark, 1984, pp. 87–8.

53 Robertson, 'The Revival of Church Worship', p. 225.

54 R. H. Fisher, *The Outside of the Inside: Reminiscences of the Rev. R. H. Fisher, D.D.*, London: Hodder & Stoughton, 1919, p. 290.

a quotation from Tennyson's 'Crossing the Bar'.[55] The *Euchologion* had also taught the Church to avoid in prayer anything that is affected or unfamiliar, and quaint oriental expressions.[56] Its chief service, though, was in keeping before the minds of the clergy the necessity of a full presentation of the wants of the people before the Throne of Grace; in teaching the correct use of scripture quotation; and also the observance of the Christian Year.[57] Perhaps the most important factor, though, was that even though it was an unofficial book, it gave the Church of Scotland a liturgy worthy of competition with the Book of Common Prayer of the Church of England.

The extent to which it was used almost verbatim, or simply as a basis for improvisations that were far removed from the base text, is an unknown. It may be that many ministers, particularly for Communion, wove together old and new. This is the case with Dr A. K. H. Boyd (1825–99), a prominent member of the Church Service Society, having become a member in 1870. Boyd trained to be an English barrister and was a member of the Middle Temple. He returned to Scotland to study at Glasgow for the ministry, and after being assistant at St George's Edinburgh, was ordained minister of Newton-on-Ayr in 1851. He was a regular contributor to *Fraser's Magazine* and became convener of the Committee on Psalmody and Hymns. Boyd was keen on the improvement of worship. In 1873, when minister of the first charge in St Andrew's, he published *A Scotch Communion Sunday*.[58] This had an order for Communion as well as Communion Addresses and other prayers. Boyd's order commenced with singing Psalm 43, which was followed by a long prayer, opened by scripture sentences, and covering praise and thanksgiving, confession and petition for pardon, ending with the doxology. A reading from Isaiah 53 was read, and then Psalm 114 was sung. The New Testament reading was from Revelation 5, followed by the singing of Paraphrase 65. A short prayer with the Lord's Prayer preceded the Action Sermon. Paraphrase 54 was sung, followed by a prayer that included within it the Apostles' Creed. Boyd included a lengthy Fencing of the Tables, beginning with the Institution narrative. It was inspired by the 1562 *Book of Common Order* and attributed to the Revd Dr T. J. Crawford, Professor of Divinity in the University of Edinburgh. It ended with the ten Commandments and the Beatitudes, and a brief exhortation ending the Sancta sanctis. While Paraphrase 35 was sung, the elements were carried into the church and placed on the communion table. Table Services (addresses) followed, leading up to the minister saying the Sursum corda. The 'Prayer of Consecration' faintly echoes that of the *Euchologion*, including 'For all Thy bounties known to us, for all unknown, we give Thee

---

55 Fisher, *The Outside*, p. 290–1.

56 Fisher, *The Outside*, p. 291.

57 Fisher, *The Outside*, pp. 292, 293 and 294.

58 A. K. H. Boyd, *A Scotch Communion Sunday. To which are added certain Discourses from a University City. By the author of 'The Recreations of a Country Parson'*, London: Henry King & Co., 1873.

thanks. Not as we ought, but as we are able, we bless Thee . . .'[59] It included the petition: 'we ask that these elements, which now in His name and by His authority we set apart from a common to a sacred purpose, may convey to Thy people the grace of the new covenant.' The prayer ended with the Sanctus and Benedictus, and then the Institution narrative was again recited. After the administration to each table, a Post-Communion Address was given, a blessing and the singing of a portion of Psalm 103. Portions were sung at the end of each table that had received communion.

This intermingling of the liturgical species may well represent a common method by which many ministers used parts of the *Euchologion* material – a local adaptation and ministerial devolution.

---

59 Boyd, *A Scotch Communion Sunday*, p. 68.

4

Nineteenth-Century Public Worship Provisions in the United Presbyterian Church, the Free Church of Scotland and a Communion Service of the Free Presbyterian Church

The Church Service Society was founded for ministers and, later, members of the Church of Scotland, though as noted in the previous chapter, a paper was contributed by C. J. Brown, who was a minister of the Free Church of Scotland. Some of the concerns of the Church Service Society were shared by some ministers of the other Presbyterian Churches. Millar Patrick wrote:

> The movement towards reform in the public worship of Scottish Presbyterianism, which began with the formation of the Church Service Society in 1865, was bound in time to affect other branches of the Church than the one to which that Society, unofficially, belonged. It was the nature of things that the first stirring of interest should appear in the United Presbyterian Church.[1]

The United Presbyterian Church

The United Presbyterian Church was formed in 1847, and was a union of the United Secession Church (itself an amalgamation of smaller groups in 1820) and the Relief Church. Apart from a willingness to use hymns alongside metrical psalmody, there was no great difference in worship forms from the Church of Scotland. Its Basis of Union stated that 'the Westminster Directory of worship continue to be regarded as a compilation of excellent rules.'[2] One minister who decided that improvement was necessary and desirable was Dr William Bruce Robertson, a poet and hymn writer, and

---

1 Millar Patrick, 'The Church Worship Association of the United Free Church', in *The Church Service Society Annual* 3 (1930–1), pp. 79–82, p. 79.

2 *Subordinate Standards of the United Presbyterian Church*, Edinburgh: United Presbyterian College Buildings, 1880, p. 94.

who had been called to Cotton Row Church, Irvine, in 1847, where his congregation built a new church, Trinity, in 1863. Of neo-gothic style, the architect was Frederick Thomas Pilkington. Arthur Guthrie wrote of Robertson's style of worship at Trinity:

> The three correlatives, as he called them – praise, prayer, and preaching – were built up by him on the principle of a progressive unity. The praise was perfectly rendered by a congregation that for many years had been taught that, of the three, praise stood highest with God. Standing statuesquely in the desk, as the singing proceeded, with countenance lit up, he would move to the rhythm of the music, while the choir, at the same time, seemed touched with a like feeling, – an electric spiritual current passing between them. The music thus took a deeper tone; and a meaning, never discerned before, unfolded itself in the hymn, to choir, singers, and congregation. The prayer which followed, naturally drew inspiration from the elevation and emotion begotten of the singing – hence his prayers can only be described as rapt utterances full of holy yearnings and aspirations, breathing as from golden censers the incense of a pure sacrifice; and, while fitting into the higher service of praise, they led up to the central thought of the discourse which, at such special times, was often a prose poem. Believing that souls were to be reached and lured heavenwards through the imagination, he waylaid and surprised his hearers with visions of beauty, and by thoughts which only a poet – and a poet inspired by the Divine Spirit – could suggest.[3]

Guthrie notes that Robertson encouraged the movement for an improved service of praise in the sanctuary, and 'for years he had contemplated framing a liturgy which would be in harmony with Presbyterian forms, and in which praise, prayer, and preaching would each receive its proper place.'[4] Robertson caused some controversy when in 1868 he held a service on Christmas Eve, celebrating the Christmas themes:

> As the beautiful building admirably lent itself to floral decorations, the [Sabbath school] teachers, with an eye to artistic effect, encircled the massive pillars with floral wreaths, and inscribed on [a?] beam of gallery, in floral characters, the words, 'A Merry Christmas'. Being Christmas Eve, the services, not altogether, but in part, naturally took their main colouring from the season's festival: sacred song blended with appropriate exercises breathing deep thanksgivings for the Child born at Bethlehem; these, again, were connected with the life and mission of Him who was the Desire of all Nations.[5]

---

3 Arthur Guthrie, *Robertson of Irvine: Poet Preacher*, New York: Thomas Nelson & Sons, 1890, pp. 247–8.
4 Guthrie, *Robertson of Irvine*, p. 255.
5 Guthrie, *Robertson of Irvine*, pp. 255–6.

The congregation sang Paraphrase 39, verses 1,6 and 7, 'to the beautiful tune Palestrina'. There was a reading from Luke 1, verses 46, 55 and 56 to 80. Then the choir sang 'O Come all ye faithful'; a reading from Luke 1:8–18, Choir, 'Hark the Herald Angels sing', a prayer of thanksgiving, Matthew 1:1–12; Choir and children, 'Brightest and Best of the sons of the morning', further prayer and congregational singing of 'Bright and Joyful'. Luke 1:68–69, 78–79 was read, and then a sermon was preached:

> The discourse was followed by, 'Praise God, from whom all blessings flow', Tune – 'Old Hundred', on key A, on which key the preacher repeated the creed, the choir responding 'Amen'; and a succession of prayers, in which the choir led the responses. The Lord's Prayer was repeated, the choir singing 'Amen', and then rendering the beautiful Christmas anthem, 'In the Beginning'. Prayer followed – the whole service concluding with Augustine and Ambrose's grand hymn, the 'Te Deum', and the benediction.[6]

Some other United Presbyterian ministers took exception, and an article in the *United Presbyterian Magazine* condemned this attempt to revive Christmas as a religious festival. The Presbytery met and issued a rebuke to the *Magazine* complaining that the writer had not himself communicated with Robertson. The editor replied that the *Magazine* was private property, and had the right to animadvert on anything taking place. Newspaper correspondence followed showing considerable public support for Robertson's endeavours, and members of the United Presbyterian Church should show sympathy with the cry for improved psalmody, more devout devotional exercises and a higher type of church service.[7] Robertson himself gave a robust defence against the charge of 'ritualism', asserting:

> We adhered to the good old forms of free prayer, read Scripture, and delivered address, the only liberty being taken, as aforesaid with the music. But the prayers throughout were free, and not liturgical; the sermons and addresses were delivered and not read; nothing was read but the hymns and Scriptures, and they were read openly. Even the music was vocal only, and nothing instrumental was allowed; and had the difficult problem been presented to you to construct a meeting that should at once be a protest against ritualism, and yet do homage to our Presbyterian ritual, to which it must adhere, and not depart from it in making that protest, how under these severe conditions could the meeting have been otherwise conducted?[8]

---

6 Guthrie, *Robertson of Irvine*, p. 262.
7 Guthrie, *Robertson of Irvine*, p. 264.
8 Guthrie, *Robertson of Irvine*, p. 268.

The Presbytery sided with Robertson but the episode pointed to changes or, to some, innovations that were taking place in United Presbyterian Church worship. Certain changes were already underway before the union, specifically with John Brown of Broughton Place Secessionist Church, Edinburgh, who had introduced Communion Services every two months and had the communicants 'in one compact body in the lower part of the church', and 'their simultaneous partaking of this ordinance – a deviation from the old Scottish custom since widely followed, though the act of Communion does not often so immediately succeed the sermon as it did in Broughton Place'.[9] Other changes that had occurred were discussed by Andrew Duncan, United Presbyterian minister of Midcalder, in *The Scottish Sanctuary as It Was and as It Is*, published in 1882. Among these he listed the use of hymn books, standing to sing and without lining out by the precentor; the use of instrumental music (organ); sitting for prayer, more frequent celebration of Holy Communion, and simultaneous Communion in place of table-by-table. Duncan concluded:

> There can be no question that some of the changes in the conduct of the services of the Church that have been adverted to, are changes to the better. But it may be doubted whether improvement in this respect has been accompanied with progress in all those things that pertain or are more intimately related to the essence of Christian worship.[10]

Further impetus came with the founding of the United Presbyterian Devotional Service Association. Founded during the meeting of the United Presbyterian Synod in 1882, the object of the Association included fostering interest in the history and literature of public worship, and three of its initial papers were published by the Provisional Committee in 1882 under the title *Devotional Services of the Church*.[11] The first paper, by Andrew Henderson of Paisley, reviewed worship in the early Scottish (Reformed) Church, giving some special place to the Westminster *Directory*. Henderson concluded his historical review:

> . . . but it may serve to show that the purity of Presbyterian worship does not depend on retaining the exact forms which were introduced in the 17th century. Our circumstances are so different from those of the early Reformers that no one would advocate the restoration of their usages; but the men who changed the forms to which they had been accustomed, in obedience to what they regarded the requirements of heir times, may

---

9 John Cairns, *Memoir of John Brown DD*, Edinburgh: Edmonston & Douglas, 1860, p. 129.

10 Andrew Duncan, *The Scottish Sanctuary as It Was and as It Is, or, Recent Changes in the Public Worship of the Presbyterian Churches in Scotland*, Edinburgh: Andrew Elliot, 1882, p. 161.

11 *Devotional Services of the Church*, Edinburgh: David Douglas, 1882.

surely be allowed to teach us the lesson that spirituality of worship is not necessarily bound up with unbending rigidity of traditional form.[12]

This seems to have been in tune with Robert Lee's point that as times change, so should worship.

The second paper, by John Boyd of Wemyss Bay, discussed the defects of Presbyterian services. He commended the Presbyterian elasticity, but because of private individual changes the time was ripe for formation of an Association to discuss improvements to current practices. The paper noted that the established Church had the Church Service Society, the Free Church of Scotland had the Public Worship Association, and hence it was appropriate for the United Presbyterian Church to have a comparable association. Defects in current practice included lack of the aesthetic element and of variety, with some elements too long and others too brief, and lack of preparation. Boyd cited the United States newspaper, the *Boston Recorder*, which listed the various categories of Presbyterian prayers, including political prayers in which jingoism run mad or ultra-radicalism found scope for censuring one or other of the great leaders.[13] Boyd suggested several improvements, including using a scriptural Benediction at the end of the service.

The third paper was by Charles Jerdan of Dundee, which outlined the aims of the proposed Association. He made a point of declaring: 'We do not desire to smooth the way for the introduction of a liturgy.'[14] What the Association hoped to do was to exalt the element of worship, that the praise and prayer should no longer be regarded as 'the preliminary exercises' or as a mere setting to the discourse.[15] It would point out defects and blemishes in the mode of worship and discuss proposals in the direction of improvement.[16]

The Constitution with office bearers was published in 1883, with an introductory letter signed by the President, Andrew Henderson, and Secretary, William Dickie, asserting that the Association had been formed to stimulate attention and 'to promote in every respect the devout and orderly expression of the worship of the Church, by the brotherly interchange of opinion and by the publication of a Periodical or Occasional Paper'.[17] The Constitution stated a remit not unlike that of the Church Service Society:

That the Object of the Association shall be to promote the Edifying Conduct of the Devotional Services of the Church. In pursuing this object the Association shall endeavour to foster an interest in the History and Lit-

---

12 *Devotional Services of the Church*, p. 10.
13 *Devotional Services of the Church*, p. 16.
14 *Devotional Services of the Church*, p. 24.
15 *Devotional Services of the Church*, p. 25.
16 *Devotional Services of the Church*, p. 25.
17 Copy in New College Library, Edinburgh.

erature of Public Worship, consider the Practice of other Denominations, indicate defects in existing usages, discuss proposals in the direction of improvement, and by such means to promote the devout and orderly expression of the Worship of the Church.[18]

A short article commending the Association appeared in the *United Presbyterian Magazine* in August 1884, which also reported that at the first annual meeting in May a paper entitled 'The Requirements for the Conduct of Public Devotions' had been given by Professor Henry Calderwood.[19]

The Association was later to compile *Presbyterian Forms of Service*, 1891, with further editions in 1892 and 1894. The Preface to the first edition drew attention to the importance of public worship, and though certainly not imposing a liturgy, it noted that there was urgent need of a *Directory* adapted 'to present-day requirements'. The forms offered in the book were 'offered merely as illustrations of the manner in which the various services may be appropriately conducted under the existing system of public worship in the United Presbyterian Church'.[20] Millar Patrick noted of the first edition that the 'modest issue of 400 copies was sold out in a few weeks, in spite of the fact that the book was viewed with such official disfavour that the Church's Publications Committee refused to allow it to be sold on the Synod's premises'.[21] The necessity of further editions proved the need.

The first edition contained a lectionary and table of selected psalms and paraphrases. For the services of public worship, a series of scripture sentences suitable for the beginning of the service were provided and a recommended outline for the service was given:

Sentences of Holy Scripture
Short Prayer of Invocation, introduced with 'Let us pray'
Psalm or hymn of adoration, invocation or thanksgiving
A Prayer of Confession and Supplication
Old Testament Lesson, with suggested introductory formula
A Prose Psalm or Scripture Sentence
New Testament Lesson, with suggested introductory formula
Prayer of Thanksgiving and Supplication, ending with the Lord's Prayer and silent Prayer
A Psalm or hymn 'of a praiseful character'

---

18 Copy in New College Library, Edinburgh.

19 See 'The Devotional Service Association', *The United Presbyterian Magazine* August 1884, p. 368. I have not been able to trace a copy of this address, and it is not listed in Calderwood's publications. See W. L. Calderwood and David Woodside, *The Life of Henry Calderwood, LL.D., FRSE*, London: Hodder & Stoughton, 1900.

20 *Presbyterian Forms of Service*, Robert R. Sutherland, Edinburgh 1891, p. vi. The Preface of the first edition was reproduced in the 1894 version: *Presbyterian Forms of Service*, Edinburgh: McNiven & Wallace, 1894, p. vi.

21 Patrick, 'The Church Worship Association', p. 80.

Brief Prayer of Illumination
Discourse
Psalm or hymn appropriate to the Discourse
Short Prayer
'Dismission' hymn or doxology
Benediction.

There were complete 'specimen services' for the Morning and Evening service, which followed the pattern of the recommended outline. The Prayer of Invocation of the Morning Service began thus: 'O Thou that slumberest not nor sleepest, we bless Thee that Thus hast watched over us during the night that is past, and brought us this day into Thy house of prayer.'[22] Like the *Euchologion* services, the Thee/Thou language of the 1662 Book of Common Prayer and the Westminster *Directory* was retained.

A further section contained selected collects, and then the book offered an outline for the Lord's Supper and two full forms for its celebration. The suggested outline was as follows:

PREPARATION AND INSTRUCTION

1 Introductory Sentences of Scripture
2 Psalm or Hymn (Introductory)
3 *Prayer of Grace*
4 Reading of Scripture
5 Psalm or Hymn referring to Christ's Atoning Work
6 Pre-Communion Address

THE COMMUNION

7 Words of Institution
8 *Eucharistic Prayer* (the Congregation responding by singing the SANCTUS or the HOSANNA)
9 Silent Prayer, and Uncovering of the Elements
10 Communion Hymn
11 *Blessing of the Bread*, and Distribution
12 *Blessing of the Cup*, and Distribution
13 Song of Thanksgiving

EXHORTATION AND DEVOTION

14 Exhortation
15 *Prayer of Self-Dedication and Intercession*
16 Concluding Hymn
17 *Benediction*.

---

22 *Presbyterian Forms of Service*, p. 19.

A footnote advised that if the communion service was to follow immediately after the sermon at Morning Worship, then items 1–6 might be omitted.[23]

The first order provided opening scripture sentences and suggested Psalm and Hymn numbers. Two forms were given for A Prayer for Grace, the first ending with the Lord's Prayer. A list of suitable biblical readings was given, as well as scripture sentences referring to the atonement. After the Words of Institution were read, a 'Eucharistic Prayer' was provided, and as has been noted earlier, this did not incorporate the 'Blessing' of the bread and cup, following the pattern established in the Catholic Apostolic Liturgy. If the Eucharistic Prayer was suggested by earlier liturgies, it is not apparent which, if any, they might be. No Sursum corda or opening dialogue was included. The prayer offered 'the gratitude of our souls for the precious memorial which Thou hast given us of our Saviour's atoning work', mentioned 'our vital union with Him' and asked: 'Increase our faith, we beseech Thee; enlarge our love, quicken our discernment, that these holy symbols may bear to us a new revelation of the love which passeth knowledge, and unfold to us the mystery of everlasting joy.'[24] This 'extended Preface' concluded with the Book of Common Prayer's form of the Sanctus, with the Benedictus in brackets as optional. The congregation were to respond by singing a version of the Sanctus, Doxology 17. The Blessing of the Bread did not actually ask for any blessing or sanctification. It thanked God that at the table Jesus Christ is 'before our eyes openly set forth crucified – wounded for our transgressions and bruised for our iniquities', and that in the bread we have the communion of Christ's broken body. It asked for inspiration that as we partake the sacramental food, we may spiritually eat of the true bread that came down from heaven.[25] The 'Blessing' over the wine was equally vague in what was requested. After all had received the elements, a brief statement by the minister picked up on the traditional opening to the Preface and alluded to the Sursum corda: 'It is most meet, right, and our bounden duty that we should praise the Lord for His goodness to us at His holy table: Therefore let us unitedly lift up our hearts unto Him in a song of thanksgiving.'[26] The prayer of self-dedication and intercession asked for a variety of qualities and gifts.

The second order's Eucharistic Prayer included the petition:

Grant, we humbly beseech Thee, that as we partake of the bread and wine, our souls may be fed with the Bread of life, and that we through the Holy Ghost may be partakers of Christ's body and blood, which are meat indeed and drink indeed.[27]

---

23 *Presbyterian Forms of Service*, p. 39.
24 *Presbyterian Forms of Service*, p. 44.
25 *Presbyterian Forms of Service*, pp. 45–6.
26 *Presbyterian Forms of Service*, p. 48.
27 *Presbyterian Forms of Service*, p. 54.

This order had no prayers or petitions for 'blessing' the elements.

Two orders for the baptism of infants were provided, with slightly different structures. Each was to follow the sermon of Sunday worship. The first order commenced with an Address that gave some definition or understanding of baptism. It 'is the sign and seal, not of anything man can accomplish, but of what God alone can do', 'teaches that all men are morally and spiritually unclean by reason of sin' and is also a 'token and pledge of the covenant love of God to his people'.[28] The children of believers are recognised by baptism as members of the visible Church – they are included in God's covenant – and so parents must acknowledge the obligations that this entails. A prayer asked God to bless the dispensation of this ordinance and, along with the outward baptism of water, to grant inward baptism of the Holy Spirit. A prayer after the baptism asked for protection and sanctification. The second order provided scripture sentences before the Address. The latter described baptism as a symbol, pledge and a means of grace, which symbolises the washing of regeneration and renewing of the Holy Ghost. A prayer referred to the parents dedicating the child to God. The post-baptismal prayer requested that as the child had been baptised into Christ, he/she might be one with Christ.

Services were also provided for admission of baptised persons to full communion, ordination of a minister and of elders, a form for dedication of a church, orders for marriage, funerals and suitable readings for departed persons of various ages.

The 1894 edition was described as 'Second Edition, Revised and Enlarged'. The revisions were modest and some material was expanded. In this edition two full 'specimen forms' were provided for Morning and Evening public worship. The first order for Evening was basically that found in 1891, except in the Confession and Supplication, where the paragraph, 'We do not seek to palliate our guilt, or to set our virtues over against our offences' was replaced by a completely new piece. The 'selected Collects' became 'Selected Prayers' and were considerably expanded in number and theme. The first order of infant baptism was provided with scripture sentences before the Address, and in the latter, the second paragraph, 'baptism', was replaced by 'ordinance'. An order for the baptism of adults and admission to communion was provided. Similar small changes to words are found in other services, and some of the readings at funerals were changed or supplemented. The copy of the 1891 edition in Princeton Theological Seminary library has hand-written additions and alterations, and this gives us some idea of how some ministers used the forms. Millar Patrick remarked that: 'By many competent judges this is regarded as one of the best books of its kind issued in Scotland.'[29] Unfortunately he did not identify the competent judges, and whether they were rating this against the *Euchologion* or the Westminster *Directory*. *Presbyterian Forms of Service* provided something

---

28 *Presbyterian Forms of Service*, p. 57.
29 Patrick, 'The Church Worship Association', p. 80.

'adapted to present-day requirements', as the Preface claimed, for the United Presbyterians, but its provisions were certainly not as extensive and rich as those of the *Euchologion*.

Some insight into more popular United Presbyterian teaching on baptism and the Lord's Supper is given in *The Church Circle*, 1871, by the Revd Andrew Morton, minister of St James Place United Presbyterian Church, Greenside, Edinburgh, from 1862 until 1894.[30] The purpose of the book was to address 'the common people' on the great duties of life.[31] Morton presented sacraments as 'signs and seals', which require material emblems and have the idea of covenant-guarantee.[32] In baptism, water is the emblem but it has no regenerative power, nor is there any evidence that God has conferred on the sign inherent virtue to communicate the thing signified.[33] Neither does the minister/priest have power to confer regeneration. Yet baptism is a sign of one of the greatest acts of consecration in which human-kind can engage or perform. 'It is so because it is the emblem of an eternal surrender to Christ, and identity with Him, and because it represents a covenant-relation which has no moral parallel. It is the *seal* or visible pledge of salvation.'[34] Baptism is an instrumental but not the efficient cause of salvation. It exhibits repentance and faith but can be the channel of a special and an abounding grace.[35]

Morton's treatment of the 'Table of the Lord' included establishing the context of its institution and the various names for it across time and trad-itions. He was critical of any suggestion that the elements could be the real body of Christ.[36] He rejected transubstantiation and attacked Puseyism and ritualism before turning to 'The Scriptural Priest and His One Sacrifice' and fastening on the teaching of the Epistle to the Hebrews. It is natural commemoration and the elements are symbols of redeeming love. The sym-bolism exhibits a sealing ordinance.[37] Morton advised his readers:

> You look at that bread, and remember that nothing can add to the in-trinsic value of His sacrifice. You look at that 'Cup of blessing' and, as you taste it, you remember that there is no sin which the blood of Christ cannot wash out – no being to whom it may not be applied. You are reminded that its sufficiency to-day is as available and inexhaustible as it was when he bowed His blessed head upon the cross.[38]

---

30 Andrew Morton, *The Church Circle*, Edinburgh: Andrew Elliot, 1871; A. Ian Dunlop, *The Kirks of Edinburgh 1560–1984*, Edinburgh: Scottish Record Society, 1989, p. 138.

31 Morton, *The Church Circle*, Preface p. v.

32 Morton, *The Church Circle*, pp. 150–3.

33 Morton, *The Church Circle*, p. 158.

34 Morton, *The Church Circle*, p. 164.

35 Morton, *The Church Circle*, p. 165.

36 Morton, *The Church Circle*, p. 183.

37 Morton, *The Church Circle*, p. 202.

38 Morton, *The Church Circle*, p. 203.

It would seem that, for Morton, the 'emblems' were to provoke a memory of the work of Christ and the divine love. Preparation and prayer were needed, as well as meditation for this spiritual communion.[39]

The Free Church of Scotland

Some ministers of the Free Church also felt that an association was needed to guide and update worship, and so they too produced a new worship manual.

Concerns about innovations in worship in the Free Church of Scotland surfaced in the Presbytery of Hamilton, Lanarkshire, in 1854. John Jaffray (1804–58) is thought to have been the author of a pamphlet entitled *Remarks on the Innovations in the Public Worship of God, proposed by the Free Presbytery of Hamilton*. Though this work was mainly concerned with psalmody and tunes, it also listed:

> unwonted postures in worship – the dispensation of the Sacrament of the Lord's Supper without *tables* – the adjournment to dinner after the morning meeting, to come back in the afternoon for the purpose of communicating – the substituting in many places in the country, worship in the *evening* in place of *the afternoon* . . . It is quite clear that, by the slightest effort, in the way of search, innumerable innovations may be found.[40]

Concerns were presumably widespread enough for a committee to be appointed to consider the legislation of the Church regarding the subject of innovations in worship. The report was presented to the General Assembly of the Free Church in 1864. The report surveyed the legislation, beginning with the immediate years leading up to the Westminster *Directory* and the letter from the Scottish Commissioners to the General Assembly of 1645. It drew attention to the 1707 Act against innovations in worship. Based on the historical review, it concluded with three principles:

> *First*, It authoritatively prescribed only what by distinct requirement, or by plain implication, it found to possess positive Scripture warrant – rejecting and prohibiting whatever forms, rites of usages were either directly opposed to the Word of God, or appeared at variance with the simplicity and spirituality which ought to characterize Christian worship. *Second*, It left, as matters indifferent, to be regulated, not by legislative enactment, but by Christian prudence and discretion, such things as

---

39 Morton, *The Church Circle*, pp. 204–7.

40 John Jaffray, *Remarks on the Innovations in the Public Worship of God, Proposed by the Free Presbytery of Hamilton; with an Appendix, containing the Translations and Paraphrases Sanctioned for use of Private Families by the General Assembly, 1751*, Edinburgh: Bell & Bradfute, 1854, p. 69.

involve no essential principle, on which no certain light is to be derived from the Word of God, and which do not break in upon the established order of worship in the Church.

Third, It discouraged any rash interference with existing usages, such as might create disturbance, or attract undue attention to the mere externals of devotion, and sought to have all conducted so as to promote the good order and edification of the Church.[41]

These principles were so general as to allow considerable interpretation, and developments continued that some regarded as unlawful innovations. Dr James Begg (1808–83), the stalwart defender of what he regarded as Reformation truth, published an attack on 'false worship' in 1875, under the title *Anarchy in Worship, or Recent Innovations contrasted with the Constitution of the Presbyterian Church and the Vows of her Office-Bearers.* Begg argued that scriptural principles of pure worship were held by Presbyterians, and must be held now. Unfortunately, so Begg opined, some Presbyterians were ignorant of what was required in worship and even ask where God has prohibited instrumental music and other corruptions of worship.[42] For Begg, 'It is not enough that a thing is not forbidden. It must be expressly commanded by God, and that as a duty binding under the New Testament dispensation, or it is absolutely inadmissible in worship.'[43] After a selective survey of Old and New Testament quotations to support this, Begg declared:

> Anything else or different from this, and especially anything borrowed from heathenism or the abolished temple-service – as pretended priests, altars, altar-cloths, incense, symbolical vestments, or instrumental music – are entirely without divine warrant, and therefore unlawful.[44]

Begg proceeded to identify different types of innovators – the presumptuous and blasphemous, the popularity-hunting, the politic and scheming, the aesthetic (who turns church into theatre) and the well-meaning innovator. Of the aesthetic innovator, Begg wrote:

> The simple worship of Scotland, coupled with a full exposition of the word of the living God, has been the means under God of elevating the common people of our land with its barren soil and inhospitable climate

---

41 *Report of the Committee appointed to Consider Generally the Legislation of the Church on the Subject of Innovations in Worship,* Free Church of Scotland May 1864, Edinburgh: Thomas Constable, 1864, p. 8.

42 James Begg, *Anarchy in Worship, or Recent Innovations contrasted with the Constitution of the Presbyterian Church and the Vows of her Office-Bearers,* Edinburgh: Lyon & Gemmell, 1875, pp. 6–7; reprint in James Begg, *Select Works of James Begg on Worship,* Puritan Reprints (CPSIA self-publishing), 2007, np.

43 Begg, *Anarchy in Worship,* p. 7.

44 Begg, *Anarchy in Worship,* p. 13.

to a moral and intellectual elevation which has left effeminate and sensuous nations far behind; and it will be the greatest crime if this is exchanged for what is called aesthetic worship, appealing to the senses but not improving the soul.[45]

He added that the recent introduction of 'sensuous and sensational worship' is only training for frivolity, apostacy and Rome.[46] Regrettably, apart from citing the Episcopal Bishop Forbes, he gave no example from his own Church. Begg believed that everything had been settled in 1644/5 and that in the 1707 Act on Innovations, worship had been fixed for all time. Attempts to introduce an organ and, in the established Church, Robert Lee's arguments in *The Reform of the Church of Scotland*, pointed to an ecclesiastical revolution. It was with apocalyptic fervour that Begg warned that while multitudes were standing consistently on the old ground, blind Presbyterians were helping forward the defection and ancient foes were imagining that Presbyterianism is effete, or is about to abdicate.[47]

Begg's conservatism was not shared throughout the Free Church. In May 1891 the Public Worship Association was formed 'to promote the ends of edification, order, and reverence in the public services of the Church, in accordance with Scripture principles, and in the light especially of the experience and practice of the reformed Churches holding the Presbyterian system'.[48] Patrick listed the leaders as Dr Douglas Bannerman, Professor William Blaikie, A. B. Bruce, A. Orrock Johnston, John Laidlaw, Hugh MacMillan, George Reith, Ross Taylor, S. D. F. Salmond, Walter C. Smith and George Steven. Blaikie's *The Work of the Ministry*, 1873, contained a chapter on leading Divine Service; A. B. Bruce was heavily involved in the *Free Church Hymn Book*, 1882; Smith was a hymn writer and Orrock Johnston, having originally been opposed to the introduction of the organ, changed his mind and was an advocate for its use. Douglas Bannerman wrote on the topic of liturgies as well as on the sacraments, and he also appealed to his father James Bannerman's work, *The Church of Christ*.[49] In his *The Worship of the Presbyterian Church, with Special Reference to the Question of Liturgies*, 1884, Bannerman took rather a different approach from that of Begg.

Bannerman began with the scriptural foundation but noted a qualification in the Westminster Confession, that 'there are some circumstances concerning the worship of God and government of the Church common to human actions and societies, which are to be ordered by the light of nature and

45 Begg, *Anarchy in Worship*, p. 24.
46 Begg, *Anarchy in Worship*, p. 27.
47 Begg, *Anarchy in Worship*, p. 48.
48 Patrick, 'The Church Worship Association', p. 80. I have not been able to locate any primary documents relating to the Association, and neither any Minutes nor documents related to *A New Directory for the Public Worship of God*.
49 James Bannerman, *The Church of Christ*, 1869, reprint, Banner of Truth Trust, np, 1960, vol. 1, Division II. I, chapters 1–3.

4.1 The Revd Dr Douglas Bannerman

Christian prudence', which he interpreted as Christian common sense.[50] Scripture was the warder at the door, but if a new element was simply a circumstantial variation, a new arrangement, then it may be admitted.[51] What was important was the need for elasticity to meet all the emergencies of life. Unlike Begg, Bannerman looked back to the *Book of Common Order* and examples of European Reformed Church liturgical books. Given that some of the Westminster *Directory* provisions had fallen into abeyance, in his view a careful revision and republication of the *Directory* would be a 'very seasonable thing, and might in many ways lead to much good'.[52] He noted that Dr Chalmers in his later years had mentioned the possibility of a book of prayers with new compositions alongside the 'pious effusions' of past ages.[53] Among his concluding proposals, he urged 'some high and chaste model service' to set before ministers, and that an optional liturgy would allow the people a more direct share in worship.[54] In many ways Bannerman's work set the stage for the Public Worship Association. Apparently, papers were issued annually for private circulation among the members.[55]

In 1898 the Association published *A New Directory for the Public Worship of God*. This book offered an outline of sixteen elements for the order of Sunday worship, comparing this with thirteen items and eleven items in the sixteenth-century *Book of Common Order* and the Westminster *Directory*, respectively. Specimen prayers of invocation, thanksgiving, confession of sins, petitions and intercessions, and prayers of illumination were offered. This format recommended an outline and then specimen forms and was followed with the other services – baptism of infants and adults, the Lord's Supper, admission of baptised persons to full communion, marriage, Burial of the Dead, Ordinations of ministers and elders, Licensing of probationers and Dedication of a Church.

Reviewing Free Church of Scotland teaching on baptism, T. F. Torrance drew attention to the clash between, on the one hand, the reassertion of hyper-Calvinism and predestination and, on the other, the moralism and semi-Pelagianism that developed out of the notion of covenant as

---

50 D. D. Bannerman, *The Worship of the Presbyterian Church, with Special Reference to the Question of Liturgies*, Edinburgh: Andrew Elliot, 1884, p. 4.

51 Bannerman, *The Worship of the Presbyterian Church*, pp. 5–6.

52 Bannerman, *The Worship of the Presbyterian Church*, p. 42.

53 Bannerman, *The Worship of the Presbyterian Church*, p. 49, note 1.

54 Bannerman, *The Worship of the Presbyterian Church*, pp. 76–7.

55 *A New Directory for the Public Worship of God*, fourth edition, Edinburgh: Macnivean & Wallace, 1900, p. viii.

contract.[56] The implications for baptism are illustrated by the different emphases found in James Bannerman and James S. Candlish.

In *The Church of Christ* Bannerman began with a treatment of sacraments in general, and having defined sacraments, proceeded to fit baptism and the Lord's Supper into his definition. Sacraments are sensible signs of spiritual blessings, teaching and representing by outward actions gospel truths, and are also federal acts affording a seal or confirmation of the covenant between God and his people.[57] They are also a means of grace to those who rightly partake of them.[58] Bannerman described baptism as a seal attesting a federal transaction between God and believer, and a means of *confirming* the faith of a believer; it is not intended for the benefit or conversion of the unconverted.[59] However, as Torrance was to point out, since this implied that the believer dedicated herself to Christ in this outward act, and that in return Christ gave himself to the believer, it was difficult to apply to infant baptism.[60] Bannerman asserted that all baptised infants have an interest in the Church as members, and are brought to the door of the Kingdom, but without personal faith baptism does not finally save. Baptism is connected to regeneration for some infants but not for infants who never in their subsequent life experience a saving change. Grace depends on human belief.

James Candlish was Professor of Systematics at the Free Church College in Glasgow, and Torrance believed that he presented a more biblical conception of the covenant will of God.[61] In *The Christian Sacraments*, 1879, Candlish wrote of the sacraments:

> Now Christianity is characteristically and pre-eminently a religion of grace: the centre and sum of its doctrine is that faithful saying which is worthy of all acceptation, 'that Jesus Christ came into the world to save sinners'; and the sum of its practical experience is 'union and communion with Christ in grace and glory'. It is a salvation wrought by God for sinners of mankind; and in it we are debtors to His grace for all spiritual blessings. God in Christ is the giver and we are receivers of His free sovereign grace and love. Hence the outward rites of Christianity are not performances by which we do something to obtain God's blessing, or render to Him a payment, or accomplish a work of our own, but rather exercises in which we receive what he freely gives.[62]

Torrance expressed the view that none of Candlish's views were carried over into the service of infant baptism in *A New Directory*, where the

---

56 T. F. Torrance, *Interim Report of the Special Commission on Baptism. Reports to the General Assembly 1959*, Edinburgh, 1959, pp. 629–62, p. 632.

57 Bannerman, *The Church of Christ*, Part III, Div.II, pp. 6, 8, in vol. 2.

58 Bannerman, *The Church of Christ*, p. 17.

59 Bannerman, *The Church of Christ*, p. 49.

60 Torrance, *Interim Report*, p. 638.

61 Torrance, *Interim Report*, p. 639.

62 James S. Candlish, *The Christian Sacraments*, Edinburgh: T&T Clark, 1879, pp. 13–14.

emphasis is on the act of parents in presenting and dedicating the child, and the congregation receiving him into membership of the Church, but mitigated slightly in the Father–child relationship in the prayers.[63] The recommended structure was Prayer, Praise, Passages of Scripture, Address, Prayer, Baptism, Anthem 'the Lord bless thee' and prayer, and was intended to be included in the order of Public Worship. The *New Directory* gave topics for the Address and exhortation, where the covenant and the duties of parents and the Church are stressed. Using language adapted from the Westminster *Directory*, the request was made that God would make the baptism a seal of adoption, remission of sin, regeneration and eternal life, and give the promises of the covenant. Using the original *Book of Common Order*, the post-baptismal prayer spoke of the sacrament as a singular token and badge of God's love.

On the Lord's Supper, James Bannerman taught that it renews the 'infeftment' of church membership, and 'attests that the covenant by which we are Christ's still holds good for the body and spirit which he has ransomed to Himself'.[64] As well as a remembrance value, it also has a pictorial significance, portraying the body broken and the wine outpoured.[65] The elements are the seals of a federal transaction between the believer and Christ, and Bannerman argued that Zwingli had been misrepresented on the Supper. Grace may be given in the sacrament, but this is dependent on our recognition of the federal transaction.[66] In contrast, Candlish followed Calvin in stressing that the ordinance 'vividly sets forth the vital union effected by faith between Christ and the believer. They are made one as truly as the food we eat becomes one with the substance of our bodies, as truly as the branch is one with the stem of the tree into which it is ingrafted.'[67] It is the communion of the body and blood of Christ; worthy receivers are made partakers of Christ's body and blood.[68]

The biblical theologian, Professor Marcus Dods, was regarded as being on the liberal wing of the Free Church, and in 1878 had been charged with unorthodoxy by more conservative members of the Church but was acquitted by the majority. He wrote no large work on sacraments but in 1884 published a pamphlet to explain the Communion to young communicants. There was nothing particularly unorthodox in this work. He appealed to the Westminster Shorter catechism and explained the Jewish background

---

63 *Interim Report*, pp. 643, 644. The convener of the Public Worship Association, Douglas Bannerman, had written tracts defending infant baptism and admission to communion, but perhaps he shared the views of his father, whose works he had edited. Douglas Bannerman, *Difficulties About Baptism*, Edinburgh: Oliphant, Anderson & Ferrier, 1898; *Grounds and Methods of Admission to Sealing Ordinances*, Perth: Andrew Elliot, 1882.

64 James Bannerman, *The Church of Christ*, II, Div. II.IV, Ch. III, p. 129. Bannerman uses the term *infeft* from Scottish legal language.

65 Bannerman, *The Church of Christ*, p. 133.

66 Bannerman, *The Church of Christ*, p. 140.

67 Candlish, *The Christian Sacraments*, p. 96.

68 Candlish, *The Christian Sacraments*, pp. 114, 115.

to the Passover celebration meal, which he believed to be the setting of the Lord's Supper. At the Supper, it was no longer the Passover that was to be commemorated but Jesus' own death.[69] Jesus had chosen the 'signs' of bread and wine 'because they are in familiar use for the nourishment of the body, and, therefore, fitly represent Him who gives us spiritual life'.[70] We may not understand how the dead bread we eat becomes life in us, or how Christ can become a living spirit in us, but regardless of our understanding, Christ says, 'He that eateth me even he shall live by me.'[71] According to Dods, Christ is present in the sacrament as he is to faith at any time and any place, but Communion is not a mere representation or a bare commemoration, but an actual present communion between Christ and the soul.[72] Perhaps because of its genre, the work is not particularly forthcoming on how young communicants might prepare themselves, or what they might encounter in a liturgical celebration of the Supper.

The Supper in the *New Directory* reproduced large sections of the *Book of Common Order* and the Westminster *Directory*. A second 'Prayer of Thanksgiving and Consecration' was suggested and in part taken from the order of Communion of St Giles', Edinburgh, itself based on the Church Service Society's *Euchologion*.[73] The prayers were patient of expressing the theologies represented by both Bannerman and Candlish.

The Lord's Supper outline allowed for a table Address before and after Communion, and examples of these are found in the edited sermons of the noted Free Church minister, Dr John 'Rabbi' Duncan (1796–1870). These are devotional, with wide-ranging biblical texts, concerned with the Christian life and witness and provide a small representation of this genre. Few of Duncan's Addresses seem to have been focused directly on the ordinance. In his Pre-Communion Address on 10 July 1864, at St Luke's Free Church, Edinburgh, Duncan stressed the substitutionary death of Christ, which meant that the Supper was a feast in commemoration of redemption from sin and death. The words of institution show that the redemption was costly bought but freely given.[74] After Communion he noted that the ancient term for the service was the Eucharist, the feast of priestly thanksgiving, and the Church offers prayers and thanksgivings.[75] On 16 July 1865, after discussing the remark 'He die, or we die', Duncan, using somewhat 'Zwinglian' language, said: 'believing communicants, I give for your believing acceptance the token of that, when I put into your

69 Marcus Dods, *The Lord's Supper Explained to Young Communicants*, Glasgow: J. N. Mackinlay, 1884, pp. 3–6.

70 Dods, *The Lord's Supper Explained*, p. 10.

71 Dods, *The Lord's Supper Explained*, pp. 12–13.

72 Dods, *The Lord's Supper Explained*, p. 19.

73 See Chapter 7 for St Giles' and its service books.

74 David Brown (ed.), *John Duncan, Pulpit and Communion Table*, Inverness: Free Church of Scotland Publications, 1969, pp. 143–5.

75 Brown, *John Duncan, Pulpit and Communion Table*, p. 145.

hands the symbols of His broken body and shed blood'.[76] After Communion he exhorted believers to contemplate all the spiritual benefits that flow from Christ's death, and he cited the Westminster Catechism that sacraments are effectual means only by the blessing of Christ and the working of the Holy Spirit in those who believe.[77]

Highlands Free Church of Scotland and Free Presbyterian Church communion services

The Highlands were still more conservative than the Scottish Lowlands and urban areas. At the end of the nineteenth century, the Communion Season celebrations were much like they had been some sixty years earlier. In an article published in 1918, the Revd Dr Donald Munro (1860–1937), minister of Ferintosh and that year Moderator of the Free Church of Scotland, described the communion service as he remembered it from his earlier years.[78] The solemn services were preceded by much preparatory work, on Wednesday, Thursday and Friday before the celebration.[79] On the communion sabbath a large congregation (thousands) had assembled, and in front of the preaching tent there were two long rows of communion tables:

> At the appointed hour, generally 11 o'clock, the presiding minister entered the 'tent'. He was generally one of the most outstanding preachers in the North, for as a rule only men of weight and experience, such as Dr. Angus MacIntosh, Mr Kenney, Killearnan, and Dr. MacDonald, were asked to preach the Gaelic Action. The preacher came direct from the 'ivory palaces' of secret communion, and the fragrance which accompanied him was diffused around. The very reading of the opening Psalm had a subduing effect on the assembled thousands, while the singing of it to one of their plaintive melodies, led by a choice precentor, was most thrilling. The prayer which followed, so fervent unctuous, found a response in many a contrite heart. . . . From the very beginning of the sermon, in which the glory of Christ's person and the merits of His atoning sacrifice were treated with rare clearness, fulness and tenderness, the interest of the hearers was aroused; . . .
>
> The 'fencing of the table' which followed was not only searching, but singularly helpful to exercised Christians, for the great preachers of those days had much of the Spirit of Him who 'breaks not the bruised reed'.

76 Brown, *John Duncan, Pulpit and Communion Table*, p. 87.

77 Brown, *John Duncan, Pulpit and Communion Table*, p. 88.

78 See Chapter 8 for the Free Church of Scotland after 1900, which was a small remnant that refused to unite with the United Presbyterians to form the United Free Church of Scotland. Munro, though, was recalling a time before 1900.

79 Donald Munro, 'The Rise and Progress of Evangelical Religion in the Northern Highlands. IV. The Communion Seasons', *The Monthly Record of the Free Church of Scotland*, November 1918, pp. 178–9.

In those days in the North Highlands the Psalm-tune associated with the table service was invariably 'Long' Dundee, which was rendered with as much feeling as the singing on the historic Stitched Brae, in the time of the Seccession, when, to use the expressive words of old Dr. Waugh of London, the singing of 'Martyrs' was almost fitted to arrest an angel on an errand of mercy 'and would afford him more pleasure than a' the chanting of a' the organs in a' the Cathedrals of Europe'.

Singularly solemn was the part of a Highland Communion Sabbath when hundreds of exercised Christians came forward slowly and reverently to take their place at the table of the Lord. But an outstanding feature of the service was the concluding address, which followed the administration of the ordinance. . . .

Sometimes the service, owing to the number of tables, had to be very prolonged. . . . Before the close of the service the stars of heaven had appeared, so that the precentor had to chant the line from memory. In those days were no evening sermons on the Communion Sabbath, but in several townships there were meetings for prayer . . . Monday was the day of Thanksgiving, and the last was often the great day of the Feast. The services were especially designed to comfort and strengthen the Lord's people in their wilderness journey.[80]

In 1892, a year after the formation of the Public Worship Association, the Free Church of Scotland General Assembly passed the Declaratory Act, relaxing the stringency of subscription to the Westminster Confession of Faith. In this the Church was following similar moves in the Church of Scotland and the United Presbyterian Church to account for the developments in biblical criticism and changing methods of theology. Dissent came from two ministers from the Highlands, Donald MacFarlane of Raasay and Donald MacDonald of Shieldag, and in 1893 they seceded to form the Free Presbyterian Church. A small number of others joined their ranks, and they ordained new ministers, including John R. Mackay. The Deed of Separation accused the Free Church of Scotland of abandoning the doctrine of the divine authorship of the Scriptures, and also had sanctioned 'uninspired' hymns, authorised instrumental music in the public worship of God, and had violated the purity of worship as understood by the Free Church of Scotland.[81]

Donald MacDonald and John R. Mackay presided over a 'communion season' at Rogart, Sutherland, in July 1894, which was described in a contemporary newspaper article, and witnesses to the more conservative culture of the Highlands.[82] The 'services' were conducted from Thursday

---

80 Munro, 'The Rise and Progress of Evangelical Religion', pp. 178–9.

81 Text in *One Hundred Years of Witness*, Glasgow: Free Presbyterian Publications, 1993, pp. 39–41.

82 All details are taken from the report in the *Northern Chronicle*, 25 July 1894, p. 6, column E.

until Monday, and the pulpit was erected between two large spreading trees. On the Thursday, the Revd Mackay preached and Friday was the 'men's day'. This was the custom of male members of the gathering being asked to address questions raised by a text of Scripture. It was reported that the gathering appreciated the exposition of the 'question' given out by James Murray of Rogart, on John 3:5. The Communion was administered on the Sunday in the presence of a large crowd (it was estimated to be between 1,500 and 2,000, and included some members of Free Church of Scotland who had decided to attend the service). The service and Table Addresses were in Gaelic, other than the last table, which was in English. A separate service in English was also conducted in the evening. The account is very similar to a reminiscence, written in 1893, of Communion in the Highlands, though which denomination was not specified.[83] A Psalm was given out, sung to one of the 'long tunes'. The minister delivered an extemporary prayer and then came the sermon. The people sat down and another short Psalm was sung, 'after which the minister explains the nature of the solemn rite and "fences" the table by reading from the Epistles who are worthy to partake, and who by coming unworthily are eating and drinking judgment to themselves'. During psalm-singing, and with repeated invitations, the tables are filled, though in this case the communicants were few (too many unworthy!), 'and in a short time the ministers return to their pulpit, and words of edification and comfort are spoken to those who have made this public profession'.

These two accounts point to a certain conservatism associated with Highland and Gaelic culture, and it is possibly no accident that subsequent secessions have been concentrated mainly in the Highlands. Equally, it may also show that a need for development and change in worship in urban areas was not felt to the same degree in rural areas. The Secessionist ministers probably felt no need of either *Presbyterian Forms of Service* or *A New Directory*. The format evolved from the 1644 *Directory* was sufficient.

Conclusion

The two smaller but significant Presbyterian Churches were both influenced by the same catalysts that required some 'genetic' change in worship forms and style. The fact that the Highland areas felt no such need suggests that this was very much a Lowland and urban movement, where the changes in Victorian culture and life were rendering the older formats less effective than they once had been. Smaller groups would break away to preserve the 'old' format, but the larger groupings – the United Presbyterians and the Free Church of Scotland – responded in 'evolutionary' fashion by making some small but significant changes.

---

83 Rebecca F. Forbes, 'A Highland Sacrament', in the *Celtic Monthly*, vol. 1, 1893, pp. 61–2.

5

Worship's Companions:
The Playing of the Merry Organ,
Hymns, and Sweet Singing in the Choir

The liturgical revival in Scottish Presbyterian churches was not confined to the compilation of printed liturgical forms. It included a change in what was sung in services and how – the introduction of the pipe organ, the widespread use of hymns from official hymnals and the formation of choirs to lead the singing.

The revival of the 'merry organ', or the 'kist o' whistles'

Looking back across the nineteenth century, Sir Archibald Geike regarded the use of instrumental music as the most remarkable change that had occurred in Scottish services. He wrote:

> Had any one in the earlier half of last century been audacious enough to predict that in a couple of generations the 'kist o' whistles', which had been long banished as a sign and symbol of black popery, would be re-introduced and welcomed before the end of the century, he would have been laughed to scorn, or branded as himself a limb of the prelatic Satan.[1]

Dr Robert Lee introduced a harmonium into Greyfriars around 1862.[2] Norman Macleod Caie wrote:

> The instrument was installed behind a screen in the vestibule. And one evening, while the choir were practising, Dr. Lee came in. An excellent musician himself, and in full sympathy with his precentor's efforts to improve the musical side of the service, he was so impressed by the blending of the harmonium with the voices of the choir that he at once discussed

---

1 Sir Archibald Geike, *Scottish Reminiscences*, Glasgow: James Maclehose, 1904, p. 94.
2 Norman Macleod Caie gives 1862 (see note below); Henry Farmer, *A History of Music in Scotland*, London: Hinrichsen, 1947, p. 369, gives 1863; *Organs in Greyfriars* (small pamphlet, ed. David Beckett, 1990), gives 1860!

with his choir-leader the idea of employing the instrument during worship. The project was carried into effect almost immediately.[3]

In 1865 Lee installed a two-manual and pedal pipe organ built by David Hamilton of Edinburgh. Although Greyfriars may have been the first church of the established Church to install and to be allowed to keep the organ,[4] the 'organ' controversy seems to have started some decades before with Dr William Ritchie at St Andrew's, Glasgow, in 1806. Ritchie, on behalf of the congregation, petitioned the Lord Provost for permission from the heritors to make alterations in the seats behind the pulpit to house an organ. The Lord Provost's attention was caught by the reference to an organ, and he referred the matter to the Presbytery of Glasgow for adjudication, on the grounds that 'Whether the introduction of Organs into our established churches, be an improvement or not, is the province of the ecclesiastical judicatories, not of the civil magistrates, to determine.'[5] Ritchie had not asked the Lord Provost for permission for an organ, but only for permission to make alterations to the seating. By August 1807, an organ had been installed and was used in worship. The Presbytery acted on the Lord Provost's letter, and also received other complaints, and in a vote on 2 September 1807 declared 'that the use of Organs in the public worship of God is contrary to the law of the land, and to the law and constitution of our established church; and therefore the Presbytery did, and hereby do, prohibit the use of Organs in all the churches and chapels within their bounds.'[6]

The controversy produced a number of essays either in support or against the organ as a church instrument. The argument against was voiced by James Begg senior, minister of New Monkland, in a treatise published in 1808, in which he maintained that although under the old dispensation musical instruments were allowed, under the new dispensation, Christians were bidden to sing with the spirit and understanding. Organs, he noted, were introduced into churches during the popish superstition and idolatry and their use was not permitted by the Church of Scotland's laws and constitution.[7] William Andrews commented: 'The organ was summarily silenced, therefore, and the grand tones of that instrument were not heard

---

3 Norman Macleod Caie, 'The Jubilee of the Church Organ in Scotland', August 1913, reprinted in *Life and Work*, 12 July 2013, www.lifeandwork.org/features/looking-back-scotland-s-first-church-organ, accessed 28.03.2018.

4 The claim of *Organs in Greyfriars* (no pagination).

5 The letters and documents relating to the whole episode are contained in *A Statement of the Proceedings of the Presbytery of Glasgow, Relative to the Use of an Organ in St. Andrew's Church, in the Public Worship of God*, Philadelphia, PA: Anderson, 1821, p. 2.

6 *A Statement of the Proceedings*, p. 18.

7 James Begg, *A Treatise on the Use of Organs and Other Instruments of Music in the Worship of God*, Glasgow: D. Niven & Co., 1808, especially pp. 19 and 27.

again in accompaniment of sacred song in the Presbyterian churches of Scotland for more than twenty years.'[8]

However, in 1829, the Revd John Johnstone, with the support of his congregation, installed an organ in the Relief Church at Roxburgh Place, Edinburgh. The Relief Synod ordered its removal, but Johnstone and his congregation seceded from the Relief Church rather than give up the organ. Once again pamphlets were published either for or against the organ, with William Anderson writing *An Apology for the Organ as an Assistance of Congregational Psalmody*, 1829, and James Russel condemning the innovation in *A Reply to an Apology for the Organ*.[9] Around the time of Lee's introduction of a pipe organ (in place of a harmonium) at Greyfriars, some other congregations seem to have had the same inspiration. According to the recent lists compiled by Stewart and Buchan, the first Church of Scotland organ to be officially opened for use in worship was at Anderston Parish Church, Glasgow on 15 January 1865, built by the London firm of William Hill.[10] St Giles Parish Church at Dundonald, Ayrshire opened its organ on 3 February 1865, built by the firm of James Hamilton, Edinburgh.[11] Both of these were earlier than Lee, the Greyfriars organ being opened in April 1865. Two organs built by Peter Conacher were opening in June 1865, at Duns and Skelmorlie parish churches.[12] According to Ian McCraw, St Mary's Church, Dundee installed an organ in 1865, and in 1866 St Andrew's, Glasgow once more made plans to do so.[13] A two-manual organ was placed in Elgin Parish Church in 1873, and an appeal to the General Assembly to prevent it was defeated.[14] An organ was erected in Glasgow Cathedral in 1879.[15]

The United Presbyterian Church allowed organs after 1872. At its May Synod of that year the following motion was carried:

That this Synod decline to pronounce a judgment upon the use of Instrumental Music in Public Worship, yet do no longer make uniformity of practice in this matter a rule of the Church; but the Synod urge upon the Courts of the Church, and upon individual ministers, the duty of guard-

---

8 William Andrews, *Bygone Church Life in Scotland*, London: William Andrews & Co., 1899, p. 105.

9 For further pamphlets and works, see Gavin Struthers, *A History of the Rise, Progress and Principles of the Relief Church*, Glasgow: A. Fullerton & Co., 1843, footnote on p. 443.

10 David A. Stewart, revised Alan Buchan, *Organs in Scotland: A Revised List*, Edinburgh: The Edinburgh Society of Organists, 2018, p. 18.

11 Stewart, *Organs in Scotland*, p. 18.

12 Stewart, *Organs in Scotland*, p. 18.

13 Ian McCraw, *Victorian Dundee at Worship*, Dundee: Abertay Historical Society, 2002, p. 96; Farmer, *A History of Music*, p. 369.

14 *Acts of the General Assembly* 1876, pp. 57–8, cited in Andrew L. Drummond and James Bulloch, *The Church in Victorian Scotland 1843–1874*, Edinburgh: St Andrew Press, 1975, p. 189.

15 Drummond and Bulloch, *The Church in Victorian Scotland*, p. 189.

ing anxiously the simplicity of Public Worship; and press on the earnest attention of all the members of the Church watchfulness over the unity of our congregations.[16]

A pipe organ had been erected in the United Presbyterian Church at Claremont, Glasgow, in 1856, but only now in 1872 could it lawfully be used in worship.[17]

Resistance was longer and stronger in the Free Church of Scotland, with a review of the Ritchie 1807 events by Dr Robert Candlish in 1859, and a 271-page diatribe against their use by James Begg junior (1806–73), minister of Newington, in 1866.[18] A committee was appointed to study the question of instrumental music in worship, and it published its report in 1883. A number of members dissented from the recommendations of the report, but the majority agreed that there was no scriptural reason for prohibiting musical instruments, no law of the Church forbidding it, and that it should be left to kirk sessions to decide the matter.[19] The Revd John Kennedy (1819–84) gave a speech against instrumental music before the Presbytery of Dingwall, raising the question, 'if the desired innovation can be shown to be utterly unscriptural, what but the utmost recklessness can account for the attempt to pollute the Church by its introduction?' He argued that it was unscriptural and inexpedient.[20] The Revd John McEwan also mounted a rearguard action against instrumental music in worship, but a good many churches took the decision to introduce either a pipe organ or a harmonium.[21] The harmonium, and by association the pipe organ, gained wider acceptance thanks to the visit of Dwight L. Moody and Ira D. Sankey in 1873. The American evangelists attracted large audiences from all the main Presbyterian churches. John Coffey explains their popularity thus:

---

16 Cited in the *Report on Instrumental Music in Public Worship May 1883, Acts of the General Assembly of the Free Church of Scotland*, vol. 37, 1883, p. 28.

17 Drummond and Bulloch, *The Church in Victorian Scotland*, p. 188, have 1855; Stewart, *Organs in Scotland*, p. 207, has 1856.

18 Robert S. Candlish, *The Organ Question: Statements by Dr. Ritchie, and Dr. Porteous, For and Against the Use of the Organ in Public Worship in the Proceedings of the Presbytery of Glasgow, 1807–8*, Toronto: Lovell & Gibson, 1859; James Begg, *The Use of Organs and other Instruments of Music in Christian Worship Indefensible*, Glasgow: McPhon, 1866. Reprint in Begg, *Select Works of James Begg on Worship*.

19 Report on Instrumental Music in Public Worship May 1883, *Acts of the General Assembly of the Free Church of Scotland*, vol. 37, 1883, pp. 1–30.

20 John Kennedy, 'The Introduction of Instrumental Music into the Worship of the Free Church Unscriptural. Unconstitutional, and Inexpedient, 1883', www.nesherchristianresources.org/JBS/kennedy/Introduction_of_Instrumental_Music.html, accessed 14.02.2020.

21 John McEwan, *Instrumental Music: A Consideration of the arguments for and against its introduction into the worship of the Free Church of Scotland. With a Preparatory note by the Rev. George Smeaton DD, New College, Edinburgh*, Edinburgh: James Gemmell, 1883.

Before they ever arrived in a town, the evangelists had been heralded from the pulpit and in the local press. They cultivated the support of clergy and laity alike, for advertising the meetings involved a great participative effort. Supporters held prayer meetings, organized committees, formed choirs, raised funds and visited every household in the locality. It was hard to avoid knowing about the evangelists.[22]

To the large audiences Sankey sang solos accompanied by the harmonium. Of an Edinburgh visit, Sankey recorded that at a meeting in the Free Assembly Hall a shocked woman cried out, 'Let me oot! Let me oot! What would John Knox think of the like of yon?' But Sankey then added:

Professor Blaikie said in the Edinburgh Daily Review at that time: 'It is almost amusing to observe how entirely the latent distrust of Mr. Sankey's "kist o' whistles" had disappeared. There are different ways of using the organ. There are organs in some churches for mere display, as some one has said, "with a devil in every pipe;" but a small harmonium, designed to keep the tune right, is a different matter, and is seen to be no hindrance to the devout and spiritual worship of God.'[23]

The writer of the Introduction to the narrative of the Moody and Sankey visits to Scotland and Ireland felt that all was fine – and acceptable – when Sankey sang out clearly 'so as to drown the organ'.[24] Robert Selby Wright noted that in 1874 the kirk session of Canongate Kirk invited Moody and Sankey to hold meetings there, and an organ was introduced in June of the same year, which he thought was possibly the result of the meetings.[25]

The survey of church services in Dundee, reported in *The Piper O'Dundee* newspaper between 1888 and 1890, showed that nearly all had an organ. The Steeple Kirk (St Clements), Bell Street and Downfield United Presbyterian, and St Paul's and St John's Free Churches were listed as having harmoniums; Ward Chapel, St Mark's, St John's (Cross) together with Tay and George's Chapel, both United Presbyterian, had organs.[26]

22 John Coffey, 'Democracy and popular religion: Moody and Sankey's mission to Britain, 1873–1875', in Eugenio F. Biagini, *Citizenship and Community: Liberals, Radicals and Collective Identities in the British Isles, 1865–1931*, Cambridge: Cambridge University Press, 1996, pp. 93–119, p. 98.

23 Ira D. Sankey, *My Life and the Story of the Gospel Hymns, and of Sacred Songs and Solos*, Philadelphia, PA: P. W. Ziegler Co., 1906, pp. 68–9.

24 Anon, *Narrative of Messrs Moody and Sankey's Labors in Scotland and Ireland, also in Manchester, Sheffield and Birmingham, England*, New York: Anson D. F. Randolph & Co., 1875, p. 11.

25 Ronald Selby Wright, *The Kirk in the Canongate: A Short History from 1128 to the Present Day*, Edinburgh: Oliver & Boyd, 1956, pp. 126 and 152–3. Canongate now has the harmonium used by Moody and Sankey.

26 *The Piper O'Dundee*, 4 July 1888, p. 54; 3 October 1888, p. 207; 27 November 1888, p. 626; 14 November 1888, p. 284; 22 May 1889, p. 246. *Organ* 25 July 1888, p. 90; 26 September 1888, p. 199; 17 October 1888, p. 236; 22 August 1888, p. 138; 31 October 1888, p. 258. St John's Free Church was raising money to purchase an organ, 5 March 1887, p. 1.

258   THE PIPER O' DUNDEE.   [OCTOBER 31, 1888.

The Kirks o' Dundee.

No. 13—GEORGE'S CHAPEL, S. LINDSAY STREET.

Rev. George Smart.

GEORGE'S Chapel, once known as School Wynd U.P. Kirk, and now better known as Gilfillan's Kirk. has had a splendid past, and since the death of George Gilfillan has passed through troublous times; but the kirk has risen above its trials, and shown itself worthy its traditions. The kirk has just

Interior of George's Chapel.

been undergoing extensive alterations, and was re-opened on Sabbath last.— The interior is beautifully proportioned, the gallery, with its fine sweep and handsome pillars being specially noteworthy. The decoration is unique, but pleasing and harmonious. The windows have been filled in with tinted glass of various and not altogether well selected shades. The organ is very handsome, and from pew to pulpit the arrangements of the kirk are of the most modern and comfortable kind. The choir is large, and although not very evenly balanced, sings well together, especially in the concerted pieces. The organ is beautifully played, but the voluntary seemed of rather a light nature for the player and the fine instrument.

The minister, the Rev. George Smart, who was inducted to School Wynd Kirk some twenty months ago, was born in the suburbs of Perth, and brought up under the ministry of the brilliant M'Owen of the North Church there. Some sixteen years ago he was a hard worker at the University of St Andrews, taking high places in the classes of Literature, Logic, Metaphysics, and Moral Philosophy. In the annual competition for scholarships at the U.P. Hall, Edinburgh, he gained the "Alexander" Bursary, and during the recess he assisted first at Whampray, Dumfriesshire, and latterly at Lochee U.P. Church. As a probationer he received calls from New Deer, Nairn, Denny, and other places. He accepted Denny, the smaller charge, at a stipend less by £100 than that of Nairn, and there he laboured for about seven years. The style of the minister of School Wynd Kirk is homely, and there is no straining after effect, but he displays fire; and in the sermon preached on Sabbath last from the words, "Beginning at Jerusalem," he displayed a grip of the salient points which insured the attention of his hearers and enabled him to drive home lessons, which were none the less valuable that they were of the simple and everyday order. For instance the idea of fixing on the hearers that their "Jerusalem was in the home, the church, and the circle," was, if not brilliant, more effective than mere brilliancy.

School Wynd Kirk with its working congregation and under the guidance of its working pastor ought to attain to the high position which as the premier U.P. Kirk of Dundee it should occupy.

The Piper's Portrait Gallery.

NO. 37.—MR WILLIAM M'FARLAND,
Of Her Majesty's Theatres, Dundee and Aberdeen.

FOR over twenty-five years Mr William M'Farland has successfully catered for the entertainment of the Dundee public. He made his first appearance in the Kinnaird Hall, when he exhibited a diorama of "The Holy Land." He was then prevailed upon by the Messrs Sangers, for whom he had previously acted as acting manager and agent in advance, to rent the large building which they had erected in East Dock Street, called the Alhambra. Mr M'Farland had only

5.1 *Piper O'Dundee*, 31 October 1888, report on George's Chapel, S. Lindsay Street

89

Hymns and hymnals

The popularity of Moody and Sankey not only made the organ more
acceptable but also further endorsed the ever-widening singing of hymns,
anthems and solos. Describing a meeting in the Barclay Free Church in
Edinburgh in 1873, Sankey said:

> As I took my seat at the instrument on that, to me, most memorable
> evening, I discovered, to my great surprise, that Dr. Horatius Bonar was
> seated close by my organ, right in front of the pulpit. The first gospel-song
> music I had ever composed, written since coming to Edinburgh, was set to
> words which he wrote – 'Yet there is room'.
>
> Of all men in Scotland he was the one man concerning whose decision
> I was most solicitous. He was, indeed, my ideal hymn-writer, the prince
> among hymnists of his day and generation. And yet he would not sing one
> of his own beautiful hymns in his own congregation, such as 'I heard the
> voice of Jesus say', or, 'I was a wandering sheep,' because he ministered
> to a church that believed in the use of the Psalms only.[27]

The Scottish tradition from the Reformation had been to sing metrical
Psalms unaccompanied, though the Psalter had included some paraphrases
of other parts of Scripture. It was the United Presbyterian Church that took
the lead in the introduction of hymns. Prior to union, the Relief Church
had published a collection of 231 sacred songs and hymns in 1798, and the
United Secession Church had printed a hymnal just as negotiations on union
with the Relief Synod had begun. After the formation of the United Presbyterian Church, the *Hymn Book of the United Presbyterian Church* was
published in 1851. Benson noted that in it the 460 hymns were arranged
in order of the scripture passages on which each was based, and it was not
easy to use.[28] The United Presbyterian Church replaced it in 1877 with
Presbyterian Hymnal. This had 366 hymns, which were collected under
fifteen headings. The section 'Church' included four for baptismal services
and six for the Lord's Supper. The section 'Ancient hymns' included the
Te Deum and the *Dies Irae*, and some of John Mason Neale's translations
of ancient Greek and Latin hymns. Benson commented that the change in
atmosphere between the collection of 1851 and that of 1877 would lead to
the conclusion that they belonged to two different denominations.[29]

The opposition to hymns in some quarters is typified by the Overture
made to the Free Church Presbytery of Hamilton by Mr Buchan in 1853,
which argued for the use of hymns. It was answered in an anonymous
pamphlet, thought to be by John Jaffray, entitled *Remarks on the Inno-*

---

27 Sankey, *My Life and the Story of the Gospel Hymns*, pp. 66–7.

28 Benson, *The English Hymn: Its Development and Use of Worship*, New York: George
H. Doran Company, 1915, p. 531.

29 Benson, *The English Hymn*, p. 531.

vations in the Public Worship of God, Proposed by the Free Presbytery of Hamilton, 1854. This author argued that the Psalms and unauthorised paraphrases were quite sufficient; as for hymn books, which may be valued by some as pretty toys in peaceful and prating times, they would be nothing but an incumbrance and a weariness in the day of battle and of suffering.[30] The author also suggested that to allow hymns would lead to chanting, intoning and the introduction of instrumental music.

The Church of Scotland and the Free Church of Scotland had the shared inheritance of the 1781 Translations and Paraphrases, some of which might be regarded as embryonic hymns. The Church of Scotland appointed committees to consider Psalms and paraphrases in 1845 and 1847 respectively, and although reports containing a collection of hymns appeared in 1854 and 1855, nothing substantial resulted. In 1860, a committee under Dr David Arnott produced a collection of hymns, which was revised and published in 1861 but little used. It was introduced at the Kirk of Canongate, Edinburgh in 1863.[31]

Dr A. K. H. Boyd was responsible for overseeing a committee that produced a much improved book, which was finally adopted in 1870 as the *Scottish Hymnal*, containing 200 hymns. It was expanded to 358 hymns, and by 1888 to 442. Boyd, it should be noted, was a prominent member of the Church Service Society, and in an article of 1889 recorded that the 1888 edition had sold two million copies.[32] He argued that a new generation had arisen that had never known the pathos of an Ayrshire Tent Preaching; the old order had gone – in fact it had gone before the hymnal was even contemplated.[33] Boyd's article was an apologia for the hymnal, and outlined the work of the committee, the decisions regarding the original words and alterations made.

5.2 The Revd Dr
A. K. H. Boyd

The hymns were placed in ten sections, similar to the *Presbyterian Hymnal* sections. The hymns for baptism and childhood, and the Lord's Supper, were grouped under the section 'Natural and Sacred Seasons', with four suitable for baptisms and five provided for the Lord's Supper.

The Free Church of Scotland continued the tradition of metrical psalmody, its first denominational psalter being published in 1845 under the

---

30 *Remarks on the Innovations in the Public worship of God, Proposed by the Free Presbytery of Hamilton*, Edinburgh: Bell & Bradfute, 1854, p. 34.

31 Wright, *The Kirk in the Canongate*, p. 151.

32 A. K. H. Boyd, 'The New Hymnology of the Scottish Kirk', *Blackwood's Magazine* May 1889, pp. 657–67, p. 657.

33 Boyd, 'New Hymnology of the Scottish Kirk', p. 658.

title *The Psalmody of the Free Church of Scotland*. This was edited by T. L. Hately (1815–67), a printer and distinguished precentor. A version of this collection that added a guide to psalm-singing was published under the title *The National Psalmist*. In the same year, Hately also published a collection of Gaelic tunes as *Old Gaelic Tunes taken down by T. L. Hately*. The Gaelic-speaking congregations had adapted and modified many of the basic melodies to better suit the language, and the singers also began to ornament them; they are known as 'Long Tunes'.[34]

Hately made a significant contribution to the Free Church musical tradition and composed forty psalm tunes, including 'Glencairns', 'Leuchars' and 'Cunningham' (the latter in memory of William Cunningham). He was also the musical editor of *The Scottish Psalmody*, 1854. In the same year he also published *The Book of Psalms and Sacred Harmonies*. This was the first of the 'split-page', or 'staff' (or 'Dutch-door') psalters, having a horizontal split throughout the collection, with the words on the top and music on the bottom half, allowing the music to be opened to match whatever text of the psalm was selected. This seems to have been inspired by the combination of his printing knowledge with the needs of precentors and congregations.

Other Free Church musicians contributing tunes included the Revd Neil Livingston (1803–91) who, in 1864, published a scholarly edition of the Scottish Psalter of 1635; and A. D. Thomson, who composed the tune 'Free Church'. In 1873 a revised *Scottish Psalmody* was published, which in turn was replaced in 1883 by *The Scottish Psalter*.

The nineteenth-century Free Church, then, was far from static, and conservation as well as renewal and development took place within the tradition of metrical psalmody. A new step was taken in 1882 with the publication of *The Free Church Hymn Book*. A committee had been appointed to examine the lawfulness of using hymns in worship, and in 1869 reported that there was nothing in Scripture or church law that conflicted with the singing of hymns.[35] A counterblast came from James Gibson, Professor of Systematic Theology and Church History at the Free Church College, Glasgow. Entitled *The Public Worship of God: Its Authority and Modes, Hymns and Hymn Books*, it said little about worship in general, and a vast amount from Scripture against hymns and instrumental music. Gibson argued that hymns smuggled in Arianism and Arminianism, betrayed the feebleness of the human being, and that the words of many were silly and meaningless bombast.[36] In 1870, the Committee presented a draft of *Trans-*

---

34 See A. P. W. Fraser, 'Praise: The Melody of Religion', in Clement Graham (ed.), *Crown Him Lord of All: Essays on the Life and Witness of the Free Church of Scotland*, Edinburgh: The Knox Press, 1993, pp. 71–90, p. 85. I am dependent on this essay for much of the information on Hately and the Free Church editions of the Psalter.

35 Benson, *The English Hymn*, p. 536.

36 James Gibson, *The Public Worship of God: Its Authority and Modes, Hymns and Hymn Books*, London: James Nisbet, 1869. See pp. 127 and 143 for the latter remarks.

lations and Paraphrases with additional hymns. Benson noted that, after some delay, this was approved and allowed for public use in 1872, amid much opposition, by a vote of 152 against sixty-one.[37] The 1882 hymnal had a Preface by a committee appointed in 1878, in which was expressed the hope that the collection would fulfil its purpose – 'the advancement of God's glory in the praise of the sanctuary'. It contained 387 hymns and thirty scriptural anthems set to music by Edward J. Hopkins, an Anglican musician. The hymns do not appear to have been arranged in any obvious sequence, but a subject index was provided at the back, giving themes and headings so that a suitable selection could be made.

Although there were differences in the hymnals of the three main denominations, there was also considerable overlap. In 1891, the United Presbyterian Church resolved to revise its hymnal and decided to approach the Church of Scotland and the Free Church of Scotland to see if they might co-operate in a common venture. A joint committee was appointed, and drafts for a new joint hymnal appeared in 1895 and 1896. The Church of Scotland decided to withdraw, but did adopt the final book, *The Church Hymnary*, 1898. The Preface claimed that the hymnal 'is catholic, as including hymns by authors belonging to almost every branch of the Church from the second century to the present day, and comprehensive, as intended for the use of various Churches and congregations'.[38] The musical editor was Sir John Stainer. As in the United Presbyterian and Scottish Hymnal, the hymns were collected under various thematic headings, broadly termed God, the Christian Life, the Church, Special Occasions, hymns for the young, dismissal hymns, doxologies and ancient hymns.

Although some congregations, particularly in the Islands, resisted the innovation, hymns now became a vital element in most Scottish Presbyterian worship. As noted, the hymnals included hymns and music from many traditions. Scottish musicians had always been ready to compose new music for the metrical psalmody, and now their scope was broadened to include hymnody. Reference has already been made to Horatius Bonar, who in 1843 had seceded to the Free Church of Scotland and was elected Moderator in 1883. According to Brownlie, though often negligent of rhyme and rhythm, Bonar was the principal hymn-writer of Scotland.[39] He published *Hymns of Faith and Hope* in three series, 1857, 1861 and 1866. In 1872 *The Song of New Creation* was published, followed by *Hymns of the Nativity*, 1879, *Communion Hymns*, 1881, and *Until the Day Break*,

37 Benson, *The English Hymn*, p. 536.

38 *The Church Hymnary: Authorized for Use in Public Worship by the Church of Scotland, the United Free Church of Scotland, the Presbyterian Church in Ireland, the Presbyterian Church of Australia, the Presbyterian Church of New Zealand*, Edinburgh: Henry Frowde, 1902 edition. By the time the hymnal was published, the United Presbyterians had united with the Free Church of Scotland to form the United Free Church of Scotland. See Chapter 8.

39 John Brownlie, *The Hymns and Hymn Writers of the Church Hymnary*, London and Edinburgh: Henry Frowde, 1911, p. 230.

1890. Among some of his best known are 'Be Still, my soul; Jehovah loveth thee' and 'I heard the voice of Jesus say'. Eighteen of his hymns were included in *The Church Hymnary*, including one of his communion hymns, 'For the bread and for the wine'. Other Free Church of Scotland hymn writers were James Grindlay Small (*Songs of the Vineyard*, 1846; *Hymns for Youthful Voices*, 1859; *Psalms and Sacred Songs*, 1866) and James Drummond Burns. The United Presbyterian minister George Jacque composed two hymns that were included in *The Presbyterian Hymnal*, 1876, and William Bruce also contributed two hymns to the same hymnal. Hymn writers of the Church of Scotland included John Ross Macduff (*Altar Stones*, 1853; *The Gates of Praise*, 1876), Archibald Charteris and George Matheson, who authored the well-known 'O love that wilt not let me go'.[40]

The Moody and Sankey mission also served to popularise hymns. Frances Wilkins noted:

> The hymns in *Sacred Songs and Solos* were printed, first using sol-fa and later staff notation, in four parts (soprano, alto, tenor and bass) to be accompanied by an organ. Most hymns were written with choruses and had simple melodies which were easy to pick up. The book, along with *Redemption Songs*, was taken up for congregational use in many churches and mission halls along the North-East coast, as in other area[s] of the United Kingdom.[41]

And choirs

The 'song schools' barely survived the Reformation, and Scottish Reformed worship was a cappella congregational singing, led by the precentor. Thomas Frost summarised thus:

> The psalm to be sung was announced by the minister, and the precentor, who occupied a smaller pulpit below him, placed in a slit in a lyre-shaped brass frame in front of him a card bearing the name of the tune in large letters, so as to be visible to all the congregation. The minister then repeated the first two lines of the verses to be sung, and the precentor struck his tuning-fork on the desk. It was a custom of long standing, probably dating from a time when few of the congregation could read, for the precentor to read and sing a line alternately, which must, to persons unaccustomed to it, have sounded strange, and certainly have destroyed

---

40 Brownlie, *The Hymns and Hymn Writers*, pp. 221–5; James Moffatt and Millar Patrick, *Handbook to the Church Hymnary, With Supplement*, London: Oxford University Press, 1929, passim.

41 Francis Wilkins, *Singing the Gospel along Scotland's North-East Coast, 1859–2009*, Abingdon: Routledge, 2018, p. 39.

what little harmony there might have been if the psalm had been sung differently.[42]

Victorian Britain saw a renewed interest in communal singing and choirs, both secular and sacred. In the Scottish Presbyterian churches, this interest coalesced with the revival of the organ and the singing of hymns and anthems. Choirs with choirmasters became more common. An early example was Thomas Lees (d.1824) who was choirmaster at the High Church, Edinburgh.[43] At Greyfriars, Joseph Geoghegan was choirmaster from 1857 to 1883, under Dr Lee, and his choir 'sang with an amount of taste, energy, and precision which rendered them locally famous'.[44] Sir A. C. Mackenzie was choirmaster at St George's Edinburgh from 1865 to 1879.[45] J. O. Sinclair was conductor of St Giles' Cathedral Choir from 1874.[46] James Finlay was organist and choirmaster at Peebles parish church, which had a purely male-voice (and boys) choir.[47] William Moodie was choirmaster at Lansdowne United Presbyterian Church until 1877, then at the Barony until 1889 and then at East Pollokshields Free Church, all at Glasgow.[48] In its reports on various Dundee churches between 1887 and 1889, *The Piper O'Dundee* listed the following as having a choir: St Andrew's Parish Church, McCheyne Memorial Church, Ward Chapel, Tay Square ('a weak choir'), St Mark's Parish Church, George's Chapel, Albert Square Free Church, Chalmers Free Church, Free St John's Kirk and Downfield United Presbyterian (a Choral Union).[49] The Moody and Sankey visit to Scotland had also encouraged hymn singing with a choir. The *Aberdeen Daily Free Press* explained:

'Praise' meetings would consist of an address from Moody, prayers and testimonies with hymn singing led by Sankey at regular intervals, accompanying himself on harmonium and joined by a choir. The choir consisted of local singers, both male and female. The hymns tended to all have choruses, which the congregations could easily join in with. It was also common in Aberdeen for hymns to be sung by congregation and choir almost non-stop whilst waiting outside the meeting places until the start of the services.'[50]

---

42 Thomas Frost, 'Church Music', in William Andrews (ed.), *Bygone Church Life in Scotland*, London: William Andrews & Co., 1899, pp. 98–107, p. 104.

43 David Baptie, *Musical Scotland: Past and Present*, Paisley: J. and R. Parlane, 1894, p. 99. My thanks to Douglas Galbraith for drawing my attention to this dictionary.

44 Baptie, *Musical Scotland*, p. 61.

45 Baptie, *Musical Scotland*, p. 111.

46 Baptie, *Musical Scotland*, p. 170.

47 Baptie, *Musical Scotland*, p. 54.

48 Baptie, *Musical Scotland*, p. 132.

49 *The Piper O'Dundee*, 7 May 1887, p. 11; 11 July 1888, p. 66; 25 July 1888, p. 90; 22 August 1888, p. 138; 26 September 1888, p. 258; 19 December 1888, p. 342; 20 February 1889, p. 90; 22 May 1889, p. 246; 27 November 1889, p. 626.

50 *Aberdeen Daily Free Press*, 15 June 1874, p. 2, cited in Wilkins, *Singing the Gospel*, p. 36.

The introduction of choirs was not without debate on their function in worship. *The Piper O'Dundee* commented on the music of St Andrew's Parish Church:

> The singing in St. Andrew's makes no pretentions to fine artistic effect. The choir, led by the choirmaster, who presides at the harmonium, give the congregation a start with the tune, the people then take the matter into their own hands, and each and all drone away at their own sweet will, approximating more or less closely to correct time and tune – mostly less. After all, joining heartily, if not very correctly, in the singing of psalms and hymns to simple, old-fashioned, well-known tunes, pleases the ordinary worshipper more, and does him more good, than merely listening to a fine musical entertainment by a highly trained choir.[51]

The correct use of a choir was the subject of some papers given at the 1894 conference of the Scottish Church Society. Hely Almond pointed out that the voices of perhaps five per cent of the congregation acting as a choir caused at least ninety-five per cent of the total sound.[52] He suggested the dismissal of all paid singers; the opening psalm sung by the choir, and then the same psalm sung by everyone; that the choir be dispersed all over the church, or behind the congregation; repeat tunes so the congregation get to know them; and to use older and familiar tunes.[53] Above all, organists and choirs should understand that their function is subordinate.[54] J. M. Nisbet complained that more attention was given to collecting pretty music than to the arrangement of acts of praise, and advocated the use of plainsong, especially for canticles, in which the congregation could sing alternative verses.[55] In contrast, he thought the anthem 'The glorious crown to our Service of Praise' should never be sung by the people. The function of the anthem was twofold: it interprets to the congregation the holy beauty of the divine message and should give expression to the emotions of the worshippers.[56] The Revd W. H. Macleod complained that often choirs savoured more of the concert-room than of the church, and advocated the founding of Choir Guilds.[57] Such discussions and suggestions were necessary because, like organs and hymnals, choirs too were 'here to stay'. Not

---

51 *The Piper O'Dundee*, 7 May 1887, p. 11.

52 Hely H. Almond, 'Church Music and Choirs', in Scottish Church Society, *The Divine Life in the Church*, Second Series, vol. 2, Edinburgh: J. Gardner Hitt, 1895, pp. 206–12, p. 207.

53 Almond, 'Church Music and Choirs', pp. 208–10.

54 Almond, 'Church Music and Choirs', p. 212.

55 J. M. Nisbet, 'Church Music and Choirs', in *The Divine Life in the Church*, pp. 213–19, p. 213 and pp. 215–6.

56 Nisbet, 'Church Music and Choirs', pp. 216–17.

57 W. H. Macleod, 'Church Music and Choirs', in *The Divine Life in the Church*, pp. 220–6.

only were the new liturgies visible signs of a change in worship style, but the music was too.

Concluding note

Although not all ministers in the three largest Presbyterian groupings embraced the new liturgical forms that the Church Service Society or denominational committees produced, ministers and congregations seem to have been more open to changes in music – instrumental accompaniment, hymns and a group of strong trained singers to sing as a choir. This, though, was not a peculiarly Scottish Presbyterian trend. In the Church of England, at the same time, the old metrical psalmody of Sternhold and Hopkins, and Tate and Brady, gave way to hymns, particularly *Hymns Ancient and Modern*, 1861, and although many churches had musical accompaniment in the form of west-gallery parish bands, these gave way to the organ and a robed choir that sat in the chancel.[58] This 'enrichment' was the influence of, and also a reflection of, the wider aesthetic tastes and developments in Victorian society and culture.

---

58 Bryan D. Spinks, *The Rise and Fall of the Incomparable Liturgy: The Book of Common Prayer, 1559–1906*, London: SPCK, 2017, chapter 5.

6

Worship and the High Church Party:
The So-called Scoto-Catholics and the
Scottish Church Society

The main purpose of the Church Service Society was the improvement of the standard of worship in the Church of Scotland, and this concern resonated with many ministers. However, the common cause was aesthetical and not primarily theological, and the theological make-up of the Society was wide and broad. As observed in an earlier chapter, when a sixth edition of the *Euchologion* was proposed, Professor Allan Menzies and 145 others made a representation to the committee, which was interpreted with some dissatisfaction by some of the 'Broad' church membership as what they regarded as Anglicanising and 'High Church' tendencies in the fifth edition of 1884. This 'manifesto' may also may have been a veiled criticism of James Cooper.

The Scottish Church Society

James Cooper became a member of the Church Service Society in 1873 and was appointed to the Editorial Committee in 1880. His diary of 9 January 1883 records: 'Church Service Society. Service for Holy Communion and Baptism well through: secured Nicene Creed and *Sursum Corda* in first service.'[1] Cooper was one of a group of churchmen who held a high doctrine of the church, ministry and sacraments, and wanted to recover more of the 'catholic liturgical patrimony' of the Church of Scotland. Although appreciative of the *Euchologion*, he would later write of the Church Service Society, 'It appears to many of us now that this Society is not likely to do much more; and that it is paralysed by the spirit of compromise arising out of the composition of its managing body.'[2] Cooper and some like-minded

---

1 James Cooper's diary, 2283/5,3 (Aberdeen University), cited in Brian A. Rees, 'James Cooper and the Scoto-Catholic Party: Tractarian Reform in the Church of Scotland, 1882–1918', PhD thesis, St Andrews University, 1980, p. 460, note 52.

2 James Cooper, *The Revival of Church Principles in the Church of Scotland. A paper read at a meeting of the North Test Valley Clerical Society, held at Ashe Rectory*, Oxford: Mowbray, 1897, p. 17.

ministers were not prepared to compromise, and held strong doctrinal convictions about the Church of Scotland being part of the wider Catholic Church. These ministers, dubbed 'Scoto-Catholics' by their detractors, founded the Scottish Church Society in 1892 to defend and propagate their ideas and theological convictions. Brian Rees writes:

> The Scottish Church Society's formation followed upon the General Assembly of 1891, at which an amendment to the Report of the Church Interests Committee had been proposed by Wallace Williamson and J. H. Crawford of Abercorn to the effect that 'the General Assembly, while rejoicing at the prospect of Presbyterian reunion, accepts such union only as a step towards the complete unity of the Church of Christ'. The consciousness that motivated this amendment soon drew to itself others of a similar orientation, and a meeting, presided over by Dr. John Macleod of Govan, was held to consider how best to proceed.[3]

As a result of discussion between James Cooper, George Sprott and John Macleod, it was resolved to found a Society for the defence and propagation of Catholic truth.[4] A committee was formed to prepare a constitution, with Macleod as convener and Cooper as secretary. The Society was formally instituted in June 1892, and Professor William Milligan was elected president. The Society took for its motto, 'Ask for the old paths and walk therein'. Its stated purpose was *to defend and advance Catholic doctrine, as set forth in the ancient Creeds, and embodied in the Standards of the Church of Scotland* and *generally to assert Scriptural principles in all matters relating to Church Order and Policy, Christian Work, and Spiritual Life, throughout Scotland*.[5] Among its special objects were the assertion of the efficacy of the sacraments, the restoration of Holy Communion to its right place in relation to the worship of the Church, the revival of Daily Services wherever practicable and the observance in its main features of the Christian year.[6]

There was considerable overlap with membership of the Church Service Society, the Scottish Church Society representing its 'High Church' membership. However, Christopher Johnson identified two main groups within the Scottish Church Society: George Sprott, Thomas Leishman and James Cooper represented one; John Macleod, William Milligan and Andrew Wallace Williamson represented another, which placed less emphasis on the traditions of the Church.[7] The story of this Society has been told in

---

3 Rees, 'James Cooper and the Scoto-Catholic Party', p. 313.
4 Rees, 'James Cooper and the Scoto-Catholic Party', p. 313, memoir 164.
5 William Milligan, *The Scottish Church Society*, Edinburgh: J. Gardner Hitt, 1893, pp. 5, 8.
6 Cooper, *The Revival of Church Principles in the Church of Scotland*, p. 22.
7 Christopher N. Johnston, *Life of Andrew Wallace Williamson*, Edinburgh, 1929, p. 152.

detail elsewhere, and the focus here is on the convictions about worship and liturgy held by particular members of the Society.[8]

William Milligan (1821–93)

6.1 The Revd Professor
William Milligan

The theological foundation of the High Church movement was provided by Professor William Milligan, who has been described as 'the Pusey of the movement'. When he was a student he had spent a year in Germany. In 1860 he was appointed Professor of Biblical Criticism at Aberdeen and in 1870 became a member of the committee appointed for the revised version of the New Testament, and so had regular contact with Church of England clergy and scholars. He was deputy clerk of the General Assembly of the Church of Scotland from 1875 to 1886, and then Principal Clerk. He had joined the Church Service Society in 1875, and in 1882 was Moderator of the Church of Scotland. He published studies on Ephesians, the book of Revelation and on the Resurrection of the Dead. His major work, which provided a theology of worship for the High Churchmen, was *The Ascension and Heavenly Priesthood of Our Lord*, 1892, which emphasised the priestly ministry of Christ and, through the Holy Spirit, the priestly ministry of the Church.[9] In this work he asked:

> Does the ascended and glorified Lord even now present to His Father in heaven anything that may with propriety be called an offering? Or are His heavenly functions summed up in the idea of Intercession? . . . Are we to confine the thought of 'offering' on the part of our Lord to His sacrificial death? Or are we so to extend the thought as to include in it a present and eternal offering to God of His life in heaven?[10]

For Milligan, the saving events of Jesus Christ were not simply a past achievement but were in a present, active state in the living Christ. There is an eternal offering in heaven before the Father. He argued:

---

8 Douglas Murray, 'The Scottish Church Society, 1892–1914: A Study in the High Church Movement in the Church of Scotland', PhD thesis, University of Cambridge, 1976; Rees, 'James Cooper and the Scoto-Catholic Party'.

9 William Milligan, *The Ascension and Heavenly Priesthood of Our Lord*, Greenwood, SC: Attic, 1977; See also Hogan L. Yancey, 'The Development of the Theology of William Milligan (1821–1893)', PhD thesis, University of Edinburgh, 1970.

10 Milligan, *The Ascension and Heavenly Priesthood*, pp. 115, 116.

There is even a sense in which Intercession is Offering, and Offering Intercession. Let it also be allowed (and no other conclusion seems possible) that, as our High-priest is Himself 'heavenly', His work must be of the same character, and it will necessarily follow that the idea of His Offering is likewise heavenly, and, as heavenly, eternal.[11]

What is offered is not death but a life that has been through death:

That offering began with the cross, with the moment when, separated from all that was material, local, or limited, the Lord who died was able to enter upon a spiritual, universal, and everlasting priesthood, and to present to the God against whom His people had sinned, His spiritual, universal, and everlasting offering.[12]

Christ now pleads the cause of his people with all-prevailing intercession on their behalf, Christ who is both human and divine, and in whom the Spirit dwells. When the Spirit is bestowed on us, Christ and the Spirit dwell in us. This has implications for the nature of the Church:

The Church exists by means of our Lord's communication to her of that Spirit which is His own Spirit. It follows that what He is His people, according to the measure of their capabilities, must also be. This principle is, indeed, a simple corollary from the fundamental conception of the Church as the Body of Christ, for the Body lives in such close communion with the Head that whatever the Head wills the Body must do.[13]

Christians have the divinely instituted sacraments and ministry, and the concept of priesthood as fulfilled in Christ must also be fulfilled in the Church.[14]

This theology had obvious implications for worship and for the Eucharist. Worship, argued Milligan, is one of the means by which Christ manifests his glory on earth. Worship should be common worship, which is an expression of the common life of the Church. It promotes the glory of God:

The service of the Church was almost exclusively joyous. Her worship consisted nearly altogether of Psalms, the Lord's Prayer, the Creed (itself a Psalm) . . . a few versicles, a few Collects, the lections from Scripture, and these interspersed with anthems, responsories, and hymns.[15]

---

11 Milligan, *The Ascension and Heavenly Priesthood*, pp. 126–7.
12 Milligan, *The Ascension and Heavenly Priesthood*, p. 138.
13 Milligan, *The Ascension and Heavenly Priesthood*, p. 228.
14 Milligan, *The Ascension and Heavenly Priesthood*, p. 243.
15 Milligan, *The Ascension and Heavenly Priesthood*, p. 301.

Worship must express itself in form, some ceremonial and ritual, as an implication of the incarnation.[16] Furthermore, the inclusion of a Creed is because it expresses the faith of the whole Church.[17]

Milligan taught that from the beginning of her history, the Church instinctively regarded the sacrament of the Holy Communion as the central act of worship.[18] The reason is that in the Supper 'the Church realised to a greater extent than in any other of her ordinances both her own deepest, that is, her sacrificial life in her glorified Lord, and His peculiar presence with her as her nourishment and strength and joy.'[19] Milligan did not pursue the concept of presence, but did outline the 'offering' nature of the Eucharist:

> As our Lord's offering of Himself to His Heavenly Father never ends, or can end; so in that offering His people, organically united to Him, one with Him, must be offered, and must offer themselves; and this they do in the expressive and touching symbols of the Eucharist. They do not simply remember what Jesus did on earth. They bring to their remembrance as a present fact what He is doing in heaven. They commemorate, they hold communion with, they accept, and at His Table are nourished by, a living Lord, – 'in remembrance of *Me*,' of Me, not as I was, but as I am, to the end of time. Christ Himself, spiritually present with them, is the life of their souls; His body and blood there given them are the substance of their feast; and living in Him, and obtaining in Him pardon, peace, and strength, they transact here below what He is transacting in the heavenly Sanctuary. In the Sacrament of the Supper, in short, they offer themselves in Him who is now and for ever an offering to the Father.[20]

Milligan's theology, orthodox in Trinitarian and Christological belief, and arguing for a high doctrine of the Church and its priestly ministry through the risen and ascended Lord, provided a theology that appealed to those ministers who formed the Scottish Church Society. As noted, Milligan was elected its first president, and in 1893 he published a pamphlet giving an account of the aims of the Society. It was perceived that some apologia was needed, since there were those who saw this as a movement to make the Church of Scotland 'Catholic' or Episcopal, or something worse. Of the faith of the creeds he wrote:

> What concerns the members of the Scottish Church Society, therefore, is simply whether these doctrines occupy their proper place in the mind of the Church taken as a whole? Are the doctrines of the Divinity, the

---

16 Milligan, *The Ascension and Heavenly Priesthood*, pp. 304–5.
17 Milligan, *The Ascension and Heavenly Priesthood*, pp. 313–31.
18 Milligan, *The Ascension and Heavenly Priesthood*, p. 309.
19 Milligan, *The Ascension and Heavenly Priesthood*, p. 309.
20 Milligan, *The Ascension and Heavenly Priesthood*, p. 266.

Incarnation, the Atoning Death, the Resurrection, the Ascension, and the Second Advent of Him whom we call the Redeemer of the world, of the presence and work of the Holy Spirit in the Church, and of the place and value of the Divine ordinances sufficiently prominent in our minds?[21]

As well as knowledge of the standards of faith, and that the Church of Scotland is part of the fuller Church of Christ, Milligan noted the Society's stress on the sacraments, particularly the Eucharist:

They are the only Christian ordinances directly appointed by our Lord (a fact which places them in a category peculiar to themselves), and they are, moreover, the special instrumentality by which the glorified Lord, human as well as divine, continually renews His union with us in our human natures, bidding us who are men appropriate by faith His manhood, His 'Body and Blood,' His 'flesh for the life of the world,' that we, entering by that portal into the marriage feast, may have both sealed and applied to us One who, as the life of the soul, is divine as well as human.[22]

Douglas Murray noted that Milligan's adhesion to the Society, and his presidency of it in its first year, were of great value and gave the movement almost an official sanction.[23] His death in December 1893 was a great loss to the Society, but his influence lived on in many of the Society's notable, if not also notorious, members.

James Cooper (1846–1922)

In his study of the Scottish Church Society, Douglas Murray observed of James Cooper, who was a student of William Milligan at Aberdeen, that although Cooper's churchmanship was certainly distinctive and diverged in certain points from Milligan's positions, yet he shared his former professor's theological views and these formed the basis of his own thinking.[24] Cooper had an admiration for the Church of England and lamented the divisions of the Christian Church. He favoured union of the divided Scottish Presbyterian churches, but as a prelude to union with the Scottish Episcopal Church and the Church of England. He looked back nostalgically to the time of the Scottish Episcopate of James VI and Charles I, with episcopacy working with Presbytery and the General Assembly. He liked the 1637 Book of Common Prayer, the so-called 'Laud's Liturgy', and published a new edition of it. He argued for the importance of the ancient creeds, as the standard of the Scottish Church as well as for use in worship.

---

21 Milligan, *The Scottish Church Society*, p. 6.
22 Milligan, *The Scottish Church Society*, pp. 10–11.
23 Murray, 'The Scottish Church Society, 1892–1914', p. 53.
24 Murray, 'The Scottish Church Society, 1892–1914', p. 53.

6.2 The Revd Professor
James Cooper

Cooper read the early works of the English Tractarians – Newman, Manning and Pusey – and his biographer, Wotherspoon, remarked that Pusey was his model.[25]

Cooper was one of the founding members of the Scottish Church Society, and his own understanding of the aims was set out in a long paper originally given to Church of England clergy.[26] In this paper, Cooper stressed the continuity of the Church of Scotland with the pre-Reformation Church, and that ordination by laying on of hands continued the apostolic succession. The Church of Scotland held to the doctrine of the Apostles' Creed, and the Scots Confession set forth a high doctrine of the sacraments. This same paper presented his audience with the work of Robert Lee and the Church Service Society. He noted the wide use of the *Euchologion* but also that it had not been approved by public authority: 'It would be a serious matter for the General Assembly to commit itself to a Liturgy that was not thoroughly good; and it is better to wait for the growth of such than to invoke a premature decision.'[27] He drew attention to the authorised hymnal, a prose psalter and the revival of a daily service in some churches. On the Lord's Supper he said:

Holy Communion had come to be celebrated only once or twice yearly; quarterly Celebrations are now common: in some churches monthly, or more than monthly. The desire, one hopes, is growing for greater frequency; and Communion is once a month (quite freely) given to the sick.[28]

The paper included a list of the objectives of the Scottish Church Society as stated in the constitution, and concluded with his own vision of their fulfilment. His concern for worship and the sacraments was made abundantly clear. In an unfinished autobiography, reflecting on the ruins of Elgin Cathedral, he wrote:

it was reared as we have heard, for the Glory of God, and for the amplification and more honourable and reverent fulfilment of His appointed worship; and the strongest admonition that its ruins read to me to-day is to my consciousness of how miserably our Reformed Church has failed in

25 H. J. Wotherspoon, *James Cooper: A Memoir*, London: Longmans, Green & Co., 1926, p. 94.
26 Cooper, *The Revival of Church Principles in the Church of Scotland*.
27 Cooper, *The Revival of Church Principles in the Church of Scotland*, p. 18.
28 Cooper, *The Revival of Church Principles in the Church of Scotland*, p. 19.

regard to Worship; which, after all, is what Our Savior tells us that God desires of us: – *The Father seeketh such to* WORSHIP HIM. Whatever else may be the duty of a Scottish Minister, he must aim at reviving the spirit of worship: this also, I may say without boasting, I have laboured through my whole ministry to do.[29]

His own liturgical contributions can be traced through his successive ministries at St Stephen's, Broughty Ferry; St Nicholas East Church, Aberdeen; as Professor at Aberdeen; and as Moderator of the General Assembly.

St Stephen's Broughty Ferry

In 1873, Cooper was offered the charge of St Stephen's, Broughty Ferry. It was a new church and so had no deeply entrenched traditions, and as Rees says, 'it was there that his unique ministry, in the sense of his movement toward the realisation of his ideals, first began.'[30] This entailed buying communion plate for the church and fittings for the communion table, including Gothic-style chalices, and communion linens from Cox & Co., London.[31] He also presented the congregation with a brass lectern.[32] Under his ministry the church was endowed and erected into a parish, and a chancel was added.[33] Christmas services were introduced from 1874 onwards, and the observance of Holy Week from 1878.[34] Rees, referring to Cooper's diaries, says:

> He composed a Baptism service for use in his church. He had the choir learn the *Te Deum* and the *Dies Irae*; the *Te Deum* being sung there for the first time on St. Stephen's Day, 1873. He pressed for quarterly Communion, and although one elder objected at first, it was instituted in February 1874.[35]

Cooper also composed a communion service for St Stephen's.[36]

---

29 Wotherspoon, *James Cooper*, p. 19.

30 Rees, 'James Cooper and the Scoto-Catholic Party', p. 173.

31 Rees, 'James Cooper and the Scoto-Catholic Party', pp. 174–5.

32 Rees, 'James Cooper and the Scoto-Catholic Party', p. 175.

33 Wotherspoon, *James Cooper*, p. 102.

34 Wotherspoon, *James Cooper*, p. 102.

35 Rees, 'James Cooper and the Scoto-Catholic Party', p. 178. The Diaries are at Aberdeen University Library.

36 I have not been able to locate a copy of this. *The Order of the Celebration of the Sacrament of the Lord's Supper in the Parish Church of St. Stephen Broughty Ferry*, printed for the congregation, Broughty Ferry, 1877. Listed in Cooper Bibliography compiled by Douglas Murray, *The Record* 29 (1995), pp. 34–40.

The East Church of St Nicholas, Aberdeen

At the beginning of 1881, the East Church of St Nicholas, Aberdeen, became vacant, and Cooper was recommended to the congregation by Professor Milligan. He was offered the charge and was inducted to the East Church on the Eve of Ascension Day.[37] Cooper wrote:

> Knowing the ways of Presbyteries and their officers I went down to the church in the morning and found that nothing had been done to provide for proper fulfilment of the sacred rite. The pulpit was where it still is. Immediately in front of it was a wide pew like a horsebox covered with cocoanut matting, with a few common chairs standing about. There was no sign of a Table. I asked the Church Officer where the Communion Table was. His answer was, 'Please, sir, in the West Lobby.' 'What is it doing there?' 'Please, sir, the gentlemen of the Choir put their hats on it.' I said, 'Its proper place is here – help me to bring it in.' I found some handsome chairs in the transepts and brought them also into the Church. At this moment my father entered the Church and great was his disappointment to see that there was neither organ nor lectern, font nor altar, such as we had in St. Stephen's. 'This will mean a great sacrifice to you'. 'We just must have it rectified,' I said.[38]

It was the attempt to rectify matters in worship that caused some difficulties between certain members of the congregation and Cooper. He had made it clear before he accepted the call that he wanted to establish quarterly Communion, and to take an active part in teaching at the church's Sabbath Schools. He attempted to do at the East Church what he had done at Broughty Ferry, but in May 1882, eleven of his twenty-seven elders sent a petition to the Presbytery of Aberdeen, complaining of 'High Church' doctrine and practices. Wotherspoon wrote of the complaint:

> It complained of their Minister's 'High Churchism' and general proclivities, of entertaining a desire to change the position of the pulpit, of having used the expression 'Christian Altar,' of varying the sequence of acts in public worship, of using a Litany in the Sunday School, of holding Daily Service and of using thereat a prayer desk and a reading desk, of thereby wasting precious time; of giving Communion to the sick; of professing a strong desire to revive the Christian Year; of holding a Christmas service for children, and of practicing for it; of preparing for it a 'Christmas Office for children'; of intending to have a brass band at the service, though on remonstrance he gave up the intention, and that in this Service Mr. Cooper intoned and the children sang responses, 'like an Episcopal Congregation'; that in those proceedings Mr. Cooper had

---

37 Wotherspoon, *James Cooper*, p. 119.
38 Wotherspoon, *James Cooper*, p. 119.

not the sanction of the Session, and that he denied that he required to have it. They had, however, 'far more serious and grave complaint' of novel and alien preaching and practice; of magnifying the Sacraments and Ministry, of dilating upon the Virginity of the Mother of our Lord, upon the Saints, the Fathers and Festivals; of teaching in effect and 'according to the opinion of many of his hearers' Baptismal Regeneration, Transubstantiation, Apostolic Succession, and ministerial absolution.[39]

He was also accused of teaching a substantial change in the state of the soul after death and prior to the resurrection and praying for the departed.[40]

The Presbytery appointed a committee, with William Milligan as convener, to examine the complaints, and Cooper agreed that in future he would inform the Session or the congregation if he intended to celebrate Communion in the houses of the sick, and would also consult regarding any changes in worship. However, the objecting elders drew up a 'Minute' complaining that their complaints had not been fully investigated. This went to the Synod, which instructed the Presbytery to reopen the case. At this stage, the elders referred to Cooper's sacerdotalism:

> There had been a priestly assumption of power, and indeed the ideas which had of late been taught among them had been strongly brought before their minds by the death of the late Dr. Pusey. The same ideas which actuated the Puseyite party seemed to be those which were inculcated, viz: – baptismal regeneration, the superiority of ordination, and the gift with it, and the change of the elements at the Communion.[41]

When the elders appeared before the Presbytery, they complained that the changes Cooper said he had made were in name only. Cooper said that he had made changes to bring peace, but declined to debate on the theological accusations on the grounds that such charges needed to take the form of a libel. Cooper finally agreed to defend his doctrinal beliefs, asking both G. W. Sprott and William Milligan to assist him. Cooper was able to draw on the Scottish standards to vindicate what he had said, and denied saying or holding certain things that the elders had accused him of. The final decision of the Presbytery was to enjoin Cooper to be careful not to give occasion for the suspicion that his opinion and practices were not in thorough accordance with the doctrine of the Church of Scotland.[42] Cooper was not able to make any alterations to the interior of the East Church, though eventually the congregation voted for an organ to be installed. He

---

39 Wotherspoon, *James Cooper*, pp. 127–8.

40 Wotherspoon, *James Cooper*, pp. 169–73.

41 *Aberdeen Journal*, 27 September 1882, cited by Murray, 'The Scottish Church Society, 1892–1914', p. 320.

42 Wotherspoon, *James Cooper*, p. 133; Murray, 'The Scottish Church Society, 1892–1914', p. 334, citing the Minutes of the Presbytery of Aberdeen, 13 February 1883.

was not successful in increasing the number of celebrations of Communion, though he did eventually establish an Easter celebration.

While at the East Church, Cooper drew up an order of service for the celebration of the Communion, entitled *The Divine Liturgy: The Order at the Holy Table*.[43] It began with the Gloria in excelsis and the Nicene Creed. These were followed by the Peace and the Words of Institution read as a warrant. An Offertory Prayer followed, which seems to have been adapted from the Catholic Apostolic Church Liturgy, and began: 'Almighty and Most Merciful Father, to Thee we offer this Bread and this Cup, of the fruits of the earth which Thou hast given for our sustenance.' This was followed by 'Prayer of the Veil', a version of which was contained in the *Euchologion*, though Cooper's version is fuller:

O God, who by the Blood of Jesus hast consecrated for us a new and living way into the holiest, through the veil, that is to say, His Flesh: cleanse us from all defilement of the flesh and spirit: and give us grace to draw near with a pure heart in full assurance of faith, and to offer Thee a sacrifice in righteousness: Through Jesus Christ our Lord, by Whom and with Whom, in the unity of the Holy Ghost, all honour and praise be unto Thee, O Father Almighty, world without end.[44]

The Eucharistic Prayer seems to have been based on that in the *Euchologion*, though much shorter, and in place of the fixed thanksgiving of the *Euchologion*, had proper prefaces for Christmas, Easter, Ascension, Pentecost, Trinity Sunday and for 'Other Times', adapted from the 1662 Book of Common Prayer. The 'consecration' follows, with the words of institution and an epiclesis, the 1637 Book of Common Prayer being the inspiration. Following the classical Eastern rites and the Catholic Apostolic Church Liturgy, there are a series of intercessions that conclude the Eucharistic Prayer. After Silent Prayer came the Agnus Dei and Lord's Prayer, and the Prayer of Humble Access from the Book of Common Prayer. The latter seems to be the inspiration for the words of delivery. Other texts at the delivery were Song of Songs 5:1 and Psalm 34:8. Provision was made for a Post-Communion Address. The service concluded with singing Psalm 103:1–5, some post-communion prayers, the Nunc Dimittis and the Blessing (one for Easter, and the usual Book of Common Prayer Blessing for other times).

James Stewart has drawn attention to begrimed order of service sheets for non-sacramental services, morning and evening, which were discovered during some renovations at St Nicholas, Aberdeen in 1987. They date from the 1890s and are probably by Cooper.[45] The Morning service was as follows:

---

43 James Cooper, *The Divine Liturgy: The Order at the Holy Table. East Church of St. Nicholas*, Aberdeen, 1892.

44 Cooper, *The Divine Liturgy*, p. 3. There were many versions in circulation that Cooper could have used.

45 James C. Stewart, 'Cooper as Liturgiologist', *The Record* 29 (1995) pp. 17–29, pp. 21–2.

Praise
Prayer (Confession, Supplication, Prayers)
The Lord's Prayer
Psalm Chant
Old Testament Lesson
Canticle
New Testament Lesson
Anthem
The Creed
Prayer for Illumination
Sermon
Praise
Prayer
Praise (Intercessions, Thanksgivings)
The Offertory
The Benediction.

The Evening Service gave the following:

Psalm (Tune)
Prayers (Invocations, Confession, Supplications, Prayers)
The Lord's Prayer after which the Choir sings Amen.
Prose Psalms Chants
Old Testament Lesson
Canticle
New Testament Lesson
Praise
Apostles' Creed
Prayers (Salutation, Kyrie, Collect of the day, Intercession)
Ending with 'Through Jesus Christ our Lord, to whom with Thee and the
Holy Ghost be glory and praise for ever.'
After which the Choir sings Amen
Anthem
Sermon
Ending with Ascription 'To God the Father, the Son and the Holy Ghost
be glory and praise for ever.'
After which the Choir sings Amen
Intimations
Praise
The Offering (Special Collections)
Benediction. After which the choir sings Amen.[46]

---

46 Stewart, 'Cooper as Liturgiologist', p. 22.

The texts of his Daily Services, which Stewart argued have their roots in the monastic tradition of offices, have also survived.[47] Cooper used a form of Communion for the sick taken from *Book of Deer*, which he later published in *Reliques of Ancient Scottish Devotion*, 1913. He also drew up a manual of the Guild of St Margaret of Scotland, a women's guild that he had founded in 1882 with his assistant, T. N. Adamson.[48] It contained services for meetings of the Guild and for 'certain Days' such as Christmas, Good Friday and Easter. These services drew on the Breviary and the Book of Common Prayer, and antiphons, Psalms, Responsories, collects and other prayers. The Christmas Day Office for Morning, for example, began with a one-sentence exhortation, followed by 'In the Name of the Father, and of the Son, and of the Holy Ghost. Amen'. The Lord's Prayer was said and then the versicles and responses from Morning Prayer of the Book of Common Prayer. This was followed by an invitatory to the 'Hymn of the Season', then an antiphon with Psalms 19, 45 and 85. Then came an Old Testament lesson, the *Te Deum* and New Testament lesson, a Responsory, the Gloria in excelsis, Creed and sermon. The Office concluded with the Kyrie, collects, versicles and responses, a further collect, hymn and the Blessing. The book also contained a selection of devotional prayers, hymns and the Psalter.

As professor at Glasgow

In 1898, Cooper was appointed to the Regius Chair of Ecclesiastical History at the University of Glasgow. There he attended Oatlands Church and St Brides, Partick. On leaving Aberdeen he was presented with an extremely ornate silver chalice, which after his death was given back to St Nicholas Aberdeen. He used it for the first time at St Bride's at Christmas 1899.[49] Brian Rees observed:

> The appointment gave Cooper far more influence and far greater scope for the dissemination of his particular type of Churchmanship. He took full advantage of the opportunity to preach at 'special services' of all kinds, and made full use of his status as Professor on various committees of the Church and the University. His classes at Glasgow were representative of his understanding of the ministerial training programme. They each began with devotions – with a Psalm and Scripture reading. At first the students joined in audibly only at the Gloria Patri, but later they

---

47 James Cooper, 'The Order of Divine Service on Week-days, Morning and Evening in the Parish Church of St. Nicholas, Aberdeen.' Typescript 1900, on permanent loan to the Kirk of St Nicholas from the Library of Christ's College, Aberdeen.

48 *The Manual of the Guild of S. Margaret of Scotland. The Parish of S. Nicholas, Aberdeen*, Aberdeen: W. Jolly & Sons, 1893.

49 Wotherspoon, *James Cooper*, p. 197. Footnote 2 gives details of its ornamentation.

recited the Psalms with him responsively. He gave everyone in his class the gift of a Revised Version of the New Testament. He arranged for Holy Communion to be celebrated at the end of each session. He took his class to Glasgow Cathedral, and there, using a formal liturgy, indoctrinated them into his High Churchism.[50]

The Office he used in Glasgow Cathedral in the 1909 edition had opening versicles and responses, Psalm 19:1–4, 7, 6 (metrical) and Psalm 84, prose version, and included antiphons. It included the 'Litany of Dunkeld', an ancient Scottish text, the Lord's Prayer, a prayer commemorating the saints, a scripture reading and the collect of the day. It was followed by prayers for the city of Glasgow, the university and commemorations of the 'fathers of the faith in Scotland' as well as of the builders of the university. The Office ended with a hymn and the Blessing.[51]

During his time as Professor, Cooper continued work on historical liturgical texts. These included, with the Episcopal Church scholar Arthur Maclean, *Testamentum Domini* and an edition of the 1637 Book of Common Prayer in 1904. As noted above, in 1913 he published *Reliques of Ancient Scottish Devotion*. This included a service for Communion of the sick (*Book of Deer*), the Litany of Dunkeld (*Kalendars of Scottish Saints*), a death-bed prayer of Saint Margaret of Scotland (Turgot's *Life of Queen Margaret*), the consecration of a burial ground (Pontifical of Bishop David de Bernham) and a children's service for Palm Sunday (*Rathen Manual*).[52]

As Moderator of the General Assembly

Cooper was elected Moderator of the Church of Scotland in 1917 and he published ('with considerable reluctance, but at the request of many') the Devotional Exercises used during the meeting of the Assembly.[53] These devotions included the communion celebration as well as prayer services used on the other days of the Assembly meeting. In the Preface, Cooper claimed that for thirty years it had been the tradition to celebrate Communion in St Giles' Cathedral on the morning of the second day of the Assembly meeting. He believed that the order he published was drawn up by (the late) Dr A. K. H. Boyd, Moderator in 1890, with the advice of two other prominent members of the Church Service Society, Thomas Leish-

---

50 Rees, 'James Cooper and the Scoto-Catholic Party', pp. 341–2.

51 *University of Glasgow. Class of Church History. Office for the Annual Visit to Glasgow Cathedral*, Glasgow: Robert Maclehose & Co., 1909.

52 James Cooper, *Reliques of Ancient Scottish Devotion*, Edinburgh and London: T. N. Foulis, 1913.

53 James Cooper, *General Assembly Prayers 1917*, Glasgow: James Maclehose & Sons, 1917, p. 5. See also Colin R. Williamson, 'General Assembly Prayers 1917', *The Record* 29 (1995), pp. 30–2.

man and G. W. Sprott. The other prayers were, so Cooper claimed, his own compilations, but drawn from other sources, including the office drawn up for use in the Church of England in 1701 during the War of the Spanish Succession, and which Cooper had published in the *Transactions of the Scottish Ecclesiological Society* for 1917.

The Communion Service has clear affinities with that which evolved in the *Euchologion*. It began with a metrical Psalm, 43:3–5, sung, and then said a prose Psalm 26:6 and 51:7–8. Then came a confession of sins and petition for pardon. Two lessons followed, Isaiah 53 and John 6:48–58, and then Paraphrase 35 was sung. This was followed by the Grace, a reading of the Institution and the Nicene Creed. The Eucharistic Prayer with Sursum corda followed, and was clearly inspired by that of the *Euchologion*. After an epiclesis and Amen came the Lord's Prayer, a reading of the Institution narrative and the distribution of the elements. After Communion came the Peace, a brief exhortation and four verses of metrical Psalm 103. A long intercessory prayer followed, allowing for special petitions for the time and thanksgiving for the departed. The service ended with Nunc Dimittis and a Benediction (as in the Book of Common Prayer).

The devotions for certain times of the day of the remaining days of the meeting varied in sequence of items, but were a mixture of collects, intercessions, praise, confessions and thanksgiving, as well as scripture lessons in some. Cooper concluded his Preface by noting that the meeting had taken place under the shadow of a war, and 'it would be well for us to hear in the Scripture Lessons, "what the Spirit saith unto the Churches" in the Name of Him, the Head of the Church, who "walketh in the midst of the Seven Golden Candlesticks."'[54]

T. N. Adamson and the Barnhill Case

Douglas Murray wrote:

> The Barnhill Case, however, was largely concerned with questions of ornamentations and ritual, and the verdict in the case by the Assembly of 1903 represents the limits which the Church of Scotland regarded as permissible in the area of ritual.[55]

Liturgy is performance and is normally accompanied by symbolic actions and symbolic church furnishings. It has already been seen that James Cooper acquired certain furnishings and accoutrements from London suppliers. Thomas Newbigging Adamson was in full support of them, and at Barnhill he attempted to introduce and sustain a type of furnishing and

---

54 Cooper, *General Assembly Prayers 1917*, p. 6.
55 Murray, 'The Scottish Church Society, 1892–1914', p. 397.

a level of symbolic ceremonial that for many seemed Episcopalian rather than Presbyterian.

St Margaret's Church, Barnhill was a new church, situated in the burgh of Broughty Ferry, but ecclesiastically it was in the parish of Monifieth to the east of Dundee. The new St Margaret's congregation had been founded by some leading high church laity, including Thomas Taylor of Cambustay, who was a jute merchant and funded the new iron church building. Taylor had also been involved in the founding of St Stephen's Church, Broughty Ferry. It appears that the parish of Monifieth did not see any need for a new church, and the petition for the new building went before the Dundee Presbytery without the knowledge and prior consent of the kirk session of Monifieth. The new church opened in 1884 and Cooper recommended his former assistant in Aberdeen, T. N. Adamson, as the minister. In his biography of Cooper, Wotherspoon wrote of Adamson: 'He was Cooper's intimate and trusted friend, more than an assistant – his counsellor and coadjutor – highly sympathetic to Cooper's ideas, a devoted and able worker, competent and instructed, but without his chief's native caution or *flair* for the possible.'[56] Adamson was duly appointed. He became a member of the Church Service Society in 1885 and was one of the founding members of the Scottish Church Society.

Since St Margaret's was a chapel of ease, it was still subject to the kirk session of Monifieth, and Adamson introduced quarterly celebrations of Communion in 1885 without permission of the kirk session. The frequency was increased to monthly in 1894. This contrasted with the twice-yearly celebration in the parish church of Monifieth. Adamson also introduced daily services. In the *Transactions of the Aberdeen Ecclesiological Society*, 1894, Adamson published an account of the furnishings of St Margaret's, under the title 'How to make something of an Iron Church'. He narrated the state of its furnishings and arrangements when purchased in 1844 and its reassembling at Broughty Ferry – lined with wood, unstained and unvarnished, with a 'hideous' pulpit and a long precentor's desk, which had been replaced by an American organ at Broughty Ferry. When Communion was celebrated, a long table had to be borrowed from private houses. 'All that could be said in its favour was that it was in good repair, clean, and not offensively ugly.'[57] Adamson then proceeded to describe its refurbishing – seats stained in a deep rich mahogany, high rafters and tie-beams at the east end, the 'altar' against the east wall on a dais of two oak steps, and with panelling on either side. Above the altar was a piece of French tapestry, and a lamp taking the place of the old speaker trumpet. On the beam over the altar was the inscription 'Gloria in excelsis Deo'. The 'altar' was described in detail:

---

56 Wotherspoon, *James Cooper*, p. 124.

57 T. N. Adamson, 'How to make something of an Iron Church', *Transactions of the Aberdeen Ecclesiological Society* 3 (1894), pp. 14–18, p. 15.

The frame of the altar – which is perfectly plain – is of teak; the slab, or *mensa*, of sweet scented cedar, inlaid with five Maltese crosses in brass. The materials were provided by the communicants each giving one shilling. The altar was made by one of them, who is now in Australia. It has three frontals, all stretched upon frames – one in plain green serge of a good shade, with orphreys, &c., of velvet to match, and a gold cross with rays, for every day use; a second, in Venetian red broadcloth and Francis I velvet, richly embroidered with mediaeval roses in silk and pomegranates in gold, and on the centre panel I.H.S., surmounted with a crown: this frontal is used on all Sundays except in Advent and Lent, and on all feast days; and a third in violet (or heliotrope) cloth and velvet with a plain gold cross. This is used during Advent and Lent, and the cross upon it was transferred from the first simple frontal which the church possessed. The materials of the red frontal, along with altar linen, were the gift of a lady who has never been in the church: the work on it was done by the same zealous daughter of the Church, who worked and presented that at Craigiebuckler. The lace for the linen was presented by an old lady in the congregation: it had been her own work in her younger days. She and her son further gifted a rare old Persian carpet for the altar steps.[58]

Adamson also described the communion plate and altar furnishings:

The altar vessels, consisting of two chalices and two patens, are of silver, entirely gilt. The chalices were a gift from the founder of the church; the patens were provided by the children of the congregation, one in memory of the child martyrs of Uganda, and the other in that of Father Damien, the leper's friend. There is also a cruet of cut crystal with gold stopper, and an alms dish of wrought copper. Besides these, the altar possesses two chalice veils and two corporals of embroidered lawn and linen. A cross of flowers or fruit is used on great occasions, such as Christmas and Easter. No space being available for a pulpit, the lectern serves in its stead. It and the prayer desk are of stained deal of a simple design. The Bible is an old folio – a copy of what is known as Brown's Bible – in an old calf binding.[59]

In this same article, Adamson described the figures of saints in the stained-glass windows and the carvings in the panels of the font.

A complaint against Adamson was made by the Revd Neil Mackenzie to the Presbytery of Dundee in 1895 after the dedication service for a new stone church. The Presbytery finally concluded that no case had been made for their intervention. However, the Revd Jacob Primmer, minister of Townhill Church, Dunfermline, a convinced puritan and sworn enemy of anything he considered to be Romanism, was prompted by the article on the

---

58 Adamson, 'How to make something of an Iron Church', p. 16
59 Adamson, 'How to make something of an Iron Church', p. 17.

Iron Church to take further legal action by circulating a letter to the Presbytery of Dundee. The Presbytery did not consider the letter, but Primmer appealed to the General Assembly, which in turn instructed the Presbytery to hear the complaint. The Presbytery requested Adamson to administer Communion in accordance with the tradition of the Church of Scotland, but Primmer felt that this ignored the ornamentation of Barnhill, and continued to agitate for further action against Adamson. The legal process dragged on from 1901 to 1904, primarily because Adamson wanted a legal representative present at the visit of the Presbytery, and when this was refused, the case went to the synod and then to the General Assembly.[60] The final ruling of the General Assembly, which upheld most recommendations and judgement of the Presbytery, stated: 'The minister . . . shall not replace on the Communion Table the cross, candlesticks, frontals, and other appurtenances which gave it the appearance of an "altar".'[61]

Murray commented on this:

Thus Adamson was able to keep the table but could not replace the items which the Presbytery had ordered to be removed. The Assembly decision, however, had made no mention of the position of the baptismal font, and Adamson was able to place the font near to the door once more. . . . An article in the *Evening Post* in June, 1903, stated that Adamson had arranged the furniture to adhere strictly to the decision of the General Assembly. The communion table was covered with a plain white cloth with vases of flowers upon it. There is no direct evidence to ascertain whether Adamson continued to adhere to the Assembly's decision. *The Book of St. Margaret's*, however, recorded the gift of an 'Altar Frontal (white)' in November, 1905, and the Rev. J. F. G. Orr recorded the use of both the cross and the frontals shortly after he succeeded Adamson at Barnhill.[62]

The Barnhill case was thus about ceremonial and furnishings, but Adamson had also used a printed liturgy for Communion, which he was also required to abandon. The service that had been used for the dedication festival of the church on St Margaret's Day, 1895, was reproduced in the papers of the General Assembly 1902.[63] It had an Introit of versicles and responses, a General Confession, which consisted of the threefold Kyrie and the General Confession of the Book of Common Prayer, an absolution and the Gloria in excelsis. Then followed some collects, and an Epistle

---

60 For the legal process, see Douglas Murray, 'The Barnhill Case, 1901–1904: The Limits of Ritual in the Kirk', *Records of the Scottish Church History Society* 12 (1986), pp. 259–76.

61 *Acts of the General Assembly*, 27 May 1903, p. 74.

62 Murray, 'The Scottish Church Society, 1892–1914', pp. 413–14; *Evening Post*, 1 June 1903; J. F. G. Orr, 'Saint Margaret's Parish Church, Barnhill, Broughty Ferry', *Transactions of the Scottish Ecclesiological Society* 4 (1913–15), pp. 259–66.

63 Appendix F in Rees, 'James Cooper and the Scoto-Catholic Party'.

and Gospel and the Nicene Creed. The offertory hymn was 'Jerusalem, my happy home!', followed by offertory sentences, and an Offertory Prayer. None of this was much different from material in the *Euchologion*. It was the 'Thanksgiving', 'Canon', 'Consecration' and 'Oblation' that probably drew the ire of the Presbytery, since they were taken straight from the 1549 Book of Common Prayer, as was some of the other material in Adamson's service. The Lord's Prayer was recited, followed by the Peace, 'Christ our Passover', the Prayer of Humble Access, and Agnus Dei. After the administration of the sacrament, a short thanksgiving and communion hymn were followed by post-communion collects and the blessing from the Book of Common Prayer. The rite was just too 'Episcopal' for the taste of the Presbytery.

Adamson had also been accused of praying for the departed. The subject of prayers for the departed had been debated by members of the Scottish Church Society in 1893 and 1894, having been raised in a paper on 'Devotional Life: Communion with God and Communion in God' by the Revd Dr H. M. Hamilton (1836–1903). It was reported that Hamilton had asserted that the Bible did not forbid prayers for the departed. Discussion was furthered by James Cooper and was reported in the newspapers. Douglas Murray noted that John Macleod and James Cooper appealed to a prayer from the 1889 edition of *Prayers for Social and Family Worship*, as well as from the first and fifth editions of the *Euchologion*, which illustrated what they both thought was permissible.[64] As to the accusation against Adamson, the General Assembly reiterated the ruling of the Presbytery of Dundee, and enjoined him to discontinue prayers of intercession for the departed. Citing the Minutes of the Presbytery, Douglas Murray summarised:

Adamson had prayed that mercy and everlasting peace might be given to the dead. He said that, since the first injunction, he had not offered prayers of intercession from the dead. He still gave thanks for the dead, but this, he said, is not a prayer since 'nothing is asked for them, but only that God is thanked for what He has already given to them.' Adamson thus came to conform to what was regarded by others in the Scottish Church Society as an acceptable remembrance of the faithful departed in prayer.[65]

---

64 Murray, 'The Scottish Church Society, 1892–1914', pp. 356–60.
65 Murray, 'The Scottish Church Society, 1892–1914', p. 421.

H. J. Wotherspoon (1850–1930) and James Cromarty Smith (1863–1944)

H. J. Wotherspoon was ordained at Burbank near Hamilton in 1880 and later was minister of St Oswald's, near Morningside, Edinburgh in 1894. At St Oswald's, Communion was celebrated quarterly, and only after 1913 did the Kirk Session agree to additional celebrations. He gradually introduced greater observance of the Christian year. He drew the ire of Jacob Primmer, who regarded him as an extreme ritualist because he was a member of the Scottish Church Society![66] According to Primmer, 'When, on 23rd June 1900, his new church was dedicated or consecrated, there was an elaborate Ritualistic performance engaged in by Drs Cooper, Wallace Williamson, and others.'[67] Wotherspoon was the biographer of James Cooper, and published a good many works on doctrine and ministry, most notably, with James Mackenzie Kirkpatrick, *A Manual of Doctrine*, in 1919. He edited the 1552 Book of Common Prayer for the Church Service Society, having been a member since 1878.[68] He also published a book of daily private prayers, devotions and intercessions.[69] His contributions considered here are the publication of a communion service; with J. M. Kirkpatrick, *A Manual of Church Doctrine*, 1919; and the Croall Lectures 1926–27, published as *Religious Values in the Sacraments* in 1928.

The Divine Service had the subtitle, *A Eucharistic Office according to Forms of the Primitive Church* and was first published in 1893, with a second edition in 1929. In the Preface, Wotherspoon explained that certain elements have always been included and with little exception have succeeded each other in a determined and logical sequence and with certain invariable formulas.[70] The form of service he presented was intended to include all the parts of the normal liturgic service, arranged in the sequence which is probably most ancient. Wotherspoon gave some explanations of the various parts of the service as well as of some of the terms. He also listed the chief sources used – *Apostolic Constitutions*, the Liturgy of St James, the Book of Common Prayer, the Liturgy of St Basil, as well as the *Euchologion* and the Westminster *Directory*. The resulting rite began with

---

66 J. Boyd Primmer, *Life of Jacob Primmer, Minister of the Church of Scotland*, Edinburgh: William Bishop, 1916, p. 210.

67 Primmer, *Life of Jacob Primmer*, p. 210. Primmer also accused Wotherspoon's brother, A. W. Wotherspoon, of dispensing the Lord's Supper in a highly ritualistic manner.

68 *The Second Prayer Book of King Edward the Sixth (1552). With Historical Introduction and Notes by the Rev. H. J. Wotherspoon, M.A., of St. Oswald's, Edinburgh; and The Liturgy of Compromise, used in the English Congregation at Frankfort. From an Unpublished MS. Edited by the Rev. G. W. Sprott*, London: Blackwood & Sons, 1905; John Kerr, *The Renascence of Worship: The Origins, Aims, and Achievements of the Church Service Society*, Edinburgh: J. Gardner Hitt, 1910, p. 200, though listed as Witherspoon.

69 H. J. Wotherspoon, *Kyrie Eleison: A Manual of Private Prayer*, Philadelphia, PA: The Westminster Press, 1905.

70 H. J. Wotherspoon, *The Divine Service: A Eucharistic Office According to the Forms of the Primitive Church*, London: Hodder & Stoughton, 1919, p. 5.

a Gathering Psalm, the Collect for Purity, and General Confession (Book of Common Prayer) and absolution. The Benedictus followed, and three lections – a Prophetic, Epistle and Gospel were provided, and the Nicene Creed. General intercessions were provided, with provision for an anthem or hymn and a collect, and optional sermon. After this a hymn may be sung, then the Grace, and scripture sentences, exhortation and the Peace. At this point Wotherspoon provided for the Gloria in excelsis or Psalm 24:7–10 or Psalm 35 Paraphrase. Then came the Words of Institution, and Offertory Prayer, the prayer of the veil and then the Consecration. Wotherspoon provided a lengthy anaphora, which included the words of institution, an epiclesis and intercessions, culled from a number of sources and including the prayer, 'Hasten, O God, the time when Thou shalt send from Thy right hand' from the Catholic Apostolic Liturgy. The administration was preceded by the Agnus Dei, the Lord's Prayer with an embolism, and the Prayer of Humble Access. The 'Holy things for the holy' and the verse 'O taste and see' preceded a further recital of the Institution narrative, and then came the words of delivery. After Communion came a bidding to thanksgiving, a thanksgiving, a ministerial apologia asking for forgiveness, a version of the 'Going on from glory to glory' from the liturgy of Malabar, the Nunc Dimittis or Paraphrase 38:8 or Psalm 103:1–5, and finally the blessing. If used, it was certainly a lengthy liturgy.

With J. M. Kirkpatrick, another member of the Scottish Church Society and its president from 1927 to 1930, Wotherspoon compiled *A Manual of Church Doctrine of the Church of Scotland*, 1919, which expounded the Scoto-Catholic interpretation of the earlier standards of faith. Ordinances (sacraments) are the 'ordinary means' of grace, and are meant for all alike.[71] Faith is the condition of our assimilation of the grace that they apply.[72] But faith creates nothing – it seeks and receives.[73] On baptism they argued:

> It is not merely for the admission of the person baptized into the visible Church: Baptism is 'into Christ'. Baptism has efficacy. It not only 'offers', but in it the Holy Ghost really 'exhibits' (i.e. applies) and confers what is promised. This grace endures; and its possession is a constant reason, on the one hand, for penitence in that we fall short of or walk contrary to it; on the other hand, it is a ground of confidence; it is a background of faith, and an ever-present motive of conduct.[74]

Most importantly, baptism is an act of God, and we passively receive.[75]

---

71 H. J. Wotherspoon and J. M. Kirkpatrick, *A Manual of Church Doctrine according to the Church of Scotland*, London: Hodder & Stoughton, 1919, p. 22.

72 Wotherspoon and Kirkpatrick, *A Manual of Church Doctrine*, p. 36.

73 Wotherspoon and Kirkpatrick, *A Manual of Church Doctrine*, p. 38.

74 Wotherspoon and Kirkpatrick, *A Manual of Church Doctrine*, pp. 39–40.

75 Wotherspoon and Kirkpatrick, *A Manual of Church Doctrine*, p. 48.

On the Lord's Supper, the teaching of Milligan is reiterated. Thus, the co-authors wrote:

> In the heavenly places the ascended Saviour, living unto God, presents Himself before the Father on our behalf, showing His Death and pleading His accomplished sacrifice. He is there the 'Lamb as it had been slain', 'a propitiation for us.' In this act we now are one with Him: He is the Head, we are the Body. What He then does personally in the Upper Sanctuary, He in like manner does by our means on earth: uniting us to Himself by His Holy Spirit and ministering also in and through us before God.[76]

> In the Lord's Supper the Church pleads the atonement, and becomes a fellow-worker with Christ in his intercession.[77] In the consecrated elements we receive Christ's Body and Blood, inwardly and spiritually.[78]

In the Croall Lectures, Wotherspoon emphasised that sacraments are more than symbols and that there is no reason in the common and rational order of our existence why sacraments should not be recognised as media of grace.[79] He argued that sacraments:

> have this religious value, that they testify that God has other ways to the soul than the dialectic. In belief the soul has contact with truth; in conscience it has contact with law; in sacraments it has personal contact with the personal Christ.[80]

Baptism and the Eucharist have a several character of their own that justifies their being called *the* sacraments.[81] Echoing Milligan, Wotherspoon asserted of the Eucharist:

> It is further the all-inclusive prayer: it is the oblation of all possible praise and adoration: and since we do it in the fellowship of the Church which is also the priesthood of humanity, it is the most comprehensive intercession. It shows Christ's sacrifice, once for all perfected and all-prevailing. It shows His Ministry in the Heavens. It manifests His presence and action among us by the Holy Spirit – for it is He Who Himself pleads His death and we are in this only His instruments. It anticipates and heralds His fulfilled Kingdom – for we do this 'till He come'.[82]

---

76 Wotherspoon and Kirkpatrick, *A Manual of Church Doctrine*, pp. 74–5.

77 Wotherspoon and Kirkpatrick, *A Manual of Church Doctrine*, p. 77.

78 Wotherspoon and Kirkpatrick, *A Manual of Church Doctrine*, pp. 78–9.

79 H. J. Wotherspoon, *Religious Values in the Sacraments*, Edinburgh: T&T Clark, 1928, p. 123.

80 Wotherspoon, *Religious Values*, p. 127.

81 Wotherspoon, *Religious Values*, p. 139.

82 Wotherspoon, *Religious Values*, p. 152.

Taking up the themes of Hebrews, he stated that Christ is our High Priest whose offering is himself, and Christ in the heavens is himself the memorial, the anamnesis before God of his passion and death.[83] To the question of what is offered in the Eucharist, he wrote:

> In the action fulfilled by our agency Christ appears in the merit of His Obedience and sacrifice; Christ pleads Atonement, declaring His will that the same be applied to believers; Christ shows His Death, – the life given a ransom for many – shows it Godward and manward; the world can see no farther than the Death, and to the world it is a proclamation of only that; but, to us, it is that He is risen and is alive for evermore and has the keys of death and the grave. He lives, but He is as though He had been slain: the scars of the Passion testify and speak for us. And in this showing and pleading He will have us with Him, and to be active in it. If we say, 'How shall we show the Lord's Death?' He puts certain things into our hands and says, 'With these: this is My Body, My Blood: DO THIS.' But in obeying, we must be aware of Him as the Doer. The Sacrament is His, not ours, nor, as some say, the Church's – it is a fatal in every relation if we let ourselves think of the Church as an entity separate from Christ, a headless body. In unity with Christ and in obedience to Him 'the act of man becomes the sacrament of the act of God'.
>
> The sacrificial in the Sacrament then is that in it Christ is set forth in the merit of His sacrifice on earth, as once crucified and now risen and ascended to appear in the presence of God for us. His death is shown, and His life. The act of Atonement is represented, as Christ represents it in His own person. It is a memorial, a witness not a memory – a memorial of Him as He is and a union with Him as He acts.[84]

This passage has been given in full since it provides a bridge between Milligan's teaching and the articulation of Eucharistic offering in later Church of Scotland communion rites.

As one might expect, Wotherspoon urged more frequent celebration of Communion.[85] For the content of the Eucharistic Prayer, he noted that in all liturgies save 'in Roman theology', the invocation of the Spirit is regarded as central to consecration of the elements. Rather optimistically, he argued that, with the exception of Zwingli and the Sacramentarians, all believe that the body and blood of Christ are given in communion, and controversy only enters when attempts are made to explain how and to philosophise.[86] The lectures and *The Divine Liturgy* offered both an ideal rite and a robust theological defence of what many in the Scottish Church Society held dear.

---

83 Wotherspoon, *Religious Values*, p. 239.
84 Wotherspoon, *Religious Values*, pp. 242–3.
85 Wotherspoon, *Religious Values*, p. 257.
86 Wotherspoon, *Religious Values*, p. 276.

James Cromarty Smith was minister of Alexandria, West Dunbarton-shire from 1888 to 1905, and then at Coatdyke near Coatbridge, North Lanarkshire from 1905 until his retirement in 1939. He became a member of the Church Service Society in 1889 and was twice president of the Scottish Church Society, 1913–14 and 1930–3. While at Alexandria he increased the twice-yearly Communion to quarterly.[87] Coatdyke was a new church in an industrial area, and from the beginning Smith instituted weekly Communion. He apparently used Wotherspoon's *The Divine Service*.[88] The Morning Service had much in common with Morning Prayer in the Book of Common Prayer.[89] His concern for frequent Communion resulted in a little booklet entitled *This Do: A Christian's Bounden Duty*.[90] Although in this booklet his aim was not so much to explain the doctrine of the Lord's Supper as to set before Christians the duty of being a communicant, much of the booklet was taken up with doctrine and took a similar line to that found in Wotherspoon: in all our prayers to God we plead what Christ has done, but in the Lord's Supper we join our actions to our words and plead the merits of our Saviour's death.[91] In this Ordinance the Church continually proclaims and pleads before God the sacrifice that Christ himself is continually presenting in Heaven, pleading it as the sinner's one hope and refuge.[92] Smith elaborated:

> The sacrifice of Calvary can never be repeated. It was once for all, but its virtue lasts on for ever, and it is being continually pleaded by our Lord in heaven. What he does openly in heaven His Church does sacramentally here on earth. In the 'Holy Place not made with hands' our High Priest leads the worship of the Church which is His Body. In union with Him and in fellowship with angels and archangels and all the company of the redeemed we make this Memorial of Him Who is the propitiation for our sins and for the sins of the whole world. This is the glory of Christian worship. We with Christ, in Christ, intercede with the Father for all mankind for the whole world. So we fulfil our priesthood.[93]

This was a succinct summary of the Milligan theology of the Eucharist.

As regards Eucharistic presence, like Wotherspoon, Smith insisted that in Communion Christ imparts to us the purity and power of his perfect humanity and makes us partakers of the divine nature, and it is wise to

---

87 Minutes of the Kirk Session of Alexandria, 6 July 1897, cited in Murray, 'The Scottish Church Society, 1892–1914', p. 435.

88 Murray, 'The Scottish Church Society, 1892–1914', p. 437, note 7.

89 Murray, 'The Scottish Church Society, 1892–1914', p. 438.

90 James Cromarty Smith, *This Do: A Christian's Bounden Duty*, Coatbridge: Alex Pettigrew, 1908 and 1911.

91 Smith, *This Do* (1911 edition), p. 12. Some manuscript lecture notes on liturgy, 1929, are held by Glasgow University Special Collections.

92 Smith, *This Do*, p. 14.

93 Smith, *This Do*, p. 15.

shun all controversy about how.[94] One of the ends of Communion is the brotherhood of humanity, but the perpetual obligation is the duty to receive Communion regularly, and the last pages of his booklet attempted to refute excuses and objections made against regular receiving of Communion.

John Charleson at Thornliebank

One of the deep fears of those who were suspicious of the true motives of the Scottish Church Society was that it was encouraging papalism and attempting to lead the Church of Scotland back to Rome. The fears were mostly just that, but in the case of John Charleson, the fear was fulfilled. John Charleson was born in 1862 in Inverness and was a member of the Free Church of Scotland. While training for the ministry he moved to the Church of Scotland and was appointed minister of a mission station in Thornliebank in 1890. This was in the parish of Eastwood near Glasgow, and the minister was George Campbell, a founder of the Church Service Society and a member of the Scottish Church Society. Charleson joined the Scottish Church Society but was never a member of the Church Service Society.

In 1896 a petition from 207 members of Thornliebank Church was presented to the Presbytery of Paisley expressing great dissatisfaction with Charleson. The complaints included the use of a service book entitled *Church Services*, alterations to the chancel, which included a tabernacle (presumably for reservation of the sacramental elements), the abolition of seat rents and the position of the baptismal font.

The service book (a copy of which I have been unable to trace) apparently contained sixteen services based on themes such a 'The Commandments' and were mainly responsive services constructed from scripture sentences.[95] The book ceased to be used after 1894 following complaints. Psalms were chanted in the services, and the Creed was also recited, though these did not form part of the complaint. The erection of a shelf over the communion table and the placement of a 'tabernacle', as well as positioning the font by the door rather than by the pulpit, may be interpreted as part of Charleson's interest in church interiors and their symbolism of past ages. In an essay dealing in some detail with the Byzantine churches and Chichester Cathedral, Charleson concluded with the observation and opinion:

Our old cathedrals, abbeys, and churches, even in their ruins, are still our country's pride, and enable us 'to suck honey out of the rock, and oil

---

94 Smith, *This Do*, pp. 21–2.

95 I am dependent on the description given by Douglas Murray in 'Scoto-Catholicism and Roman Catholicism: John Charleson's conversion of 1901', *Scottish Church History Society Records* 24 (1992), pp. 305–19. The liturgy by John Charleson was entitled *Church Services*, and printed in Glasgow in 1890.

out of the flinty stones.' Vain now are our regrets that our fathers did not listen to the gentle voices that pleaded with them to lay no spoiling hands on that magnificence of symbolic stonework, that splendour of sacred art, that solemn grandeur of time-honoured and holy ritual.[96]

In attempting to resolve the dispute, Charleson defended the position of the font since that was the medieval position.

In 1897 a service book entitled *Matins and Evensong* was published, which included prayers for the dead and intercessions to Mary and the saints. *The Glasgow Herald* attributed it to the Scottish Church Society but later Charleson admitted that he was the author and said that he had used the services at Thornliebank.[97] It appears that at this point George Sprott and John Macleod requested Charleson to resign from the Scottish Church Society, which he did.[98] In 1901 he left the Church of Scotland and became a Roman Catholic priest.[99]

Concluding note

With the exception of Charleson, the members of the Scottish Church Society attempted to be loyal to the Church of Scotland's wider and older traditions, and gave the liturgical renewal a doctrinal underpinning. The various members made their own significant contribution by publishing older liturgies, authoring new ones, and encouraging more regular celebration of Holy Communion.

96 John Charleson, 'Rationale and Symbolism of Christian Churches', *Transactions of the Glasgow Ecclesiological Society*, 1895, pp. 39–52, p. 52.

97 *The Glasgow Herald*, 22 May 1897; 1 June 1897, cited in Murray, 'Scoto-Catholicism and Roman Catholicism', p. 313, note 43.

98 Scottish Church Society, Annual Report, 1901–2, p. 18, cited in Murray, 'Scoto-Catholicism and Roman Catholicism', p. 312.

99 John Charleson, *Why I Left the Church of Scotland*, London and Edinburgh: William Hodge & Co., 1901.

7

Integrating Some of the Pieces: Culture, Ecclesiology, Architecture and Case Studies

The nineteenth-century Scottish Presbyterian liturgical renewal was not an isolated phenomenon. It had a parallel in the Church of England with the Tractarians, the rise of ritualism, the replacing of parish bands with the organ and the wide adoption of hymns in place of metrical psalms.[1] But there are other parallels. The Catholic Apostolic Church, whose liturgy was a source for the Church Service Society *Euchologion*, represented a church that developed from a simple Presbyterian style of worship to a complex liturgy based on historic sources from the east and west, with an exotic ceremonial.[2] In the German Reformed Church in the USA, the Mercersburg theologians drew up the provisional liturgy, 1857, which used pre-Reformation sources.[3] In the French Reformed l'Église d'Étoile in Paris, Eugène Bersier introduced a liturgy in 1884, which drew on the Book of Common Prayer and the Catholic Apostolic Liturgy.[4] The Roman Catholic Church, too, had a liturgical movement, with a wrestle between diocesan use or Roman use, as at Solesmes with Dom Prosper Guéranger, who had a love of the Middle Ages and championed the antiquity of the Roman use over the 'neo-Gallican' innovations of the French diocesan liturgical books.[5] In England, the Roman Catholic hierarchy was re-established in 1850, and A. W. N. Pugin and Fr Daniel Rock advocated the restoration of the medieval Sarum use, whereas those such as Cardinal

---

1 Bryan D. Spinks, *The Rise and Fall of the Incomparable Liturgy: The Book of Common Prayer, 1559–1906*, London: SPCK, 2017, chapter 5.

2 Gregg Alan Mast, *The Eucharistic Service of the Catholic Apostolic Church and Its Influence on Reformed Liturgical Renewals of the Nineteenth Century*, Lanham, MD: Scarecrow Press, 1989.

3 Jack Martin Maxwell, *Worship and Reformed Theology: The Liturgical Lessons of Mercersburg*, Pittsburgh, PA: Pickwick Press, 1976.

4 Bruno Bürki, 'Reformed Worship in Continental Europe since the Seventeenth Century', in L. Vischer (ed.), *Christian Worship in Reformed Churches Past and Present*, Grand Rapids, MI: Eerdmans, 2003, pp. 32–65.

5 Cuthbert Johnson, *Prosper Gueranger (1805–1875): A Liturgical Theologian. An Introduction to his liturgical writings and work*, Analecta Liturgica 9, Rome: Pontificio Ateneo S. Anselmo, 1984; R. W. Franklin, *Nineteenth-century Churches: The History of a New Catholicism in Württemberg, England, and France*, New York and London: Garland Publishing, 1987.

Wiseman wanted Roman use.[6] This raises the broader question as to what the external changes were that triggered these varied liturgical movements. Yitzak Hen, a historian of medieval liturgy, has remarked: 'Scholars who submerged themselves in the study of liturgy too often tend to ignore the context in which the liturgy evolved, as if liturgical texts were produced in a political and cultural vacuum.'[7] Though certainly true, it is often difficult to demonstrate a direct link between culture and liturgical texts. Better indications are liturgical bricks and mortar. This chapter explores some of the characteristics of the Romantic Movement, which was the nineteenth century's 'cultural turn', and its expression in ecclesiastical architecture, and presents some cases studies where the building and liturgical developments went hand in hand.

Romantic medievalism and gothic

H. G. Schenk characterised the essence of nineteenth-century Europe thus:

> Utopian dreams for the future side by side with nostalgia for the past; a marked nihilistic mood accompanied by a fervent yearning for a faith; serious attempts to bring about a Christian revival followed, in an admittedly marginal case, by the very abandonment of faith on the part of the former apologist; the tug-of-war between the old religion and new ideologies – these are some of the unresolved contradictions which lie at the core of the movement. No shorter formula can be devised to define the essence of Romanticism.[8]

It is far from easy to pinpoint what the concept of Romanticism designates, and in his study of the history of ideas, Arthur Lovejoy concluded that the word 'romantic' had come to mean so many things that by itself it meant nothing.[9] Indeed, the era so designated represents continuities as well as changes, contrasts and contradictions, and encompassed the agrarian and industrial revolutions. There are, however, some characteristics and links between the romantic aesthetics, a concern for art and beauty, and trends in nineteenth-century ecclesiastical architecture. The concern for art and beauty, found in the early German romantics such as Hölderlin and Schlegel, was expressed in British writers such as Keats and Coleridge, and in Burke's concept of the sublime. At the heart of Romanticism was

---

6 See James R. Joseph, 'Sarum Use and Disuse: A Study in Social and Liturgical History', unpublished MA thesis, University of Dayton, Ohio, 2016, pp. 17–24.

7 Yitzhak Hen, 'Key Themes in the Study of Medieval Liturgy', in Alcuin Reid, *T&T Clark Companion to Liturgy*, London: Bloomsbury T&T Clark, 2016, pp. 73–92, p. 73.

8 H. G. Schenk, *The Mind of the European Romantics: An Essay in Cultural History*, London: Constable, 1966, p. xii.

9 Arthur Lovejoy, *Essays in the History of Ideas*, New York: Capricorn, 1960, pp. 234–5.

nostalgia for a perceived earlier richer epoch. Its expression greatly varied, but the movement is summed up succinctly by Jeremy Morris:

> Romanticism was a broad movement of sensibility which shaped not only art and literature in the nineteenth century, but philosophy, theology, and anthropology, critically challenging what had come to be seen as the orthodoxies of an earlier age. Despite its consonance with what is sometimes assumed to be a distinct English tradition, it also helped to undermine notions of national distinctiveness, highlighting or recovering aspects of a vision of Catholicity in particular that instead drew attention to affinities with other historic church traditions such as Eastern Orthodoxy and of course Roman Catholicism, and with the medieval past.[10]

In England, Horace Walpole, who was an eighteenth-century advocate of Romanticism, exemplified his architectural expression in his Strawberry Hill residence. In Scotland, some of these cultural characteristics were typified in the person of Sir Walter Scott in his novels such as *Ivanhoe* and *The Lady of the Lake*. Scott also gave architectural expression to his interests in the Baronial style of his house, Abbotsford. Particular concern with medievalism and Gothic in the nineteenth century was epitomised by A. W. N. Pugin, who designed Big Ben and the Palace of Westminster, and undertook secular and religious work both sides of the border. Pugin's conversion to Catholicism meant that he was regarded with suspicion by protestants, but his crusade for Gothic church architecture and ornamentation was shared by many.[11] Though perhaps exaggerating the break with rationalism and empirical science, Chris Books claimed:

> Gothic – as historical discourse, as architecture, as literature – was an originating and shaping force of the Romantic Movement. At Romanticism's core was a repudiation of the rationalist assumptions that had governed European high culture since the seventeenth century. To its opponents, the rationalist project had divorced people from feeling and imagination, turned knowledge into a lifeless mechanism, reduced the universe to a vast machine running inexorably on laws proclaimed by empirical science. Romantic reality was different, centred not in external prescription but in the individual's dynamic engagement with the encompassing world. Naturalness was set against artificiality, the organic against the mechanical, creativity against academic rule, uniqueness against generality. And on the radical wing, personal freedoms – political, religious, artistic – were paramount, even if they meant overthrowing

---

10 Jeremy Morris, *The High Church Revival in the Church of England: Arguments and Identities*, Leiden: Brill, 2016, p. 27.

11 Michael Fisher, '*Gothic For Ever*': *A. W. N. Pugin, Lord Shrewsbury, and the Rebuilding of Catholic England*, Reading: Spire Books, 2012; Rosemary Hill, *God's Architect: Pugin and the Building of Romantic Britain*, London: Penguin Books, 2008.

established order. Romanticism twined with gothic and medievalism in a dense semantic texture.[12]

After Pugin, the movement for Gothic churches and Gothic furnishings in England was led by John Mason Neale and Benjamin Webb who, in 1839, founded the Cambridge Camden Society, later to become the Ecclesiological Society.[13] Particularly influential in Scotland were John Ruskin (whose parents were Presbyterian) and William Morris. Commenting on Ruskin, Kristine Garrigan wrote:

> The relationship between Pugin and Ruskin is a revealing one. Although they were not personally acquainted, they shared many attitudes: their disdain for restorations and eclecticism, for classic, Renaissance, and nineteenth-century architecture; their sense that the Victorian social structure was the root of all architectural evils, and that only pious men in a healthy society can build good buildings; their scholarly, lifelong interest in Gothic art; their belief that Gothic was the only truly Christian architecture.[14]

In *The Stones of Venice*, Ruskin, contrasting the Renaissance classical architecture, wrote:

> The Gothic was good for God's worship, but this was good for man's worship. The Gothic had fellowship with all hearts, and was universal, like nature: it could frame a temple for the prayer of nations, or shrink into the poor man's winding stair. But here [Renaissance architecture] was an architecture that would not shrink, that had in it no submission, no mercy.[15]

In *The Seven Lamps of Architecture*, Ruskin argued that on the one hand, Gothic was characterised by 'preciousness and delicacy' and, on the other, 'a severe, and, in many cases, mysterious, majesty, which we remember with an undiminished awe, like that felt at the presence and operation of some great Spiritual Power'.[16]

In his early years, William Morris had absorbed the ideas of Thomas Carlyle and Ruskin, and had briefly worked for G. E. Street, a Gothic revival architect. Poet, artist and writer, Morris was one of the founders of the Arts and Crafts movement, which idealised the medieval craftsmen

---

12 Chris Brooks, *The Gothic Revival*, London: Phaidon Press, 1999, pp. 121–2.

13 Christopher Webster and John Elliott (eds), *'A Church as it Should Be': The Cambridge Camden Society and its Influence*, Stamford: Shaun Tyas, 2001.

14 Kristine Ottesen Garrigan, *Ruskin on Architecture: His Thought and Influence*, Madison, WI: University of Wisconsin Press, 1973, p. 19.

15 John Ruskin, *The Stones of Venice*, Volume the Third, xxxix, New York: John Wiley & Sons, 1887, pp. 60–1.

16 John Ruskin, *The Seven Lamps of Architecture*, Orpington: George Allen, 1889, p. 70.

(which supported his Socialist convictions). He had no immediate Scottish roots, but lectured widely in Scotland and received many commissions for stained glass there.[17] Furthermore, although there certainly were 'home-grown' Scottish architects, some of the more prominent nineteenth-century Scottish architects studied in England under Gothic revival specialists such as George Frederick Bodley and George Gilbert Scott.[18]

Scottish ecclesiology, Scottish church architects and Gothic

The nineteenth-century English Ecclesiology movement, represented by Pugin, Neale and Webb, focused on details of medieval Gothic buildings and the need to preserve and reproduce the style as the 'authentic' Christian style. Documenting the historical data required that they be 'church tourists'.[19] In Scotland, comparable pioneering work on antiquities can be traced to Thomas S. Muir of Leith (1803–88).[20] Muir wrote four books on the ancient ecclesiastical architecture of Scotland as well as some pamphlets and articles. He visited the remotest parts of Scotland, finding both Celtic and medieval ruins. In *A Ramble from Edinburgh to Durham*, 1843, Muir wrote:

> I am not speaking of our Church as a body, not of its individual members, many of whom, like myself, entertain a more catholic freedom of thought in spiritual concerns than she admits of in her rule and practice . . . God has endowed the mind with many noble faculties and refined affections, which our Church talks largely about, but refuses to give employment to in her service. In the construction of her places of worship, she makes unceasing efforts at accommodation, but without much regard to character of shape or arrangement.[21]

In *Descriptive Notices of Some of the Ancient Parochial and Collegiate Churches of Scotland*, 1848, he wrote:

> Compared with those of other countries, the ancient ecclesiastical structures of Scotland are certainly of small repute: scanty in number, and

---

17 Annette Carruthers, *The Arts and Crafts Movement in Scotland: A History*, New Haven, CT: Yale University Press, 2013.

18 Michael Hall, *George Frederick Bodley and the Later Gothic Revival in Britain and America*, New Haven, CT: Yale University Press, 2014; Gavin Stamp, *Gothic for the Steam Age: An Illustrated Biography of George Gilbert Scott*, London: Aurum Press, 2015.

19 John Mason Neale, *Hierologus, or the Church Tourists*, London: James Burns, 1843.

20 I am deeply indebted to the late Tom Davidson Kelly for the information on Muir, and for two pages of a never completed article entitled 'The pre-Disruption ecclesiology of Thomas Smyth Muir of Leith (1 Jan 1803–10 Oct 1888)'.

21 Thomas S. Muir, *A Ramble from Edinburgh to Durham*, Edinburgh: Edinburgh Printing Company, 1843, pp. 102–3.

sorely impaired by mutilation, neglect, and barbarous adaptation to modern taste or convenience, in few cases only are they in a condition to give to the spots they occupy that distinctive character which everywhere forms so beautiful an element in the composition of the English landscape; and seldom, when nearly inspected, are they found to present much but what is likely to awaken more of regret than admiration in the mind of the observer.[22]

His preference for the medieval is clear in his comment on Glasgow Cathedral, that 'the choir, which is used for Presbyterian worship, is destroyed by galleries and pues (*sic*)', but the crypt is 'very beautiful and perfect'.[23] Dunblane's interior presented 'a melancholy spectacle of parsimony and corrupt taste'.[24] Of St Giles', Edinburgh Muir observed:

The whole of this interior is in a miserable condition. Its proportions and architecture are all but destroyed by galleries and other unsightly erections; and many of the ornamental details, particularly those on the bases of the decorated piers, have been shamefully mutilated to accommodate a species of pew-work which appears to be contrived for no end but that of impairing the ancient character of the building and bringing it into contempt.[25]

Although he himself was not Scottish, R. W. Billings also provided crucial Scottish historical material in his *The Baronial and Ecclesiastical Antiquities of Scotland*, published in four volumes between 1845 and 1862, which contained 240 illustrations, with explanatory text. Billings also wrote *An Attempt to define the Geometric Proportions of Gothic Architecture, as illustrated by the Cathedrals of Carlisle and Worcester* in 1840. His work on Scotland documented survivals and lamented the ruins of once spectacular abbeys and churches. The antiquary Joseph Robertson gave a lecture in 1856 in which he outlined his opinions on the matter of Scottish medieval church architecture. He distinguished three periods: the earliest, with Irish influence; a second, the richest, during which 'we' followed England; and a third, borrowed from France.[26] The second, the Anglo-Scottish era, was 'the great age of ecclesiastical architecture in Scotland, the noontide at once of the spiritual glory and earthly grandeur of the Medieval Church in the north'.[27] This was contrasted with the sacred edifices built during the last

---

22 Thomas S. Muir, *Descriptive Notices of Some of the Ancient Parochial and Collegiate Churches of Scotland*, London: John Henry Parker, 1848, pp. vii–viii.

23 Muir, *Descriptive Notices*, p. xi.

24 Muir, *Descriptive Notices*, p. xiii.

25 Muir, *Descriptive Notices*, p. 8.

26 Joseph Robertson, 'Sketch of the History of Architecture in Scotland, Ecclesiastical and Secular, previous to the Union with England 1701', *Archaeological Journal* 13 (1856), pp. 228–44, p. 229

27 Robertson, 'Sketch of the History', p. 230.

150 years of Scotland's existence as an independent realm, which 'were as few in number as they were worthless in art'.[28]

These archaeological works provided information, guidance, opinion and inspiration for nineteenth-century Scottish church design and construction. Not all architects enthused over Gothic. In an attack on Sir Gilbert Scott's design for Glasgow University, the distinguished architect Alexander Thomson, a United Presbyterian, complained:

The Gothic revivalists are fond of catching hold of people by their prejudices. They say that theirs is the national style, and this assertion has come to be admitted almost generally. Yet nobody seems to understand exactly what it means. It certainly had not a national origin, and although it was practised in this country for some centuries, and assumed national and local peculiarities, the same may be said for the Classic styles. But they tell us that it suits the national taste. Now this argument, if it be worth anything at all, can be admitted only after it has been proved that Gothic is the best style, otherwise it is no compliment to the nation. We are next told that we should adopt it because it is the Christian style, and, strange to say, this most impudent assertion has also been accepted as sound doctrine even by earnest and intelligent Protestants; whereas it ought only to have force with those who believe that Christian truth attained its purest and most spiritual development at the period when this style of architecture constituted its corporeal frame.[29]

He was known as 'Greek' Thomson because he preferred the Classical style. His last surviving church that remains intact is St Vincent Street Church, Glasgow (1857–59), originally United Presbyterian), which incorporated Egyptian columns.[30] However, Thomson was one of the few hold-outs against the Gothic style that was sweeping the architectural landscape, as illustrated by the later near-neighbour to St Vincent Street Church. St Columba's Gaelic Church, Glasgow, was built by William Tennant (1902–4) in Gothic of the early decorated period. James Gillespie Graham (1776–1855) had designed the Tolbooth Church, Edinburgh, in 1839, in Gothic style, and he was assisted by Pugin.[31] James Brown (1813–78) designed the now demolished Renfield Street Church, Glasgow, in 1849, which Gavin

28 Robertson, 'Sketch of the History', p. 234.

29 Alexander Thomson, 'An Inquiry as to the Appropriateness of the Gothic Style for the Proposed Buildings for the University of Glasgow, with some Remarks upon Mr. Scott's Design', *Proceedings of the Glasgow Architectural Society* 1865–6, p. 46.

30 See John R. Hume, *Scotland's Best Churches*, Edinburgh: Edinburgh University Press, 2005, p. 99.

31 Gavin Stamp, 'The Victorian Kirk: Presbyterian Architecture in Nineteenth-Century Scotland', in Chris Brooks and Andrew Saint (eds), *The Victorian Church: Architecture and Society*, Manchester and New York: Manchester University Press, 1995, pp. 98–117, p. 101; James Macaulay, *The Gothic Revival 1745–1845*, Glasgow and London: Blackie, 1975, chapter 13.

Stamp described as reminiscent of Thomas Rickman's Regency iron Gothic experiments in England.[32] James Salmon senior (1805–88) designed the Gothic-style St Matthew's, Bath Street, Glasgow (1849).[33] Hippolyte Jean Blanc won the competition for Christ Episcopal Church, Morningside, in 1875, and in 1876 for Mayfield Free Church, the latter being in French Gothic style. Other notable examples are Dowanhill United Presbyterian Church of 1864 and Camphill Church of Scotland church.[34]

Honeyman, Anderson, Pilkington and Leiper

Among the leading architects who promoted some style of Gothic in Scotland were John Honeyman (1831–1914), Robert Rowand Anderson (1834–1921), Frederick Pilkington (1832–98) and William Leiper (1839–1916).[35]

Honeyman was a graduate of Glasgow University and had originally intended to be ordained. He obtained a place in William Burn's office in London, and became acquainted with David MacGibbon, whose interest in Scottish architecture and things medieval he was to share. In 1854, he published *The Age of Glasgow Cathedral, and of the Effigy in its Crypt*. His Gothic-style churches included Free West Church, Greenock, 1861. *The Builder* reported:

> The chief peculiarity in the building, is one to which some interest might be attached in connexion with the question of arrangement of the plans of churches suitable for the congregational uses that are more or less characteristic of the different forms of 'Protestantism', a question to which we have several times lately called attention. The peculiarity in previous cases, it may be remembered, consisted of the use of aisles so narrow as to serve only for passages, whereby the piers were not obstructions. A similar arrangement is observed here, in what may be described as side-corridors outside the main walls of the church, and having the appearance externally of low aisles. The clerestory walls, or rather the side walls proper of the church, are supported, it is hardly necessary to repeat, on stone piers; whilst the pews communicate directly with the corridors.[36]

---

32 Stamp, 'The Victorian Kirk', p. 103. A photograph of the interior is to be found in Andor Gomme and David Walker, *Architecture of Glasgow*, London: Lund Humphries, 1968, p. 173 (photo 153).

33 Gomme and Walker, *Architecture*, p. 172.

34 Gomme and Walker, *Architecture*, pp. 172–4.

35 The details that follow are mostly from the *Dictionary of Scottish Architects*, online www.scottisharchitects.org.uk, accessed 18.09.2017.

36 *The Builder* 1863, http://archiseek.com/2010/1863-free-west-church-greenock-scotland/, accessed 18.09.2017.

Other Gothic-style churches by Honeyman included Lansdowne United Presbyterian Church, Glasgow, 1862, which has been described as 'the first full-blooded piece of indigenous Gothic . . . perhaps the most attractive Victorian Gothic church in the city'.[37] At Park Free Church in Helensburgh and St Andrew's Free Church, Glasgow, he showed 'how the Puginian three-aisle plan could be adapted to Presbyterian worship, the former with masonry arcades for a wealthy congregation and the latter with cast-iron columns supporting galleries for a less affluent one'.[38]

Rowand Anderson was a devotee of Coleridge and the theology of Edward Irving, and studied art and design at the Royal Scottish Academy. Between 1857 and 1860 he worked as an assistant to George Gilbert Scott and, like Scott, was committed to Gothic revival architecture.[39] Many of Anderson's church commissions were episcopal, but he was hired for a number of restorations of pre-Reformation Scottish churches, such as St Vigeans, Arbroath, and designed a number of new Presbyterian churches, including North Berwick Parish Church, for G. W. Sprott, and Glencorse Parish Church. Of the latter building, Sam McKinstry wrote:

> Here a clergyman of the Established Church with ecclesiological leanings insisted on his new church being correctly oriented, forcing Anderson to rotate his plans through 180 degrees. The result was a church in a vigorous Butterfieldian mould incorporating the saddleback tower Anderson had so many times offered clients in vain. Inside the walls were clad in dark red brick, the communion table sat in the chancel, and a gallery ran along the back of the west wall.[40]

Anderson was also the architect for John Macleod's Govan Old Church. McKinstry commented, 'If Macleod raised Scoto-Catholicism to prominence at Govan, Anderson housed it in a building that would set standards for Scottish ecclesiology for years to come.'[41]

Frederick Pilkington was born to a local architect in Lincolnshire, England, and the family moved to Edinburgh in 1854. Pilkington probably trained as an architect in London. By the 1860s, his career in church design had blossomed. Hugh Dixon noted:

> Pilkington adhered closely to Ruskin's principals, and in the High Victorian tradition which they promoted he evolved a highly personal style by mixing northern medieval elements with those from the Gothic archi-

37 Gomme and Walker, *Architecture*, p. 173.

38 John Honeyman, 'Directory of Scottish Architects 1660–1980', www.scottisharchitects. org.uk, accessed 18.09.2017.

39 See Sam McKinstry, *Rowand Anderson: The Premier Architect of Scotland*, Edinburgh: Edinburgh University Press, 1991 for these and other details.

40 McKinstry, *Rowand Anderson*, p. 103.

41 McKinstry, *Rowand Anderson*, p. 107.

tecture of Northern Italy as published by Ruskin and George Edmund Street.[42]

·Among Pilkington's churches were Moray Free Church, Canongate, Edinburgh, 1862, South Church, Penicuik, 1862–3, Trinity Church, Irvine, 1861–3, Barclay Church, Edinburgh, 1862–4 and McCheyne Memorial Church, Dundee, 1868–71. Gavin Stamp claimed that Pilkington exploited the theoretical functional flexibility of the Gothic revival more than anyone else. In the Barclay Memorial Free Church, 'he created a sculptural, organic Gothic, enriched with creeping naturalistic sculpture. Outside, the church is distinguished by projecting curved walls rising to spiky gables supporting roofs with ridges running in all directions.'[43] But Pilkington made no attempt to create a medieval interior at Barclay – it is something like a squashed pear, to accommodate a theatre-like auditorium focusing on a central pulpit.[44]

William Leiper won the competition for Dowanhill United Presbyterian Church, Glasgow, in 1864, and the foundation stone was laid in 1865. He was influenced by French and High Gothic styles, and the interior of this church had richly coloured wall paintings as well as stained glass.[45] Other examples of his Gothic style are Bloomgate United Presbyterian Church, Lanark and Camphill Church, Queen's Park, Glasgow. This latter was described as built in French Gothic, the spire being modelled on S. Pierre, Caen.[46]

Arts and Crafts

These architects built for the established Church as well as the Free and United Presbyterian Churches. Sometimes only the exterior was Gothic, but frequently the interior also reflected a return to an older style. With the latter, the Arts and Crafts Movement became a useful partner. Peter Cormack has written:

> The catalyst for regeneration was the Arts & Crafts Movement, which originated in the 1880s as a reforming campaign to unify the visual arts. Inspired by the writings of John Ruskin and the practical example of William Morris, the movement emphasized common aims and methods across all fields of artistic activity thereby seeking to abolish conventional

---

42 Hugh Dixon, 'The Churches of Frederick Pilkington', *Liturgical Review* 2 (1972), pp. 8–15.

43 Stamp, 'The Victorian Kirk', p. 108, photo p. 109.

44 Stamp, 'The Victorian Kirk', p. 108.

45 Simon Green, 'William Leiper's Churches', *Architectural Heritage: The Journal of the Architectural Heritage Society of Scotland* 12 (2001), pp. 38–51.

46 W. Hunter MacNab, 'Leiper's Obituary', *RIBA Journal*, 26 August 1916, p. 303, cited in Green, 'William Leiper's Churches'.

distinctions between 'fine' and 'applied' arts. Since stained glass is an *art* form that can only be articulated through *craft* means, it can be seen as occupying an especially significant position – arguably a more illuminating one than any other – within Arts & Crafts discourse.[47]

James Ballentine set up as a glass-stainer in Edinburgh in 1837, but Scottish Presbyterianism at that point in time was still steadfastly against such 'popish' ornamentation.[48] Dr Robert Lee had installed coloured windows in the rebuilt Greyfriars, Edinburgh. Supplied by Ballentine and Allan in 1857, they were roundels telling the story of the Good Samaritan. Ballentine and Allen also installed the windows of Sandyford Church, Glasgow, the latter being described as 'dense Gothic Revival geometric and floral patterns in deep colours'.[49] Stained-glass windows were also installed in Glasgow Cathedral, and these were ordered from the Royal Bavarian Glassworks in Munich. This proved controversial – not so much now over stained glass itself, but foreign stained glass. This became a catalyst for a revival of this art in Scotland.[50] William Morris and Phillip Webb began to attract commissions in Scotland; for example, a large stained-glass window for Old West Kirk, Greenock, in 1865.[51] Glasgow quickly became the centre of the renewed Scottish stained-glass production. Firms founded by Daniel Cottier (1838–91), Stephen Adam (1848–1910) and J. & W. Guthrie & Andrew Wells made significant contributions – Cottier the Jamieson Memorial window in St Machar's, Aberdeen; Adam the west window in Clark Memorial Church, Largs; and the Guthrie family (designed by Robert Anning Bell) windows for Crathie Church. Other crafts were also developed, with Rowand Anderson designing the communion plate for St Vigeans, Arbroath.[52] 'Decorated with finely wrought Celtic ornament', it is, according to McKinstry, 'still highly prized by the congregation'.[53]

Architects, stained-glass designers and makers and other Arts and Crafts devotees worked with congregations and ministers, and the return to 'things medieval' in churches found focus and encouragement in the founding of the Ecclesiological societies. A concern about the state of the interior of Church of Scotland churches was voiced by one of the prominent members

47 Peter Cormack, *Arts and Crafts: Stained Glass*, New Haven, CT: Yale University Press, 2015, p. 1.

48 Michael Donnelly, *Scotland's Stained Glass: Making the Colours Sing*, Edinburgh: Historic Scotland, 1997; chapter 1 for fuller details.

49 Elizabeth Williamson, Anne Riches and Malcolm Higgs, *Glasgow*, London: Penguin Books, 1990, p. 295. See also Carruthers, *The Arts and Crafts Movement in Scotland*. I am also grateful for the notes of Tom Davidson Kelly.

50 Richard Fawcett (ed.), *Glasgow's Great Glass Experiment: The Munich Glass of Glasgow Cathedral*, Edinburgh: Historic Scotland, 2003.

51 Carruthers, *The Arts and Crafts Movement in Scotland*, pp. 27–8.

52 Carruthers, *The Arts and Crafts Movement in Scotland*, p. 35.

53 McKinstry, *Rowand Anderson*, p. 58.

of the Church Service Society, George W. Sprott. In his *The Worship of the Church of Scotland*, 1882, Sprott wrote:

> huge square barns with immense galleries, and seats crowded close to the pulpit . . . The interior of some of these Churches resembles a circus, classroom or music-hall. If the last, on entering you see a stage or platform, with a reading desk and sofa in place of an ecclesiastical pulpit, while behind there is a huge organ – the principal object in the building, – and you tremble for the Clergyman in front, who reminds you of those unfortunate Sepoys who, after the Indian Mutiny, were lashed to the mouths of cannon and blown into a thousand fragments. Strange devices, too, one sometimes hears of for the administration of the Sacraments, such as a font on the top of which a board is screwed to do duty as a table at times of Communion.[54]

The antiquarian work completed by Muir and Billings became the raw material that both architects and ministers could hold as the gold standard for renovations and new building. James Cooper, a member of the Church Service Society from 1873, and the first secretary of the Scottish Church Society, founded the Aberdeen Ecclesiological Society in 1886.[55] By 1888 it had 186 members, and from the beginning membership was not confined to the Church of Scotland. A third of its members in the first year were also members of the Church Service Society, including George Campbell and George W. Sprott. The aims of the Society were twofold:

> *First* – For the study of the Principles of Christian Worship, and of Church Architecture and the allied Arts which minister thereto; and
> *Second* – For the Diffusion in the North of Scotland of sound Views, and the Creation of a truer taste in such matters.[56]

The Glasgow Ecclesiological Society was founded in 1893, with Cooper addressing the first general meeting of the society in 1894. Architects John Honeyman and Rowand Anderson were members of the Aberdeen Society, and Hippolyte Blanc was a member of the Glasgow Society. The two societies merged in 1903 to form the Scottish Ecclesiological Society, with Cooper as president. At the inaugural meeting of the amalgamated Society, Cooper summarised its purpose, neatly weaving together worship, architecture and art:

---

54 George W. Sprott, *The Worship and Offices of the Church of Scotland*, Edinburgh: Blackwood, 1882, pp. 232–4.

55 For details, see John Sanders, 'Ecclesiology in Scotland', in Christopher Webster and John Elliott (eds), *'A Church as it Should Be'*, pp. 295–316; Tom Davidson Kelly, 'The Manna of Ecclesiology: Contributions by Members of the Church Service Society in the Development of Scottish Ecclesiology from 1863', *The Record* 42 (2006–7), pp. 3–32.

56 Reprinted in *Transactions of the Aberdeen Ecclesiological Society* 11 (1896), p. 2.

We do not think that the Public Worship of Almighty GOD is a matter of trifling importance. We believe that worship should be rendered with the fullest understanding of its principles, and with the utmost care to make it expressive of our Christian faith, and reverence, and gratitude, and love. We do not deem it to be for the glory of GOD, or for the honour of Scotland, that her ancient sanctuaries should lie waste; or her newer ones be mean, their appurtenances wretched, their decorations unmeaning and incongruous, or their music lacking in real solemnity and grandeur.

We are of opinion that all things deserve, and require, more study and attention than have been given them in Scotland: that the crave of our Reformers in their *First Book of Discipline*, 'for the reparation of all parish kirks not only in the walls and fabric, but also in all things needful within, for the people, and decencies of the place appointed for GOD'S service,' still awaits its perfect satisfaction: that information is still lacking in regard to some of our Cathedrals, Abbeys, and Collegiate Churches, which Scottish History and Scottish Archaeology, (I am old-fashioned enough to regard these two as sisters, and not foes!) should be able to furnish: and that neither the architecture, the adornments, not the music of our churches (I speak generally), are at present all that Scottish Art might be expected to produce, if only it would give its mind to these things.[57]

Cooper stated that the executive of the Aberdeen Society had never faltered in its advocacy of a worship in which the supremacy of the Eucharist would be clearly recognised, and of churches designed and built on that principle.[58] The model of the early Christian church in Scotland was attractive since it was non-Roman, but Cooper expressed the view that there was nothing Christian or truly Catholic that could not be used in the Church of Scotland.[59] Scotland's medieval churches were the model for new constructions, considering not just the exterior but also the interior. This implied the removal of galleries, the use of pews with kneeling-boards (after the style of Butterfield), a sensible placing of the organ (not in the chancel), a fine pulpit and lectern, a decent baptismal font and a large, rich Holy Table as well as well-designed bells, books, communion-plate and bookmarks and such like, which also deserved attention.[60]

57 Inaugural address in *Transactions of the Scottish Ecclesiological Society*, 1 (1904), p. 2.
58 James Cooper, 'Ecclesiology in (of) Scotland', *Transactions of the Aberdeen Ecclesiological Society* 2 (1895), pp. 31–48, p. 48.
59 James Cooper, 'A Minister's Thoughts in Regard to the Arrangement and Furnishing of a Scottish Parish Church', *Transactions of the Edinburgh Architectural Association* 4 (1908), pp. 29–40, p. 30.
60 Cooper, 'A Minister's Thoughts'.

From building to worship: case studies

Brian Rees noted that three societies – The Church Service Society, The Scottish Church Society and the Scottish Ecclesiological Society – were moving in the same direction because they shared the same ideals and, to a large extent, the same principal figures.[61] The Scottish Ecclesiological Society was very much the mortar between the bricks, bringing together liturgical, architectural and Arts and Crafts persons and ideals, and those ideals were exemplified at St Giles', Edinburgh, Govan Old Church and, at a lesser level, at St Oswalds' Woodside, Glasgow and Hyndland Church, Glasgow.

St Giles' Edinburgh

St Giles' was a medieval parish church that later had been made a Collegiate Church.[62] Only after the Reformation with Charles I and Charles II was it briefly a cathedral with a bishop. Since the Reformed churchmen had no need of either a large Collegiate Church or a cathedral, the building had over the centuries been partitioned by walls to provide spaces for four separate congregations in the single medieval building. In 1562, the Tolbooth (municipal building), which had been built at the north-west corner of St Giles', was demolished, and part of the west end of the Collegiate Church was partitioned off to serve certain municipal functions.[63] In 1578, a portion of the east end was partitioned to form the Little, East or, later, High Kirk. The nave became the Great, or Old Kirk.[64] In 1598 the town council decided to transform the upper part of the Outer Tolbooth into a third church, known as the West or Tolbooth Kirk. Later still, in 1699, the north end of the Tolbooth Church, which was still being used as a court-room, was converted to form the New North, or Haddo's Hole Church.[65] Galleries, pews and pulpits had been erected for each of these churches within the Church. The East Kirk was the largest, and attracted the more professional and municipal officers. One of the English pioneers of Gothic, Thomas Rickman, wrote in 1825:

> St. Giles, or the High Church, Edinburgh is divided for four congregations, and some smaller portions are separated for other purposes. The plan of

---

61 Brian Rees, 'James Cooper and the Scoto-Catholic Party: Tractarian Reform in the Church of Scotland, 1882–1918', PhD thesis, St Andrews University, 1980, p. 256.

62 James Cameron Lees, *St. Giles', Edinburgh: Church, College, and Cathedral, from the Earliest Times to the Present Day*, Edinburgh and London: W. & R. Chambers, 1889; Rosalind K. Marshall, *St. Giles: The Dramatic Story of a Great Church and its People*, Edinburgh: Saint Andrew Press, 2009.

63 Marshall, *St. Giles'*, p. 65.

64 Lees, *St. Giles'*, p. 168; Marshall, *St. Giles'*, p. 69.

65 Marshall, *St. Giles'*, p. 99.

the edifice is a nave, choir, and transepts, with aisles and chapels, both north and south; a large portion of the building is of Decorated character, with later additions and insertions, and much modern alteration. The choir is the principal church, and has good groining; some of the piers have flowered capitals, and some of the arches have good mouldings; a few of the windows have the tracery remaining, but from most of the them it has been cut away. On the south side a large chapel, perhaps the ancient chapter-house, is used for the meetings of the General Assembly. It has octagonal piers with good flowered capitals, and is richly groined. The south transept is separated for another congregation, and is galleried and otherwise arranged, so as to make a very awkward place of assembly, the pulpit being immediately opposite, and within a few feet of a pier; this portion has some good groining. In the nave and aisles two congregations are accommodated, and on the north side are several rooms used for various purposes. The exterior appearance of the church is much deteriorated by its windows being despoiled of tracery, the destruction of battlements, parapets, and pinnacles, and various modern alterations; but it is in contemplation to restore it, and of this it is very capable, as the substantial part of the building is not much injured, and if the interior divisions were cleared, it would make one or even two very fine churches.[66]

A renovation was undertaken between 1829 and 1833, under the architect William Burn. He certainly worked with some Gothic inspiration, and probably saved the building from collapse, but posterity has viewed his work more as destruction than restoration. It involved the demolition of three chapels at the south of the nave and another chapel adjoining the north porch. Walls and ceilings were plastered over, columns replaced, galleries inserted and many monuments were swept away. The exterior of the building was re-faced (with the exception of the tower), resulting in the loss of mediaeval ornaments. Provision was made for two churches with a central vestibule, and an Assembly Hall. The latter was found to be unsuitable for the General Assembly, and was changed into accommodation for the Old Church parish.[67] The building now housed three congregations – the Collegiate or High Kirk; the Old Kirk; and West Kirk.[68]

Restoration to make it once more a single building, while conserving and restoring some of the medieval features, was the inspiration and mission of

---

66 Thomas Rickman, *An Attempt to Discriminate the Style of Architecture in England, from the Conquest to the Reformation*, London: Longman, Hurst, Rees, Orme & Co., 1825, p. 365.

67 Architectural Drawings of St Giles' Cathedral, Edinburgh, *Scotland's Places*, https:// scotlandsplaces.gov.uk/record/nrs/RHP6512/architectural-drawings-st-giles-cathedral-edinburgh/nrs, accessed 9.10.2017.

68 Marshall, *St. Giles'*, p. 115. In 1866 the ministers were listed as the Revd David Arnott, DD, and the Revd James M'Letchie for the Collegiate Church; the Revd John Clark, AM, the Old Church; and the Revd Robert Nisbet, DD, for the West Church; Robert W. Fraser, *The Kirk and the Manse*, Edinburgh: A. Fullarton & Co., 1866, p. 1.

William Chambers, a publisher who also became provost of Edinburgh. Chambers himself explained how one day when at a service in the High or Collegiate Kirk:

> There and then, when seated in that elevated gallery close to the carved shields of the boy-prince James and his mother the inestimable Mary of Gueldres, we conceived the idea of attempting a restoration of the building, and producing a church in which the people of Edinburgh might feel some pride – a shrine fitting for the devotional exercises of Royalty.[69]

Chambers first proposed the idea in 1867, but it was not until 1871 that a Restoration Committee was appointed. The plan was to restore as far as practicable the whole interior of St Giles' but to do it step by step as circumstances permitted. It was accomplished in three stages and began with the choir (the Collegiate or High Kirk), where Chambers had the full support of Dr David Arnott, who had been minister there since the Disruption. This first stage entailed the removal of galleries and the royal pew, and in addition a number of old gravestones that had been used as flooring. The architect was William Hay, who had been an assistant to George Gilbert Scott and had already been involved in the restoration of some English cathedrals and had built new Gothic-style churches. The walls and vaulted roofs were cleaned and the floors re-laid with fashionable encaustic tiles. Hay designed a new hexagonal pulpit, carved from Caen stone by the Edinburgh sculptor John Rhind. New oak seating was installed. The restored choir reopened for services on Sunday 9 March 1873, with Dr David Arnott preaching on the text, 'The Lord is in his holy temple: let all the earth keep silence before him'.

David Arnott had been appointed in 1855 by the General Assembly as convener of the Committee on Paraphrases and Hymns. In 1872 he had persuaded his kirk session at the High Kirk to take on trial an oak Alexander's First Class Harmonium, and they later purchased a two-manual organ from Harrison & Harrison, Durham. Stained-glass windows by James Ballentine were also installed from 1874 onwards.[70] Arnott had been a member of the Church Service Society since its founding in 1865. Shortly after his death in 1877, a book entitled *Prayers for Public Worship with Baptismal and Communion Services, used in St. Giles' Cathedral (High Kirk) Edinburgh* was published.[71] It contained a selection of the prayers

---

69 William Chambers, *Historical Sketch of St. Giles' Cathedral Edinburgh*, Edinburgh: W. & R. Chambers, 1890, p. xliii.

70 Marshall, *St. Giles'*, p. 126. A list of the windows is found in William Meikle, *Illustrated Guide to St. Giles's Cathedral, Edinburgh, and the Chapel of the Thistle*, Edinburgh: H. & J. Pillans & Wilson, 1919, pp. 30–2.

71 David Arnott, *Prayers for Public Worship with Baptismal and Communion Services used in St. Giles' Cathedral (High Kirk) Edinburgh*, Edinburgh: William Oliphant & Co, 1877. Arnott was a graduate of St Andrews, and had been assistant minister at Ceres before being translated to St Giles' (High Kirk) in 1843, and was awarded the DD. He was a sculptor and poet, and published some sermons.

7.1 The Revd Dr David Arnott

that Arnott had composed for regular use in the High Kirk. Thus, although Arnott never provided a printed liturgy for regular use, he did compose prayers that were regularly used. Orders of service were provided for Forenoon and Afternoon for five Sundays, a Prayer for the New Year, as well as services for the Lord's Supper and baptism. The Forenoon and Afternoon services followed a common structure of Metrical Psalm, Paraphrase or Hymn, First Prayer, Old Testament lesson, Prose Psalm (or *Te Deum* in the morning) chanted, New Testament Reading, Second Prayer, Hymn, Paraphrase or part of a metrical Psalm, Third Prayer, Sermon, Hymn, Prayer after the Sermon, Intimations, Collection and anthem, and final Benediction. The Lord's Supper had the format of the Forenoon service, but after the sermon and collection, Paraphrase XXXV was sung, during which the minister took his place at the table, and the elders placed the elements before him. The minister read Words of Institution. A Prayer over the bread and wine followed. This prayer alluded to the words of 1 Corinthians 10:16, and spoke of the elements as 'symbols of redeeming love' and requested the Lord to grace his own institution with his presence.[72] The Institution narrative was repeated at the fraction, and during the administration, suitable scripture sentences were provided for recitation. After Communion, the tradition metrical Psalm 103 was sung, and the order ended as other Sunday services. The service of baptism, which was to come after the Sunday sermon, began with a hymn, 'A little child the Saviour came', then an exhortation, which explained that this holy ordinance was a seal of the covenant of grace, and that the sprinkling of water represented the saving efficacy of Christ's death. After the father or sponsor made his promise, a short prayer followed, and then following the baptism, the Aaronic blessing sung as an anthem and a further prayer, with the service concluding 'in the usual way'.[73]

Dr Arnott died in 1877. His successor was James Cameron Lees, one of the founding members of the Church Service Society. Lees came to St Giles' from Paisley Abbey, where, with Dr Andrew Wilson, he had overseen further restoration to the Abbey.[74] This included the removal of unsightly galleries, clearing the floor of accumulated rubbish, providing new seating, the opening up of the clerestory windows and transept walls and the

---

72 Arnott, *Prayers for Public Worship*, p. 83.

73 Arnott, *Prayers for Public Worship*, p. 95.

74 A. R. Howell, 'The Restoration of Paisley Abbey', *Church Service Society Annual* 1 (1928–9), pp. 56–66.

restoring of windows.[75] The worship was enriched and an organ had been installed and dedicated in 1874.[76] It was during Cameron Lees's time at St Giles' that the second and third phases of restoration were completed and the building became once more a single worship space. Plans submitted by Hay were approved, on the understanding that the cost would be met by Chambers. In February 1879, the galleries and pews were removed, partitions were taken down, the floor raised and the aisles opened up. The Chepman aisle, which had been divided into three floors, with the lower part being a coal cellar, was restored, with floor tiles by Skidmore of Coventry.[77] The Preston aisle and Moray aisle were also restored. The third phase, the restoration of the nave, was dependent on the West Kirk vacating the space. An Act of Parliament was procured to that end, an iron church was provided for the West Kirk congregation, and the work finally began in July 1881.[78] The pulpit was repositioned and a baptismal font in Caen stone, by Rhind of Edinburgh, based on the model of Thorwaldsen's font in Copenhagen, was presented by Lees to St Giles'. Here the concerns of the early and later Ecclesiologists converged.

The restored St Giles' was solemnly reopened on 23 May 1883, its major benefactor, William Chambers, having died three days before. Maclean summarised the service thus:[79]

After the Hundredth Psalm came the call to prayer and Prayer-Confession of sin, Invocation, thanksgiving, and supplications. Then was sung Ps.24: 'Ye gates lift up your heads on high' to 'St. George's Edinburgh'. After the Old Testament lesson, 2 Chronicles vi.12–42, came the *Te Deum*. The New Testament lesson was St. Luke xix. 37–48, after which came the Intercessory prayer. Then was sung, 'Christ is made the sure foundation,' during which Dr. Macleod gave place to Dr. Cameron Lees in the pulpit. Before the sermon Dr. Lees offered this prayer:

Almighty God, our Heavenly Father, who hast promised that in all places where Thou dost record Thy name Thou wilt meet with Thy people to bless them, grant, we beseech Thee, that Thy rich blessing may rest upon this church now opened for the worship of Thy holy name. Accept the work of Thy servant's hands. May this house be the House of God. Here may Thy true Word be preached, and Thy holy sacraments faithfully administered. Here may men be fed with the Bread of Life, and the weary and heavy laden find rest. And when we

75 Norman Maclean, *The Life of James Cameron Lees*, Glasgow: Maclehose, Jackson and Co., 1922, p. 102.

76 Maclean, *The Life of James Cameron Lees*, pp. 111, 112. One may assume that the worship was enriched by material from or inspired by the *Euchologion*.

77 Chambers, *Historical Sketch*, pp. xlvii–xlix.

78 Details in Marshall, *St. Giles'*, pp. 131–7; Chambers, *Historical Sketch*, pp. lvii–lxi.

79 Maclean, *The Life of James Cameron Lees*, p. 205. Much of the text of the service and the sermon is found in JLees, *St. Giles'*, pp. 405–11.

have served Thee humbly in our day and generation, may others enter into our labours, seeking to extend the blessed kingdom of Thy Son in this world – working, and waiting until he come again. Grant this, O Lord, for His Sake.

The text for the sermon was from Joshua 4:21, 'What mean these stones?' The sermon encapsulated Lee's understanding of what St Giles' represented. It was to be for Scotsmen what Westminster Abbey was for England – the temple of silence and reconciliation. But the sermon also wove together some of those characteristics of romanticism: the stones 'mean the relation of beauty to religion and to worship. These are three aspects of the ideal of infinite perfection – the good, the true, and the beautiful, and these three cannot be disjoined one from the other.'[80]

Then followed the Lord's prayer. After the sermon, the second Paraphrase, 'O God of Bethel', was sung to the tune Salzburg, followed by a commendatory prayer. After the offertory, Handel's Anthem, 'Halleluiah, for the Lord God omnipotent reigneth' was sung. Then the Benediction and the Threefold Amen ended the service.

The indefatigable protester against innovations and popery, Jacob Primmer, attacked the 'images' (figures in the screen) at St Giles' in 1887, and also the General Assembly's Holy Communion Service in St Giles' in 1898 as the popish mass in masquerade.[81] As noted earlier, the Church Service Society *Euchologion* was used for the General Assembly Communion, but that was not the usual use at St Giles'. It is not known whether Lees, when first appointed, continued using Arnott's service, or (which would seem more likely) whether he used prayers from the *Euchologion*. However, Lees compiled and had printed his own *Book of Common Order for use in St. Giles'*, and it seems to have been a form available in the pews. Maclean explained that Lees, in the compilation of the *Euchologion*, had wanted the intercessory prayer before the sermon. Since he failed to get that (until much later editions), he concluded that he must have a prayer book of his own and 'thus it came that Dr. Lees compiled his own book for use in St Giles'.'[82] This book, 'to be used until such time as "another formulary be set forth by the proper authority"', was apparently used in other congregations too.[83] The first edition was published in 1884 and the final sixth in 1922.[84] The first edition contained twelve orders of service and twenty-six

---

80 Lees, *St. Giles'*, p. 409.

81 J. Boyd Primmer, *Life of Jacob Primmer, Minister of the Church of Scotland*, Edinburgh: William Bishop, 1916, pp. 70 and 188.

82 Maclean, *The Life of James Cameron Lees*, p. 115. Cecil T. Thornton, 'The St. Giles Book of Common Order 1884–1926', *Church Service Society Annual* 24 (1954), pp. 35–40.

83 Thornton, 'The St. Giles Book of Common Order', p. 35; J. C. Carrick, *Cameron Lees: Queen Victoria's Soul-Friend*, Selkirk: George Lewis & Co., 1914, p. 47.

84 Copies of the 1884, 1886 and 1889 editions are held in New College Library, Edinburgh. The fourth edition of 1894 is available in modern reprint; copies of the 1902 and 1922 editions are held by Greyfriars Kirk, Edinburgh. The leather-bound copy of 1922 has

special prayers. The second edition was expanded to include services of the Infant baptism, the Lord's Supper, Marriage and Burial of the Dead; small alterations were made in subsequent editions.

As might be expected, the structure of the services was similar to that in the *Euchologion*, other than that the intercessions came after prayers of invocation, confession, for pardon, and thanks, at the beginning of the service and before the Old Testament reading, with further supplications after the New Testament reading, but all before the sermon. The First Service of the fourth edition, 1894, began with a call to prayer, which was used as the second part of the call to prayer in the First Service of the *Euchologion*. Lees then used a prayer for Divine Presence from the Eastern Orthodox Church. In some places Lees lifted some parts of a prayer from the *Euchologion* (e.g. Third Service, 'Remember, O Lord, the whole body of the people'), but added his own compositions. This was probably how many ministers used the *Euchologion*, the difference being that Lees put his devolution of the book into print. The Baptismal rite was much more succinct than that of the *Euchologion*, though perhaps curiously, Lees referred to the water as an 'emblem', and equally curious was the petition for God to 'sanctify what of the element of water is to be used to this purpose'. The 'Celebration of the Communion or Sacrament of the Lord's Supper' was another example of Lees' own reworking of material from different sources. It began with the Peace, and then a Prayer of Access and words of institution. Following the lead of the Catholic Apostolic Church, Lees differentiated between a Eucharistic Prayer and the Prayer of Consecration. The second Eucharistic Prayer and the opening of the Prayer of Consecration were from the *Euchologion*, but the latter prayer was altered to read:

> now vouchsafe unto us thy gracious presence and the effectual working of thy Spirit in us, and so to sanctify by thy Word and Spirit these elements both of bread and wine, and to bless thine own ordinance, that we may receive by faith the body and blood of Jesus Christ crucified for us, with all his benefits to our spiritual nourishment and growth in grace.[85]

In the sixth edition, the order was remodelled and it included a fuller invocation nearer the form in the *Euchologion*:

> And we most humbly beseech Thee, O merciful Father, to look upon us, as we do now make that memorial of His most blessed sacrifice which Thy Son hath commanded us to make; and send down Thy Holy Spirit to bless and consecrate these Thine own gifts of bread and wine which

---

an inscription to say it was presented to Dr Andrew Wallace Williamson at his installation, though Williamson was installed in 1910! The inscription seems to have been transferred to this leather-bound 1922 edition from an earlier original presentation copy, probably the 1902 edition.

85 1894 edition, pp. 181–2.

we set before Thee, that the bread which we break may be to us the communion of the Body of Christ, and the cup of blessing which we bless the
communion of the Blood of Christ; that we, receiving them, may by faith
be made partakers of His Body and Blood, with all His benefits, to our
spiritual nourishment and growth in grace, and to thy glory of Thy most
holy name.

Lees resigned the ministry of St Giles' in 1909, after a ministry of thirty-
two years. He was succeeded by Dr Andrew Wallace Williamson, then
at St Cuthbert's, Edinburgh. Wallace Williamson and St Cuthbert's had
both been the objects of an attack by Jacob Primmer in 1906, and then
again in 1908, on account of a stone replica of 'a Popish baptismal font,
twenty feet high and surmounted by a life-sized image of the Virgin and
Child, executed in bronze'.[86] Wallace Williamson had joined the Church
Service Society in 1885. He also came under the influence of John Macleod
of Govan and was one of the founders of the Scottish Church Society,
though he found it necessary later to resign from the Society.[87] His views
on worship were set out in his *Ideals of Ministry*, 1901. The minister's task
in worship was to allow the congregation to be absorbed in contemplation
of the glory and majesty of the Trinity.[88] He gave an outline of worship
inspired by the *Directory*, but argued:

> If we have rescued from the hymnology of the past the great songs of
> the Church universal – the Te Deum, the Magnificat, the Benedictus, the
> Gloria in Excelsis – why should we not also take to ourselves what is best
> and most helpful in all the devotions of the Christian ages, those ancient
> prayers which seem to breathe a spirit almost unattainable in our feverish
> and worldly time – a spirit redolent of the age of martyrs – a calm, high,
> and reverent adoration untainted by local or selfish considerations, but
> expressing in language universally true the needs and aspirations of the
> Christian soul?[89]

He urged that ministers should acquaint themselves with the main features
of the Eucharistic service which had been characteristic of the historic
worship of the Church.[90] The climax of the Eucharist was the invocation
on the elements, 'which ought to be rendered with the greatest possible
reverence of manner and tone'.[91] That is, it was the words of institution

---

86 Primmer, *Life of Jacob Primmer*, p. 285.

87 John Kerr, *The Renascence of Worship: The Origins, Aims, and Achievements of the
Church Service Society*, Edinburgh: J. Gardner Hitt, 1910, p. 204; The Hon. Lord Sands, *Life of
Andrew Wallace Williamson*, Edinburgh: William Blackwood & Sons, 1929, pp. 116, 169, 182.

88 Andrew Wallace Williamson, *Ideals of Ministry*, Edinburgh: William Blackwood &
Son, 1901, p. 70.

89 Wallace Williamson, *Ideals of Ministry*, pp. 106–7.

90 Wallace Williamson, *Ideals of Ministry*, p. 153.

91 Wallace Williamson, *Ideals of Ministry*, p. 166.

and the prayer of invocation that were effectual in rendering the elements fit to be instruments by which Christ's body and blood were imparted to the faithful. 'Something less than material change we see, something higher than symbol – even seal as well as sign – "This is My Body", "This is My blood".'[92]

It was during the tenure of Wallace Williamson that the Thistle Chapel at St Giles' was completed, in 1911. It was linked to St Giles' by an antechapel, and the architect, Robert Lorimer, who had trained in the office of Robert Rowand Anderson, designed a Gothic building to blend with the rest of the building.[93] In 1911 a new communion table, designed by Robert Lorimer and elaborately carved and painted with angels and the Lamb of God, was given by an anonymous donor.[94] In 1913, Williamson announced a monthly communion service, and new silver cups were donated to St Giles'. More stained-glass windows were also added.

Wallace Williamson did not himself draw up a new liturgy for St Giles' but continued the services of Cameron Lees. However, he had written that, 'there is no sufficient justification for a liturgy which does not submit to periodic revision or addition', and in keeping with his own advice, he made some alterations to Lees's forms.[95] His biographer noted in 1929:

While he retained Dr. Lees' Book of Common Order in use, and the general character of the service which Lees had introduced into St. Giles' – largely out of a feeling of loyalty to his predecessor, – he did make some minor changes, which, while generally approved by the congregation, were not quite universally so. One of these was the repetition by the congregation of the Apostles' Creed at every service, but it is proper to explain that he had made this addition to the Order of Service a matter of express stipulation when he agreed to accept the ministry of St. Giles', and it is still continued with general acceptance and approval by his successor. Lees was in favour of a service of simplicity, Wallace Williamson of one rather more ornate, perhaps, and his judgment more suited to a church like St. Giles'. But in all essential particulars the service which Lees introduced remained, and still remains, the recognised service of the church.[96]

Given the alterations made in the 1922 St Giles' Service Book, it is probable that Wallace Williamson was responsible for that edition. A copy of the 1922 sixth edition in the possession of St Giles', and marked as 'Minister's stall', has a number of crossings out and additions that may well represent some of the ongoing additions he made until his resignation from St Giles'

92 Wallace Williamson, *Ideals of Ministry*, pp. 167–8.
93 Marshall, *St. Giles'*, pp. 147–8.
94 Marshall, *St. Giles'*, pp. 151–2.
95 Wallace Williamson, *Ideals of Ministry*, p. 77.
96 Sands, *Life of Andrew Wallace Simpson*, p. 198.

in 1925. Something of his practice in celebrating Holy Communion may be gleaned from his *Ideals of Ministry*, written when he was at St Cuthbert's, Edinburgh and had been university lecturer in Pastoral Theology. 'It does not seem fitting', he wrote, 'that any minister should remain in ignorance of the main features of the Eucharistic service which has been characteristic of the historic worship of the church.'[97] Williamson gave a summary based on that of the *Euchologion*, 'which is at least in harmony with the recommendations of the *Directory* and consistent with our national traditions, though enriched by materials drawn from the ancient services'.[98] On the epiclesis he quoted almost verbatim the *Euchologion*:

> Finally there comes the invocation of the Spirit and the solemn memorial of the sacrifice of Christ, in which we ask God to grant His holy Spirit, and so to sanctify the Elements, both of bread and wine – that the bread which we break may be the communion of the body of Christ, and the cup of blessing which we bless the communion of the blood of Christ. This part of the prayer, it need hardly be said, is the climax of the great spiritual act in which we are engaged, and ought to be rendered with the greatest possible reverence of manner and tone. It is, indeed, 'the central and essential prayer' of the whole service.[99]

Williamson was succeeded by Charles Warr, who (at least according to Lord Sands; see note 87 above) continued to use Lees' forms. Greyfriars Church, Edinburgh, has a leather-bound copy of the 1922 edition, inscribed with the words of presentation to Warr on his induction to St Giles' in 1926. Warr seems to have been elected to the Council of the Church Service Society in 1919, and later served as its President.[100] There were no further editions of Lees' forms.

John Macleod and Govan Old (1875–98)

John Macleod became minister at Duns in 1862 and left to be minister at Govan in 1875. He joined the Church Service Society in 1870 and was one of the main architects of the Scottish Church Society. At Duns he made several changes in worship.[101] He installed an organ in 1866, and in 1868, with the consent of the kirk session, he introduced standing for singing and sitting for prayer. He introduced additional weekday services,

---

97 Williamson, *Ideals of Ministry*, p. 153.
98 Williamson, *Ideals of Ministry*, p. 159.
99 Williamson, *Ideals of Ministry*, pp. 166–7.
100 It is disappointing that Warr's *The Presbyterian Tradition*, London: Maclehose & Co., 1933, has practically nothing about worship.
101 Douglas Murray, 'The Scottish Church Society, 1892–1914: A Study of the High Church Movement in the Church of Scotland', PhD thesis, University of Cambridge, 1975, chapter 10.

7.2 The Revd Dr John
Macleod of Govan

observed the main festivals of the Christian year and in 1871 introduced monthly Communion. In 1875 he left for Govan, but at Duns a petition was presented to the kirk session complaining of certain changes made in worship. The complaint made its way to the General Assembly, who remitted the case to the Presbytery of Duns. After a second phase of the judicial process, the Presbytery and the General Assembly upheld the complaints, which included the use of symbols and letters on the cloth of the communion table and the font, the observance of festivals of the Christian year, the monthly Communion, as well as kneeling at the Benediction. However, this ruling concerned only Duns, and since Macleod had left the parish, the case did not personally involve him. It is no surprise that he made similar changes at Govan Old.[102] An organ was introduced, and standing for singing and keeling for prayer. A quarterly Communion was introduced in October 1875 in place of the twice-annual celebration. This was incrementally increased in 1879 and 1882, to become once a month. Holy Week services were introduced in 1884. Although a few parishioners complained to the Presbytery of Glasgow, in 1884 and again in 1885 (the latter included concern over his view on prayer for the departed), the complaints were dismissed.

These changes in worship coincided with the decision to replace Govan Old Church. The church had been designed in 1825 by James Smith and was in a late Gothic style.[103] However, since its erection, Govan had changed considerably. Roger S. Kirkpatrick noted that its interior was mean and depressing, its dimensions were inadequate to the altered circumstances of Govan and a church much larger in size, more ecclesiastical in its arrangements and modelled with a view to reasonable developments in worship, was obviously needed.[104] Rowand Anderson was consulted, and the first proposal was to enlarge and refurbish the existing church. However, in 1880 the decision was taken to erect a new church instead. A new design was drawn up and the last service in the old church was in March 1884. It was dismantled stone by stone and rebuilt as the Elderpark Parish Church. The new building combined Anderson's views on Gothic with Macleod's ideas on worship. McKinstry writes:

---

102 Murray, 'The Scottish Church Society, 1892–1914', chapter 10; Roger S. Kirkpatrick, *The Ministry of Dr. John Macleod in the Parish of Govan*, Edinburgh: William Blackwood, 1915.

103 Sam McKinstry, 'The Architecture of Govan Old Parish Church', www.govanold.org.uk/reports/1992_architecture.html, 11 March 1992, accessed 11.09.2017.

104 Kirkpatrick, *The Ministry of Dr. John Macleod*, p. 18.

The final result undoubtedly conformed to Macleod's broad wishes: it possessed *a large and subduing majesty of form and was plain and unvitiated by florid decoration*, totally appropriate to the Mother Church of an important Parish growing apace as a result of Macleod's tireless efforts. It also conformed closely to the pattern established by Anderson in his earlier churches. In common with so many of these, it consists of a lofty nave in the Early Gothic style, heavily buttressed with shallow side aisles and leading to a chancel, originally some two thirds of its present length, which results from an extension of 1908. On the church's west (liturgical north) side, the foundations of a tower were laid, but as yet it remains unbuilt. Between these foundations and the chancel lies the Steven Chapel, where daily services instituted by Macleod are still carried out. The composition, realised in cream squared sandstone rubble, is articulated by delicate hood mouldings, and is given a sense of gravitas by its general proportion, the loftiness of the lancets and the pitch of the roof. In accordance with Anderson's functionalist beliefs, inherited from his former employer, Sir George Gilbert Scott, the building's external form expresses the internal deployment of space, and in consequence, its function.[105]

McKinstry noted that the glory of the interior was the view towards the giant oculus and triple lancets of the chancel, modelled on Pluscarden Priory, together with the wall lined in dark red brick, offset by the stone of arcades and dressings.[106] The nave was lit by stained glass, mainly by Charles Eamer Kempe. The organ case, pulpit, communion table, desks and choir stalls were all designed by Anderson and made by Whytock & Reid of Edinburgh.[107] As McKinstry notes, 'the communion table was placed in the Chancel *as a witness*, the pulpit placed at the side, prayers were to be offered from the prayer desk, these and other details coinciding with the developing involvement of the congregation in the services.'[108] The new parish church was dedicated on 19 May 1888 with an elaborate service, and many special services took place in the octave. Kirkpatrick commented:

Such as they were, however, in that memorable Dedication Octave, the services of the New Parish Church of Govan exhibited an immense advance upon any previous use in the Church of Scotland under Presbyterian government; and they established, for the encouragement and imitation of all who desired and sought after liturgical improvement, a standard and a pattern.[109]

105 Sam McKinstry, 'The Architecture of Govan Old Parish Church', pp. 3–4.
106 McKinstry, *Rowand Anderson*, p. 106.
107 McKinstry, 'The Architecture of Govan Old Parish Church', p. 5.
108 McKinstry, 'The Architecture of Govan Old Parish Church', p. 5.
109 Kirkpatrick, *The Ministry of Dr. John Macleod*, p. 98.

From November 1888, daily services were introduced, at 3pm each day, and from 1892, twice a day, at 10am and 5pm.[110] The order used was based on the Daily Offices issued by the Church Service Society.[111]

In public worship, Macleod encouraged congregational participation, expected the congregation to say an audible Amen in response to prayers and blessings, and to join in the Lord's Prayer and the recitation of the Creed. In the communion service, the Sanctus and Agnus Dei were also sung by the congregation. In common with many of the Church Service Society, and probably all members of the Scottish Church Society, for Macleod, Communion was central to worship, and ideally should be the main Sunday service. He managed to increase the celebrations to monthly and on major festivals. In a sermon series, published under the title *The Gospel of the Holy Communion*, he taught that the Holy Communion was both a commemoration of and communion with the work of Jesus Christ. He suggested that there were six actions in the institution of the Supper: separation of the elements; thanksgiving; blessing (consecration); the sacrificial fraction; giving of the sacrament; and receiving the sacrament.[112] For 'thanksgiving', Macleod cited the Preface and Sanctus, which may suggest the influence of the Catholic Apostolic Church. This would be no surprise since Macleod was at the same time a Church of Scotland minister and a member of the Catholic Apostolic Church. The liturgiologist of the Catholic Apostolic Church, John Cardale, argued that thanksgiving and blessing were quite distinct acts and that thanksgiving corresponded to the Preface and Sanctus.[113] In the consecration, Christ 'is really, though spiritually, present to us as these elements are to our outward senses, so that there is an actual Memorial of the sacrifice on the Cross, and in the use of it we are, in body, soul and spirit, nourished in that body in which we are now living to God, and shall finally be raised'.[114] He was sacramentally but *really* present with us, and his body and blood were sacramentally exhibited in the bread and wine.[115] In line with other founding figures of the Scottish Church Society, he also stressed the High Priesthood of Christ.[116]

Although Macleod used printed services for certain occasions, he did not compose his own liturgical book. Kirkpatrick observed:

There can be little doubt that Dr Macleod intended in due course to complete, collect, and issue the series (of printed services) in the shape of a

---

110 Kirkpatrick, *The Ministry of Dr. John Macleod*, p. 112.
111 Kirkpatrick, *The Ministry of Dr. John Macleod*, p. 113.
112 John Macleod, *The Gospel of the Holy Communion*, Glasgow: The Scottish Church Society, 1927, pp. 25–7. The sermons were originally preached in 1888–9.
113 Macleod, *The Gospel of the Holy Communion*, pp. 39 and 42ff; J. Cardale, *Readings upon the Liturgy and other Divine Offices of the Church*, 2 vols, London: Barclay, 1874–5, vol. 1, pp. 169–70.
114 Macleod, *The Gospel of the Holy Communion*, p. 51.
115 Macleod, *The Gospel of the Holy Communion*, pp. 62–3.
116 Macleod, *The Gospel of the Holy Communion*, pp. 96–111

Service book for Govan Parish Church. But modifications, adjustments, and additions were found desirable from time to time. In particular, the special services for the principal days and seasons of the Christian Year required elaboration. And the intention to publish, deferred until more definite fixity had been reached, was never carried into execution.[117]

One of the factors that prevented Macleod from completing this intended service book was the need to continue raising funds to build more daughter churches of Govan Parish, and to find like-minded ministers to exercise ministry in them.[118] His early death in 1898 ended any prospect of a 'Macleod Service book'. However, Tom Davidson Kelly found at Govan Old a copy of the fifth edition of the *Euchologion*, 1884, which has a pencil annotation of Roger S. Kirkpatrick, one of Macleod's assistants: 'This is the copy of the Book of Common Order used latterly by Dr. Macleod in conducting the Services. The pencil markings are in his hand.' The markings identified by Tom Davidson Kelly include alterations to prayers on page 67, pencil text additions on pages 56, 57, 59, 119 and 132, and deletions on pages 44, 95 and 98.[119]

David Watson and St Oswald's Woodside, Glasgow[120]

David Watson was ordained to Middle Parish Church, Paisley in 1874, and made changes in the worship there; in 1875 an organ by Bridley & Foster was installed. Watson became a member of the Church Service Society in 1876. In 1877 until 1916 he was minister of the newly formed congregation of Woodside, Glasgow, whose meeting place 'was then an unpicturesque tin structure in a corner of Burnbank drill-ground'.[121] He became a member of the Aberdeen Ecclesiological Society, then of the Glasgow Ecclesiastical Society and finally the Scottish Ecclesiological Society, becoming a vice-president of the latter in 1906.[122]

Woodside was a chapel of ease for the parish church, and under Watson a new church building was erected and opened in 1882, the architect being Henry Higgins junior. Although now demolished, *The Building News* described the church thus:

---

117 Kirkpatrick, *The Ministry of Dr. John Macleod*, p. 98.

118 See John C. Macfarlane, *An Outline History of Govan Old Parish Church*, Kirk Session, Glasgow: Outram, 1965; Tom Davidson Kelly, *Living Stones: The Daughter Churches of Govan Parish 1730–1919*, The Friends of Govan Old, Glasgow, 2007.

119 'CSS books in use in Govan Parish', note given to the writer by the late Tom Davidson Kelly.

120 I am indebted to the late Tom Davidson Kelly for much of the information about Woodside and David Watson.

121 *The Bailie* (newspaper), No. 1480, Glasgow, 27 February 1901, p. 1.

122 *Transactions of the Scottish Ecclesiological Society*, vol. 2, Part 1, 1906–7 (1907), p. xv.

It is cruciform on plan, consisting of nave, aisles, transepts, and octagonal chancel. . . . The style is Romanesque, and the building is of local stone. There is no tower, but the principal front is flanked by spirelets. The stalls are of solid oak and the pewing of pitch-pine, the total number of seats provided, including three small galleries in transepts and over vestibule, being 1,040. The clerestory windows to nave, from which the church is directly lighted, are occupied with stained-glass memorials of recent Scotch and English divines. Arcades of stone divide the nave and aisles into five bays, and support a high-pitched roof, panelled in timber and treated with stencilled ornament.[123]

The stencilled ornamentation was by McCulloch & Gow. Watson himself painted some murals or 'wall cartoons'.[124] The pulpit and other furnishings were Italian marble. The two-manual organ was by Harrison & Harrison. Preaching at the opening service, Dr A. K. H. Boyd declared that both the building and the order of service typified 'the high-water mark of Presbyterianism'.[125] Certainly there was something 'high' about the services, as a 'shocked Episcopalian', A. G. Townshend, reported to Jacob Primmer:

On the Lord's table were vases of flowers. On the wall behind, my eyes rested on a large cross, apparently of marble. Across the chancel was fixed what we Episcopalians would call a Rood Screen, surmounted by two more crosses. Behind this screen sat a choir of men and boys, all (including the organist) arrayed in scarlet cassocks and short surplices. When the minister announced a chapter, either from the Old or New testament, the choir sang, 'Lord have mercy upon us, and incline our hearts to keep Thy laws,' and part of their performance was to sing the Lord's Prayer, the organ accompanying them. I could not help asking myself, Am I really in the land of Knox?[126]

Something of Watson's liturgical preferences are illustrated by the printed form of services used at St Oswald's, Woodside, *Common Prayer and Praise*, 1902. In the Preface Watson explained: 'Of late years quite a number of Prayer-Books have been prepared for Church use. And that fact ought to be helpful and encouraging to all who are quietly and anxiously endeavouring to improve the worship of the Church.'[127] Many people believed, so he suggested, that the Church needed to provide a sufficiency of serviceable prayers as well as suitable hymns so that believers' varied necessities could

---

123 *The Building News*, 20 January 1882, p. 88.

124 *Transactions of the Glasgow Ecclesiological Society*, vol. 1, 1894 (1895), opposite p. 66.

125 *The Bailie*, 27 February 1901, p. 1.

126 Primmer, *The Life of Jacob Primmer*, p. 214. It is difficult to understand why an Episcopalian should have been so shocked! 'Pleasantly surprised' would have been more logical.

127 David Watson, *Common Prayer and Praise*, at the University Press, Glasgow: Robert Maclehose & Co, 1902, p. vii.

find utterance when they approached the throne of grace. Eleven services were provided – five each for Sunday Morning and Evening worship, and a Communion service. The Morning and Evening services had a common structure: a Call to Worship (scripture sentences, with all standing); Kneeling for the opening prayer; a metrical psalm; sentences of Scripture recited as versicles and responses; prayer (for forgiveness of sins); hymn; Old Testament reading; versicles and responses, and prayer; hymn, New Testament reading; versicles and responses and prayers of intercession with congregational response, ending with Lord's Prayer, Canticle or hymn, or Psalmody; prayer of illumination; sermon; prayer; offertory; hymn; and Benediction. At Evening Prayer, after the Benediction the choir sang 'Vesper', which was a brief anthem or verse of an appropriate hymn.

The 'Solemn Commemoration and Communion' began in a similar way to the Morning and Evening Services, with a Call to Worship, prayer, and metrical psalm, versicles and responses, with a prayer for forgiveness and the recitation of the Ten Commandments as in the 1662 Book of Common Prayer. This was followed by a prayer and the Lord's Prayer, a hymn and a scripture reading. This was followed by versicles and responses with a series of short collects, and Heber's Hymn 'Holy, Holy, Holy' and J. B. Dykes' 'Nicaea tune', or the Benedictus. This liturgy of the Word reached its climax with a prayer of illumination and the sermon. During the singing of Paraphrase XXXV, ''Twas on that night, when doom'd to know', the elements were brought in and placed on the communion table. The Institution narrative was read, followed by a section entitled 'Consecration'. This consisted of a verse of Scripture and then a prayer broken up with congregational responses such as, 'O God, graciously hear us'. The third section of the prayer requested:

> And here to-day would we specially remember Him, – After this manner would we. Do Thou bless and sanctify these elements of Bread and Wine, and set them apart to this Holy use. And grant, we pray Thee, that together eating if that Sacred Bread we may remember how veritably His Holiness and Truth were aforetime the disciples' bread of life: and together tasting of that Sacred Wine, we may remember how unfailingly His quickening Spirit was the disciples' strength and joy: and how through the ministry of Apostle and Saint, Christ Himself has become the Light and Life of all of us.[128]

For all the accusations of Ritualism, this was not a particularly 'high' understanding of the Lord's Supper. The communion rite continued with the words of institution and the declaration of Peace. It ended with a few words of exhortation, post-communion prayers with congregational responses, hymn, offertory and final Benediction.

---

128 Watson, *Common Prayer and Praise*, p. 134.

Some of Watson's phraseology throughout the collection was quaint and awkward, but when the book is set within the building in which it was used, together they represent another local manifestation of the flowering of the nineteenth-century liturgical revival.

John Service and Hyndland Church, Glasgow

One of the daughter churches of Govan Old was Hyndland Church, built as a result of new housing. A 'Tin Church' was moved from Byres Road and re-erected at the junction of Hyndland Road and Great Western Road in 1878. The first minister appointed to Hyndland was Dr John Service, in 1878, who was called from Insch in Aberdeenshire and remained until his death in 1884. He had become a member of the Church Service Society in 1878. Some idea of his public services may be gleaned from the posthumously published *Prayers for Public Worship*, 1885. The prefatory notes explained that his singular influence as a religious teacher was thought by many to be due, to some extent, 'to an unusual combination of qualities in his sermons and in the prayers which he composed for public worship'.[129] It was further explained:

> He wrote them out with extreme care, and it is plain that he attached great importance to the adequate expression of the feelings by which he thought a Christian congregation should be animated. It is, however, difficult to present these prayers in such a form as he himself might have chosen. They are nowhere arranged for particular days of the month, for morning or evening services, or for special Church occasions. As he thought them suitable he was accustomed to select portions of one prayer, and combine them with parts of others.[130]

These are not printed liturgies but prayers that he compiled for public worship and used and continually recycled, rather like Arnott's collection from St Giles'. Twenty-four prayers were printed in this collection, although only the final one has a title, 'Burial of the Dead'. The opening of Prayer II gives a good example of the style of Service's very scriptural compilations. It opens with several verses from Psalm 27 and then continues: 'O Thou who art everywhere present in heaven and earth, and art the life of all that live, we beseech Thee who art near to us to enable us to draw near to Thee and to feel that Thou art near.'[131] The fact that these prayers were used and reformulated many times results in a semi-liturgical service.

Service was succeeded by Henry Grey Graham, who had joined the Church Service Society in 1868. It was during his tenure that the Tin

---

129 John Service, *Prayers for Public Worship*, London: Macmillan & Co., 1885, p. v.
130 Service, *Prayers for Public Worship*, pp. vi–vii.
131 Service, *Prayers for Public Worship*, pp. 13–14.

Church was replaced by the present Hyndland Church, opened in 1887. William Leiper was the architect. It was built in red Ballochmyle sandstone and was a wonderful example of Gothic style. It was to have a steeple, although because of the costs, this was never realised. Likewise, high costs meant that only limited stained glass was added, in 1889. It was fitted with a marble pulpit and communion table, as well as a Willis pipe organ. Graham was a man of letters and wrote several books, though there seems no record of his public worship services. As a long-standing member of the Church Service Society it is legitimate to conjecture that they reflected the style of the *Euchologion* and were appropriate for Leiper's Gothic interior.

Concluding remarks

As with other nineteenth-century liturgical revivals, it is possible to see that of the Scottish Presbyterian churches as part of the cultural tendencies that we call Romanticism, with Gothic-style churches, concern for liturgical furnishings and decoration and the crafting of printed liturgical services. However, at least in the Established Church, the need for local printed liturgies was declining, in part because of the publication in 1923, by authority of the General Assembly of the Church of Scotland, of *Prayers for Divine Service in Church and Home*. This was combined with rising costs of printing and the changing fashion in church building. Most importantly, however, the First World War of 1914–18 took a heavy toll on the optimism of Romanticism.

8

Forms of Worship Between Two Unions and Two World Wars, 1900–40

Virginia Woolf remarked that in or about December 1910, human character changed. She explained:

> I am not saying that one went out, as one might into a garden, and there saw that a rose had flowered, or that a hen had laid an egg. The change was not sudden and definite like that. But a change there was, nevertheless; and, since one must be arbitrary, let us date it about the year 1910. The first signs of it are recorded in the books of Samuel Butler, in *The Way of All Flesh* in particular; the plays of Bernard Shaw continue to record it. In life one can see the change, if I may use a homely illustration, in the character of one's cook. The Victorian cook lived like a leviathan in the lower depths, formidable, silent, obscure, inscrutable; the Georgian cook is a creature of sunshine and fresh air; in and out of the drawing-room, now to borrow *The Daily Herald*, now to ask advice about a hat. Do you ask for more solemn instances of the power of the human race to change? Read the *Agamemnon*, and see whether, in process of time, your sympathies are not almost entirely with Clytemnestra. Or consider the married life of the Carlyles, and bewail the waste, the futility, for him and for her, of the horrible domestic tradition which made it seemly for a woman of genius to spend her time chasing beetles, scouring saucepans, instead of writing books. All human relations have shifted – those between masters and servants, husbands and wives, parents and children. And when human relations change there is at the same time a change in religion, conduct, politics, and literature. Let us agree to place one of these changes about the year 1910.[1]

Iain McGilchrist has remarked that this specificity of the date is designed to suggest not so much the swiftness as the abruptness of the disjunction between the end of the Romanticism of the Victorian era and the beginning of the Modern era or Modernism.[2] The attempt to define 'eras' and

---

1 Virginia Woolf, 'Mr. Bennett and Mrs. Brown', a paper read to the Heretics, Cambridge, 1 May 1924, London: Hogarth Press, 1924, pp. 4–5.

2 Iain McGilchrist, *The Master and His Emissary: The Divided Brain and the Making of the Western World*, New Haven, CT: Yale University Press, 2009, p. 389.

shifts in culture by dates is always somewhat arbitrary and Woolf's choice of 1910 is, as she admitted, no exception. Whatever the date, significant changes in British society did take place in the first years of the twentieth century, with the growth of labour movements, the First World War, the Russian Revolution and rise of Communism, the Great Depression and then the Second World War, all of which witnessed to a different ethos from Victorian Romanticism and had their impact on Christian life and faith. For the Scottish Presbyterian Churches, two other events frame the period 1900–40: the union of the United Presbyterian Church with the Free Church of Scotland to form the United Free Church of Scotland, 1900; and then the union of the United Free Church of Scotland with the Church of Scotland in 1929. The period 1900–40 saw the publication of a variety of worship resources as both aids and as standards for the united churches in the age of Modernity.

The United Free Church

The Free Church of Scotland had left the established Church in 1843 over patronage. The Church of Scotland abolished patronage in 1874, and hoped to woo back the Free Church. However, as Rolf Sjölinder remarked, 'the leaders of the Church of Scotland failed to take into account the change of viewpoint which is always the result of existence as a separate denomination.'[3] The Free Church had by that date moved to embrace voluntary ecclesiology, was anti-Establishment and agitated for the disestablishment of the Church of Scotland. In 1863, conversations about union began between the Free Church of Scotland and the United Presbyterian Church. Union eventually came in 1900. Sjölinder noted that when the new united Church came into being, the United Free Church, 'it had over 1,600 parishes and some 500,000 members, over 296,000 of whom were drawn from the Free Church, and rather more than 200,000 from the United Presbyterian Church.'[4] However, a minority from each held aloof, and in the case of the Free Church, ten ministers and eleven elders left the Church and declared themselves to be 'The' legal Free Church, and demanded all the property. They lost their case in the Scottish courts, but they appealed to the House of Lords, where judgement was given in their favour in 1904. The small minority, mainly from the Highlands, was not able to administer all the property and Parliament intervened with a more sensible distribution, giving the small Free Church an amount of property that it could reasonably maintain, with the bulk going to the new United Free Church of Scotland. The few ministers who remained as the Free Church tended to be conservative in theology and worship and continued the pattern of services

---

3 Rolf Sjölinder, *Presbyterian Reunion in Scotland 1907–1921*, Uppsala: Almqvist & Wieksells Boktryckeri AB, 1962, p. 83.
4 Sjölinder, *Presbyterian Reunion*, p. 109.

inherited from the Westminster *Directory*, eschewing written forms. Some small glimpses can be gleaned from the diary of Kenneth MacRae, Free Church minister of Lochgilphead, Argyll. There were three services on a Sunday, in Gaelic at 11am and in English at 2pm and 6:30pm. The congregational singing of psalms was hearty. MacRae recorded his reflections on a communion season on Arran, 1–5 June 1916, on the preparatory services, and he noted that there was an English and a Gaelic table, with an Action sermon and a short Address after the Gaelic Table had been served. He did not record the substance of any of the prayers.[5]

In the new United Free Church of Scotland, the union of 1900 led to the amalgamation of the United Presbyterian Devotional Service Association and the Public Worship Association of the Free Church of Scotland to form The Church Worship Association of the United Free Church of Scotland. Its first publications seem to have been *Children's Services for Church and Sabbath School*, 1901, and *Prayers for Christian Homes*, 1901. The Preface to the former claimed that the first condition of successful education is the infusion of a spirit of worship before Sabbath lessons begin.[6] The publication provided hints for improvement for the service, practical notes on its conduct, suggestions for prayer, and included some prayers. It also contained an Order of Service and Services for Special Occasions – the Birth of Christ, the Crucifixion and Resurrection, New Year and a 'Flower Service'. Interestingly, the compilers felt unable to name the first of these as Christmas, Good Friday and Easter. One feature was the encouragement of participation by the provision of a litany as well as responses to the scripture sentences and responsive readings. An example of the latter is the reading of the Beatitudes with the response, 'Grant us this grace, we beseech Thee, O Lord'. Some are compilations from a variety of books of the Bible, and are quite imaginative.

A contribution to Eucharistic thinking was made by the Revd Robert Morgan Adamson (1866–1940), formerly of the Free Church of Scotland and then of the United Free Church, in *The Christian Doctrine of the Lord's Supper*, 1905. After a broad historical survey from the Old Testament onwards, Adamson turned his attention to what he called a constructive restatement of the doctrine. Although he acknowledged that since Herculean labours were so repeatedly expended on the subject, it seemed futile to dream of saying anything essentially new, he nevertheless attempted to do so.[7] Starting with the sacrament as a human ceremony, Adamson dialogued with many authors, old and contemporary, to assert that the gift in the sacrament is Jesus Christ who offers and gives himself in some true and real

---

5 Iain H. Murray, *Diary of Kenneth A. MacRae*, Edinburgh: Banner of Truth Trust, 1980, pp. 75, 83–9.

6 *Children's Services for Church and Sabbath School*, Edinburgh: McNiven & Wallace, 1901, p. vi.

7 Robert M. Adamson, *The Christian Doctrine of the Lord's Supper*, Edinburgh: T&T Clark, 1905, p. 133.

sense – himself as he is now, the risen and ascended God-Man. He appealed to the Church of England sixteenth-century divine, Richard Hooker, that the presence is not to be sought for in the sacrament but is realised in the worthy receiver of the sacrament.[8] The sacrament is the means whereby Christ makes himself 'felt' by his people.[9] The presence is in the sacrament (apparently contradicting Hooker), not in the elements. The rite might be called a sacrifice, because it is the work of all Christians who are a king-dom of priests, though he rejected the argument of William Milligan about linking sacrifice with the heavenly intercession.[10] In a subsequent chapter, Adamson reviewed many different liturgies, including Greek Orthodox, Roman Catholic, Lutheran and Unitarian. He found some commendable things in many of the rites, including the *Euchologion* of the Church Service Society and *A New Directory for the Public Worship of God*. Adamson ended his study with a review of practical aspects of the Communion.

Another contribution was in a small booklet by David Purves, entitled *The Sacraments of the New Testament*.[11] Purves was a minister in Belfast, but his work had a recommendatory note by Principal Thomas Lindsay of the United Free Church College, Glasgow. The booklet was intended to present a simple statement of the sacraments as held by the Presbyterian Church, and to be a work that ministers could present to confirmation candidates after their first Communion. Purves appealed to the teaching of Robert Bruce, that a sacrament is a holy sign and seal that is annexed to the preached Word of God, to seal up and confirm the truth contained in the same Word. In sacraments, Christ and his benefits are represented, sealed and applied. They exhibit and deliver the thing that is signified.[12] On baptism, Purves asserted that it is a precious and useful seal of the covenant and a token of God's love.[13] In the Lord's Supper, Jesus declared bread and wine to be sacramentally his body and blood: 'They were taken to represent, seal, and apply His death to all believing souls; and Christians are thereby enjoined, by a frequent repetition of the action done that night by Jesus, to keep alive His memory, and specially the remembrance of His Cross and passion, until His second advent.'[14] Christ and his benefits are 'exhibited' – not in the elements but *'in the sacrament.'*[15]

The publication of *Anthology of Prayers for Public Worship* came in 1907, with groups of prayers and formulae under the headings Prayers

---

8 Adamson, *The Christian Doctrine*, p. 165.

9 Adamson, *The Christian Doctrine*, p. 166.

10 Adamson, *The Christian Doctrine*, p. 187; Bryan D. Spinks, *Two Faces of Elizabethan Anglican Theology: Sacraments and Salvation in the Thought of William Perkins and Richard Hooker*, Lanham, MD: Scarecrow Press, 1999.

11 David Purves, *The Sacraments of the New Testament*, Edinburgh: Oliphant, Anderson & Ferrier, 1904.

12 Purves, *The Sacraments*, pp. 18, 19 and 24.

13 Purves, *The Sacraments*, p. 40.

14 Purves, *The Sacraments*, pp. 48–9.

15 Purves, *The Sacraments*, p. 58.

of Invocation, Confession of Sins, Petition, Adoration and Thanksgiving, Intercession, Illumination, Close of Public Worship and Doxologies and Benedictions. These prayers and formulae comprised Part I. Part II had prayers for use at baptism, admission to full communion and the Lord's Supper. Part III had prayers for special times and seasons, and occasions such as ordination. The exceedingly brief Preface explained that the prayers are taken 'for the most part' from recognised sources and were designed to provide material for the enrichment of the Public Prayer of the Sanctuary. An Appendix listed the sources, which ranged from Bishop Andrewes' *Private Devotions* and *Bright's Ancient Collects*, to the *New Directory* of the former Free Church and the *Euchologion*, to Archbishop Benson's *Prayers, Public and Private*.

In 1909 the Church Worship Association published the *Directory and Forms for Public Worship*. The Preparatory Note explained that this was an attempt to combine the methods found in the *Presbyterian Forms of Service*, 1891 and *A New Directory for the Public Worship of God*, 1898, 'in the belief that the assistance desired will be thus most acceptably and effectively supplied'.[16] Part I provided material for Morning and Evening Sunday worship. An outline for each was set out prior to the anthologies from which a choice might be made. The recommended order for Morning Service was as follows:

1 Sentences of Scripture
2 Prayer of Invocation
3 Praise
4 Prayer of Thanksgiving:
　 Confession
　 Supplication
5 Reading from the Old Testament
6 Praise
7 Reading from the New Testament
8 Praise
9 Prayer of Intercession: Lord's Prayer
10 Praise
11 Prayer for Illumination
12 Discourse
13 Prayer
14 Praise
15 Benediction.

The Evening Service was a simpler outline, with Praise, Prayer, Praise, Reading from Holy Scripture, Praise, Prayer, Discourse, Prayer, Praise and Benediction. After the anthologies of scripture sentences, intercessions and so on, two fuller orders of service were provided for Morning and Evening.

---

16 *Directory and Forms for Public Worship*, Edinburgh: McNiven & Wallace, 1909, p. v.

Part II contained the administration of the sacraments. Baptismal orders for both infants and adults were provided. In the former, the prayer immediately before the act of baptism stated that the sacrament had been 'ordained for a sign and seal of the covenant of grace' and requested: 'And while we baptize outwardly and with water, do Thou, of Thy great mercy, follow the ordinance with the thing signified, baptizing inwardly and with the Holy Ghost.'[17] A similar petition was included in the baptism of adults – 'we beseech thee, to join the inward baptism of the Spirit with the outward baptism of water' – though it is not clear why the phraseology in the service for infants distinguished 'baptizing inwardly' from 'and with the Holy Ghost'.[18]

The section on the Lord's Supper provided outline services for when Communion was part of the Ordinary Service, I, and for when it was a separate service, II, and for the latter, two outlines were given, A and B. For I, the Words of Institution were recited from 1 Corinthians 11, and then came an exhortation adapted from the *Book of Common Order*, 1562. A hymn was to be sung, and then coming to the table, the minister prayed a prayer of thanksgiving, which made the request:

> Bless and sanctify with thy Word and Spirit these thy gifts now set before us, and grant that we may become partakers of the body and the blood of Jesus, with all His benefits, to our spiritual nourishment and growth in grace.[19]

The final paragraph ended with the reference to angels and archangels and concluded with the Sanctus. Communion followed, with words of administration, and then after an optional brief Address, a post-communion thanksgiving was provided, which included thanks for the communion of saints. For II there was quite a different emphasis, with separate prayers for the bread and its distribution, and then for the wine. That for the bread asked that in the broken bread 'we have the communion of his broken body' and then requested that 'as we partake of this sacramental food, we may spiritually eat of the true Bread which came down from heaven'. The prayer over the wine spoke of it as a symbol of Christ's precious blood, and seemed to cater for those who held a purely symbolic understanding of the Eucharistic elements.

Part III included the marriage rite, Burial of the Dead, as well as ordination and licensing services and for the Dedication of a church. Part IV provided a lectionary. As the Preparatory Note had announced, the book had attempted to combine suggested orders of service with an anthology of materials, as well as to allow for a much freer Directory-style of service.

---

17 *Directory and Forms*, p. 101.
18 *Directory and Forms*, p. 109.
19 *Directory and Forms*, p. 120.

An example of a communion service outline is preserved in a book about Broughton Place United Free Church, 1914, which had been opened in 1821. A section was entitled 'A Communion Sabbath in Broughton Place'.[20] The attendance averaged 800 at the one and only 'table' that was provided at these 'solemn Communion Sundays', though the frequency was not recorded.[21] The writer boasted that unlike Anglican High Church and Roman Catholic celebrations, which 'are far removed from the original pattern of the upper room at Jerusalem', that at Broughton Place was administered with 'Presbyterian simplicity'.[22] According to the writer, 'The Presbyterian form may not be an exact replica of that pattern, but it follows it closely enough to be scriptural, and yet suitable to the circumstances of the times in which we live.'[23] With a somewhat memorialist tone, the account stated:

What emotions stir, or at least ought to stir, those who take part in this great Christian festival! The broken bread and the poured out wine may be only symbols, but they wonderously move the soul all the same. And why should they not? Have we not all been moved at the sight of the faded letters or personal relics of some departed relative or friend? The sacred symbols of bread and wine speak to us audibly enough, and bring our dear Lord wondrously near us, and within the radius of our best affections.[24]

After explaining that under Dr Smith the service had lasted two hours, but was now somewhat shorter, the book outlined the celebration of Sunday 1 March 1914, when the Revd James Black presided:

Prayer of Invocation
Praise – Psalm 103, v.1–5, *O thou my soul*
First Scripture Lesson – Psalm 113
Praise – Hymn 70, *We sing the praise of Him who died*
Second Lesson – Matthew 26, v.26–30
Prayer of Confession, Thanksgiving, and Intercession
Praise – Paraphrase 2, *O God of Bethel*
Sermon – Psalm 113, v.5, 'Who is like unto the Lord our God, who dwelleth on High?'
Praise – Paraphrase 35, *Twas on that night*
Read warrant for observance of Supper – 1 Cor. 11, v.23–29

---

20 Charles Irvine, *Thirty Years of Broughton Place Church*, Edinburgh: Howie & Seath, 1914.
21 Irvine, *Thirty Years*, p. 75.
22 Irvine, *Thirty Years*, p. 78.
23 Irvine, *Thirty Years*, p. 78.
24 Irvine, *Thirty Years*, p. 79.

Praise (Congregation seated) – Hymn 306, v.2, *O Christ! He is the fountain*; v.3, *O I am my Beloved's*
Dispensation of the sacred elements
Post-Communion Address
Praise – Hymn 295, *Guide me, O thou great Jehovah*
Benediction.[25]

Strangely, no 'Thanksgiving' over the elements is listed in this order.

On 4 August 1914, only a few months after this celebration of Communion, the United Kingdom was at war with Germany. The hitherto unchallenged belief in progress and art died on the fields of Flanders, and the British state gradually assumed more control over the social and economic life of the country. J. M. Winter noted:

War losses touched virtually every household in Britain, and nearly every family was diminished by the death in combat of a father, a son, a brother, a cousin, or a friend. Four years of bloodletting had created a bond of bereavement which transcended distinctions of class or caste, for what mattered was not that the war had destroyed potential leaders or poets, but that it had cut a swathe through an entire generation.[26]

It is estimated that Scotland lost some 110,000 men.[27]

In response to the national crisis, the Church Worship Association published *Forms of Prayer for Use in War Time* and *Hymns for Use in Time of War*, 1914.[28] A pastoral response to the crisis from a United Free Church minister and army chaplain, the Revd A. Herbert Gray, appeared under the title *As Tommy Sees Us*.[29] Gray wrote, 'Sooner or later all chaplains came to realise that the majority of men prefer to appear indifferent. They do not like religious services, and do not respond to the definitely religious part of a chaplain's work.'[30]

Gray noted that soldiers found the atmosphere of churches stiff and uncongenial, they found sermons boring and having to keep quiet and silent for an hour and a half was a severe trial for them.[31] He found that the Scottish soldiers knew by heart some of the tunes of the metrical Psalms and felt that singing the right words of praise and petition to the right tunes

25 Irvine, *Thirty Years*, p. 81.

26 J. M. Winter, *The Great War and the British People*, London: Macmillan, 1986, p. 305.

27 Christopher Harvie, *No Gods and Precious Few Heroes: Scotland 1914–1980*, London: Edward Arnold, 1981, p. 24.

28 For the former, see Millar Patrick, 'The Church Worship Association of the United Free Church', in *Church Service Society Annual* 3 (1930–1), pp. 79–82, p. 81. I have not been able to consult a copy of *Forms of Prayer for Use in War Time*, which was published by McNiven & Wallace, Edinburgh.

29 Arthur Herbert Gray, *As Tommy Sees Us*, London: Edward Arnold, 1919.

30 Gray, *As Tommy Sees Us*, p. 13.

31 Gray, *As Tommy Sees Us*, p. 17.

scarcely ever missed its mark. Hymns from the *Church Hymnary* he also found very useful.[32] He mentioned as well a book of psalms and hymns called *With the Colours*. However, beyond singing, Gray had little to offer on the words of worship. The booklet he referred to, *With the Colours: For God, King and Country* (enlarged edition 1918), provided servicemen with the text of the Lord's Prayer, some scripture sentences and a prayer used by Lord Roberts (which referred to King, Country and Colours). The scripture sentences were arranged under various heads, such as 'our Captain' and 'the Route or Orders of March'. It contained eighty-two paraphrases and hymns in English, and nine in Gaelic.[33]

The huge death toll of the war raised questions about how to remember the dead and their great sacrifice, and this was a challenge to Reformed teaching regarding prayer for the departed. War memorials to individual soldiers and to all those from a parish were erected. This is reflected in the 1920 revised edition of the *Directory and Forms of Worship*. In Part III of the book there were two additions – Dedication of a Church Sister or other Mission Agent, and for the Dedication of a Memorial. The first recognised the growing place of women in the mission of the Church, as well as their changing status brought about by the war. The second was a short service that contained hymns and an anthem or the *Te Deum*, and allowed for a statement respecting the deceased as well as thanks to the donors. The Dedication Prayer had the following paragraph:

We bless Thee for all who, having loved not their own lives unto the death, fought and died for our sakes, and are now among the noble army of the martyrs who praise Thee. Especially do we now give thanks for Thy servant here commemorated, for whom, we humbly trust, there us henceforth laid up a crown of righteousness that fadeth not away.[34]

Given the paucity of any mention of the departed in the Westminster *Directory*, this was a huge shift, and represents the need to say something in the face of the vast casualty figures.

A gradual acceptance of the Holy Week observance is glimpsed in the Preface to *Passiontide*, by the United Free Church minister the Revd Nahum Levison, a convert from Judaism. He wrote: 'It is my fond hope that we of the Free Churches will forget the associations which "Lent" and "Passiontide" have had; that we will restore Christ's steps with minds disabused of all superstition and ignorance.'[35] In other words, it was time the 'Puritan' backlash of the Reformation gave way to the restoration of

---

32 Gray, *As Tommy Sees Us*, pp. 70–5.

33 *With the Colours: For God, King and Country*, Edinburgh: Thomas & Archibald Constable, 1918. My thanks to Douglas Galbraith for locating a copy for my use.

34 *Directory and Forms*, 1920 edition, p. 212.

35 N. Levison, *Passiontide, or The Last days of the Earthly Life of the Master*, Edinburgh: T&T Clark, 1927, p. ix. I am grateful to the late Tom Davidson Kelly for this reference.

the Christian year. Levison's book was a commentary on the Gospel events of Holy Week. On the Last Supper, he noted that the disciples hardly understood the ritual as consubstantiation or transubstantiation, but 'they considered these elements as the vehicles of the new covenant of the Messianic kingdom, and further, that after his death and resurrection, at their meetings they partook of bread and wine, and were by means of them vividly reminded of His last meal with them.'[36]

In 1922, the Chalmers Lectures (named after Thomas Chalmers, who led the Disruption Party of 1843) had been given by the Revd Dr Robert Stephenson Simpson and were published in 1927 under the title *Ideas in Corporate Worship*.[37] Simpson had been minister of the High United Free Church, Edinburgh.[38] The lectures were rather general, to suit the needs of a wide audience. A keen supporter of the reunion conversations, Simpson emphasised the importance of corporate worship and of the Lord's Supper as the apex: 'In the Communion Office the culmination of the Service is not simply the act of reception, but linked with it is that other act by which, in the fellowship of Christ's whole Church, we offer ourselves unto Him a living offering.'[39] Simpson stressed the importance of the psalms in worship and argued for a liturgy that allowed for free prayer and variation but also much more congregational participation. He made much of 'the Scottish tradition', though without much elucidation, and he also imagined a simplicity of New Testament worship, which he thought would have been similar to the worship of the Quakers. He urged the singing of the Creed in worship and argued that at the heart of Scottish (Presbyterian) worship was the emphasis on the supernatural presence of Christ. Reaching out to laity as well as ministers, it was a forceful argument for the importance of public worship.

Millar Patrick explained that, by 1923, the supplies of the *Directory and Forms* were nearing exhaustion, and he urged the General Assembly to authorise the preparation of an official *Book of Common Order*. The Assembly agreed, and Patrick was appointed convener. A draft was completed in 1927 and the final revised version was published in 1928 as *Book of Common Order*. Patrick was an accomplished musician, and the most prominent of liturgical scholars in the United Free Church.

The 1928 *Book of Common Order* was an official publication of the United Free Church and was published by Oxford University Press, which probably gave this book a certain standing that previous worship books

---

36 Levison, *Passiontide*, pp. 110–11.

37 Robert Stephenson Simpson, *Ideas in Corporate Worship*, Edinburgh: T&T Clark, 1927.

38 The High Kirk of the Free Church had been former members of St Giles' High Kirk. The building became the Library of New College, and the congregation moved to the Reid Memorial Church in 1934. Simpson died in 1926. See A. Ian Dunlop, *The Kirks of Edinburgh 1560–1984*, Edinburgh: Scottish Record Society, 1989, pp. 274–6.

39 Simpson, *Ideas in Corporate Worship*, p. 34.

had lacked. In the Preface, Patrick advised that the provision of forms and aids for worship should not be interpreted as a desire to surrender or supersede 'the priceless ministry of free prayer'. He noted:

> It is not intended to be used as a liturgy, nor is there any obligation to follow, scrupulously or in exact detail, the orders it supplies. Its aim is to express the mind of the Church with regard to its offices of worship, in orders and forms which, while not fettering individual judgement in particulars, will set the norm for the orderly and reverent conduct of the various public services in which ministers have to lead their people.[40]

The Acknowledgments of sources listed not only the earlier worship books of the Free Church (1898) and United Presbyterian Church (1891) and the now United Free Church (1907 and 1909), but the *Euchologion* of the Church Service Society and the *Book of Common Order* of St Giles' Cathedral, Edinburgh. It also drew on the books of other Presbyterian Churches, as well as the Congregationalists John Hunter and W. E. Orchard and the Book of Common Prayer.[41]

As with many of the previous worship books, it was divided into parts: Part I The Order of Public Worship; Part II The Holy Sacraments and ordinances of the Church; Part III Prayers for Times and Seasons, the Lord's Prayer and Creeds, Ascriptions of Glory and Benedictions; Part IV the Lectionary (and Acknowledgements). This was by far the most extensive and comprehensive of the United Free Church books.

The Orders for Morning and Evening services presented two full orders for each and both varied slightly in the sequence of elements of the worship. The first order for Morning Service began with a call to worship, beginning with the old Reformed votum, 'Our help is in the name of the Lord'. A Prayer of Invocation followed, and then a psalm or hymn. A form of Confession and Supplication followed and then an Old Testament Reading, praise, New Testament lesson and permissible Apostles' Creed. A children's Address could be given at this point and, if so, followed by a psalm or hymn. A lengthy prayer of thanksgiving and intercessions followed, with 'praise', which might be an anthem, after which came the Intimations and offering. The prayer for hearing the word preceded the sermon, after which was an Ascription of Glory to God, a Blessing, a hymn and the Grace.

As with the 1909/1920 *Directory and Forms*, forms of baptism for infants and adults were provided. The rite for infants included a prayer that asked, 'Set apart this element of water from a common to a sacred use, and

---

40 United Free Church of Scotland, *Book of Common Order*, Oxford: Oxford University Press, 1928, p. 4.

41 For Hunter and Orchard, see Bryan D. Spinks, *Freedom or Order? The Eucharistic Liturgy in English Congregationalism 1645–1980*, Allison Park, PA: Pickwick Publications, 1984.

grant that what we do now on earth may be confirmed in heaven.' Oddly, no such prayer or petition was provided in the rite for adults.

Three Orders for the Lord's Supper were provided. The first has considerable dependence on the *Euchologion*, though has some eccentricities by scholarly standards of the day. After some 'Comfortable words', suggested by the Book of Common Prayer, the Sursum corda and response (*only* Sursum corda) was followed by a brief exhortation to hear the words of institution from 1 Corinthians 11. After a declaration that the minister was obeying this warrant, the minister said 'Let us Pray', and a prayer of thanksgiving was provided, which included the Sanctus and the familiar words from *Apostolic Constitutions* 8 via the *Euchologion*: 'Not as we ought, but as we are able'. The prayer asked the Father: 'grant us Thy Holy Spirit, and so to sanctify these thy gifts of bread and wine, which we now set apart to their sacred use, that the bread which we break may be to us the communion of the Body of Christ, and the cup of blessing which we bless the communion of the Blood of Christ.' An abbreviated summary of the words of institution was repeated at the fraction.

The second order seemed to be aimed at those with a more memorialist view of the Eucharist. The rite spoke of Christ ordaining bread and wine to be 'the symbols, throughout the ages, of His Body and Blood'. The prayer of Thanks over the elements asked God to 'grant us Thy Holy Spirit, that the secret of the Lord may be with us, and that we may so receive by faith Christ crucified, that the bread which we break etc.'. The third order had an extremely short prayer over the elements, which included the Sanctus and asked:

Let Thy Spirit, taking of the things of Christ and showing them unto us, so help us to receive these elements of bread and wine, which we now set apart to their sacred use, that we may receive Christ by faith to be the meat and drink of our souls.[42]

As with previous books, it is likely that it was the occasional services that were used more verbatim than the orders for Morning and Evening services. The copy I have in my possession shows clear regular use of the Burial service. The book included an order for the dedication of an organ – showing that the 'kist o' whistles' was now an accepted part of worship in most congregations. It also incorporated an order of service for Remembrance Day/Celebration of Peace.

Millar Patrick, the convener of the committee, gave a paper on the First Communion Order in the 1928 book to a group of ministers in Edinburgh, and after the 1929 reunion, this paper was published by the Church of Scotland Committee on Public Worship and Aids to Devotion in 1933. Patrick emphasised that the previous Scottish tradition of having the sacrament separate from the Word service had been overcome and that the two parts

---

42 *Book of Common Order* 1928, p. 78.

were reunited. He commented on the various components of the service and urged that the intercessions should close with a devout commemoration of the faithful departed: 'There is something to be said for reserving it to the end of the last prayer of the service; it is deeply solemnizing to remember then the blessed ones who are within the veil, and to ask for grace so to be faithful like them that at the last we, with them, may inherit the promises.'[43] Commending the entrance of the elements, Patrick wrote:

> Anyone who has seen the dignified procession of the elders, bearing the cups and patens with the covered elements, must agree that it contributes a piece of beautiful ceremonial to a service which is apt to suffer from a lack of stateliness which accords with and helps express its high solemnity.[44]

Patrick regarded the Consecration Prayer as the supreme act of the service, with Sursum corda, and commemoration of creation and redemption. The 'consecration' was the invocation of the Holy Spirit, 'to bless and consecrate into a means of grace the bread and wine, which are now set apart to their sacred use'.[45] The fraction, he believed, should be done in the sight of the people and he discussed the pros and cons of silence or readings during the administration. This official publication was certainly designed to promote and inform about the order of the Communion as it was shaped in the 1928 *Book of Common Order* and the *Prayers for Divine Service* of the Church of Scotland.

The Church Hymnary, revised edition

In 1927 there appeared a revised edition of *The Church Hymnary*. This edition was authorised for use in public worship by the Church of Scotland, the United Free Church of Scotland, the Presbyterian Church in Ireland, as well as in England, Wales, Australia, New Zealand and South Africa. Missing was the Free Church of Scotland, since this now small Church was formed by those of a very conservative nature, allowing only metrical psalmody. The Preface to the edition reveals little, other than that a draft had been approved in 1925 and had undergone some adjustments. The secretary to the Joint Revision Committee was Mr W. M. Page, and Dr David Evans, Professor of Music at the University of Wales, was the music editor. In a note on the music, Evans explained:

> A widespread reaction has set in against much of the music that was in vogue and popular at the beginning of this century. It has been generally

---

43 Millar Patrick, *The Order of Holy Communion*, Edinburgh: The Church of Scotland Committee on Publications, second edition (1933), pp. 11–12.
44 Patrick, *The Order of Holy Communion*, p. 16.
45 Patrick, *The Order of Holy Communion*, p. 21.

realized that religious feeling demands for its expression, the best and noblest music, and that the number of weakly sentimental tunes retained in use should be reduced to a minimum.[46]

The tunes included 'noble spiritual songs' from various countries and ages.

More details of the revision and its rationale were contained in the *Handbook to the Church Hymnary*, edited by James Moffatt and Millar Patrick. Patrick and William Cairns explained that the lapse of a generation stales even the best of hymn books, and demands for revision of the 1898 book became urgent: 'In the interval there had been a great advance in general musical culture, and several almost epoch-making new books had appeared, bringing into use so much fine ancient and modern music that the late-Victorian *Hymnary* came to be seen as very much out of date.'[47] Although some of the Churches involved were hesitant, solidarity prevailed. A full list of the members on the Committee was given. First, the contents of the old book were sifted and then a list of new hymns was submitted. It altered the texts only with the utmost reluctance and most sparing of hands. The final revision process and musical choices were explained. Patrick and Cairns noted:

The preparation of the *Hymnary* occupied the Committee for four and a half years. In all, they had fifty-four whole-day meetings; the Music Sub-Committee had twenty-three further whole-day meetings, and the other Sub-Committees had numerous and often prolonged meetings as well. . . . Without exception, however, they brought enthusiasm to the task, and their eagerness in the common interest made the work an unalloyed delight.[48]

Hymns now were firmly established and the claim was made by Patrick that to Presbyterians, the hymn book, with the Psalter, occupied the place of a liturgy, and gave a voice in the offices of public worship.[49] For the hymnal, this place had been established in only a few decades.

---

46 *The Church Hymnary, Revised Edition*, Oxford: Oxford University Press/Humphrey Milford, 1927, p. vi.

47 James Moffatt and Millar Patrick, *Handbook to the Church Hymnary, Revised Edition with Supplement*, London: Geoffrey Cumberlege/Oxford University Press, 1935, p. xxx.

48 Moffat and Patrick, *Handbook to the Church Hymnary, Revised Edition with Supplement*, p. xxxix.

49 Moffat and Patrick, *Handbook to the Church Hymnal, Revised Edition with Supplement*, p. xvi.

The Church of Scotland and forms for worship

The established Church moved into the twentieth century still without any officially authorised book of worship. In many ways there was no need because the Church Service Society's *Euchologion* had proved extremely popular with Church of Scotland ministers. However, the Church did have to respond to the First World War. In her thesis 'Ritual and Remembrance', which focused on the Church of Scotland's response to four wars of the twentieth century, Fiona Douglas wrote:

> The First World War thus precipitated a great deal of heart-searching and questioning in the Church (of Scotland). Now was the time to make a real and lasting impact on the life of the nation at a time of great personal and national crisis. The crisis which lay at the very heart of civilian and military experience was the sheer scale of human loss and grief.[50]

Douglas has shown how the Church of Scotland, through various committees of the General Assembly, attempted to address the liturgical, moral and spiritual issues raised by the war. The Committee on Aids to Devotion was instructed by the 1915 General Assembly 'to have regard to their future work to the circumstances and spiritual needs of the people at this grave time in our national need'.[51] *A Form and Order of Divine Service for the Day of Humble Prayer, Intercession, and Thanksgiving* was issued for 31 December 1916. It began with the traditional votum and other scripture sentences, followed by a prayer of contrition and the Lord's Prayer. Specific psalmody, hymnody and scripture lessons were provided, and then came a series of long collect-type prayers of intercession, including one for sailors and soldiers. A sermon was specified with appropriate prayers before and after, and the service concluded with a hymn, the offering, the national Anthem and the Benediction.[52]

Throughout the war, the Committee did issue services as the need arose. At the end of the war, a Scottish national service of thanksgiving and remembrance was held in St Giles' Cathedral, Edinburgh. It was entitled 'Order of Divine Service' and was attended by the King and Queen. In her

---

50 Fiona Carol Douglas, 'Ritual and Remembrance: The Church of Scotland and National Services of Thanksgiving and Remembrance after Four Wars in the Twentieth Century', PhD thesis, University of Edinburgh, 1996, pp. 25–6. See also Stewart J. Brown, '"A Solemn Purification by Fire": Responses to the Great War in the Scottish Presbyterian Churches, 1914–19', *Journal of Ecclesiastical History* 45 (1994), pp. 82–104; David Coulter, 'Garrisoning the Nation's Soul: Calvinism, Douglas Haig and Scottish Presbyterian Chaplaincy on the Western Front', in Michael Snape and Edward Madigan (eds), *The Clergy in Khaki: New Perspectives on British Army Chaplaincy in the First World War*, Farnham: Ashgate, 2013, pp. 75–93.

51 Douglas, 'Ritual and Remembrance', p. 22, with reference to 'Report of the Committee on Aids to Devotion', in *Reports on the Schemes of the Church of Scotland with Legislative Acts Passed by the General Assembly, 1916*, Edinburgh: William Blackwood & Sons, 1916, p. 782.

52 My thanks to Douglas Galbraith for tracking down a copy for me.

study of the national services in Scotland, Douglas has argued that this particular service was drawn up by Dr Andrew Wallace Williamson of St Giles', though any direct documentary evidence does not seem to have survived.[53] It began with Psalm 100, 'All People that on earth do dwell', and then Wallace Williamson led the congregation in prayer, ending with the Lord's Prayer. The congregation sang the call to thanksgiving, which was taken from Psalm 106. An Old Testament lesson from 1 Chronicles 29:10–13 was read by the Revd Dr Drummond, Moderator of the United Free Church. Psalm 46 was sung, and the second reading from Revelation 21:1–4 was read by the Revd S. J. Ramsay, Minister of Crathie. Psalm 124 was sung, and Wallace Williamson led a prayer of commemoration and thanksgiving. According to a report in *The Scotsman* newspaper, he 'gave thanks for the vision of a better world, for the devotion of the king, the honour of statesmen, the willing submission of all parties to authority, and the unity of national life realized in the presence of danger'.[54] A wreath was laid on the steps in front of the communion table. Paraphrase 66 was sung, followed by the Doxology and Benediction. The National Anthem was sung as the King and Queen left by way of the Thistle Chapel. Fiona Douglas expressed the opinion that the distinction between the nation and God tended to be blurred and the service lacked any specific reference to the sacrifice of those who had died in the war, or to a martyr's death equated with the saints.[55]

The reports of the Committee on Aids to Devotion between 1903 and 1923 mainly reported on sales of publications and divulge very little on the work of the Committee. However, the report of 1923, with Wallace Williamson the convener, stated: 'The Committee have pleasure in submitting to the General Assembly the volume entitled "Prayers for Divine Service in Church and Home" which the last General Assemblies authorised them to publish.'[56] The Preface noted that the prayer of the Committee 'is that it will prove a real aid to devotion, and that by the blessing of God it will foster a deeper spirit of worship in the hearts of our people'.[57] The publication of *Prayers for Divine Service in Church and Home*, 1923, represented the first substantial service book for public worship that the Church of Scotland had officially sponsored. As with the books of the United Free Church, the contents of this book were divided into several parts. Part I contained orders for Morning and Evening for five Sundays as well as two services for the young. Part II contained services for the

---

53 Douglas, 'Ritual and Remembrance', p. 37. The service is included in an appendix, pp. 237–40.

54 As summarised by Douglas, 'Ritual and Remembrance', p. 40, citing 'Thanksgiving in St Giles': An Impressive Service', *The Scotsman*, 22 November 1918, p. 6.

55 Douglas, 'Ritual and Remembrance', p. 45.

56 *Reports of the Schemes of the Church of Scotland with the Legislative Acts Passed by the General Assembly 1923*, Edinburgh: Blackwood, 1923, pp. 945–6, p. 946.

57 *Prayers for Divine Service in Church and Home*, Edinburgh: William Blackwood & Sons, 1923, p. vi.

sacraments and ordinances, such as burial. Part III had prayers for family worship, and Part IV, prayers for the sick. Parts V, VI and VII had, respectively, prayers for sacred and natural seasons, prayers for occasional and special use and additional material for Divine (Sunday) worship. The book also contained a lectionary. The inspiration of the *Euchologion* is evident, though American and South African Presbyterian worship books were also sources. The order for Sunday Morning services was by now an established pattern, if not always followed. It began with a call to worship with the Reformed votum, 'Our help is in the name of the Lord, etc.', opening prayer of invocation, confession and prayer for pardon, supplication and the Lord's Prayer. A psalm might be chanted before the Old Testament Reading, with a psalm or hymn before the New Testament reading. The Apostles' Creed might be recited. Intercessions followed, a psalm or hymn, prayer before the sermon, sermon, prayer, the offering, a further psalm or hymn and the blessing or grace. The copy in my possession indicates that the owner used the fifth orders for Morning and Evening with some permanent emendations. For example, in the Pardon at Morning Service, the last lines have words crossed through: 'but according to Thy mercy remember Thou us, and for Thy goodness' sake pardon and bless us; through Jesus Christ our Lord.'[58] In the Evening Service, in the supplications, the words 'with enlarged hearts may' have been crossed through – perhaps they were too suggestive of a heart disease rather than largesse.[59]

The Communion Service began with a Call to Prayer (scripture sentences), and then the Collect for Purity from the Book of Common Prayer. After a Confession and Prayer for Pardon, the Prayer of the Veil was recited. A psalm could then be said or sung, followed by the lections – an Old Testament prophetical book, then praise, followed by the Epistle and Gospel readings. These were followed by the Nicene Creed and then intercessions. After a hymn, sermon and Collects, the Offerings might be received and an invitation to the Lord's Table given. A rubric entitled 'The Entrance' suggests an imitation of the Great Entrance of the Eastern orthodox rite: 'Then, during the singing of Paraphrase xxxv. the elements shall be brought into the Church and reverently laid upon the Holy table; and the Minister shall say . . .'[60]

This was followed by the reading of the Institution narrative as a warrant. An Offertory Prayer encapsulated an idea of Eucharistic offering – 'we offer and present unto Thee this bread and this cup, in token that we are thine'. This collect wove together some material from the post-communion prayer of the Book of Common Prayer. Sursum corda with responses followed, and a Eucharistic Prayer, which was an abbreviated version of that in the *Euchologion* and, as with previous rites, did not include the

58 *Prayers for Divine Service*, p. 43.
59 *Prayers for Divine Service*, p. 48.
60 *Prayers for Divine Service*, p. 66.

Institution Narrative within the prayer. The epiclesis asked the Father to send the Spirit 'to bless and consecrate' the gifts of bread and wine. Intercessions followed, and then a twofold Agnus Dei, the Lord's Prayer and the Sancta sanctis. The Words of Institution were repeated for the fraction and lifting of the cup. After Communion, the Peace was given (not exchanged), followed by a thanksgiving, Psalm 103:1–4 and a blessing, as in the Book of Common Prayer.

The service of baptism began with the votum and an exhortation, the Apostles' Creed and questions to the sponsors. A prayer requested that the candidate 'being received by Thee in Holy Baptism, may be washed in Thy washing and renewed in Thy renewing'.[61] The prayer included a petition to sanctify the water 'to the holy use unto which Thou hast ordained it'.

Whereas the United Presbyterian Church, in its 1920 edition of *Directory and Forms*, had provided a form for dedicating memorials, no such service was included in this Church of Scotland book.[62] However, in the wake of the huge death toll of the war, we do find more references to the departed. First Morning Service included the petition: 'O Lord most high, we thank Thee for the great multitude of the redeemed, and for all dear to us whom thou hast taken to Thy nearer presence', with space for names. The communion service included: 'and rejoicing in the communion of saints, we remember with thanksgiving all Thy faithful servants, and those dear to us who are asleep in Jesus'. The Burial Service contained the petition:

> We thank Thee, O Father, for all Thy faithful servants departed this life in Thy faith and fear, and especially for *him* whom Thou hast now taken to Thyself. For all thy loving-kindness towards *him* through *his* earthly life we give Thee thanks. . . . we thank Thee . . . that *he* is entered into the rest that remaineth for Thy people.[63]

Whereas prior to the war there was opposition to James Cooper and T. N. Adamson's prayers associated with the departed, the sheer numbers of deaths in the war had served to make some reference a pastoral necessity.

There was some unease with parts of *Prayers for Divine Service*, especially the Holy Communion service, and the 1923 book was remitted to a special committee for further consideration. This committee reported in 1925 and, with regards to the Communion service, put forward the following alterations:

---

61 My copy has pencil lines through these words, though the line slips to below the line – it is unclear whether this was for study purposes, or for omission. *Prayers for Divine Service*, p. 75.

62 There was, however, an Advisory Committee on war memorials whose Report of 1919 offered a guide for suitable objects and materials for such memorials. James Cooper was the convener.

63 *Prayers for Divine Service*, pp. 96–7.

1. Deletion of all marginal rubrics.
2. The words 'may' and 'shall' replaced in all directions by the present tense.
3. Insertion of Apostles' Creed, the Nicene Creed being printed as an alternative.
4. The Triumphal Hymn [Sanctus] printed as part of the Eucharistic Prayer.
5. Certain prayers transferred and other alterations made, which will be found indicated in the printed form in the Appendix.[64]

The Committee also recommended adding a shorter form of Communion, a service for Adult baptism, and that in the section devoted to Family Worship, prayers commemorating the departed should be inserted.[65] As a result of the recommendations, a second edition of *Prayers for Divine Service* was published in 1929. In the full Communion service, the Prayer of the Veil now came immediately before the Sursum corda in place of the 1923 Offertory Prayer. The intercessions that followed the petition for consecration were transferred to after Communion. A second, much shorter form for Communion was added, though it contained the same Eucharistic Prayer and petition for consecration as the fuller service.

The fact that the Church of Scotland had a service book authorised by the General Assembly did not, and was never intended to, curtail private individual publications. Even while work had begun on compiling material for *Prayer for Divine Service*, Hugh Cameron (1855–1934), minister of Newington, Edinburgh, published *Prayers for Use in Public Worship* in 1921. Cameron's church, 'a typical Georgian building', in 1873 was the first church in Edinburgh to install an organ after Lee's at Old Greyfriars.[66] Cameron was minister there from 1898 until 1932. In the Preface to *Prayers for Use in Public Worship*, he stated that, 'This volume is not a compilation from other published sources, but a selection from the devotional services which the author has prepared for his own use during a ministry of thirty-eight years.'[67] His collection resembles more the 'specimens' of the previous century and shows little if any influence of the *Euchologion*. Morning and Evening Services for five Sundays were given, as well as services for special occasions such as Christmas. It also contained Cameron's services for baptism, Communion, marriage, visitation of the sick, burial of the dead and ordination and induction of ministers, and

64 'Report of Special Committee Appointed to Reconsider the Volume "Prayers for Divine service, 1923"', in *Reports to the General Assembly*, May 1925, Edinburgh: Blackwood, 1925, p. 1022.

65 *Reports to the General Assembly*, 1925, p. 1023.

66 A. Ian Dunlop, *The Kirks of Edinburgh 1560–1984*, Edinburgh: Scottish Record Society, 1989, p. 480; David A. Stewart, revised by Alan Buchan, *Organs in Scotland: A Revised List*, Edinburgh: Edinburgh Society of Organists, 2018, p. 160 (under Queens Hall).

67 Hugh Cameron, *Prayers for Use in Public Worship*, Edinburgh: Alexander Brunton, 1921, p. 3.

ordination and appointment of elders. His style may be illustrated from the first prayer from Morning Service for the first Sunday of the month:

> Almighty God our heavenly Father whom none but the pure of heart can know; keep us this day without sin we beseech thee, shelter us from the strain and clamour of common cares, open our minds to the truths and inspiration of the Gospel, through the exercises of public worship unite us with all them that serve thee in truth and sincerity, and so cause thy presence to abide with us that our worship may be of the spirit and the fruit of it eternal life; through Jesus Christ our Lord.[68]

The Communion was entitled 'An Order for the Sacrament of the Supper when there is no Sermon'. It began with scripture sentences, a short prayer of thanksgiving for Christ, the metrical Psalm 23 or some other, followed by a prayer for forgiveness of sins, and intercessions. The doxology, Old Testament lesson, Hymn, New Testament lesson and hymn were followed by an Address. The Institution narrative from 1 Corinthians 11 was read as a warrant, and then Cameron provided a prayer of Christological praise and intercession for the Church and for the communicants. The petition relating to the bread and wine was circumspect about divine presence associated with the elements:

> Almighty God who hast made of things outward and visible, types and symbols of things inward and spiritual; grant that this bread and wine which we now set apart to a sacred use may become to us the very presence and sustaining spirit of our Lord and Redeemer, and that we, partaking of them, may grow in faith and knowledge, in meekness and charity, in love and obedience; through the same Jesus, who also taught us to pray, [Lord's Prayer].[69]

The word 'spirit' is not capitalised, and thus is not referring to the Holy Spirit. Cameron's doctrine and forms are a reminder that many ministers stood aloof from the ideas of the Church Service Society and Scottish Church Society and wrote prayers that were fine literary pieces but closer to the older early nineteenth-century tradition of sacramental belief and liturgical expression.

Another 'private' enterprise was that of Lauchlan MacLean Watt (1867–1957). Watt was a prolific prose writer and poet, known as the piping padre from his service as a chaplain in the First World War. He was minister of Turriff (1897–1901), of Alloa and Tullibody (1901–11), St Stephen's, Edinburgh (1911–23) and of Glasgow Cathedral (1923–34). He was elected Moderator of the Church of Scotland in 1933. In 1903, Watt published a collection of Communion Addresses, which are beautifully written and

---

68 Cameron, *Prayers for Use in Public Worship*, p. 7.
69 Cameron, *Prayers for Use in Public Worship*, p. 119.

8.1 The Revd Lauchlan
MacLean Watt

tend towards a memorialist concept of the Eucharist.[70] In 1904 he published a book of prayers, though in the brief preface he wrote that it was not so much a book of prayers as a book of prayer, and the prayers were emotions rather than forms that had all been lived and felt.[71] He was a member of the Joint Revision Committee that produced *The Church Hymnary, Revised Edition*, 1927. When he was at St Stephen's, Edinburgh, Watt published *The Minister's Manual*, undated, but published by W. F. Henderson, Edinburgh, 1920, which used Old English script for certain headings and scriptural formulae; a second revised, augmented and also undated edition in very plain type was published by Allenson & Co, London, in 1934. This book contained services for the sacraments and ordinances and special services.

In 1924 he published *Prayers for Public Worship*, which was advertised as the 'Service Book, Glasgow Cathedral'.[72] Since the Preface of this latter referred readers to *The Minister's Manual* for orders of those specific services, it may be assumed that Watt also used these forms in Glasgow Cathedral.

St Mungo's Cathedral, Glasgow, had undergone restoration in the nineteenth century, rather like that of St Giles', Edinburgh. It had at one time been divided to house three churches – the Inner High Kirk in the choir and presbytery; the Outer Kirk in the nave; and the Barony in the crypt. In 1835 the Outer Kirk and Barony were moved, and the galleries of the Inner Kirk were removed and so the building became home to a single cathedral congregation. In the 1860s, the Munich stained glass was installed,

8.2 Pulpit, Glasgow Cathedral

70 L. MacLean Watt, *The Communion Table*, London: Hodder & Stoughton, 1903. They are meant, so the Preface says, to be plain and practical teachings.

71 *By Still Waters*, Edinburgh: Blackwood & Sons, 1904. Some are suitable for public worship.

72 Watt's own copy, with some handwritten additions and emendations, survives at Glasgow Cathedral. Andrew G. Ralston, *Lauchlan MacLean Watt: Preacher, Poet and Piping Padre*, Glasgow: Society of Friends of Glasgow Cathedral, 2018, p. 42.

and in 1879 so was an organ. It was the Glasgow counterpart to St Giles', Edinburgh, with many civic services. Watt had become a member of the Church Service Society in 1905 when minister of Alloa, and so it may be presumed he was acquainted with the *Euchologion*. When minister of St Stephen's, Edinburgh, he must also have been acquainted with Cameron Lees's *Book of Common Order for use in St. Giles*, and this may well have prompted him, when becoming minister at Glasgow Cathedral, to establish a comparable form there with his *Prayers for Public Worship*. Andrew Ralston, drawing on back issues of the congregational magazine, writes:

> At the start of MacLean Watt's ministry there were three diets of worship every Sunday, at 11 am, 2 pm and 6.30 pm, in addition to a service in the Royal Infirmary next door at 4.30 pm and a mission service in the Halls at 5.30 pm . . . During the week and on Saturdays a short daily service took place in the cathedral at 3 pm.[73]

The Minister's Manual had no Preface and so its rationale is not disclosed, though facing the contents page was printed 1 Corinthians 14:40, 'Let all things be done decently and in order'. The service of baptism is brief and included the hymn 'A little child the Saviour came', a statement on the meaning of baptism, the Apostles' Creed, questions, the act of baptism, the Aaronic blessing, the hymn 'When He cometh, when He Cometh' and the final Benediction. A rubric prior to the statement on the meaning of the sacrament directed: 'Then shall follow a prayer asking the presence of God in the Holy Sacrament, with the consecration of the elements used in the sacred rite.' This suggests Watt used his own extemporised form, and although he speaks of 'consecration of the elements', it allowed other ministers to use the service without being tied to Watt's theology of the prayer over the water.

The Order of Holy Communion was also brief, and in contrast to the form of Cameron Lees for St Giles', sits lightly to the *Euchologion*'s order. The choir might sing the hymn 'According to Thy gracious word', and during the entry of the clergy, Paraphrase 30, 'Come, let us to the Lord our God', was sung. Prayer and a scripture reading followed. Then Watt provided more scripture sentences, Psalm 23 (cf. Cameron), the Lord's Prayer, Psalm 116:13–19, sermon and prayer. Paraphrase 35 was then sung, during which the elements were brought in. In the 1934 edition, a brief Prayer of Access was provided:

> O Jesus, brightness of eternal glory, and comfort of the pilgrim soul, come nigh to us, for without Thee our days are devoid of gladness, our night has no promise, and our table is bare. Open the door of our prison-house, barred with our sin, and enter in and possess us, for Thy love's sake.[74]

73 Ralston, *Lauchlan MacLean Watt*, p. 41.
74 L. MacLean Watt, *The Minister's Manual*, London: Allenson & Co, 1934, pp. 18–19.

The Pauline warrant followed, an exhortation and the 'Prayer of Thanksgiving and Consecration'. In the 1920 edition, this was simply a heading, leaving the minister to extemporise. However, in the 1934 edition a brief form was provided, with nine lines of thanks and a four-line petition for consecration: 'Bless, we beseech Thee, these elements of bread and wine in this Holy Sacrament; and give us now, through faith, true communion in the Body and Blood of Him who died for us. For His Name's sake, Amen.'[75] Directions for the fraction and distribution were given:

> Thereafter the Minister shall say –
> According to the example, institution, and command of Jesus Christ, I take this bread and break it. This is the body of Christ, broken on the Cross, for your sins, and for the world.
> Here he shall himself partake and give to the Elders on either hand.
> Again, according to the example, institution, and command of Jesus Christ, I take this cup. This is the New Testament in the blood of Christ, shed upon the Cross, for your sins, and for the world.
> Here he shall himself partake and give to the Elders on either hand.[76]

Watt made provision for a Post-Communion Address, Psalm 103 and Benediction.

Both the baptismal and the communion service show Watt's concern for ordered worship, but rather like Cameron's services, illustrate an independence from the *Euchologion*, thus giving Glasgow Cathedral its own distinct 'Watt use'.

Prayers for Public Worship provided twenty-one 'General' services as well as special services of Christmas Sunday, Christmas Day, Epiphany, Easter and for municipal occasions. The service structure was almost the same as assumed by Cameron and in other Sunday services, though Watt had an unvarying Benediction.

Two other publications are also of importance. In 1936, James Ferguson, minister of Crieff, published *Prayers for Common Worship*. This was an anthology of prayers for the church year 'as an aid to ministers in their preparation for the service of the Sanctuary week by week'.[77] The sources were listed at the back and included one from Watt. Prayers were provided for morning and evening and an outline service was also offered by the author.[78]

The Revd J. G. Grant Fleming, a later successor to James Cooper at East Church of St Nicholas, Aberdeen, published *Prayers for Every Day*

---

75 Watt, *The Minister's Manual*, 1934, p. 19.

76 Lauchlan MacLean Watt, *The Minister's Manual*, Edinburgh: W. F. Henderson, 1920, pp. 14–15; this edition used Old English script for 'According to the example . . . bread', 'According to the example . . . cup', but it was not used in the 1934 edition.

77 James Ferguson, *Prayers for Common Worship*, London: Allenson & Co., 1936, p. ix.

78 Ferguson, *Prayers for Common Worship*, p. xi.

in 1938. It offered the forms of daily Prayer that had been resumed in St Mary's Chapel and the Preface appealed to Cooper's Daily Service. This collection also included services for 'certain Seasons in the Christian Year', as well as an Order of Communion, baptism and marriage. The communion service was modelled closely on that of *Prayers for Divine Service*. After an Invocation (Collect for Purity), Confession and Supplication, Psalm, Epistle and Gospel, came intercessions with congregational response and then the Nicene creed. The Pauline Warrant was read, followed by the Prayer of the Veil. The Eucharistic Prayer was almost identical to that of *Prayers for Divine Service*, save it omitted the final intercessory part and added a few lines from the Book of Common Prayer self-oblation. The remainder followed *Prayers for Divine Service*, minus the alternative post-communion thanksgiving. The baptismal rite too was mainly that of *Prayers for Divine Service*, with some emendations and omissions.

Mention must also be made of the *Chapel Service Book* of the University of St Andrews, 1931, and the *Order of Service* of St Bride's Parish Church, Partick (no date). St Andrews already had a psalter with canticles and psalms pointed for chanting by Frederick Sawyer, the organist to the University in 1928. The editorial committee of the *Chapel Service Book* drew on a variety of sources. It provided five orders for morning worship and a form for evening worship, as well as special prayers for the university. The services were patterned on the Church of England forms, as well as the services of the *Euchologion*. The typical order consisted of opening scripture sentences, confession and prayer of pardon, versicles and responses, Psalm, Old Testament reading, hymn or canticle, New Testament reading, prayer, hymn or anthem, collect, sermon, collect, offertory, hymn or Paraphrase and Benediction. No Communion Order was given.[79]

St Bride's, Partick, was one of the churches founded by John Macleod of Govan, an 'early Gothic' building designed by Peter MacGregor Chalmers and dedicated in 1897. The church closed in 1975. The first minister, James Mackenzie Kirkpatrick, was a member of the Scottish Church Society, the Church Service Society and the Aberdeen Ecclesiological Society.[80] The order provided an outline for Morning Worship and then for Holy Communion, which seems to have been celebrated once a month.[81] It bears no date but has similarities to Cooper's form for the General Assembly and to Wotherspoon's order. The service began with a metrical psalm or hymn, followed by a call to prayer, confession of sins, collect for purity, collect for sanctification, followed by the Benedictus or Gloria in excelsis. Provision was made for an Epistle and Gospel reading, Nicene Creed, hymn and

---

79 *The St Andrews University Psalter*, St Andrews: W. C. Henderson & Sons, 1928; *University of St Andrews Chapel Service Book*, St Andrews: W. C. Henderson & Son, 1931.

80 Tom Davidson Kelly, *Living Stones: The Daughter Churches of Govan Parish 1730–1919*, Glasgow: Friends of Govan Old, 2007, p. 42. Kirkpatrick was co-author of *A Manual of Church Doctrine*, 1919.

81 C. G. Inglis, 'St Bride's Parish Church', *Liturgical Studies* 1 (1971), pp. 45–8.

sermon. An invitation was extended to 'All Christians' to partake. After the Offering came the grace, Psalm 24:7–10, salutation, dedication of the offering, and Sursum corda leading to the Sanctus. Then came the Prayer of Consecration, during which the bread was broken and the cup was shown. The prayer continued with intercession and remembrance of the faithful departed, the Lord's Prayer, Prayer of Humble Access and 'Holy things for holy persons'. Agnus Dei and the Peace preceded Communion. The rite finished with a prayer of thanksgiving, Psalm 103:1–5 and a Benediction. It expressed the 'Scoto-Catholic' tradition of the Govan churches.

These private enterprises once again illustrate survival of older usages alongside devolution of newer forms and material that was recovered from the wider and older traditions of the pre-Reformation Church.

The Reunited Church of Scotland and 1940 *Book of Common Order*

Douglas Murray wrote:

On Wednesday, 2nd October 1929, the city of Edinburgh witnessed yet another important event in the history of Scotland, the union of the two largest Presbyterian Churches after almost two centuries of separation. The day began with separate meetings of the general assemblies of the Church of Scotland and the United Free Church of Scotland. The ministers and elders then filed out of their respective assembly halls in the Lawnmarket and on the Mound to meet at the junction of the High Street and Bank Street. In the view of at least one observer, the moment when the two moderators met and clasped hands seemed to be the 'practical consummation' of union.[82]

Discussions on reunion between the Church of Scotland and the United Free Church had been underway for many years, interrupted by the First World War. The Church of Scotland prepared Articles Declaratory that were confirmed by Parliament in 1921 and cleared away many of the objections of the United Free Church regarding an established national church. The two main final architects of union were the two moderators, Alexander Martin of the United Free Church and John White of the Church of Scotland. The spontaneous response to the now famous handshake of 1929 by the two moderators was that spectators broke out in singing the words of Psalm 133:

---

82 Douglas M. Murray, *Rebuilding the Kirk: Presbyterian Reunion in Scotland 1909–1929*, Edinburgh: Scottish Academic Press, 2000, p. 1. Murray gives a full account of the discussions and legalities.

Behold, how good a thing it is,
And how becoming well,
Together such as brethren are
In Unity to Dwell.

After the two assemblies met, they processed to St Giles' for a service of thanksgiving. The service was a printed form, entitled *Union of the Church of Scotland and the United Free Church of Scotland: Form and Order of Divine Service in the cathedral Church of St. Giles on Wednesday, 2nd October at 11a.m.* The service began with Psalm 122 to the tune 'St Paul'. A brief exhortation followed and Psalm 100, the 'Old Hundreth'. The votum and another scripture sentence introduced short prayers of praise, confession, pardon and intercession, ending with the Lord's Prayer. Psalm 118:1–7 to the tune 'St Andrew' was sung, and an Old Testament lesson from Isaiah 61. The *Te Deum* was sung, followed by the New Testament lesson, Ephesians 4:1–16, and the Apostles' Creed was recited by all standing. Intercessory prayers followed, ending with the Veni Creator and the Blessing. The National Anthem was then sung, followed by the recessional hymn, 'The Church's One Foundation'. The brief service followed what was the common outline of Morning Worship. Furthermore, both Churches were at a point where, for special occasions, it was quite acceptable to use a printed set form of service and to recite the Apostles' Creed.

Clearly, what was acceptable in a form of service, at least for special occasions, had by 1929 come a long way from a typical service in 1843.

When the Church of Scotland and the United Free Church amalgamated, the 1929 edition of the Church of Scotland *Prayers for Divine Service*, and the United Free Church of Scotland *Book of Common Order*, 1928, were both new and many copies had just been printed. However, something new for the united Church would sooner or later be needed. The year 1931 saw the publication of the *Ordinal and Service Book for use in Courts of the Church*, which in addition to services for licensing and ordaining ministers and special meetings, included the service of Holy Communion for use at the General Assembly meetings. This was very similar to the form in the 1929 edition of *Prayers for Divine Service*.[83] *Prayers for the Christian Year* was published in 1935 and *Prayers for Use at Sea* in 1936. During the 1930s, the Committee on Public Worship and Aids to Devotion published a series of Occasional Papers on historical and practical aspects of worship, such as 'The Scottish Collects', 'The Choir Master and the Choir', 'On the Improvement of Public Worship' and 'The Christian Year'.[84] Another short

---

83 *Ordinal and Service Book for use in Courts of the Church*, Edinburgh: The Church of Scotland Committee on Publications, 1931, pp. 43–54; *Ordinal and Service Book of the Use of Presbyteries*, Edinburgh: The Church of Scotland Committee on Publications, nd, pp. 43–54.

84 These are undated. I am aware of twelve. 1. George T. Wright, *Choir Unions*; 2. Millar Patrick, *The Story of the Scottish Psalm Tunes*; 3. W. W. D. Gardiner, *On the Improvement of Public Worship*; 4. Millar Patrick, *The Order of Holy Communion*; 5. Millar Patrick, *The*

pamphlet, printed by Blackwood of Edinburgh in 1931, was a sermon by the Revd Ninian Hill (1861–1946), an assistant minister of St Cuthbert's, Edinburgh, who became the first chaplain (1930–1) of St Andrew's Church, Jerusalem. Entitled *The Scottish Communion Service*, the pamphlet gave a historical outline of how the service had developed in the Church of Scotland tradition, noting the importance of the Church Service Society *Euchologion*, now 'largely superseded by the book of "Prayers for Divine Service"', and how the communion service was substantially the same as that used in St Giles' Cathedral for the General Assembly.[85] Hill argued that at the Last Supper there were six actions that the Church replicates – taking the bread and cup; giving thanks; blessing the bread; breaking the bread; giving the bread and cup; and receiving the elements.[86] He illustrated some of these with quotations from the communion liturgy in *Prayers for Divine Service*, and an appendix to the published sermon gave the Prayer of the Veil and the Eucharistic Prayer from that.

Although the experience of the First World War had led to remembrance of the departed, that it was still controversial in some quarters is evidenced by the experience of Dr Charles Warr of St Giles', Edinburgh. Warr noted:

The following words occurred in the prayer I offered at the Stone of Remembrance on Armistice Day, 1931: 'We remember before thee with reverence our fellow-citizens who laid down their lives in the cause of justice and freedom; to thee we commend each one of them: evermore look upon them in the fullness of thy tender love and mercy.' The following day the trouble began.[87]

The Moderator of the Free Church of Scotland, who had been officially present, sent a letter of protest to the Press, the Press turned it into a debate and the Revd Nahum Levison wrote a tract condemning prayer for the dead.[88] Warr opined:

Scottish Collects: From the Scottish Metrical Psalter of 1595; 6. (no author) *A Course of Reading for the Church Organist*; 7. Thomas Marjoribanks and John Wilson Baird, *A Year's Praise*; 8. G. Wauchope Stewart and G. T. Wright, *Musical Services*; 9. Alexander Smart, *The Choir Master and His Choir*; 10. Alexander Chisholm, *A Primer of Psalmody*; 11. Thomas Majoribanks, *The Christian Year*; 12. Oswald Milligan, *The Scottish Communion Office and its Historical Background*. This last appears to be c.1939. Mention should also be made of the Kerr Lectures given by D. H. Hislop, published in 1935 as *Our Heritage in Public Worship*, T&T Clark, Edinburgh. This was a broad study of Christian worship, and Hislop argued that the Church of Scotland was an inheritor of all that is valuable in the worship of Christendom.

85 Ninian Hill, *The Scottish Communion Service: A Sermon*, Edinburgh and London: William Blackwood & Sons, 1931, p. 9.

86 Hill, *The Scottish Communion Service*, pp. 10–11.

87 Charles Laing Warr, *The Glimmering Landscape*, London: Hodder & Stoughton, 1960, p. 172.

88 Frederick Levison, *Christian and Jew: The Life of Leon Levison 1881–1936*, Edinburgh: The Pentland Press, 1989, pp. 232–4. Leon was brother of Nahum. I have not been able to access a copy of his tract.

The collapse of the old geocentric conception of the universe, the mellow-
ing influence of enlightened Biblical criticism and scientific thought upon
rigid theological dogma and the ascendancy of the evolutionary theory as
regarded both spirit and matter had successfully removed the antiquated
conceptions of a geographical heaven and hell from the speculations of
temperate and intelligent Christians.[89]

Warr cited Dr John White of the Barony, Dr Norman Maclean of St Cuthbert's, Dr Archibald Fleming of London and Professor A. J. Gossip as those
who also included the departed in their intercessory prayers.[90]

In 1936, the Committee on Public Worship and Aids to Devotion
reported that the time was right for the preparation of a new *Book of
Common Order*. It calculated that the 1929 and 1928 books would be out
of print within the next five years. It advised:

In several respects these books show a divergence in practice between
the two sections of the now united Church, and it is felt that opportunity
should now be taken to prepare a new Book of Common Order representative of the mind of the united Church. It is desirable that a work of such
importance should not be hurried, and that every effort should be made
to give most careful consideration to its various parts. It is estimated that
the work may occupy a period of four years.[91]

The convener, Dr Oswald B. Milligan, was minister of Corstorphine, Edinburgh, and the son of the late Professor William Milligan.[92] Following in
his father's footsteps, Oswald Milligan was a member of the Church Service
Society (1907), becoming President 1938–40, and was also a member of
the Scottish Church Society. In 1938 he published *The Practice of Prayer*,
which was a series of Addresses on private prayer and meditation.[93] In
1939 he wrote a short pamphlet entitled *The Scottish Communion Office*,
which charted a history from Knox through 1637 and to the *Directory*.
The last two pages mentioned the 1923/29 and the 1928 books of the two
united Churches, and announced that a new communion service had been
drawn up for the new *Book of Common Order, 1940*. He added that the
gospel 'finds its highest expression in the sacrament of the Lord's Supper'.[94]
He also wrote a pamphlet for the Committee on Youth, entitled *Holy
Communion*. In this little work he taught his readers that the sacrament

---

89 Warr, *The Glimmering Landscape*, p. 173.

90 Warr, *The Glimmering Landscape*, p. 174.

91 *Reports of the General Assembly 1936*, Edinburgh: Blackwood, 1936, pp. 881–2.

92 D. M. Thomson, *The Corstorphine Heirloom: A History of the Old Parish Church of
Corstorphine*, Edinburgh: John Blackie, 1946.

93 Oswald B. Milligan, *The Practice of Prayer*, Edinburgh: Church of Scotland Committee
on Publications, 1938.

94 Oswald Milligan, *The Scottish Communion Office and Its Historical Background*,
Edinburgh: The Church of Scotland Committee on Publications, nd (*c*.1939), p. 20.

not only 'represents' but also 'seals' and 'applies' Christ and his benefits. The sacrament was explained under the headings 'memorial', 'communion', 'thanksgiving and pledge' and 'membership of the Body of Christ'.[95] Milligan died quite suddenly in 1940. He had given the Warrack Lectures for 1940 and these were published posthumously in 1941. They drew on and explained much of the theological thinking behind the 1940 *Book of Common Order*. Whatever might be the case in actual Church of Scotland practice, Milligan gave pre-eminent place to the communion service, writing:

> Whether celebrated with all the gorgeous ceremonial of Rome or with the severe simplicity of the Scottish parish church, the merely outward accompaniments of this service make an appeal to the senses which is more vivid, more moving then in any other service.[96]

Echoing his father, Milligan stressed that in the Eucharist it is Christ himself who, acting through his Church, consecrates the bread and wine to be vehicles whereby his presence is communicated to us.[97]

Another member of the Committee on Public Worship and Aids to Devotion was W. D. Maxwell. Maxwell had served as a minister in Canada and England and in 1931 had published a detailed study and commentary on the *Genevan Form of Prayers*, 1556, and in 1936 *An Outline of Christian Worship*. The Secretary of the Committee, W. M. Page, was a noted hymnologist, who, like Milligan, died in 1940.

The Book of Common Order was set out in eleven sections. Section II contained orders for Morning and Evening worship and services for children. Section III contained the sacraments and ordinances, which included not only marriage and burial but ordination of elders and deacons and a variety of dedication services.

The structure of the Morning and Evening services followed the standard sequence represented in the *Euchologion* and the respective denominational books prior to the reunion. The baptismal rite was compiled from the 1928 and 1929 liturgies and incorporated revisions made in 1939. A prayer requested: 'Sanctify this water to the spiritual use to which Thou hast ordained it.'[98] The book provided for a first order for Communion, a short order for a second table, an alternative order and a short order. The first order and the shorter order were based on those in *Prayers for*

---

95 Oswald B. Milligan, *Holy Communion*, The Church of Scotland Committee on Youth, Edinburgh: William Blackwood & Sons, nd.

96 Oswald B. Milligan, *The Ministry of Worship*, Oxford: Oxford University Press, 1941, p. 92.

97 Milligan, *The Ministry of Worship*, p. 111.

98 A detailed commentary on the sources of baptismal and confirmation rites is found in William Desmond Bailie, 'The Rites of Baptism and Admission of Catechumens ('Confirmation') according to the Liturgy and History of the Church of Scotland', PhD thesis, Queen's University Belfast, 1959.

Divine Service, 1929 edition, and the *Ordinal and Service Book for use in Courts of the Church*, 1931. The alternative order was based on the *Book of Common Order*, 1928. Attention here will be focused on the first order, the sources for which were tabulated in detail by John H. Barkley.[99]

After a call to worship, a psalm or hymn was to be sung, followed by scriptural sentences from the 1929 book, which was also the source for the Book of Common Prayer Collect for Purity. A confession of sin and prayer for pardon were followed by a canticle, psalm or hymn, lections, Nicene Creed, intercessions and sermon. Scripture sentences of invitation were read, followed by Psalm 24:7–10, Paraphrase 35 or Hymn 320, or another suitable psalm or hymn. During the singing the elements were brought into the church and placed on the 'Holy table'. The Prayer of the Veil and a prayer offering the bread and wine were from the 1929 book. The Institution was read as a warrant, followed by the Sursum corda and Eucharistic Prayer. This was primarily the prayer found in the 1931 *Ordinal and Service Book*. However, the paragraph that was originally inspired by *Apostolic Constitutions* 8, 'Not as we ought, but as we are able', was expanded the anamnesis paragraph underwent a rephrasing and included the new, interesting additional phrase:

Not as we ought, but as we are able, do we bless thee for His Holy incarnation, for His perfect life on earth, for his precious sufferings and death upon the Cross, for His glorious resurrection and ascension, for His continual intercession and rule at Thy right hand, for the promise of His coming again, and for His gift of the Holy Spirit.

Wherefore, having in remembrance the work and passion of our Saviour Christ, and pleading His eternal sacrifice, we Thy servants do set forth this memorial, which He hath commanded us to make; and we most humbly beseech thee to send down Thy Holy Spirit to sanctify both us and these Thine own gifts of bread and wine which we set before Thee . . .[100]

This section of the prayer could be claimed to be the triumph of the William Milligan–James Cooper–H. J. Wotherspoon school of thought. Central to their theology was the eternal heavenly intercession of Christ, where Christ shows and pleads his sacrifice before the Father. As Wotherspoon expressed it, 'in his showing and pleading he will have us with Him, and to be active in it.'[101] It is possible that the phrase 'pleading His eternal sacrifice' was imported by W. D. Maxwell from the 1932 *Book of Common Order* of the

---

99 John H. Barkley, 'The Eucharistic Rite in the Liturgy of the Church of Scotland', DD thesis, University of Dublin, 1949.

100 *Book of Common Order* 1940, pp. 127–28.

101 H. J. Wotherspoon, *Religious Values in the Sacraments*, Edinburgh: T&T Clark, 1928, pp. 242–3.

United Church of Canada.[102] Maxwell had studied with Richard Davidson, who was Principal of Emmanuel College, Toronto, and heavily involved in the compilation of the 1932 liturgy, and it seems that Maxwell himself had been a member of the drafting committee between 1926 and 1928. After he moved to Scotland and became a member of the Aids to Devotion Committee, the minutes of the meetings of 30 October and 27 November 1935 indicate that he had a considerable hand in the drafting of the communion rite.[103] Commenting on the phrase later, Maxwell was to write:

> What now, we may ask, is the doctrine of sacrifice in the Eucharist? This is not mentioned in our standards, but is implicit in the words of the consecration prayer contained in the *Book of Common Order*. The determinative words are 'pleading His eternal sacrifice, we thy servants do set forth this memorial'. The Scottish rite lays emphasis not upon 'the oblation once offered', though this, of course, is there in recollection and theology, but specifically upon the eternal quality of our Lord's sacrifice: it happened once for all time, but it belongs to eternity where He continually presents Himself before the Father. Similarly, the Eucharist is of eternity, and when we plead 'His eternal sacrifice', we desire Him to unite our offering and prayers with His, which is eternal, and 'this memorial' in time and space is a part of that eternal memorial. His sacrifice is not repeatable, but it is continually renewed; the 'remembering' is not mere recollection in the psychological sense (which, in fact, is never the biblical sense), but a real uniting, possible by grace and through faith, faith which is not mere intellectual assent, but a committal of the whole person to Him. It is, thus, as Calvin declares, a *vera communicatio* with Him.[104]

The Lord's Prayer was followed by the fraction, the threefold Agnus Dei and the administration. The Peace was given after Communion and four post-communion prayers were provided, the last, according to Barkley, composed by Dr William McMillan of Dunfermline drawing on unofficial Anglican sources.[105] The service concluded with Psalm 103:1–5, Paraphrase 60 or another psalm or hymn of praise, and the Anglican Blessing.

---

102 *The Book of Common Order of the United Church of Canada*, Toronto: The United Church Publishing House, 1932, p. 80.

103 John Dow, 'Richard Davidson: Churchman', in Harold W. Vaughan (ed.), *The Living Church*, Toronto: The United Church Publishing House, 1949, pp. 1–26; Minutes of Meetings of the Aids to Devotion Sub-Committee, pp. 176–7 – copies furnished to me by the Revd Colin Williamson. For fuller theological discussion, see Bryan D. Spinks, 'The Ascension and Vicarious Humanity of Christ: The Christology and Soteriology Behind the Church of Scotland's Anamnesis and Epiklesis', in J. Neil Alexander (ed.), *Time and Community*, Washington DC: The Pastoral Press, 1990, pp. 185–201. For the Canadian liturgy, see Thomas Harding and Bruce Harding, *Patterns of Worship in the United Church of Canada 1925–1987*, Toronto: Evensong Publications, 1996.

104 W. D. Maxwell, 'The Elements of Reformed Worship', in P. Edwall, E. Hayman and W. D. Maxwell (eds), *Ways of Worship*, London: SCM Press, 1951, pp. 111–24, pp. 115–116.

105 Barkley, 'The Eucharistic Rite', pp. x, 57.

A final rubric allowed for the singing of the Nunc Dimittis or Paraphrase 38:8,10–11, as the elements were removed from the church.

Maxwell, in his revised edition of *An Outline of Christian Worship*, wrote glowingly of the new book's communion rite:

> This noble and notable rite indicates the richness, centrality, and unique-ness of the Scottish liturgical tradition, its catholicity yet independence. It is not a creation de novo, but a long tradition brought to its perfec-tion. An action of the whole company, it possesses a simple but solemn ceremonial chiefly utilitarian rather than symbolic; and the celebrant normally (but not invariably) adopts the basilican posture. In its dignity of action, felicity of expression, and adequacy of content, it provides a worthy vehicle of worship entitling it to a place amongst the great rites of Christendom.[106]

Charles Warr felt vindicated, noting that eight years after the commotion about his prayers on Armistice day, 'under the editorship of Dr Oswald Milligan, and with the official imprimatur of the General Assembly, the Book of Common Order of the Church of Scotland appeared. It con-tains two prayers of intercession for the departed!'[107] John Wilson Baird expressed satisfaction with this order of Communion, but he did not think the book itself was beyond criticism. He wished for more vestry and choir prayers, was not fond of the Evening Orders and far from satisfied with the baptismal and marriage rites.[108]

Far more critical was the National Church Association. This body had been founded in 1932 'for the safeguarding of the protestant and Pres-byterian witness of the Church of Scotland', and continued the stance of Begg and Primmer in opposing anything too liturgical and that might be 'Scoto-Catholic'.[109] The Association published a small pamphlet entitled *The Book of Common Order of 1940 Examined*. In the Preface, the secre-tary, Thomas Mackenzie Donn, claimed that the publication would explain why the 1940 book ought not to have been authorised by the General Assembly and should be replaced as soon as possible by another book more compatible with the doctrine and worship of the Church of Scotland.[110] The

---

106 William D. Maxwell, *An Outline of Christian Worship*, Oxford: Oxford University Press, 1952, p. 136. It was first revised in 1945. See also W. D. Maxwell, 'The Book of Common Order of the Church of Scotland, 1940', in W. J. Kooiman and J. M. van Veen (eds), *Pro Regno Pro Sanctuario* (Festschrift for G. van Der Leeuw), Nijkerk: G. F. Callenbach N.V., 1950, pp. 323–31.

107 Warr, *The Glimmering Landscape*, p. 175.

108 John Wilson Baird, 'Second Thoughts on the Book of Common Order', *Church Service Society Annual* 19 (1949), pp. 3–10.

109 Nigel M. de S. Cameron (ed.), *Dictionary of Scottish Church History and Theology*, Edinburgh: T&T Clark, 1993, p. 619.

110 *The Book of Common Order of 1940 Examined*, Inverness-shire: The National Church Association, 1955.

whole 'atmosphere' of the book was too liturgical, and evidently had been compiled by a committee of liturgical experts, which was not fully representative of the Church.[111] The Association objected to calling the church building and the communion table 'holy', to the word 'celebrate' and the chanting of prose psalms.[112] It also singled out references to the departed in prayer, the liturgical use of creeds, the epiclesis in the Eucharistic Prayer and use of the Agnus Dei.[113] The criticisms seem to have come from a group committed to the older forms of worship represented by the Westminster *Directory*, and a suspicion of anything used by Anglicans, Roman Catholics and Eastern Orthodox as being a priori anti-Presbyterian. The Association had a small membership but nevertheless gave voice to a more conservative constituency that was unhappy about the nature of a liturgy given an official status as representing the mind of the Church. More representative was the sentiment expressed by Baird:

> For the first time since 1644, in a very real sense since the Reformation, the Church of Scotland possesses a service-book of her own, increasingly recognized, increasingly used, increasingly known throughout the world as the book which sets forth the Church of Scotland's view as to how the services of the sanctuary ought to be conducted.[114]

It remained *the* official standard until 1979, which is itself a testimony to the book's popularity and durability.

---

111 *The Book of Common Order of 1940 Examined*, pp. 4–5.
112 *The Book of Common Order of 1940 Examined*, pp. 7, 9.
113 *The Book of Common Order of 1940 Examined*, pp. 10, 11, 14–15.
114 Baird, 'Second Thoughts on the Book of Common Order', pp. 5–6.

9

The Ecumenical and Liturgical Movements and the 'Last Years of Modernity': 1940–79

The 1940 *Book of Common Order* was drawn up and produced in the first months of the Second World War. Wartime austerity was followed by post-war austerity, since the price of victory was one quarter of Britain's national wealth.[1] It was not until the mid-1950s that the United Kingdom began to enjoy a time of prosperity. The immediate post-war Labour government had created a better welfare state, with National Insurance to guarantee pensions, the creation of the National Health Service and a National Railway. A series of wartime reports by a 'Commission for the Interpretation of God's Will in the Present Crisis' for the General Assembly were republished as a single volume in 1946 and sounded an optimistic hope:

> For grounds of encouragement are by no means absent. What the Church has always had most to fear in the world is the stony soil of apathy and worldly complacency, but it is undoubtedly true that as a people we have to some extent been shaken out of such complacency by the terrible events and experiences of the last five years. There is a greater readiness among us to ask questions about the deeper foundations of our nation's life. There is evidence, both among our fighting men and among those at home, of an increased interest in what we may call the ultimate background of our human existence.[2]

Callum Brown has noted that in Scotland the period 1946 to 1956 was characterised by a frenzy of evangelical Protestant missions and revivals, and it was not until the 1960s that church membership began to decline.[3] The 1960s were a time of considerable cultural and social change, which gave rise to an ever-growing secularism where religion was regarded as outmoded and irrelevant. The influence of popular television broadcasts,

---

1 Mark Donnelly, *Sixties Britain*, Harlow: Pearson Education, 2005, p. 15.

2 Church of Scotland, *God's Will for Church and Nation. Reprinted from the Reports of the Commission for the Interpretation of God's Will in the Present crisis as Presented to the General Assembly of the Church of Scotland during the War Years*, London: SCM Press, 1946, p. 178.

3 Callum G. Brown, *The People in the Pews: Religion and Society in Scotland since 1780*, Glasgow: The Economic and Social History Society of Scotland, 1993, pp. 44–5.

increased prosperity and the rise of pop culture all contributed to what Hugh McLeod has called 'a period of decisive change in the religious history of the Western world'. This included an enormous increase in the range of beliefs and world views accessible to a majority of the population; a shift from identity in a 'Christian country' to a pluralist society, leading to changes in attitudes and the law towards divorce and abortion; and a weakening of 'socialising' into a membership of a Christian society.[4] The result was that, as with the Church of England south of the border, the Church of Scotland began to have less and less place in the nation's political and social life. At the same time, within Christian circles, there was growing optimism about the progress of ecumenism, especially in the wake of the Roman Catholic Church's Second Vatican Council. There was also much activity in liturgical revision, brought about by the Liturgical Movement and the renewed interest in sacramental theology. These various cultural and theological factors all had influences on worship in the Church of Scotland.

The 1940 *Book of Common Order* consolidated

The 1940 *Book of Common Order* was firmly established as expressing the mind of the Church of Scotland, even if many ministers used only small parts of it. The secretariat was taken over in 1940 by F. Nevill Davidson Kelly, a layman and solicitor, who oversaw the work of the Committee on Public Worship and Aids to Devotion until his sudden death in 1979, providing considerable continuity.[5] The *Ordinal and Service Book* was revised in 1954 and again in 1962; and a revised edition of *Prayers for the Christian Year* was published in 1952 (second impression 1954). Minor changes occurred – for example, in the provisions for Holy Week Thursday, the second prayer of the 1935 edition was replaced, psalms followed 'O Saviour of the world' and the collect 'O Lord Jesus Christ, who in a wonderful sacrament didst leave Thy Church a memorial' was altered.[6]

Another important resource was provided by Colin Miller, minister of Auchtergaven, Perthshire, in his *Prayers for Parish Worship*, 1948. Miller provided material for services throughout the Christian year, for Sundays and festivals, as well as Holy Week. In an Introduction, inspired by W. D. Maxwell's studies, he highlighted the fact that the Church of Scotland had failed to establish the communion service as the regular Sunday worship

---

4 Hugh McLeod, *The Religious Crisis of the 1960s*, Oxford: Oxford University Press, 2007, pp. 1–2.

5 His papers have been given to the National Archives of Scotland by his son, the late Tom Davidson Kelly. Tom and his wife Kim kindly hosted me in 2015 so that I could look at these papers.

6 See *Prayers for the Christian Year*, Oxford: Oxford University Press, 1935, pp. 39–40 and *Prayers for the Christian Year*, Oxford: Oxford University Press, 1954, pp. 97–8.

and in many parishes the normal Sunday worship was a 'decimated form of Matins'.[7] His proposed services had a threefold structure:

The Approach – Purgative
The Liturgy of the Word – Illuminative
The Liturgy of the Upper Room – Unitive

Realising that few parishes would be willing to have a weekly communion, 'The Liturgy of the Upper Room' was a 'dry form', which presented a prayer with the form of the Eucharistic Prayer but without a reference to bread/wine and body/blood.[8] Miller explained:

> The Liturgy of the Upper Room in the 'dry' form presented here is a 'great prayer' with certain distinct notes or moods. The thanksgiving in the preface and Sanctus leads on to the consecration, which is here a consecration and offering of the congregation and 'Christ in them'; and they in turn are linked with the Church militant and triumphant in the great intercession, which is completed by the Lord's Prayer standing in the place of honour as the completion and summary of all prayer, just as the Creed was the completion and summary of the Word.[9]

The Epiclesis in his great prayer prayed, 'and to send upon us thine Holy Spirit, the Lord and giver of life, to bless and consecrate our bodies, minds, and spirits, that we may give ourselves to thee, a living sacrifice, holy and without blemish'.[10]

Miller drew on a wide range of sources for his prayers. His main concern was to heed Maxwell's historical conclusions regarding the fact that Calvin's Sunday rite was the Liturgy of the Word of the old mass, and begged for completion with a Lord's Supper. Miller's form restored the pattern as a 'bridge' service to the full Communion and made the form of the Eucharistic Prayer familiar, so that when Communion was celebrated, that prayer with Sursum corda and Sanctus was not totally strange to the congregation.

Another important contribution was by Allan McArthur who, in *The Christian Year and Lectionary Reform*, argued for a more systematic liturgical calendar based on the life of Christ.[11]

---

7 Colin F. Miller, *Prayers for Parish Worship*, Oxford: Oxford University Press, 1948, p. xii. Maxwell was cited on pp. ix and x.

8 Miller, *Prayers for Parish Worship*, pp. xii and xiii.

9 Miller, *Prayers for Parish Worship*, p. xiii.

10 Miller, *Prayers for Parish Worship*, e.g. pp. 4, 8, 12.

11 Allan McArthur, *The Christian Year and Lectionary Reform*, London: SCM Press, 1958.

A Free Church of Scotland service 1957

The Free Church of Scotland, being the successors of those who had refused to enter the 1900 union with the United Presbyterian Church, continued the tradition of the Westminster *Directory* as practised in the nineteenth century and allowed neither hymns nor musical accompaniment. Public prayer continued to be extemporary. We do, however, have the full text of a Gaelic service, which was broadcast on radio on 24 February 1957 and has been translated into English.[12] Given the constraints of a broadcast, it may well have been shorter than the typical service, but does follow the normal pattern. The minister was the Revd Murdoch Campbell (1900–74), who wrote Gaelic poetry. He was born on the Isle of Lewis, was a singer, and studied at Edinburgh University and the Free Church College. He served parishes in several places, including Glasgow, and then in later life returned to rural ministry at Resolis on the Black Isle. He served as Moderator of the Free Church in 1956.

The broadcast service began with Psalm 65:1–5 to the tune 'Kilmarnock'. The opening prayer (ET is in the traditional mock Tudor-Stuart liturgical style), praised God for creation, gave thanks for the saving work of Christ and thanked God for faith, reconciliation and peace. There followed a reading of Psalm 25, then singing of Psalm 72:4–6 and a further reading from Ephesians 2:1–14. A second prayer acknowledged sin and asked for the Holy Spirit so that the congregation could plead the cause of Christ. It also contained intercessions for the sick and suffering, those who were bereaved and the Queen and her counsellors. The style and content may be illustrated from the opening paragraph of this second prayer:

> Most Holy One, in many things we fall short. Who can understand all his errors? The heart is deceitful above all things; who can know it? Thou hast set our secret sins and our faults in the light of thy countenance. Cleanse us in heart, and purify is from all the evil practices of our lives. Grant us grace that we may serve thee with reverence and godly fear.[13]

This was followed by Psalm 86:10–12 to the tune 'Martyrdom'. The sermon followed, on Job 19:25 and 27, and although it spans several pages, was probably shorter than the norm. A prayer followed (no text given), Psalm 34:3–7 to the tune 'Stornoway' and a final Benediction. This is an important witness to the format of most Free Church of Scotland services.

---

12 Murdoch Campbell, *Wells of Joy: Gaelic Religious Poems with Translations by Kenneth MacDonald and Notes by David Campbell*, Kilkerran: Covenanters Press, 2013, pp. 64–74 Gaelic, pp. 75–84 English. There may be many other broadcast services that invite further investigation.

13 Campbell, *Wells of Joy*, p. 78.

George MacLeod and the Iona Worship

Another important contribution to worship stemmed from the Iona Community. Iona was the site where, in 563, St Columba and his twelve followers had established a community on the east side of the island off the west coast of Mull. Over the succeeding centuries it was destroyed several times by Viking attacks before being refounded by the Benedictines at the beginning of the thirteenth century. In the fifteenth century, the Abbey Church became the Cathedral of the Bishop of the Isles. At the Reformation the Abbey was abandoned, fell into disrepair and became one of Scotland's ancient ruins. The ownership was under the Duke of Argyll, who decided to relinquish ownership of the Abbey and nunnery ruins and transfer them to a public trust linked to the Church of Scotland.[14] Thus it was in 1899 that a group of churchmen gathered at 123 George Street, Edinburgh, to form the Iona Cathedral Trust and the decision was taken to repair the Abbey Church (Cathedral). In 1902 plans were submitted by architects MacGibbon and Ross of Edinburgh for the roofing of the choir, the tower, the south aisle and transept and the glazing of the windows.[15] By 1903, John Honeyman had been engaged alongside MacGibbon and Ross. The work was finished by P. MacGregor Chalmers. The first service in the restored Abbey was on 26 June 1910. The Trust Deed had expressly excluded the parish minister and the kirk session of Iona from involvement in management and worship in the Abbey, though the parish congregation did worship in the Abbey on some Sundays during the summer. As Mac-Arthur comments, however, it was inevitable that once the Abbey choir and nave were returned to full use, speculation about the adjoining monastic buildings would soon follow, and as early as 1903, James Cooper had proposed that it be rebuilt as a seminary for training young Highlanders intending to go into ministry.[16] This rebuilding came to fruition due to the vision and determination of George MacLeod, minister of Govan Old.

George MacLeod came from a dynasty of distinguished churchmen, including his distant relative, John Macleod of Govan. He had served with distinction in the First World War in the Argyll and Sutherland Highlanders and received the Military Cross and the Croix de Guerre. He had been educated in England, at Winchester and at Oriel College, Oxford, and so he had experienced Anglican worship.[17] After the end of hostilities he trained for the Church of Scotland ministry at Edinburgh University. During the war he had been influenced by Tubby Clayton, who had founded Toc H, and MacLeod was ordained to serve as a Toc H padre in Glasgow. He

---

14 E. Mairi MacArthur, *Columba's Island: Iona from Past to Present*, Edinburgh: Edinburgh University Press, 1995, p. 83.

15 MacArthur, *Columba's Island*, p. 85.

16 MacArthur, *Columba's Island*, p. 133. MacArthur uses the term 'cathedral' throughout, whereas today 'Abbey' seems the preferred name.

17 His studies at Oxford were halted by the War but qualified him to be awarded a BA after the Armistice.

9.1 Iona Abbey

had a bitter falling out over the Anglican 'closed communion' and in 1926 accepted a call to St Cuthbert's, Edinburgh, one of the 'High Places' that had drawn the wrath of Joseph Primmer. George MacLeod established himself as a powerful preacher. In 1929 he turned down a call to Govan Old, only to accept it in 1930, and there he established a strong ministry, with a focus on the deprived areas and those affected by high unemployment. In 1933, an encounter with Russian Orthodox worship in Jerusalem made a deep impression on him and he also took interest in the Celtic Christian tradition, even if in an idealised manner. Ron Ferguson wrote:

> George was not a historian: he was a man with a profound sense of history, which is a different thing. It was natural that the Celtic period should hold enormous appeal for a romantic MacLeod. Its poetry, its love of beauty, its sense of nature shot through with spirit, its wholesome earthiness and profound holiness made it an attractive model, all the more so because many of its sources were so imprecise. George could make of it what he willed – and he did, he did.[18]

As a child, MacLeod had been to Iona for holidays, and when at Govan Old, he turned his thoughts to the restored Abbey and the remaining monastic ruins. In a private paper circulated in 1935 he urged the need for the Protestant Church to recover its Catholic heritage, and proposed the establishment of a brotherhood within the Church of Scotland, of no permanent vows, into which men could come for the first two or three years of

---

18 Ronald Ferguson, *George MacLeod: Founder of the Iona Community*, second edition, Glasgow: Wild Goose Publications, 2001, p. 137.

their ministry. 'The base would be Iona, and unemployed craftsmen would be invited to restore the Abbey buildings.'[19]

It was not until 1938 that the vision began to be a reality, and over many years the buildings were restored, and as well as a community at the Abbey, a wider Iona Community was established.[20] By the time he began the rebuilding on Iona, the war hero had become a pacifist, and his concern for social justice was perceived by some as extreme socialism and communism. His concern for liturgy identified him as a Scoto-Catholic who was trying to smuggle into the Church of Scotland Anglican or even Roman Catholic worship.

MacLeod's 'philosophy' on the community and worship was outlined in his book *We Shall Re-Build*, 1945. By this time, the influence of the Liturgical Movement was becoming apparent, and MacLeod made explicit reference to it. He wrote:

> If you study the Liturgical Movement, as it is exemplified in the Benedictine Monastery of Prinknash, and as it is spreading in Scotland, you will see that it is all designed to recover the 'apostolate of the laity'; to prevent anyone being 'an individual' while in Church; that all may know their membership 'together.' If you can get a look at the design for the new Anglican Coventry Cathedral, you will see the same movement gaining force. There is no far-distant chancel. Right out from the wall stands the holy Table, in the very centre of the place where the congregation will gather. And if you study the liturgical movement of the Church of England, you will find their new insistence on what they call 'the Corporate Communion.' No longer are individuals encouraged to go disintegratedly to 'make their communion'; hours are being changed that the whole body of the people may be present at the celebration; while Parish breakfasts are arranged, that those who have declared their spiritual brotherhood may, if only by symbol, seal it with a demonstration of its human meaning and its total challenge.[21]

He urged the recovery of the Christian year, and to reinstate the Holy Communion into the centrality it had in the early Church.[22] Of the social implications of the Eucharist, he wrote:

> There is One Bread in wheat ship, market-place and altar. Christ's presence in the world declares all bread to be holy; and if we fear to distribute

19 Ronald Ferguson, *Chasing the Wild Goose: The Story of the Iona Community*, second edition, Glasgow: Wild Goose Publications, 1998, pp. 51–2.

20 For the Iona Community's development, see T. Ralph Morton, *The Iona Community Story*, London: Lutterworth Press, 1957; *The Iona Community: Personal Impressions of the Early Years*, Edinburgh: Saint Andrew Press, 1977; Norman Shanks, *Iona: God's Energy. The Vision and Spirituality of the Iona Community*, Glasgow: Wild Goose Publications, 2009.

21 George MacLeod, *We Shall Re-Build*, Philadelphia, PA: Kirkridge, 1945, pp. 84–5. The first edition was c.1944, Iona Community, Glasgow.

22 MacLeod, *We Shall Re-Build*, pp. 30 and 49.

it, restrict the machinery whereby ever more bread may go round, and seek in fear to hoard what is not ours to hoard, then, like the manna in the wilderness that was hoarded, it begins to stink.[23]

MacLeod's Iona community combined work and prayer, and at least for those intending the ordained ministry, included a rule of life around daily prayer. Morning Prayer was at 8am, with Meditation at 9:30am and evening worship at 9pm. On Sundays, Communion was celebrated at 10:15am, and later at 10:30am.[24] The forms were adapted from the daily liturgy at Govan Old, themselves developed from the forms introduced by John Macleod.

The Iona forms first used by George MacLeod do not seem to have been kept, but *The Abbey Services of the Iona Community* of the 1950s probably preserves forms very similar, if not identical, to those introduced by MacLeod.[25] Morning Prayer began with a fixed responsory, to which other versicles and responses might be added. A hymn followed, with Prayer of Confession, silence and Prayer of Pardon. This was followed by the Lord's Prayer and a Bible Reading. A hymn of praise followed and then prayers of thanksgiving and intercession.

The Order of Service for the Holy Communion was outlined in *We Shall Re-Build*, and the excerpted service provided in *The Abbey Services* seems to agree with that outline. Although it was prepared to be the 'Iona use', there are reasons to believe that MacLeod used the order in the 1923 edition of *Prayers for Divine Service* as the source. The Prayer of the Veil came after the Declaration of Forgiveness, as in the 1923 edition (it was moved to before the Eucharistic Prayer the 1929 edition), and it had a two-fold Agnus Dei, found in both editions of *Prayers for Divine Service*, but which in the 1940 *Book of Common Order* had become the usual three-fold version.

The original community and its rule of life was quite independent from the Church of Scotland, and its independence, and political leanings of its leader, brought the whole enterprise under suspicion. Ferguson wrote:

Many ministers were suspicious of this charming, charismatic, Scoto-Catholic, with his dynastic pedigree, privileged upbringing and Winchester accent redolent of the English ruling class. His allegedly Anglican and Roman Catholic ways, along with his pacifist and socialistic tendencies, made him a confusing suspect as well as fascinating figure. Not a few ministers were simply jealous of this dynamic preacher and broadcaster who was popular with the masses.[26]

---

23 MacLeod, *We Shall Re-Build*, p. 14.

24 The sources differ! Morton, *The Iona Community Story*, p. 60; Ferguson, *George MacLeod*, p. 182; George MacLeod, *We Shall Re-Build*, p. 116.

25 *The Abbey Services of The Iona Community*, Glasgow: The Iona Community, no date, but which John Harvey dates as 1956 (email 7 January 2019). The services did not change for some years after George MacLeod had stood down as leader.

26 Ferguson, *George MacLeod*, p. 165.

In fact, because of his pacifism, for a time MacLeod was banned from radio broadcast. In 1951 the Iona Community was finally brought under the jurisdiction of the Church of Scotland. An Iona Board was established, with members from the General Assembly as well as community members, and it reported to the General Assembly every year. Even so, suspicion and controversy continued, especially when the community accepted a statue of the Virgin, which was set in the centre of the restored buildings.

George MacLeod's vision for Iona to be part of training for the Church of Scotland ministry did not materialise. However, those who had the Iona experience wanted to continue something of that experience and vision when they left the island, and so the Iona Community was established. In 1945, John Oliver Nelson wrote:

> The Community is a brotherhood of men – ministers and craftsmen – who fulfil their Christian vocation in regular paid jobs, but who are bound together by a common Rule which brings them into constant economic and spiritual dependence upon each other, thus far some 40 ministers and craftsmen are members, other forms of the Rule binding 180 minister associates and 380 women associates to Iona.[27]

The founding of 'associates' was in 1943, and they were encouraged to spend thirty minutes in reading a consecutive lectionary, as well as in prayers, and by implication, to follow in some way the Morning Prayer forms of Iona, available in the *Abbey Services* booklet.

The Order for the Kirk of Canongate, Edinburgh

Canongate Kirk serves the parish of Canongate in Edinburgh and is also the place of worship for the royal family when in residence at the palace of Holyroodhouse. The church was founded in 1688 and completed in 1691. From 1937 until 1977 the minister was the Very Revd Dr Ronald Selby Wright. He was a friend of George MacLeod and the manse of Canongate was used for a time by the Iona Community. When Selby Wright was away as an army chaplain during the Second World War, MacLeod served as locum. Selby Wright served as Moderator of the General Assembly and he also served as President of the Scottish Church Society. During his time at Canongate, he reordered the building. He wrote:

> By 1950 the dummy wall had been removed, and with it the old organ, showing once more the apse, and displaying the church in its rightful proportions. The side galleries had already been removed and a centre aisle had been made. Flat stones had been put into the apse bearing the

---

27 American Foreword to *We Shall Re-Build*, no pagination.

9.2 Interior of Canongate Kirk, Edinburgh

names of all ministers of Canongate since the Reformation, beginning with John Craig, and various gifts were given to adorn and beautify the newly opened up and renovated building. . . .

The beautifying of the sanctuary under the expert guidance of Mr Ian Gordon Lindsay and Mr George Hay, with its bright colours of blue and white; the reopening of the old apse; the light and simple dignity; the robed choirboys; the heraldically coloured coats of arms; the beautiful flowers given Sunday by Sunday (the responsibility of a different member of the church each week); the *Order Book*, of which five thousand copies have now been printed since it first appeared in 1947, enabling members not only to follow the service intelligently but to become a part of it; even the 'true blue Presbyterian' cassock and white stole presented to the minister by the congregation and worn by him at frequent and appropriate times – all these and many more 'innovations' contrast favourably in all eyes with the old dull building, heavy and dark with galleries and brown paint, the fluctuating (not least in the evenings) size of an adult and largely female choir; the service conducted entirely from the pulpit; the almost complete sacerdotalism of the minister, without a word, except for the hymns, from the people, not even the Lord's Prayer (though occasionally that was sung); and above all, and symbolizing so much, the aspidistra in a scarlet bowl placed in the middle of a table that could scarcely be called 'Holy'![28]

---

28 Ronald Selby Wright, *The Kirk in the Canongate: A Short History from 1128 to the Present Day*, Edinburgh: Oliver & Boyd, 1956, pp. 141, 143–4.

As he noted above, in 1947 Selby Wright produced *The Order of Divine Service* for use in Canongate Kirk. It has been enlarged over various editions.

In the Foreword to the third edition, 1957, Selby Wright claimed:

The orders contained in the present book are the same central structure as those in the first Scottish Service Book of 1562 (commonly known as John Knox's Liturgy) and the Book of Common Order of 1940 authorized by the General Assembly of the Church of Scotland for the use and guidance of Ministers of our Church.[29]

The Foreword encouraged more frequent celebrations of Communion and the book provided short orders for morning and evening, inspired by prime and Compline.

An outline for a Daily 'Word' service was given, followed by the Order of Morning Worship when there was no Communion. It was patterned after the first part of the communion liturgy, in accordance with the arguments of W. D. Maxwell. The full communion service was based very much on the 1940 *Book of Common Order*. It had three opening scripture sentences of the shorter order of 1940. There was a shorter confession, but otherwise the same opening prayers. Selby Wright provided his own form of intercessions. Patterned after Eastern Orthodox use, the Communion itself began with the Creed. The words of institution followed as a warrant. The Eucharistic Prayer was that of the 1940 *Book of Common Order*. The book also provided for a Christmas Eve Watchnight Service, as well as some doxologies and conclusions. It seems to have been a popular book, since by the 1957 edition, over 5,000 copies had been printed. Some copies, no doubt, were taken as souvenirs, but it seems likely that fellow ministers obtained a copy as a resource for their own worship services. A full description of the Sunday worship was given by Selby Wright in an address to the Church Service Society.[30] He wrote of the opening service:

The service is introduced by the solemn *Entry of the Bible* carried by one of the Choir Boys, the lighting of the lamps at the Holy Table by another boy, and then the Head Boy enters and, standing in front of the Holy Table, says *Let us Worship God*, and announces the first hymn.

While the hymn is being sung the choir of fifty boys and young men enters in procession followed by the ministers. The choir is robed in scarlet cassocks (as befits a Royal foundation), nearly all of which have been

---

29 *The Order of Divine Service and Sundry Other Services as used with the Canongate Kirk (the Kirk of Holyroodhouse) and Edinburgh Castle*, third edition, Edinburgh: Oliver & Boyd, 1957, p. 3. This edition was dedicated to George MacLeod. I have not had access to other early editions.

30 Ronald Selby Wright, 'Peace and Safety', *Church Service Society Annual* 25 (1955), pp. 9–21.

made, from a pattern, by members of the congregation. Each chorister wears a white ruff round his neck and, for those who have 'earned' them, the silver badge of the Canongate is worn on a pale blue ribbon. There is nothing 'high church' about a choir of boys and young men.[31]

The All-Scotland Crusade 1955

For George MacLeod, one of the prime purposes of the Iona Community was as training for mission in Scottish parishes, and he led a series of parish missions. Other notable leaders of home missions were D. P. Thomson and Tom Allan. There were also 'Radio Missions' organised by BBC Scotland in 1950 and 1952. Out of these came the Tell Scotland Movement, which had ecumenical backing, and the Revd Tom Allan was appointed full-time Field Organiser. After the success of Dr Billy Graham's 1954 crusade in Harringay, London, the decision was taken to invite Graham to undertake a similar crusade in Scotland – though George MacLeod was opposed to the idea. The result was the 1955 All-Scotland Crusade, based in Glasgow at Kelvin Hall. On the Sunday afternoon prior to the crusade, a Service of Dedication was held in Glasgow Cathedral, led by the minister, Dr Nevile Davidson, who was a member of the sponsoring committee.[32] The crusade meetings in Kelvin Hall followed a common pattern. Tom Allan wrote:

> The meeting began as often as not with the singing of one of the old Scottish psalms, and no one who attended Kalvin Hall will ever forget St. George's, Edinburgh, sung by the immense congregation. Then followed prayer, a solo from Mr. Beverly Shea, intimations, and the extraordinary expeditious uplifting of the offering by the capable and superbly drilled stewards, another hymn, another solo by Mr. Shea, and so to the sermon.[33]

In preparation for the crusade meetings, a *Song Book* was compiled by Cliff Barrows. Given the large numbers that attended the meetings, the *Song Book* had a wide circulation.[34] It consisted of 108 'songs', old and new – and some certainly new to Scotland. Nine Scottish metrical psalms were included. William Fitch noted that there was a wide selection of the best-loved gospel hymns, many of them going back to the time of Moody and Sankey.[35] In the brief foreword, Cliff Barrows wrote:

---

31 Selby Wright, 'Peace and Safety', pp. 11–12; Cf. *The Kirk in the Canongate*, p. 149.

32 Tom Allan (ed.), *Crusade in Scotland . . . Billy Graham*, London: Pickering & Inglis, 1955. See also Alexander C. Forsyth, 'The Apostolate of the Laity: A Re-Discovery of Holistic Post-War Missiology in Scotland, with reference to the Ministry of Tom Allan', PhD thesis, University of Edinburgh, 2014.

33 Allan, *Crusade in Scotland*, p. 13.

34 For the total of 1,185,360 people (not all of whom of course bought a copy), see Allan, *Crusade in Scotland*, p. 8.

35 Allan, *Crusade in Scotland*, p. 46.

Every great moving of God's Spirit has been accompanied by the songs of the redeemed. Join with us in singing these favourites – both new and old – and I'm certain you too will know the joy and blessing that they can bring.[36]

Some of these would seep into Scottish public worship.

The Ecumenical and Liturgical Movements: The Joint Liturgical Group

Though two separate movements, the Ecumenical and Liturgical Movements became closely linked. The origin of the Ecumenical Movement is usually traced to the Edinburgh World Missionary Conference in 1910, from which came the Faith and Order movement, and later the World Council of Churches. Its aim and goal was the reunion of the divided churches. At the 1937 Edinburgh Conference a committee was appointed to consider the traditions of worship in the various member churches. Its report, delayed by the Second World War, was published in 1951, entitled *Ways of Worship*. Church of Scotland delegates were fully involved. It stated: 'In the course of this enquiry we have been struck by the extent to which a "liturgical movement" is to be found in Churches of widely differing traditions.'[37] The report continued:

There is a widespread genuine unrest, a very definite feeling that worship ought to regain its central place in life, and that it can only do this if Churches return to the primitive patterns. To this end many Churches turn away from the habits and practices of their recent past in order to regain the purity and strength of worship as it was practiced in their classic periods. Often it is not clear whether this return to the past constitutes any definite theologically justified movement. There is need to discriminate between the claims of tradition and the authority of Holy Scripture, between the felt attraction of what is old or 'classic', and the need to base what is done on obedience to divine commandment. But in one way or another there is a desire to recover the 'original pattern'.

For this reason worshippers in Reformed Churches are rediscovering the liturgical principles and orders of service of the primitive Reformation, while members of all Churches, including the Roman Catholic, are studying afresh the worship of the early Church. More important still, the New Testament is being studied for the information it gives concerning worship. Arising out of this we may discern some abatement of the ruling

36 Foreword, *Billy Graham Song Book: All-Scotland Crusade 1955*, compiled by Cliff Barrows, Glasgow: Pickering & Inglis, 1955 (np).

37 P. Edwall, E. Hayman and William Maxwell (eds), *Ways of Worship: The Report of a Theological Commission of Faith and Order*, London: SCM Press, 1951, p. 16.

passion for representing the ways of worship of other people as 'degenerate'. At long last we are beginning to see that, measured by the standards of the New Testament and the early Church, none of our current ways of worship is fully adequate.[38]

The Liturgical Movement as it developed in the twentieth century was a movement in the Roman Catholic Church that was concerned with the laity, as the body of Christ, praying the liturgy rather than just being present and busy with private devotions. It encouraged regular reception of Communion at Mass. The pastoral concerns were shared by other Western churches, and the ideas were adapted for the appropriate Church. There was also a renewed interest in liturgical history and a shared ecumenical approach emerged.[39] Section IV of the Faith and Order Conference at Montreal, 1963, under the title 'Worship and the Oneness of Christ's Church', stated:

> Among the many recent blessings of the ecumenical movement, one in particular is of decisive importance for the common mission of the churches in our time. It is the current 'rediscovery' of Christian worship – of that twofold 'service' to God and to the world which is expressed in the biblical term leitourgia – as the central, determinative act of the Church's life. There is no clearer evidence of this than the joint theological work produced since the last Faith and Order Conference at Lund in 1952, the growth of the Liturgical Movement in virtually all Christian traditions, and the common recognition of an essential connection between the worship of the Church and its missionary task. It is heartening to realize that, at a time when Christians are perhaps more aware of the tragic estrangements of the world from the Church than ever before, God is so plainly calling us to discover together the joy, the depth and the power of Christian Worship.[40]

Ecumenical liturgical cooperation in the United Kingdom led to the founding of the Joint Liturgical Group (JLG) in 1963. At the suggestion of Dr R. C. D. Jasper, a member of the Church of England Liturgical Commission, the Archbishop of Canterbury invited participation of eight Churches in England, Scotland and Wales, under the chairmanship of Dean Douglas Harrison. The Roman Catholic Church originally sent observers but these later became full members. The Church of Scotland responded to the invitation, and was represented by the Revd Dr John Lamb and the Secretary of the Committee on Public Worship and Aids to Devotion, F. Nevill Davidson Kelly. The Group published (and still publishes) several booklets

---

38 *Ways of Worship*, p. 21.
39 See further in John Fenwick and Bryan Spinks, *Worship in Transition: The liturgical Movement in the Twentieth Century*, Edinburgh: T&T Clark, 1995.
40 Text in *Studia Liturgica* 2 (1963), pp. 243–55, p. 243.

with services for ecumenical use. The first publication was a set of essays, which included one by John Lamb, revised from a version in the *Church Service Society Annual*, entitled 'Liturgy and Unity'.[41] At the beginning of the collection the aim of the JLG was set out as follows:

1 The planning of a Calendar, Forms of daily Service, and a Lectionary which the Churches might be glad to have in common.
2 The planning of joint forms of service which might be used with the approval of the several Churches on occasions for united worship, such as the Week of Prayer for Unity and Holy Week.
3 The consideration of the structure of the service of Holy Communion.[42]

In 1967, *The Calendar and Lectionary* was published, inspired in part by the study of the Revd A. Allan McArthur, *The Christian Year and Lectionary Reform*, 1958. McArthur had proposed a lectionary based on a calendar concerned with the events of Christ's life, which was partly adopted in the JLG publication and would be eventually adopted by the Church of Scotland in 1994. It was a two-year lectionary with themes for each Sunday, and provided an Old Testament, Epistle and Gospel reading. In 1968, *The Daily Office* was published, by which time Stuart Louden had replaced John Lamb as one of the Church of Scotland representatives; and 1971 saw the publication of *Holy Week Services*.[43] In 1972, the JLG published *Initiation and Eucharist*, which set out an outline service for each sacrament. The outline for Baptism was:

The Scriptural Warrant, with specimen form
The Act of Renunciation
The Prayer at the Font or Baptistry
The Act of Baptism
The Laying on of hands/Anointing with Chrism.[44]

For the Eucharist, it suggested for 'The Word of God':

Scripture
Sermon
Intercessions.

---

41 Ronald C. D. Jasper (ed.), *The Renewal of Worship*, Oxford: Oxford University Press, 1965.
42 Jasper, *The Renewal of Worship*, pp. vii–viii.
43 Ronald C. D. Jasper (ed.), *The Daily Office*, London: SPCK and Epworth Press, 1968; *Holy Week Services*, London: SPCK and Epworth Press, 1971.
44 Neville Clark and Ronald C. D. Jasper (eds), *Initiation and Eucharist*, London: SPCK, 1972, pp. 15–17.

For 'the Supper':

> Presentation and taking
> Eucharistic Prayer, and it noted the different places among churches for
> the words of Institution
> Fraction and Communion.

It also acknowledged the elements of praise of God, confession and dismissal as parts of the structure. A fuller outline was provided at the end of the publication.[45] In 1978, the JLG published a 'Eucharistic canon', which was in part inspired by the *Te Deum*.[46] Membership of the JLG did not require participant churches to adopt any of these, but they were an added ecumenical resource in which the Church of Scotland had participated.

Theologians and the Sacraments: Donald Baillie, John Baillie, David H. Cairns and Thomas F. Torrance

The World Council of Churches grew out of the earlier missionary movements, and under its auspices, dialogue between the divided churches led both to denominational theologians re-examining their own traditions and to a willingness to learn from other traditions. In the 1950s and 1960s, four theologians of the Church of Scotland made significant contributions internationally and denominationally on sacramental theology – Donald Baillie; John Baillie; David H. Cairns; and Thomas F. Torrance.

Donald M. Baillie (1887–1954) was born into a Highland manse of the Free Church of Scotland, 'presided over by a Calvinist divine of strong character', but his father died when Donald was three years old.[47] His mother brought him and his brothers up in the same strict Calvinist tradition. He studied literature and philosophy at Edinburgh University and then theology at New College Edinburgh, and spent two semesters at the Universities of Marburg and Heidelberg. He served as assistant minister at Morningside United Free Church, Edinburgh, and with the YMCA in France in 1917. After the war he served as a parish minister until 1934, when he was appointed to the chair of Systematic Theology at St Andrews. Baillie's ecumenical interests and contributions were highlighted by his participation as a steward in the World Missionary Conference in Edinburgh in 1910, as a Church of Scotland delegate to the Second World Conference on Faith and Order in Edinburgh in 1937, and as chairman of the Theological Commission of the Third World Conference on Faith and

---

45 Clark and Jasper, *Initiation and Eucharist*, pp. 23–31.

46 Text in Max Thurian and Geoffrey Wainwright (eds), *Baptism and Eucharist: Ecumenical Convergence in Celebration*, Geneva: World Council of Churches, 1983, pp. 182–3.

47 Donald M. Baillie, *The Theology of the Sacraments and Other Papers*, with a biographical essay by John Baillie, London: Faber & Faber, 1957, p. 13.

Order in Lund, Sweden, in 1952. In preparation for the latter he co-edited (with John Marsh) *Intercommunion* (1952). His lectures on the sacraments were published posthumously by his brother, John Baillie.

Donald Baillie confessed that one reason for the infrequency of celebration of Communion in the Church of Scotland was because 'we do not really possess a theology of the sacraments'.[48] He argued that the universe itself was sacramental and that:

> when Christianity took the common elements of water and bread and wine and made sacraments of them, it was because this universe is the sacramental kind of place in which that can fitly happen; because these elements, these creatures of God, do lend themselves to such a use; and because we men and women, who are another sort of God's creatures, do require in our religion such a use of material things and symbolic actions.[49]

Yet the sacraments are of the Church, a visible society, and have a social and corporate aspect.[50] Baptism and the Eucharist are the dominical sacraments and have an integral continuity with the incarnation.[51] In both, the Church looks back to the death and resurrection of Christ and forward to the full enjoyment of the Kingdom.

Baillie acknowledged that baptism had problems concerning its institution (Matthew 28:19), the mode of administration (immersion, submersion, sprinkling) and the subject of administration (believers' baptism versus infant baptism), but argued for its dominical origin. He debated each of the questions and defended infant baptism on the grounds that the sacrament is about bringing someone into a new environment – that of the community of the Church.

In his discussion on the Eucharist, Baillie cited scholars ranging from P. T. Forsyth and Gregory Dix, to Ildefons Herwegen and Ronald Knox. He argued that God's presence is not a local or spatial presence, but a spiritual personal relationship that we have to symbolise by spatial metaphors.[52] He appealed to Calvin that although the body and blood of Christ are not locally present in the elements, they are spiritually present and truly and really present to the faith of the believer. And he appealed to the recent studies on the meaning of anamnesis to make present the salvific work of Christ. In his final section on Eucharistic offering, he again returned to the discussion of anamnesis and also of *poiein*, where 'Do this' might also carry the meaning of 'Offer this'. He was dubious that *poiein* in the Last Supper context implied that meaning. However, he argued that when we

---

48 Baillie, *The Theology of the Sacraments*, p. 40.
49 Baillie, *The Theology of the Sacraments*, p. 44.
50 Baillie, *The Theology of the Sacraments*, p. 50.
51 Baillie, *The Theology of the sacraments*, p. 60.
52 Baillie, *The Theology of the Sacraments*, p. 98.

offer praise, we can only do so in union with Christ's eternal sacrifice. He cited with approval the view of William Milligan, and asserted:

> Now if we gather all that we have been thinking about the Real Presence of Christ in the sacrament, about the offering that we make to God in the sacrament, and about the eternal sacrifice of Christ whose high-priestly work continues for ever at the heavenly altar, may we not say something like this: that in the sacrament, Christ Himself being truly present, He unites us by faith with His eternal sacrifice, that we may plead and receive its benefits and offer ourselves in prayer and praise to God? If we can say this, then surely we Protestants, we Presbyterians, have our doctrine of eucharistic sacrifice. . . . When in the sacrament we plead the sacrifice of Christ, and in union with Him offer ourselves to God, the whole of that process is a giving and receiving in one.[53]

Behind this was the anamnesis of the *Book of Common Order*, 1940, with 'pleading His eternal sacrifice'. His brother John wrote:

> He was ever loyal to his own Scottish and Presbyterian tradition; but within that tradition, from a very early date, and increasingly, his learning was towards the more liturgical mode. The Christian Year meant very much to him. To the proper order of worship he attached the greatest importance, and his own private prayers in public were always prepared with the most scrupulous attention to this. He shrank from any form of expression, in himself or others, which (as is unfortunately only too common) represents rather the particular temperament of the ministrant than the universal need, or which degenerated into a sentimentality and subjectivity of feeling which he regarded as foreign to the true Christian temper.[54]

John Baillie (1886–1960) was also a minister and theologian. He studied at Edinburgh University and then New College, and was appointed to the chair of Systematics at New College Edinburgh in 1934. He was a student steward at the epochal World Missionary Conference in Edinburgh in 1910, went on to become an active worker in the Faith and Order Movement from the early 1930s, and a member of the British Council of Churches. In 1943 he was elected moderator of the Church of Scotland and convener of its very influential Committee for the Interpretation of God's Will in the Present Crisis, whose report was later published as *God's Will for Church and Nation* in 1946. He was also a member of the central committee of the first assembly of the World Council of Churches in Amsterdam in 1948, and was elected one of its six presidents at the second assembly in Evanston, Illinois, in 1954. His *A Diary of Private Prayer*,

---

53 Baillie, *The Theology of the Sacraments*, pp. 118, 122.
54 Baillie, *The Theology of the Sacraments*, p. 31.

1936, a collection of daily devotions, was very popular. His lectures on baptism were published posthumously in 1964 under the title *Baptism and Conversion*. In these lectures he explored the observation of Stephen Neill that there were two antithetic approaches to the beginning of the Christian life: conversion and baptism. Baillie reviewed the concept of baptismal regeneration in the New Testament and various ecclesiastical traditions. His own conclusions were that, as taught in the Westminster Confession, the grace of baptism is not inseparably annexed to the washing in water. He quoted from the baptismal rite in the *Book of Common Order* that in baptism a child is 'now received into the membership of the holy Catholic Church', arguing that we are unable to posit an age when the disposition of faith appears:

> When a child is born and baptized into the household of faith, and acquiesces in the manner of his upbringing, the disposition of faith, by the grace of God operating through his Christian home, is already being formed within him.[55]

Much of the substance of the lectures was devoted to conversion, from its wider meaning in antiquity, in the Old Testament and in the various Christian traditions. He concluded that by whatever steps and stages, and whatever the experiences, a believer must be committed to 'the whole fulness of Christ and the whole breadth of the new outlook on life with which He came to endow us'.[56]

David H. Cairns (1904–92) was the son of the Revd David S. Cairns, a theologian and Principal of Christ's College, Aberdeen. He studied first at Aberdeen University but then transferred to Oxford, returning to Aberdeen to study theology. In 1933 he became an assistant to George MacLeod at Govan Old Parish. After serving as a chaplain in the Second World War, he became Professor of Practical Theology at Christ's College, Aberdeen, and lecturer in Systematic Theology at the University of Aberdeen. In 1967 he published a book on the Lord's Supper, *In Remembrance of Me*. He built on the work of Joachim Jeremias's book, *The Eucharistic Word of Jesus*, asserting that the Passover setting of the Last Supper pointed to the Supper being a renewing of a covenant, in God's presence.[57] The Lord's Supper is a covenant of forgiveness that creates a new relationship of intimate worship between God and humanity and between a person and his neighbour.[58] Throughout *In Remembrance of Me*, at appropriate points, Cairns cited the Eucharistic liturgy in the 1940 *Book of Common Order*.

On the subjects of Presence and Gift in the sacrament, Cairns cited Jeremias to assert that in the words, 'This is my body', 'This is my blood',

---

55 John Baillie, *Baptism and Conversion*, Oxford: Oxford University Press, 1964, p. 47.
56 Baillie, *Baptism and Conversion*, p. 112.
57 David H. Cairns, *In Remembrance of Me*, London: Geoffrey Bles, 1967, p. 17.
58 Cairns, *In Remembrance of Me*, p. 21.

Jesus was comparing himself to the Passover Lamb.[59] The presence of Christ in the sacrament is the presence of the Lord, who is now exalted to the Father, yet is still the same Jesus, drawing on both Donald Baillie and the sixteenth-century Scottish divine, Robert Bruce. Another important aspect that Cairns discussed was 'fellowship', drawing attention to the other meals of Jesus, with a messianic meaning in the banquet of fellowship and reconciliation. Appealing to Church of Scotland practice, Cairns wrote:

> And the participation of the elders and the worshippers, who pass the bread and wine from hand to hand, should continually remind us that it is not only the Lord himself who gives to each member of the family, but that he does it through our neighbour's giving and fellowship.[60]

Citing the Intercession Prayer in the *Book of Common Order* Eucharist, Cairns noted that the fellowship includes those servants who have departed in the faith.[61] On the controversial topic of sacrifice, Cairns stressed the complete sacrifice on the cross, but in the Milligan tradition, appealed to Hebrews 9:24–28, and argued that the offering is not only the death but the incarnation and the life of Christ, and that although the sacrifice is complete, the priesthood of Christ is not finished but continues in heaven under the form of intercession.[62] Cairns explained:

> having said this about the sacrifice that it is complete, once for all offered, and once for all accepted, we must go on to say that Christ's sacrifice is present with his intercession; eternal, not being eternally offered, but because once offered and accepted, it is the eternal basis and foundation of the intercession. It is to the Son who has completed his offering that the Father grants the prayers which he prays in filial confidence.[63]

Applying this to the Eucharist, he wrote:

> His sacrifice is present with him in the sense that he is the Christ who in his life and death offered his sacrifice. Therefore the words in the Consecration Prayer of our Communion Service where we speak of – 'Pleading his eternal sacrifice' – cannot mean that we plead with the Father to accept the Son's sacrifice. They must express our admission that without this gift we would not have this access to the Father, and they must come from a background, as it were, of humble gratitude that we do in fact have this gift, which we never could have seized for ourselves.[64]

---

59 Cairns, *In Remembrance of Me*, p. 29.
60 Cairns, *In Remembrance of Me*, p. 55.
61 Cairns, *In Remembrance of Me*, pp. 58–9; 1940 *Book of Common Order*, p. 115.
62 Cairns, *In Remembrance of Me*, p. 67.
63 Cairns, *In Remembrance of Me*, p. 71.
64 Cairns, *In Remembrance of Me*, p. 71.

We offer ourselves and our praise, 'Not as we ought, but as we are able'.[65] In a further chapter, Cairns explored the Eucharist as a sign of hope. What is most interesting is the interplay here of *lex orandi* with *lex credendi*, with the *Book of Common Order* illustrating (and in turn suggesting) Eucharistic doctrine.

Perhaps the most influential Church of Scotland theologian was Professor T. F. Torrance (1913–2007). Torrance was Professor of Christian Dogmatics for twenty-seven years at New College, Edinburgh, and shaped the theological thinking of a whole generation of ministers. He was also Moderator of the Church of Scotland 1976–77 and a President of the Church Service Society. As convener of the Special Commission on Baptism 1955–62, he was responsible for drafting much of the material for the reports that were published, and also wrote important essays on baptism.[66]

The 1955 report considered first the then current position of biblical studies which, common in the era of 'biblical theology', contrasted the Hebraic and Hellenistic minds. However, even at this stage the report grounded baptism in Christology: 'The doctrine of Baptism is grounded in the Person and Work of Christ. What He was, what He taught, and what He did are the facts that determine and shape the Sacrament of Baptism and give it its significance.'[67]

The institution of baptism was addressed with a stress on its trinitarian dimension, and the Report also examined the use of *baptisma* rather than *baptismos*, suggesting that it is similar to *kerygma*, and describes an event of God. *Baptisma* refers not only to the ritual action in water but is used of Christ's impending death. The Apostolic Church spoke of the Spirit bringing redemption and creation together. Jewish proselytes baptised themselves but children were baptised by someone else; in Christian baptism, all are baptised as though they are dependent children. Baptism is also in the Name, which means into the sphere where the mighty acts of God in the incarnation, birth, life, death, resurrection and ascension are operative for our salvation.

This does not mean, of course, that the Sacrament of Baptism automatically saves us, but that it places us in Christ, where his death and resurrection are operative, though we may fall away from him with terrible consequences (2 Corinthians 10:1–12). Baptism requires the response of faith, and a whole life of faith, for we cannot be saved without faith; yet baptism tells us that it is not our faith that saves us but Christ alone.[68]

---

65 Cairns, *In Remembrance of Me*, p. 72.

66 The report is found in *Reports to the General Assembly*, Edinburgh, 1955; see also Bryan D. Spinks, '"Freely by His Grace": Baptismal Doctrine and the Reform of the Baptismal Liturgy in the Church of Scotland, 1953–1994', in Nathan Mitchell and John Baldovin (eds), *Rule of Prayer, Rule of Faith: Essays in Honor of Aidan Kavanagh*, Collegeville, MN: Liturgical Press, 1996, pp. 218–42; T. F. Torrance, 'The One Baptism Common to Christ and His Church', in *Theology in Reconciliation*, London: Geoffrey Chapman, 1975, pp. 82–105.

67 *Reports to the General Assembly 1955*, p. 611.

68 *Reports to the General Assembly 1955*, p. 626.

Ultimately, baptism is grounded in the Incarnation, in which the eternal Son of God immersed himself in our mortal humanity and assumed it into oneness with himself that he might heal it and through the whole course of his obedience reconcile us to God.[69] A final section of the report noted two aspects needing further elucidation: the relation between God's covenant faithfulness and our faith; and the Christological pattern of the doctrine. The ground of our baptism is not our faith but the faithfulness of Christ. In him, God has kept covenant and faith with his people and the promise is to us and our children. In baptism Christ stands surety for us.

Since this report was to be the cornerstone of the Commission's work, it was rewritten and published in book form under the title *The Biblical Doctrine of Baptism*, 1958. Though this perhaps had less of Torrance's stamp on it, it nevertheless forcefully stated his position:

> our salvation ultimately depends upon something other than our faithfulness within the covenant relationship; that would be a salvation by works, and who then would be saved? To be baptised is to be baptised out of self and into another, into Christ. It is he who saves us, and he alone. The ground of baptism is therefore not our faith, but the faithfulness of Christ.[70]

Many of the arguments of this report were presupposed and reiterated in Torrance's essay, 'The One Baptism Common to Christ and His Church'. Agreeing with Karl Barth and Karl Rahner that the primary *mysterium* or sacrament is Jesus Christ himself, Torrance stressed that baptism is into the *koinonia*, or participation in the mystery of Christ and his Church. It cannot be interpreted as a flat event in itself – either as a ritual event or ethical event, but in a dimension of depth going back to the saving work of God in Christ, for 'when the Church baptises in his name, it is actually Christ himself who is savingly at work, pouring out his Spirit upon us and drawing us within the power of his vicarious life, death and resurrection.'[71]

Torrance unfolded again the distinction between *baptisma* and *baptismos*, noting that *baptisma* includes Christ's incarnation, birth, life, death and resurrection. He received a baptism meant for sinners on our behalf, and received divine judgement on our behalf. Baptism is always into his one vicarious *baptisma*. Baptism is administered to us in the name of the Triune God, and all we can do is receive it, for we cannot add anything to Christ's finished work. Through baptism we are united to him through the Spirit and participate in his saving life:

> It is not a separate or a new baptism but a participation in the one all-inclusive baptism common to Christ and his Church, wrought out

---

69 *Reports to the General Assembly* 1955, p. 637.
70 *The Biblical Doctrine of Baptism*, Edinburgh: Saint Andrew Press, 1958, p. 58.
71 Torrance, *Theology in Reconciliation*, p. 83.

vicariously in Christ alone but into which he has assimilated the Church through the baptism of one Spirit, and which he applies to each of us through the same Spirit. It is *baptisma* in the Name of the Triune God.[72]

The one *baptisma* brings together the baptism of Jesus in water and the Spirit at the Jordan, his baptism in blood on the cross and the baptism of the Church in his Spirit at Pentecost. When we receive baptism we are granted God's grace to participate in the one all-inclusive incarnational *baptisma* of Jesus Christ and to become members of his Body and children of the heavenly Father. The baptism of the Spirit may precede or follow baptism with water but the focal point of both is the invocation of the name of Christ, for it is in him that both baptisms find their unity. In baptism it is not so much that we confess Christ as that he confesses us before the Father. We are presented before God as subjects of his saving activity and are initiated into a mutual relation between the act of the Spirit and the response of faith. Baptism is in, with and through Christ.

The emphasis is that baptism is grounded objectively in the saving work of Christ, which is also the work of the divine Trinity. Baptism is an act of God in his Church, and the faith confessed is Christ's obedient faithfulness in his saving ministry and mission. A trinitarian dimension is crucial, as is the Christological/incarnational soteriology, which allows us to participate in the life of the divine.

Torrance approached the Eucharist from the more general supposition that all worship is properly a form of the life of Jesus Christ ascending to the Father in the life of those who are so intimately related to him through the Spirit; and when they pray to the Father through Christ, it is Christ the Incarnate Son who honours, worships and glorifies the Father in them. The Eucharist is the paschal mystery of Christ, which he set forth for the participation of all who believe in him.[73] The Supper is both an act of Christ and the act of the Church in his name. It is not an independent act in response to what God in Christ has done, but 'as act towards the Father already fulfilled in the humanity of Christ in our place and on our behalf, to which our acts in his name are assimilated and identified through the Spirit'. For Torrance, it is being in Christ or 'Christ in us' that is vital:

It is in this union and communion with Christ the incarnate Son who represents God to us and us to God that the real import of the Lord's Supper becomes disclosed, for in eating his body and in drinking his blood we are given participation in his vicarious self-offering to the Father. As we feed upon Christ, the bread of life who comes down from above, eating his flesh and drinking his blood, thereby receiving his eternal life

72 Torrance, *Theology in Reconciliation*, p. 88.

73 T. F. Torrance, 'The Paschal Mystery of Christ and the Eucharist', in *Theology in Reconciliation*, pp. 106–38.

into our actual life, and living by Christ as he lives by the Father who sent him, he unites us and our worship with his own self-consecration and so offers us to the Father in the identity of himself as Offerer and Offering.[74]

Two lengthy passages illustrate what Torrance thought about both presence and sacrifice. Christ is present through:

[T]he same kind of inexplicable creative activity whereby he was born of the Virgin Mary and rose again from the grave. Because it really is the presence of the Lord Jesus Christ in his living, creative reality, in his personal self-giving to us, it is a presence over which we have no kind of control, ecclesiastical, liturgical or intellectual. It is the same kind of presence that confronted the disciples on the first Easter morning at Emmaus or in the upper room at Jerusalem, and indeed it is the same presence except that now it takes another form, the eucharistic form specifically appointed by Jesus as the particular empirical form in which he has promised as the risen and glorified Christ to meet his people in the closest and most intimate way, throughout all history, in anticipation of his unveiled form when he will come again in great power and glory. It is the whole Jesus Christ who makes himself specifically and intensely present to us in this eucharistic form in his oneness as Gift and Giver, the whole Jesus Christ in the fulness of his deity and in the fulness of his humanity, crucified and risen, not a bare or naked Christ, far less only his body and blood, but Jesus Christ clothed with his Gospel and clothed with the power of his Spirit, who cannot be separated from what he did or taught or was in the whole course of his historical existence in the flesh. What he has done once and for all in history has the power of permanent presence in him. He is present in the unique reality of his incarnate Person, in whom Word and Work and Person are indissolubly one, personally present therefore in such a way that he creatively effects what he declares, and what he promises actually takes place: 'This is my body broken for you', 'This is my blood shed for many for the remission of sins'. The real presence is the presence of the Saviour in his personal being and atoning self-sacrifice, who once and for all gave himself up on the Cross for our sakes but who is risen from the dead as the Lamb who has been slain but is alive for ever more, and now appears for us in the presence of the Father as himself prevalent eternally propitiation.[75]

As to the manner in which the Eucharist is a sacrifice, Torrance wrote:

. . . that we *through the Spirit* are so intimately united to Christ, by communion in his body and blood, that we participate in his self-consecration

---

74 Torrance, *Theology in Reconciliation*, p. 111.
75 Torrance, *Theology in Reconciliation*, p. 120.

and self-offering to the Father and thus appear with him and in him and through him before the Majesty of God in worship, praise and adoration with no other sacrifice than the sacrifice of Christ Jesus our Mediator and High Priest. Conversely, the eucharistic sacrifice is the self-consecration and self-offering of Jesus Christ in our nature ascending to the Father from the Church in which he dwells through the Spirit he has poured out upon it, uniting it to himself as his Body, so that when the Church worships, praises and adores the Father through Christ and celebrates the Eucharist in his name, it is Christ himself who worships, praises and adores the Father in and through his members, taking up, moulding and sanctifying the prayers of his people as they are united to him through communion in his body and blood.[76]

Christ has put himself in our place so that we may be put in his place; through the Spirit we participate in his vicarious self-offering as the real agent of our worship and through our prayers and thanksgivings in the Eucharist we offer Christ to the Father. It should be recalled that Torrance was able to draw on the Eucharistic Prayer of the 1940 *Book of Common Order* (and its 1979 successor), which had the phrase 'pleading his eternal sacrifice'; in many ways Torrance's theology was an exegesis of those words. His son, Professor Iain Torrance, writes:

My father's practices of worship took place at several levels. After our family breakfast, all his life until he suffered a disabling stroke at the age of 89, my father presided at family prayers around the breakfast table. He would read a short passage of scripture (guided by the Revised Common Lectionary), and then he would read one of the weekday prayers from the volume *Prayers for Divine Service in Church and Home* (Edinburgh, William Blackwood, 1923). My father's copy had earlier been owned by Professor William Manson . . . He kept a Bible (Authorized Version) and a copy of the 1662 Book of Common Prayer on the shelf of [his] prayer desk.

As children, our father gave us our own copies of *Kyrie Eleison: A Manual of Private Prayers* by H. J. Wotherspoon (Edinburgh, William Blackwood, 1948) . . . The sacraments of baptism and Holy Communion were immensely important to my father. They were absolutely not simply memorial but the outward signs of the decisive action of God in Christ.[77]

In some ways, Torrance builds on and brings to fruition the theology found in Wotherspoon and Kirkpatrick's *A Manual of Christian Doctrine*.

---

76 Torrance, *Theology in Reconciliation*, p. 134.
77 Private communication, email 29 March 2019.

Some Orders of Service from the Presbytery of Dumbarton and other parishes in the 1960s

In the 1960s, the Revd James C. Stewart undertook a survey of worship in the Presbytery of Dundee and collected the worship bulletins from several parishes. These are outlines, not full texts of every prayer. That of Drum-chapel St Andrews for 15 March 1964, Passion Sunday, had as follows:

> Assembling Verse Hymn 535, vl. Onward! During which the Bible was carried in. Hymn 108 (Regent Square 7) Sing my tongue, call to Prayer, followed by Prayers of Adoration, Confession and Supplication. The Old Testament reading was Isaiah 63:1–9, and the (Metrical) Psalm 143 ii 6–8 (tune: St. Cecilia, RCH 152), followed by readings from Hebrews 9:11–15, and St. John 10:7–18. Then came Prayers of Intercession, and Hymn 415, followed by the sermon. The Offering was accompanied by the Doxology, 'Praise God from whom all blessings flow'. Then came the Sursum corda, with Dedication and Lord's Prayer, followed by Hymn 106. If there was a baptism or celebration of communion, this came next. Provision was made for a further hymn when a sacrament was celebrated. On this occasion the service ended with a Benediction, and a 'Dispersal Hymn', 535 v.5, during which the Bible was carried out.[78]

A very similar order was printed for use at Drumchapel St Mark's, and the minister of Rowton, the Revd John Shaw, in a handwritten letter of 16 May 1966, gave a very similar outline that he used. The Revd Andrew Scobie of Cardross had a printed outline with Psalm, Call to Prayer, Prayer and Lord's Prayer, Hymn, Old Testament lesson and then a Children's Address. The New Testament lesson came next, followed by Prayers and the Intimations. After a paraphrase was sung the Sermon was preached, followed by prayer, dedication of offering, a hymn and the Blessing with choral Amen. Andrew Scobie noted (letter of 16 June 1966) that the congregation were not used to standing for the call to Prayer and only joined in the final choral Amen. The main variation between the orders was the placing of the Children's Talk, the Intimations and the Offering. At New Kilpatrick, Communion was celebrated on the third Sunday of each month and baptism on the last Sunday, though no indication was given of what orders of service were used for these (letter of 11 May 1966).

---

78 I am indebted to the Revd James C. Stewart for providing me with these bulletins and accompanying correspondence. From the Presbytery of Dumbarton, orders of service were provided by Drumchapel St Andrew's, Drumchapel St Mark's, Rowton, Knightswood, Cardross, Cairns Church Milngarvie, Trinity, Duntocher, Balfron North Church, St James', Clydebank, Knoxland, Alexandria Bridge Street Church, Strathblane Church, Killermont Parish Church, Bearsden, Craigrownie Parish Church, Bearsden North Church, Carelochland Parish, Helensburgh Old and St Andrew's Parish Church, New Kirkpatrick, Bearsden, St Paul's Milngarvie, Killearn, Linnvale Clydebank, St Matthew's Yoker, Bearsden South, and Westerton.

Among the orders from other churches is that of The Old Kirk Edinburgh, which provided a text for the continuation of Morning Worship when there was Communion.[79] After an Invitation to Communion came Psalm 24:7–10 and then the Words of Institution. A Heading 'Prayer of Thanksgiving' gave the text of the Sursum corda, the heading 'Thanksgiving for the making of the world' and Sanctus with Benedictus. The rest of the prayer was explained as follows:

Thanksgiving for the gift of Jesus;
Thanksgiving and remembrance of the life and work of Jesus;
Prayer for the Coming of the Holy Spirit to make real this action;
Offering of ourselves and our work to God;
Prayer for God's blessing on his world;
Lord's Prayer.

It would appear that the 1940 *Book of Common Order* was the underlying source for this local devolution.

The *Church Hymnary* 1973

A third edition of the *Church Hymnary* was published in 1973, the first meeting of the revision committee having been held on 24 October 1963 and the Revd Dr Thomas H. Keir appointed convener. Other members of the Church of Scotland included the Revd A. Stewart Todd and the Very Revd Ronald Selby Wright. F. N. Davidson Kelly was appointed Secretary. The committee had representatives from the United Presbyterian Church as well as the Presbyterian Churches of England, Ireland and Wales. Thomas Keir wrote: 'The Church Hymnary: Third Edition is, strictly speaking, not a revision but a new conception in modern hymn-books. It runs to 695 items, but the figure includes 79 psalms or psalm portions.'[80] John M. Barkley wrote an essay in the *Handbook*, 1979, to explain the rationale behind this revision. The committee decided that the purpose of a hymn book '*is a book for the use of the people of God in the public worship of God*'.[81] This dictated the structure, which was based on The Order of Public Worship: 'CH3, in other words, is not a collection of hymns under various headings, as was the case with RCH [Revised Church Hymnary 1927], but a hymn-book – a book for the use of the people of God in the public worship of God.'[82] This, in turn, meant that the content of the book must be decided

---

79 This is undated but is either late 1950s or early 1960s.

80 Thomas H. Keir, 'The Church Hymnary: Third Edition', *Liturgical Review* 3 (1973) pp. 26–33, p. 26.

81 John M. Barkley, 'The Revision, 1963–1973', in John M. Barkley (ed.), *Handbook to the Church Hymnary Third Edition*, Oxford: Oxford University Press, 1979, pp. 55–67, p. 56; italics original.

82 Barkley, 'The Revision', p. 56.

first – words and hymns – and then fitting musical settings. The structure of the first three parts was:

1 Approach to God. Hymns 1–134
2 God's Mighty Acts. Hymns 135–344
3 Response. Hymns 345–545.

The remaining items were:

4 The Sacraments. Hymns 546–590
5 Other Ordinances. Hymns 591–610
6 Times and Seasons. Hymns 611–633
7 Close of Service. Hymns 634–662
8 Personal Faith and Devotion. Hymns 663–695.

The committee also pondered the question of 'Who are the Church?' It agreed that it is both the Church triumphant and those who believe in Christ in all lands, and their children. 'In all lands' meant that hymns from 'younger' churches in Asia and Africa became a resource, and hymns for children were also included, but integrated throughout the hymnary and not in a special children's section.

The inclusion of seventy-nine psalms (sixty-five metrical) was not to reduce the Psalter from 150 to seventy-nine but to increase the usage in public worship from about twenty-three 'usual' psalms to seventy-nine. Liturgical material such as Kyrie eleison, Sanctus and the Creed were included, and a wider selection of hymns for both Baptism and Holy Communion was offered. Contemporary composers were commissioned to write new tunes for some of the hymns. The preface to this third edition announced that the collection was 'sent out in the prayerful hope that it may enrich the worship of congregations to the greater glory of God'.[83] It was widely criticised for omitting many favourite hymns, though it did introduce many new hymns to the Church of Scotland. While acknowledging some positive points, John Bell has written:

> On the negative side, it paid scant attention to the social and theological shifts of the twentieth century. It grudgingly included songs of personal devotion and caused offence both by omitting stock favourites such as 'What a friend we have in Jesus' and by changing the tunes to other revered texts, it exhibited no awareness of contemporary developments in religious verse and music happening in the 1960s and 1970s. The Taizé Movement, the songs encouraged by Vatican II, the faith and folk movement whose most prestigious exponent was Sydney Carter – none of these were represented; nor was there yet anything of significance from the global Church whose hymnody was beginning to be shared via

---

83 *The Church Hymnary*, third edition, Oxford: Oxford University Press, 1973, p. vi.

international gatherings of the World Council of Churches and related organizations.[84]

As was the case with other revisions of worship begun in the 1960s and completed in the 1970s, when they were published they were already out of date.

Towards revision of the 1940 *Book of Common Order*

The 1940 *Book of Common Order*, like all official English-language liturgies of the time, had been written in the style of the Authorized Version of the Bible of 1611, with God addressed as thee and thou and with antiquated grammar and syntax. One of the decisions taken by the Roman Catholic Church after Vatican II was that the vernacular translations of the Latin editions of the revised liturgies should be in modern language, and so new texts in contemporary English appeared. This inspired other English-speaking churches to make a similar transition. In May 1965, the Presbytery of Edinburgh's Special Committee on Worship and Fellowship's Report reviewed patterns of Morning and Evening Worship, and made some recommendations. The report also noted:

> Fifty per cent of our people seemed content with prayers in the A.V. language, the other half were dissatisfied with them. There was a widespread view that the prayers offered in Church were too long. It was evident that a great many ministers felt they could not use the prayers in the B.C.O. as they are at present. There is ground for a radical revision of our present B.C.O.[85]

The need for a revision, radical or otherwise, was a sentiment shared by many ministers. In 1967 a remit from the General Assembly to the Committee on Public Worship and Aids to Devotion, convened by R. Stuart Louden, requested that the committee examine the nature, sources and function of public worship in the Reformed Churches in the light of contemporary scholarship. This in order to:

1 make clear the purpose and principles of public worship;
2 provide a source of teaching material about the meaning and practice of public worship; and

---

84 John L. Bell, 'Scottish Hymnody: An Ecumenical and Personal Perspective', in Duncan B. Forrester and Doug Gay (eds), *Worship and Liturgy in Context: Studies and Case Studies in Theology and Practice*, London: SCM Press, 2009, pp. 259–78, pp. 261–2.
85 Presbytery of Edinburgh, *Report of Special Committee on Worship and Fellowship*, May 1965, pp. 3–4.

3 suggest ways in which the form of public worship in the Church of Scotland can be developed, so as to become a more adequate means of grace to the people of this generation.[86]

This was with a view to drawing up a report and provide teaching material about the meaning and practice of worship. The report was presented at the May 1970 General Assembly, prefaced by an account of discussions on worship with other Churches.[87] The report noted the latest work of the Joint Liturgical Group and inter-Church co-operation over material prepared by the International Consultation on English Texts (ICET). Informal contact had also been made with Scottish Episcopalian and Roman Catholic churchmen engaged in parallel work. Members of the committee had also attended the Societas Liturgica conference in Ireland, where the subject of the congress was 'The Language of Christian Worship'. The Committee observed:

A radical approach to the language of worship was apparent in many quarters, but there was a consensus among the English language personnel in favour of aiming at a language for public worship, lying somewhere between the traditional and formal Elizabethan English found in the Authorized Version and the Book of Common Prayer, and a crudely colloquial and modern jargon: this implied a flexible Revised Standard Version type of English for use in public worship. . . . The results of all these wider contacts are very much before the Committee, as work and study are initiated and promoted towards an eventual full revision of the *Book of Common Order 1940*. The complexity of the task of finding 'simple, direct and meaningful language' which is appropriate to the corporate worship of Almighty God, has to be recognised.[88]

The ICET Lord's Prayer was cited in the report. It also noted that some experimental *Orders of Evening Service* and a service for Remembrance Sunday had been issued.

An appendix contained the report *Doctrine and Practice of Public Worship in the Reformed Churches*. The Preface drew attention to the fact that a number of experimental works on worship were being tried out in the Church of Scotland and that a 'Common Order' was required to express the mind of the Church. It also noted the 1968 Uppsala *Report on Worship* of the WCC, which observed that 'there is a crisis of worship, and behind that a crisis of faith.'[89] The theological principles that the committee set down had a Christological and Trinitarian basis:

The Gospel of grace is that [Jesus] assumes our life, takes on our responsibilities, offers to the Father a life of unbroken communion and obedience,

---

86 Stated in *Reports to the General Assembly 1970*, p. 190.
87 *Reports to the General Assembly 1970*, pp. 183–205.
88 *Reports to the General Assembly 1970*, p. 184.
89 *Reports to the General Assembly 1970*, p. 190.

dies our death, rises in our humanity, returns to the Father as the One True Man before God, the One True servant of the Lord, the One True Worshipper who now by His Holy Spirit leads us in our worship. As our One High Priest, He is the Head of all creation, the Head of the Church, the Leader of the worshipping community, who lives in communion with the Father to intercede for all His creatures.[90]

The whole life of Christ, so the report affirmed, is a life of self-offering to the Father on behalf of the world, culminating in the One True Sacrifice of love and obedience on the Cross, which alone is acceptable to God, for all men, for all nations, for all times.[91] The Church, through grace, prays in the Holy Spirit through the Son to the Father. Jesus Christ is both High Priest and Mediator, and he becomes our worship. The report asserted that worship recapitulates salvation history, leads to mission and bears witness to the Kingdom. A draft report of a working party on worship of December 1971 urged that General Assembly enjoin all ministers and kirk sessions to consider how best to move as speedily as possible towards making the Lord's Supper the regular weekly Sunday Service.[92]

Together in Worship, published in 1969, was to help lay persons conduct worship for small groups, fellowships and meetings, and offered material in both contemporary and traditional liturgical language. It also offered some 'new approaches' in music, recommending some suitable folk, off-beat and pop songs as well as some non-biblical readings.[93]

The desire for services in contemporary English spurred the publication of *Worship Now* in 1972. It was compiled by the Revd Professor David Cairns, the Revd Professor Ian Pitt-Watson (1924–95, Professor of Practical Theology, Aberdeen), the Revd Professor James A. Whyte (1920–2005, Professor of Practical Theology and Christian Ethics, St Mary's College, St Andrews), and Mr T. B. Honeyman of Saint Andrew Press.[94] It had been inspired in part by the contemporary prayers published in England by Caryl Micklem of the Congregational Church in England and Wales.[95] The *Worship Now* collection was divided into five sections, A–E. Section A contained Prayers for Morning Service; B, Sacraments and Ordinances; C, New Forms of Worship (e.g. family worship, Meditation, a Dance Drama of the Holy Spirit); D, The Christian Year and Occasional Services; and E, An Anthology of Prayers and Introductory Sentences. A list of the contributors was given at the back of the book.

90 *Reports to the General Assembly* 1970, p. 192.
91 *Reports to the General Assembly* 1970, p. 193.
92 Working Party on Worship, Draft Report to Assembly (as appendix to Committee's report), typescript, dated 15 December 1971.
93 *Together in Worship*, Edinburgh: Saint Andrew Press, 1969.
94 David Cairns, Ian Pitt-Watson, James A. Whyte and T. B. Honeyman, *Worship Now: A Collection of Services and Prayers for Public Worship*, Edinburgh: Saint Andrew Press, 1972.
95 Caryl Micklem, *Contemporary Prayers for Public Worship*, London: SCM Press, 1967.

The orders followed a usual Church of Scotland pattern but experimented with modern language. Thus, the third order for Morning Service: 'O God, we give thanks for all your goodness to us: for your goodness to us in our life together with other men.'[96]

Professor David Cairns provided 'Holy Communion – First Order', with a Eucharistic Prayer on the 'classical' model, inspired by Scripture, and one of the Roman Catholic Eucharistic Prayers for Reconciliation. Cairns did not utilise the phrase 'pleading His eternal sacrifice'. His anamnesis and epiclesis read:

> Having in remembrance all that Christ has done for us,
> We rest in confidence on your eternal love
> Declared to us once for all in him,
> And we rely on his continual intercession for us.
> And now, O Father, remembering these things,
> We pray you to send your Spirit,
> To bless both us and this bread and this wine,
> That through them, in faith, we may receive the life of Christ.[97]

This Eucharistic Prayer, reflecting liturgical devolution, was adopted by the Revd William Whitson for Coatbridge in a specifically cyclostyled service book for that parish in 1974.[98]

A somewhat experimental order was authored by Professor William Barclay. The Eucharistic Prayer was more in the form of intercessions than the traditional model.[99] Another Communion Order was provided by the Revd David Ogston, Assistant at St Giles' Cathedral, Edinburgh. This had some 'traditional' features, such as Psalm 24:7 for the entry of the elements. A traditionally shaped Eucharistic Prayer was given, though the content was mainly petition for the community, and any divine presence invoked was indirect: 'come to us . . . and be our guest, the guest of sinners', which actually suggests that the Church, and not Christ, is the host of the feast.

Other devolved services are illustrated by the service bulletins in the collection of Mr Harold Mills of Edinburgh, mainly for St Giles' Cathedral, but also a few for Glasgow Cathedral. Mostly they followed what had become the standard non-sacramental service, as in the parish bulletins in the collection of James C. Stewart.[100]

---

96 *Worship Now*, p. 11.

97 *Worship Now*, pp. 48–9.

98 William Whitson, *Sunday Morning: A Guide to the Christian Celebration*, Coatbridge, 1974, pp. 23–4. My thanks to the Revd James S. Stewart, who furnished me with this booklet.

99 *Worship Now*, pp. 54–5.

100 My thanks to Harold Mills for allowing me access to his collection in 2015. He was at that time intending to present them to the National Archives of Scotland.

The 1973 Report of the Committee on Public Worship and Aids to Devotion – and now Dr Alastair K. Robertson was convener – noted that, as part of the work to revise the 1940 *Book of Common Order*, the committee had prepared draft orders of service for funerals, discussed the position of the Agnus Dei in the communion service, announced that it had now been placed in its threefold form, after the fraction, and announced its forthcoming publication, *The Divine Service*.[101] This latter was also published in 1973. The Preface, written in the name of the committee by Alastair Robertson, described the sixty-page booklet as a contribution towards the revision of the 1940 *Book of Common Order*. It further explained:

> The booklet is entitled *The Divine Service* because the Committee is convinced of two things: (1) That the Lord's Supper is the central, typically Christian act of public worship; and (2) that the celebration of the Lord's Supper has historically and doctrinally been so closely allied to the observance of Sunday that, as the Universal Church in general and the Reformers in particular have clearly demonstrated, the Lord's Supper should be the principal act of worship Sunday by Sunday.[102]

The booklet contained three full orders for Holy Communion, a Shorter Order, the JLG Lectionary with minor modifications and collects to fit the titles of the JLG Sunday calendar. With regard to the three main Orders for Communion, Robertson explained that each differed considerably in language, roughly corresponding to the language of the Authorized Version, Revised Standard Version and New English Bible translations.[103] The first was compiled by Alastair Robertson, the second by A. Stewart Todd and the third by James C. Stewart and Alex Sawyer.[104] One new development was that the words of institution were incorporated into each of the Eucharistic Prayers. The phrase 'Pleading his Eternal Sacrifice' was contained in the Eucharistic Prayers of Orders 2 and 3. What was slightly odd was that only the third Order was in modern language. The Church of England 'Collect for Purity' was rendered:

> Every heart is open to you, our God, our every wish and secret is known to you: send your Spirit to make pure our inmost thoughts so that we may love you truly, and give you thanks and praise: through Jesus Christ our Lord.[105]

---

101 *Reports to the General Assembly* 1973, pp. 207–12.
102 Committee on Public Worship and Aids to Devotion of the General Assembly of the Church of Scotland, *The Divine Service*, Oxford University Press, 1973, p. iv.
103 *The Divine Service*, p. iii.
104 This information was given to me verbally, I think by Douglas Galbraith.
105 *The Divine Service*, p. 29.

In 1974, two booklets providing teaching material were published: *Weekly Communion in the Church of Scotland* and *Learning Together about Christian Worship*.[106] The report of the Committee on Public Worship and Aids to Devotion to the 1976 General Assembly summarised the work being done towards revision of the 1940 *Book of Common Order* and also drew attention to a forthcoming book containing sets of prayers for Morning Service. It was at this General Assembly Meeting that the long-serving secretary, F. Nevill Davidson Kelly, who had served from 1940 until 1975, collapsed and died. A. Stewart Todd rightly acknowledged that his contribution to the liturgical and musical well-being of the Church of Scotland was monumental.[107]

In 1977, with A. Stewart Todd as convener, *Prayers for Contemporary Worship* was published. The Introduction recognised that there was not one universally applicable modern English idiom and that the collection was an attempt to compose prayers in a language with which those who are worshipping can honestly associate themselves. Contemporary, though, was not to be equated with 'casual' or 'conversational'.[108] The collection provided a complete set of prayers for a Sunday Service; Additional Prayers for Sunday Worship; Intercessions for the Christian Year; and Thematic Prayers, such as 'Joy' or 'In time of depression'.

The new *Book of Common Order* was published in 1979. It was a 'partial' volume, to be supplemented by other volumes. It contained the orders of communion from *The Divine Service*, an outline Order for Public Worship, services for baptism and confirmation, marriage, funerals and ordination of elders. It also included the modified JLG Lectionary, and collects as in the Divine Service, but now also a second set in modern English. It also provided some Proper Prefaces for the Christian Year.[109] The supplementary/companion volumes were *Prayers for Sunday Services*, 1980 and *New Ways to Worship*, 1980.

Of note is the baptismal rite. Though claiming that it followed the 1968 order fairly closely, changes had been made so that the word of God could be heard rather than 'the din of theological words'.[110] However, in the opening exordium, the 1968 section covering salvation history from the Jordan to the Cross – inspired by the Christological basis of baptism stressed in the biblical report on baptism – was omitted. Two baptismal prayers were provided, both shorter than 1968. The first version used the 1940 words 'that this child may be born anew of water and the holy Spirit' and the second used the 1968 words, suggesting that not all ministers in the Church of Scotland had been persuaded that the sign and the thing signified

106 Published by St Andrew Press, Edinburgh, 1974.

107 A. Stewart Todd, 'The Ordering of Eucharistic Worship', *Liturgical Review* 7 (1977), pp. 11–19, p. 11.

108 The General Assembly's Panel on Worship, *Prayers for Contemporary Worship*, Edinburgh: Quorum Press, 1977, pp. 9–10.

109 *The Book of Common Order (1979)*, Edinburgh: Saint Andrew Press, 1979.

110 *The Book of Common Order (1979)*, p. xii.

were united in the sacramental rite. In some ways the 1979 rite might be seen as a retreat from the textual gains made in 1968. There would seem to be a gulf between the Christocentrism and sheer grace of the reports of the Special Commission, and the more guarded rite of 1979 which, albeit loosely and anachronistically, might be termed semi-federalist.

The Eucharistic rites, under the guidance of A. Stewart Todd, were based on 'state of the art' liturgical scholarship of the 1970s, Stewart Todd referencing Willy Rordoff and articles by Louis Ligier, a leading Roman Catholic liturgical scholar. In spite of this, or perhaps because of it, Duncan Forrester stated:

> The *Book of Common Order* 1979 was not greeted with great enthusiasm, either by reviewers or by many in the Church of Scotland. It is on the whole canny and sometimes pedestrian, perhaps because it is the fruit of so many compromises. Whether it will do much to encourage that most desirable of reform in worship – 'the Lord's Supper every Sunday' – depends on its ability to commend itself to ministers and congregations.[111]

Indeed, only a lukewarm review was offered by the English United Reformed Church minister, John Huxtable.[112] He was dubious as to whether it would lead to more frequent celebration of Communion. He was also very uncertain that the book had 'got it right' on baptism, and felt that the initiation services were less satisfactory that the communion services. His main doubts were about the effects of modern-language prayers on worshippers. In general, he thought the language used was fitting, but of the Eucharistic Prayer of the Third Order, he opined that the 'graceless' expression 'Your Son Jesus Christ is to be thanked and praised' sounded like a reminder for a vote of thanks. The 1979 *Book of Common Order* was never embraced with the same enthusiasm as that of 1940 and had a much shorter lifespan.

While in the press, a criticism came from the National Church Association in the form of an alternative service book entitled *Reformed Book of Common Order*, 1977. In the Preface the Revd George M. Dale wrote that the 1940 *Book of Common Order* was in many respects 'not in accord with the doctrine and practice of the Church of Scotland' and expressed the opinion that *The Divine Service* was an even greater departure from the Kirk's doctrine. Citing the anamnesis 'we offer unto thee this bread and this cup' (propitiatory sacrifice), the epiclesis (for the purpose of changing the elements) and Agnus Dei (teaching transubstantiation), he concluded that 'the inspiration and source of such material are not Reformed doctrine

---

111 Duncan Forrester, 'Worship since 1929', in Duncan B. Forrester and Douglas M. Murray, *Studies in the History of Worship in Scotland*, second edition, Edinburgh: T&T Clark, 1996, p. 186.
112 Review in *Liturgical Review* 9 (1979), pp. 72–5.

based upon the Scriptures, but Anglo and Roman Catholic doctrine.'[113] Dale was critical of the Scoto-Catholics led by Sprott and Leishman, and then by W. D. Maxwell. The *Reformed Book of Common Order* was based on the *Form of Prayers* (*Book of Common Order* 1562) and the Westminster *Directory*. There was no concession to modern English. This compilation was made by those who seem to have had no interest in the Liturgical and Ecumenical Movements, and for those who did, this book seemed 'quaint and conservative' and 'turgid and insular in content'.[114] The 'quaint' character was illustrated by the service titles, 'Public Worship, The Morning Diet', and the 'turgid' by such cumbersome sentences as in the 'Eucharistic Prayer':

> Therefore, at the invitation and command of Our Lord and Saviour, we present ourselves at His table to remember Him; to declare and witness before the world that by Him alone we have received forgiveness and eternal life, that by Him alone Thou dost acknowledge us as Thy children and heirs, that by Him alone we have access to Thy throne of grace, that by Him alone we have our citizenship in heaven, that by Him alone our bodies shall be raised from the dust and share with Him that endless joy which Thou, our Father, hast prepared for Thine elect before the foundation of the world.[115]

No doubt the publication was popular among some conservative groups, since a second edition was published, but it was hardly a bestseller. Furthermore, Forrester correctly pointed out that in the sacramental services, the book had substantially toned down the teaching of the standards of the Church of Scotland.[116]

Concluding remarks

The forty years between the two *Books of Common Order* were marked by many changes in Western society and culture, and churchgoing began its steady decline. The fruits of the Ecumenical and Liturgical Movements encouraged Churches, including the Church of Scotland, to renew their official liturgical service books and to provide prayers in a modern vernacular. For many, though, the new services were uninspiring and quests for dignified, resonating language in modern English were not all that successful. The removal of archaic 'thee, thou, and verbs ending with -eth' removed a certain mystique, which the liturgical language of the 1960s and 1970s could not replicate well. On the ecumenical front, great

---

113 *Reformed Book of Common Order*, Edinburgh: Brunswick Impression, 1977, pp. iv–v.
114 Forrester, 'Worship since 1929', p. 186.
115 *Reformed Book of Common Order*, p. 39.
116 Forrester, 'Worship after 1929', p. 186.

progress was hailed in the publication of the World Council of Churches Faith and Order report, *Baptism, Eucharist and Ministry (BEM)*. It was celebrated and commended to the Churches for comment and response at the 1982 meeting in Lima. A special Eucharistic liturgy was composed, which was regarded as expressing the consensus that had been reached. The Eucharistic Prayer was one which, in theory, should have appealed to the Church of Scotland, since the anamnesis drew on Hebrews and the high priestly ministry of Christ, which had been promoted by William Milligan and was also key to some of the leading Church of Scotland theologians in the 1940s through to the 1970s. The Churches were not asked to respond to the Lima liturgy but to the theology of *BEM*. The Church of Scotland welcomed the basic theological agreement that had been reached and gave a positive response to much of the report. It expressed the view that less than justice had been done to the case for infant baptism. On the Eucharist, the Church of Scotland noted:

(1) While there is agreement on the primary matter of the *fact* of 'real presence', further work is clearly necessary on the secondary matters of modes of interpretation, particularly regarding
the nature of the uniqueness of the real presence of Christ
the nature of His relation to the elements as distinct from His relation to the action
the nature of any change in the elements
the change within ourselves in response to the presence of Christ in the celebration.
(2) The same is true of the precise nature of the sacrifice element in the memorial and the sense in which Christ's sacrifice is 'represented'.[117]

The period saw no publication of service books in the smaller Presbyterian Churches. The United Free Church of Scotland (11,750 members and seventy-two ministers) response to *BEM* was three paragraphs, stating that it found much to disagree with, but received the document 'with interest'. It further noted that the views in the report 'will not find ready acceptance in our congregations'.[118] The smaller Scottish Presbyterian bodies tended to stand aloof from the Ecumenical Movement, and the Liturgical Movement seems to have made little or no impact on them.

---

117 Max Thurian (ed.), *Churches Respond to BEM: Official Responses to the 'Baptism, Eucharist and Ministry' Text*, vol. 1, Geneva: World Council of Churches, 1986, p. 95.
118 Max Thurian (ed.), *Churches Respond to BEM: Official Responses to the 'Baptism, Eucharist and Ministry' Text*, vol. 4, Geneva: World Council of Churches, 1987, p. 183.

10

Into Postmodernity

In an essay reflecting on the Church of Scotland's *Common Order*, 1994, William Storrar noted that worship and culture have always been closely intertwined in the history of church and nation in Scotland. He wrote:

> The problem facing the Church of Scotland today is *not* the fact of its decline as a mass-membership modern institution but its failure to develop the kind of social analysis, theological reflection and missionary ecclesiology which will enable it to steer its way through those rapids of social change that we call the postmodern world in the 1990s; just as George MacLeod offered the Church of Scotland in the 'modern world' of the 1930s. That postmodern world is one which is experienced as a contradictory social existence.[1]

Commentators on cultural trends discerned, or announced, that the period of modernity, which had begun in the late Victorian era and reached a peak in the 1960s and 1970s, had by the 1980s morphed into 'late modernity' or postmodernity.[2] Some of the many 'symptoms' of this cultural turn include the questioning of evolutionary and scientific progress, of the hegemony of Euro-North Atlantic cultural norms and values and of the monopoly of 'experts' in their respective disciplines. It is also the world of more sophisti-cated computers, smartphones, social media – the digital age. There is a new appreciation for plurality and difference and a move away from a universal perspective. Multiple choices have become the new norm. These cultural trends have arisen as the mainline churches continue to decline. The 1980s also saw a retreat from the optimism on the fruits of ecumenism, and Churches began to be more concerned about identity and their specific traditions. There has also been a continuing decline in church membership in the United Kingdom.[3]

This has had an impact on worship styles. Churches find themselves

---

1 William Storrar, 'From *Braveheart* to Faint-Heart: Worship and Culture in Postmodern Scotland', in Bryan D. Spinks and Iain R. Torrance (eds), *To Glorify God: Essays on Modern Reformed Liturgy*, Edinburgh: T&T Clark, 1999, pp. 69–84, pp. 79–80; italics original.

2 David Lyons, *Postmodernity*, second edition, Minneapolis, MN: University of Minne-sota Press, 2005; Steven Connor, *Postmodern Culture: An Introduction to Theories of the Contemporary*, second edition, Oxford: Blackwell, 1997.

3 For a detailed discussion, see Grace Davie, *Religion in Britain: A Persistent Paradox*, Oxford: Blackwell, 2015.

with a 'mixed economy' in worship, from some clergy and people adopting praise-worship style music with informal liturgies, to those who experiment with 'alt.worship', to the enriching of previous older traditions, as well as reformulating older historic denominational forms.[4] These are all reflected in the various evolving forms and provisions for worship in the Scottish Presbyterian Churches.

The Church of Scotland's *Common Order* 1994/96

The dissatisfaction with the 1979 *Book of Common Order* has already been noted, and many ministers in the Church of Scotland preferred that of 1940. The Panel on Worship had already been instructed to look again at the theology of baptism and issued a report in 1983. It endorsed much of the theology of the 1966 *The Doctrine of Baptism*. Its emphasis on grace is illustrated in the following:

> Baptism does not arise out of any work of ours, but is baptism into the work of Christ on our behalf, and must be linked with the presence of the word which tells of that divine work. It is not offered to us as the authentication of anything we have done, or as an expression of anything we have done, or an approval of anything we have done or promised. None of these is the thing signified by the sign. What is signified is what God has done, does and will do. On this alone can human lives be grounded.[5]

The report also considered some pastoral issues. In its wake a revised baptismal rite appeared in 1986. Although based on that of 1979, 1986 represented a revision in phraseology and structure. The setting of the rite was after the normal Liturgy of the Word. In the opening explication a connection between the baptism of Jesus on the Jordan and the 'baptism' suffered on the cross was made. It included an address to the child taken from the rite of baptism of the French Reformed Church:

> N . . ., It was for you that Jesus Christ came down into the world, struggled and suffered; for you he endured the agony of Gethsemane and the darkness of Calvary; for you he cried, 'it is accomplished'; for you he died and for you he conquered death; yes, for you, little one, you who know nothing of it yet. Thus the Apostle's words are confirmed: 'We love God because he loved us first'.[6]

---

4 For fuller discussion, see Bryan D. Spinks, *The Worship Mall: Liturgical Initiatives and Responses in a Postmodern Global World*, London: SPCK, 2010; Church House Publishing USA edition, 2011.

5 *Reports to the General Assembly* 1983, p. 156.

6 For further on the report and this Order, see Bryan D. Spinks, '"Freely by His Grace": Baptismal Doctrine and the Reform of the Baptismal Liturgy in the Church of Scotland, 1953–1994', in Nathan Mitchell and John F. Baldovin (eds), *Rule of Prayer, Rule of Faith: Essays in Honor of Aidan Kavanagh, OSB*, Collegeville, MN: Liturgical Press, 1996, pp. 218–42.

In 1987, the Panel on Worship noted that the 1940 *Book of Common Order* would soon be out of print, and after discussion, the General Assembly requested the Panel to proceed without delay to produce a new *Book of Common Order*.[7] In the meantime, other resources for 'contemporary' worship had been published. In 1989 a second volume of *Worship Now* appeared, with compilations from a number of those who were either connected with or had been involved in both the Panel for Worship and the Church Service Society. The editors noted:

> Our aim is not to provide an alternative to the more official service books and publications on worship, but to complement them. Nor do we aim to lay down some new norm for contemporary worship, but rather to open up new possibilities by showing the varied work of some of those who are seeking a contemporary idiom in worship. The material is meant to be seen as flexible and adaptable. Not all of it will be appropriate to everyone in the different settings in which we worship. But all that is published here has been used and is in use, and none of it has been specially written for this publication. We hope that the book may be seen as a resource, and that it will encourage others to 'conceive their own prayers'. It may be that some of the material stimulated by this book will find its way into our hands for inclusion in a future volume, and we will be happy if it does.[8]

This compilation is a good example of both devolution and evolution. The prayers that were included had all been used in worship services and so give some idea of the breadth of form, style and content of public worship. At the same time, they were offered for use and as paradigms for others to use. The variety is illustrated by two examples from Opening Prayers for Worship. Form 3, by W. J. G. McDonald of Mayfield Church, Edinburgh, began:

> Father, this is our worship –
> To turn away from the daily duties and the passing show,
> And from the work that awaits us tomorrow;
> To stand in the presence of what is real,
> To bow in the presence of the Eternal.[9]

Form 5, by T. Graeme Longmuir, chaplain of Strathallan School, began:

> Glorious God, before whom the mountains salute with mist-capped peaks, rivers run their cascading courses, lochs pulsate with silent ripples, trees

---

7 *Reports to the General Assembly of the Church of Scotland*, Edinburgh: Pillars & Wilson, 1987.

8 *Worship Now Book II*, compiled by Duncan D. Forrester, David S. M. Hamilton, Alan Main and James A. Whyte, Edinburgh: Saint Andrew Press, 1989, p. vii.

9 *Worship Now Book II*, p. 7.

of the field clap their hands, and rolling hills cry aloud for joy; your glory shines through tinted colour, breezes through leaf-filled woods, sparkles in the rushing stream, and wakens shores from peaceful slumbers.[10]

The compilation had four sections covering an anthology of prayers for opening worship, adoration and confession, thanksgiving and intercession, as well as a complete Sunday Service; worship for the seasons of the Christian year; Sacraments and ordinances; and Acts of Worship for special services, including small group and family worship. The material for Holy Communion seems to have been 'experimental' in the sense that none followed the 'classical' pattern found in the *Book of Common Order* of 1940 and 1979, and there was no classical pattern of the Eucharistic Prayer. Form 8 included a contemporary form of the 'Reformed Sursum corda' of William Farel, John Calvin and the 1556 Genevan *Form of Prayers*:

> And thus, as one community, members of the one Body of Jesus Christ, and baptized by the one Spirit, we together take this bread and wine, and call upon the Spirit of Christ to descend upon us, be among us, and raise us up to heaven, that *this* may be for us the bread of life, and *this* the cup of our salvation.[11]

One of the characteristics of much of the material was that it took the form of statements responsively said by minister and congregation, or words addressed to the congregation rather than being cast in the form of prayer addressed to God.

In its report to the General Assembly in May 1990, the Panel on Worship, with Andrew J. Scobie as its convener, noted a Gaelic publication for children, reported on the progress of the revision of the *Book of Common Order* and commended a publication, *Together in Worship*. It also outlined the provisional Table of Contents of the new *Book of Common Order*. The report also noted that many ministers felt that their training in music and worship was inadequate and that 'Ordination does not bestow omnicompetence'.[12] The term of office expired for both the convener and the vice-convener, David C. MacFarlane, and they were succeeded by John Bell and T. Graeme Longmuir respectively.

In the light of *Together in Worship*, in 1991 the Panel on Worship published *Worshipping Together*, to assist worship conducted by kirk session teams. It offered guidelines for planning and conducting worship, with a recommendation to follow the liturgical calendar as set out in the Joint Liturgical Group's two-year lectionary, as well as a recommended outline for the Order of Worship. Since it was intended for lay-led worship, there

---

10 *Worship Now Book II*, p. 9.
11 *Worship Now Book II*, p. 160; italics original.
12 *Reports to the General Assembly* 1990, pp. 199, 201 and 209.

were no sacramental services included. The copy I have was certainly used and has changes to the wording and additions in pencil – a reminder of how both laity as well as ministers would 'tweak' published prayers.[13]

The Panel on Worship report of 1993 expressed the hope that the new *Book of Common Order* would be on its way to publication and drew attention to the growth of 'spirituality' and revived interest in the Celtic expression of the Christian faith. It also advised that the *Church Hymnary* be revised; in fact most of the report was taken up with discussion of music and hymnals. Of note was the observation:

> In some of our churches, there is increasing use of a shared scriptural call to worship; in some there may be the use of a phrase such as, 'Lord, in your mercy,' 'hear our prayer'; or of a sung response such as, 'O Lord. Hear my prayer', during intercessions. In other places, the recitation of the Apostles' Creed at Holy Baptism or the Nicene Creed at Holy Communion is being encouraged, as is the more frequent observance of Holy Communion itself.[14]

Responsorial prayers and litanies were becoming increasingly common, and there was also the recognition that a growing number of congregations were celebrating Communion more regularly.

A new book with the title *Common Order* was published in 1994, and an emended edition was published in 1996. In the Preface, John Bell, who had become convener of the Panel on Worship in the late stages of its preparation, explained the title thus:

> This is a *common* book, because it belongs to all the people of God. . . . it is also a book of *order*. In worship we engage as the Body of Christ in an encounter with almighty God. This engagement should never become a rambling incoherence of well-meaning phrases and gestures. It should exhibit that deliberate and historical patterning of sentiment and expression which befits the meeting of the sons and daughters of earth with the King of Kings.[15]

The secretary, Charles Robertson, wrote:

> The new book is for the whole Church, not just for ministers. Provision has been made for the people to participate, either by offering a substantial part for them to say in the service or by making some of the material responsorial. The Panel wishes it to be known that, in the early days of

---

13 The Panel on Worship, *Worshipping Together*, Edinburgh: Saint Andrew Press, 1991. Pencil changes made on p. 10 to the confession, and to the prayers, pp. 53, 55 and 69.
14 *Reports to the General Assembly* 1994, p. 291.
15 *Common Order*, Edinburgh: St Andrew Press, 1994, p. x; italics original.

the new book's life, there will be no bar to photocopying or duplicating the Panel's copyright material for congregational use.[16]

This was an invitation for local adaptation and parish personalising of the material. Charles Robertson has recounted something of the genesis of this liturgical compilation:

> The Committee was always aware that, in a telling phrase, it could 'no more devise living worship than build a tree'. Creative activity is not generally the hallmark of committees, and the Liturgical committee of the Panel knew it was no exception to the rule. While it was determined to produce the best book it could, there was no guarantee that the protracted and painful process of hammering out drafts (provided by members of the committee), levelling and receiving criticism and framing revisions would result in peerless prayers and matchless liturgies. But eventually, the principal services, forms of prayer and other worship material did emerge, with whatever felicity the readers and users can best judge. When the work was about half-way finished, a group of four (messrs Scobie, Longmuir, and Robertson, together with Dr John Shaw Dunn, a lecturer in anatomy at the University of Glasgow, a keen churchman and a know-ledgeable liturgist) spent three days together, reviewing the material, identifying gaps and sketching out the orders and prayers necessary to complete the book. The committee thereafter, and in particular the smaller group of four, continued the work until a complete first, and then a second, draft of the book was presented to the Panel. Final adjustments were made to the text and the book was published by the Saint Andrew Press in May 1994.[17]

The committee felt free to draw on the whole range of Christian experience from whatever source so that the book could reflect the insights of the Christian spirituality of the whole Church, which included not only historical liturgies, but Roman Catholic, Anglican and Reformed.[18]

By the late 1970s, the issue of inclusive language in English-language worship was becoming an issue. In 1982, there had been a controversy over the use of a prayer by the Congregationalist Brian Wren in which God was addressed as 'Mother'.[19] In the wake of the controversy, and a report by the Panel on Doctrine, an explicit undertaking was given to the General Assembly in 1986 and 1988 to use inclusive language wherever possible, and the committee tried to be sensitive in its use of language to describe

---

16 *Common Order*, p. xvii.

17 Charles Robertson, '*Common Order*: An Introduction', in Spinks and Torrance (eds), *To Glorify God*, pp. 1–11, p. 3.

18 Robertson, '*Common Order*: An Introduction', p. 6.

19 Finlay MacDonald, *From Reform to Renewal: Scotland's Kirk by Century*, Edinburgh: Saint Andrew Press, 2017, p. 198.

God.[20] A. Stewart Todd regretted that the Panel had not included material with the older 'thee/thou' form of address.[21]

Common Order commenced with private prayers for the minister and also with the choir. It contained five orders each for Sunday Morning and Evening services, orders for baptism (for a child and for an adult), for Confirmation and included five orders for Holy Communion, orders for marriages, funerals and various ordinances, as well as seasonal prayers, a daily devotion, lectionary and collects of the day. Morning and Evening Services followed the pattern that W. D. Maxwell had championed, namely the fore-mass or *missa sicca* rather than the Anglican form based on the Divine office, though the exact sequence and provisions varied.[22] The fourth Morning Service attempted to emulate the 'Celtic' tradition that was becoming popular, the call to Worship being as follows:

> God is the King of moon and sun;
> God is the King of stars beloved.
> He knows our every need;
> He is the kindly God of life.[23]

Common Order retains separate baptisms for child and adult candidates. The rite for a child begins with scriptural warrants. A Statement follows, the final paragraph of which stresses the love of God in baptism. The parents are asked if they receive the teaching of the Church, and the Apostles' Creed is recited. The prayer over the water follows – it places in brackets the rehearsal of the mighty deeds of God in the flood, Noah and Moses and the baptism of Jesus; these may be omitted. However, when the minister pours water into the font he asks God to:

> Send your Holy Spirit
> upon us and upon this water,
> that N . . .,
> being buried with Christ in baptism,
> may rise with him to newness of life;
> and being born anew of water and the Holy Spirit
> may remain for ever in the number of your faithful children;
> through . . .[24]

---

20 Robertson, '*Common Order*: An Introduction', p. 7.

21 A. Stewart Todd, '*Common Order*', *The Record* 27 (1994), pp. 22–6, p. 22.

22 See Chapter 9.

23 *Common Order*, 1994, p. 35; see also Graham Woolfenden, '"Everyday will I bless you, and praise your name forever and ever": Daily Prayer in *Common Order* and the *Book of Common Worship*', in Spinks and Torrance, *To Glorify God*, pp. 213–25.

24 *Common Order*, 1994, p. 89.

The original draft omitted the concept of rebirth, and may reflect the influences of David Hamilton's *Through the Waters*.[25] Hamilton, Lecturer in Practical Theology at the University of Glasgow, examined the biblical images used for baptism and although he commended the use of the Address from the French Reformed rite, lamented the fact that its 'Instruction' of that rite had been replaced by the 1979 introduction, and lacked reference to the destroying power of water and dying and rising in baptism. Although he discussed the image of rebirth, he argued that dying and rising was more appropriate. In *Common Order* reference to rebirth was added after a telephone conversation between the present writer and Charles Robertson.

The Address from the French Reformed rite was retained, though rephrased:

N . . .,
for you Jesus Christ came into the world:
for you he lived and showed God's love;
for you he suffered the darkness of Calvary
and cried at the last, 'It is accomplished';
for you he triumphed over death
and rose in newness of life;
for you he ascended to reign at God's right hand.
All this he did for you, N . . .,
Though you do not know it yet.
And so the word of Scripture is fulfilled:
'We love because God loved us first'.[26]

The Baptism follows, and a blessing, and then the promises of the parents and their duties. The 1996 emended edition allowed for the baptismal formula to be either 'baptised *in* the name' or 'baptised *into* the name'. The overall theological emphasis on sheer grace is forcefully expressed. The commitment of the congregation follows and then the prayers. For adult baptism, the rite is very similar, except that after the baptism, in place of parental promises, the candidate makes his or her own promise. There is a short form if Confirmation is not taking place; otherwise the candidate makes the Confirmation promises. *Common Order* was still working out liturgically the implications of its reports on baptism overseen by T. F. Torrance, and in many ways could be seen as the liturgical expression of Torrance's baptismal theology.[27]

---

25 David S. M. Hamilton, *Through the Waters: Baptism and the Christian Life*, Edinburgh: T&T Clark, 1990.

26 *Common Order*, 1994, p. 89.

27 See Bryan D. Spinks, '"Freely by His Grace"', in Mitchell and Baldovin, *Rule of Prayer, Rule of Faith*, pp. 218–42. See also Iain Torrance, 'Fear of being Left Out and Confidence in being Included: The Liturgical Celebration of Ecclesial Boundaries. A Comment on the Baptismal Liturgies of the *Book of Common Worship* (1993) and *Common Order* (1994)', and James F. Kay, 'The New Rites of Baptism: A Dogmatic Assessment', both in Spinks and Torrance, *To Glorify God*, pp. 159–72 and pp. 201–12.

Five forms for Holy Communion were provided. Robertson explained:

The principal Order follows a more or less classical pattern and offers three Thanksgivings or Eucharistic Prayers, thus allowing for variety and frequency of celebration. Each one of these is different in character: the first follows the classical pattern in structure and language; the second is drawn from our own Reformed tradition, from the *Genevan Service Book*; and the third comes from the world Church (English Language Liturgical Consultation, ELLC).

The second Order reflects the Celtic tradition; the third is a shorter Order to be used at a second Service or other similar occasion; the fourth is for use when children communicate; and the fifth is for use at home or in hospital.[28]

The Eucharistic Prayers reverted to the 1940 and older format, omitting the words of institution, instead having them read as a warrant prior to the prayer and again at the fraction, a feature that was criticised by the convener for the 1979 book, A. Stewart Todd.[29] The 1996 edition added a note: 'The narrative of the Institution (n.22) may be incorporated within the Thanksgiving', and it gave the introductory wording to facilitate this.[30] The omission of the Sancta sanctis was criticised by Tom Davidson Kelly, who argued that it weakened our common celebration: 'First, the element of paradox, secondly, the sense of majesty and the greatness of God and thirdly, the ecumenical dimension of common witness with the eastern Churches.'[31] This liturgical item was restored in the 1996 edition, after the Lord's Prayer and before the fraction.[32]

In the principal Order, alternative Eucharistic Prayer A had the 1940 version 'pleading his eternal sacrifice', and contained an epiclesis asking God to 'bless us and these your gifts of bread and wine' so that they may be the communion of the body and blood of Christ.[33] Alternative C echoed a Eucharistic Prayer that originated as an ecumenical prayer in the USA, and the epiclesis asked to send the Holy Spirit 'upon us and upon this bread and wine that we who eat and drink at this holy table may share the life of Christ our Lord'.[34] The 'Celtic flavour' of the second order caught the attention of the Swiss Reformed liturgist, Bruno Bürki, who wrote: 'Remarkable here are not only the concrete and natural prayer language, but also the image of humans urgently approaching God in prayer and the

---

28 *Common Order*, 1994, p. xv.
29 Todd, '*Common Order*', pp. 25–6.
30 *Common Order*, 1996, p. 143.
31 Tom Davidson Kelly, 'What happened to the Sancta Sanctis?', *The Record* 27 (1994), pp. 30–2, p. 32.
32 *Common Order*, 1996, p. 138.
33 *Common Order*, 1994, pp. 133–4.
34 *Common Order*, 1994, p. 137.

close relationship among those praying, aspects we are not used to in the more reserved and detached Western liturgy.'[35]

An example of the style is illustrated from the last paragraph of the opening prayers:

As we receive the word and knowledge
of your forgiveness,
enshield, encircle us,
each day, each night,
each dark, each light.
Uphold us,
be our treasure,
our triumph everlasting;
strong Son of God most high.[36]

A. Stewart Todd felt the 'Gallican' (*sic*) exuberance was heart-warming, but Peter Thomson believed that since the Celtic tradition is only a small part of the whole, the Celtic material stood out somewhat awkwardly.[37]

The marriage rites show influence from the Church of England's *Alternative Services Book*, 1980. Three different marriage orders were given and a form for blessing a civil marriage, though A. Stewart Todd believed that the wording might suggest two tiers of marriage, when in fact all marriages are a gift of God.[38] For funerals, plenty of options and provisions were given, with two Orders and an Order for a Funeral of a Child. However, in comparison with the funeral orders in the 1993 *Book of Common Worship* of the Presbyterian Church of America, *Common Order* had a less confident soteriology, summed up by William Young:

It is not honest to speak and pray as though you took for granted that someone is in glory when you are fairly sure he isn't. Of course, there are many cases when you don't know, and while you cannot speak with the same measure of assurance, you have at least to give the deceased 'the benefit of the doubt' and to speak of any signs of God's grace in his life of which you have been conscious.[39]

---

35 Bruno Bürki, 'The Celebration of the Eucharist in *Common Order* (1994) and in Continental Reformed liturgies', in Spinks and Torrance, *To Glorify God*, pp. 227–39, p. 236.

36 *Common Order*, 1994, p. 146.

37 Todd, '*Common Order*', p. 25; Peter D. Thomson, '*Common Order*', *The Record* 27 (1994), pp. 27–9, p. 28.

38 Todd, '*Common Order*', p. 24. See also, Kenneth Stevenson, 'The New Marriage Rites: Their Place in the Tradition', in Spinks and Torrance, *To Glorify God*, pp. 173–86.

39 William Young, 'Funerals in a rural parish', *The Record* 14 (1986) pp. 2–8, p. 2; Bryan D. Spinks, 'Ecclesiology and Soteriology Shaping Eschatology: The Funeral Rites in Perspective' in Spinks and Torrance, *To Glorify God*, pp. 187–99.

A major step was taken with the lectionary. In 1979, the Church of Scotland, as a member of the Joint Liturgical Group (JLG), had used the group's two-year lectionary. However, another ecumenical lectionary, the Revised Common Lectionary (RCL), inspired by the three-year Roman Catholic Lectionary, was becoming popular. *Common Order* adopted RCL. This influenced the Church of England. A proposal had been made for the liturgical revision that would become *Common Worship* 2000 to use the RCL, but the House of Bishops was reluctant to break from the JLG lectionary, which had been upgraded to a four-year cycle. Once the Church of Scotland had adopted the RCL, the House of Bishops agreed that the Church of England should be in step with the other national Church in the United Kingdom.

Common Order remains the current Church of Scotland liturgical exemplar; a further edition was published in 2005.

Iona Community and Wild Goose Publications

Norman Shanks notes that when George MacLeod founded the Iona Community in 1938, few would have predicted that it would be flourishing seventy years later.[40] Shanks explains:

> Within the Community we often wonder at the Community's continuing existence, when so much has changed – 280 members now and still growing; as many women members as men (it was not until 1969 that women could become members and now we have a woman leader); no longer do the majority of members live in Scotland; there are now more non-ordained people than ministers of Word and sacrament among the membership; and an increased proportion belongs to a tradition other than the (Presbyterian) Church of Scotland from which the majority came for many years – although particular denominational loyalties are of little consequence alongside our sense of belonging together around our shared purpose.[41]

Both the community and its publishing house, Wild Goose Publications, have continued to make significant contributions to worship. *The Iona Community Worship Book* continues to be expanded and updated, including the use of modern language. That of *c.*1984 had for its opening versicles:

Leader: The world belongs to the Lord.
All: The earth and its people are his.

---

40 Norman Shanks, 'The Worship of the Iona Community and its Global Impact', in Duncan B. Forrester and Doug Gay (eds), *Worship and Liturgy in Context: Studies and Case Studies in Theology and Practice*, London: SCM Press, 2009, pp. 230–45, p. 230.

41 Shanks, 'The Worship of the Iona Community', p. 231.

L: How good and how lovely it is
All: To live together in unity
L: Love and faith come together
All: Justice and peace join hands
L: If the Lord's disciples keep quiet
All: These stones would shout aloud.
L: Lord, open our lips
All: And our mouths shall proclaim your praise.[42]

Compared with the earlier forms, there is a greater variety, newer hymns and the addition of a hymn or psalm before the scripture reading. The collection, though, is always a work in progress, with periodic revisions and expansion; for example, in the 1991 edition, the last versicle quoted above becomes 'Open our lips, O God'.[43] Shanks notes that since 1999 there has been a shift in the Community to a six-day week, with the commitment service taking place on Wednesday and the Communion on Thursday, with a flexible service on Friday. He explains:

None of these services is exclusive: on each occasion it is 'public worship' that is offered, and invariably, as well as guests and staff, visitors to the island and often some of the local island community attend also. In addition, for many years one of the highlights each week has been the 'Pilgrimage', now held on Tuesdays, a guided walk around Iona, stopping at places of historical/religious significance for a brief act of worship – typically involving a reading, a reflection, a prayer and a song. And each weekday afternoon at 2 p.m. there are brief prayers for peace and justice, provided particularly so that day-visitors may share in the Abbey worship, but usually attended also by some guests and staff.[44]

Provision for these devotions were already present in the 1991 revised edition of the *Worship Book*, which also included a 'Creation Liturgy' and 'A Celtic Evening Liturgy' as well as prayers for justice and peace, for healing and 'The Iona Pilgrimage'.

An important contribution from the Wild Goose Worship Group, in which John Bell and Graham Maule have been key authors, has been the *Wee Worship Books*. The recent editions have been listed as 'incarnations'. The fourth edition, 1999, went through many reprints until 2014. The Introduction explained that it was 'not intended to replace denominational service books, but to enable people from a diversity of backgrounds to share forms of prayer which are not bound to the canons and sensitivities of one Christian tradition'.[45] It gave some guidelines on how to use the

---

42 *Iona Community Worship Book*, np and nd, but inscribed by the purchaser July 1984.
43 *The Iona Community Worship Book*, Glasgow: Wild Goose Publications, 1991 revised edition, p. 9.
44 Shanks, 'The Worship of the Iona Community', p. 234.
45 *A Wee Worship Book*, Glasgow: Wild Goose Publications, 1999, p. 7.

liturgies, covering planning, leadership, environment, music, the use of the Bible, conversations, symbolic actions and Holy Communion. Five liturgies were provided each for Morning and Evening and two for Daytime. Two Orders of Communion were included and a service of healing. The Prayer before the scripture readings in Morning Liturgy A gives an excellent idea of the style:

> In you, gracious God,
> The widowed find a carer,
> The orphaned find a parent,
> The fearful find a friend.[46]

The communion liturgies did not have the exact same structural sub-headings, though the differences are not of great significance. Communion A recommended a gathering song or silence, a responsorial call to worship and an optional invitation, which included: 'But here, at this table, [Jesus] is the host.'[47] A Song was sung, during which the bread and wine may be brought forward. This was followed by 'the story', which was a dialogue between celebrant and a reader and included the Institution narrative. The Eucharistic Prayer followed, with traditional dialogue. A Festal Preface was provided as an alternative to the fixed Preface, which gave thanks for the world. The third paragraph prayed:

> And grateful as we are
> for the world we know
> and the universe beyond our ken,
> we particularly praise you,
> whom eternity cannot contain,
> for the coming to earth and entering time
> in Jesus.[48]

The phrase 'beyond our ken' seems antiquated to English ears, but is a common one in Scottish dialect. The prayer asked God to send the Holy Spirit 'to settle on this bread and wine and fill them with the fullness of Jesus', and it asked that the Spirit rest on the communicants.[49] A most interesting responsorial fraction was provided:

> **Fraction**: (*Taking and breaking bread*)
> *Celebrant*: Among friends, gathered round a table,
> Jesus took bread, and broke it, and said,
> 'this is my body – broken for you'.
> (*Holding up a cup of wine*)

---

46 *A Wee Worship Book*, 1999, p. 14.
47 *A Wee Worship Book*, 1999, p. 84.
48 *A Wee Worship Book*, 1999, p. 86.
49 *A Wee Worship Book*, 1999, p. 88.

Later he took a cup of wine and said,
'This is the new relationship with God
Made possible because of my death.
Take it, all of you, to remember me.'
Jesus, firstborn of Mary.
ALL: HAVE MERCY ON US.
Celebrant: Jesus, saviour of the world.
ALL: HAVE MERCY ON US.
Celebrant: Jesus, monarch of heaven,
GRANT US PEACE.
Celebrant: He whom the universe could not contain,
Is present to us in this bread.
He who redeemed us and called us by name
Now meets us in this cup.
So take this bread and this wine.
In them God comes to us
So that we may come to God.[50]

A fifth 'incarnation' was published in 2015, now providing six services each for Morning and Evening and a single communion liturgy with alternative prefaces and an alternative Eucharistic Prayer. It also provided modern 'affirmations of faith'. In the main text of the Eucharistic Prayer, the lead into the Sanctus included joining voices, not only with angelic hosts but also with the Church throughout the world, 'Orthodox and Lutheran, Catholic and Reformed'.[51] Jesus is the one 'who was born among us incognito'.[52] The fraction was more traditional than in 1999, focusing on the Institution narrative, and was for the celebrant alone.[53]

Other members of the Iona Community have also made significant contributions. Kathy Galloway edited *The Pattern of Our Days*, 1996, which offered liturgies for a wide variety of themes, such as Pilgrimages and Journeys, Healing and Acts of Witness and dissent. Norman Shanks has noted that following this as a model, an increasing number of books with liturgies, worship resources and reflective material composed by a remarkable range of other members, associate members and staff of the community have appeared. 'It is notable,' says Shanks, 'that among these are many women, whose distinctive voice has in a variety of ways added a significant dimension both to the Community itself and to what in the Community's worship is valued by the wider Church.'[54] John Bell and Graham Maule have also contributed many collections of modern hymns

---

50 *A Wee Worship Book*, 1999, pp. 88–9.
51 *A Wee Worship Book*, Glasgow: Wild Goose Publications, 2015, p. 90.
52 *A Wee Worship Book*, 2015, p. 90.
53 *A Wee Worship Book*, 2015, p. 91.
54 Shanks, 'The Worship of the Iona Community', p. 243. Examples are *Cloth for the Cradle*, 1997 and *Fire and Bread*, 2005. A full list of publications is available on the Wild Goose Publications website: www.ionabooks.com/.

and songs, such as *When Grief is Raw: Songs for Times of Sorrow and Bereavement, The Courage to Say No* and *A Road to Roam*. Bell has also defended and encouraged congregational song, as well as sketches and scripts for worship.[55] In conversation, both John Philip Newell and John Bell have shared with the author that they, as invited speakers, and the Iona worship resources, enjoy far greater popularity in England and the USA than in Scotland.[56] It may well be that the Iona material is too avant-garde for many Presbyterian parishes' worship, and it might also be a hangover from the suspicion towards George MacLeod and his pacifism. The result is that, like certain Scottish whiskys, much of the material seems to have a greater market abroad than at home.

Hymnody, *Church Hymnary* fourth edition, and the places where they sing

As noted in the previous chapter, the third edition of *Church Hymnary* was already out of date when it appeared, and never achieved wide popularity. Supplemental publications appeared as *Songs for the Seventies* and *Songs for a Day*. In 1988, *Songs of God's People* was published, with a preface by John Bell, who was convener of the Supplement Committee. Bell explained that to increase the practicality and appeal of the book, guitar chords were included and well-known tunes were offered as alternatives to new melodies.[57]

Elsewhere, Bell has noted that although it was vilified by some musical elites, it sold nearly a quarter of a million copies, though that was not necessarily an endorsement of aesthetic or theological value.[58] In 1998 an ecumenical compilation, *Common Ground*, was published. Charles Robertson, in a brief Introduction, singled out John Bell and Douglas Galbraith, who had undertaken the editing of the material and preparation for publication. The collection included global songs, popular choruses and hymns, as well as liturgical material, such as the Agnus Dei. However, already in

---

55 John Bell and Graham Maule, *When Grief is Raw: Songs for Times of Sorrow and Bereavement*, Glasgow: Wild Goose Publications, 1997; *The Courage to say No: Twenty-three Songs for Lent and Easter*, Glasgow: Wild Goose Publications, 2004; *A Road to Roam: A Way of Celebrating Sacred Space*, Glasgow: Wild Goose Resource Group, 2006; John L. Bell, *The Singing Thing: A Case for Congregational Song*, Glasgow: Wild Goose Publications, 2000; *Wild Goose Prints No.1*, Glasgow: Wild Goose Publications, 1989.

56 John Philip Newell is a former warden of Iona and editor of *The Iona Worship Book*, Glasgow: Wild Goose Publications, 1991, as well as collections of Celtic-style prayers for morning and evening; John Bell is a member of the Iona Community, and an accomplished musician and composer, as well as having served as convener of the Panel on Worship. See also Liz Graham, 'The Evolution and Impact of the Worship of the Iona Community 1938–1998', dissertation for the BD Hons, University of Edinburgh, 1998.

57 *Songs of God's People*, Oxford: Oxford University Press, 1988.

58 John Bell, 'Scottish Hymnody: An Ecumenical and personal Perspective', in Forrester and Gay (eds), *Worship and Liturgy in Context*, pp. 259–78, p. 266.

1994, the General Assembly had approved the appointment of a committee to produce a replacement for the 1973 *Church Hymnary*. John Bell was the convener and Charles Robertson the secretary. The completed hymnal was published in 2005. In the Introduction, John Bell explained that the world of 1973 had dramatically changed, that this new edition was intended to be used for the worship of God in the twenty-first century and so needed 'to reflect the contemporary experience of humanity and the contemporary fruits of God's creative spirit'.[59] Elsewhere Bell has identified the hallmarks of the collection of 825 texts with 658 tunes as having a genuine Scottish character, an international perspective and an explicit incarnational theology.[60] The first 109 items in this hymnal contain psalm versions and a selection of doxologies, and most of these are intended for singing. Of the non-metrical psalms, the new hymnal included material from Taizé, plainchant, Anglican chant and material from Roman Catholic sources (Bernadette Farrell, James Quinn and Joseph Gelineau). Graham Deans noted that the music for the Psalmody included traditional and modern Scottish tunes, Gaelic and Lowland melodies, Scottish chants and other pieces by John Bell and Ian White.[61] Ten items were provided in the section for baptism, including the Apostles' Creed in the version of the English Language Liturgical Consultation (ELLC). The section for Holy Communion included the texts of the Gloria and Sursum corda and musical settings for the Sanctus, Benedictus and the Agnus Dei (ELLC texts), and several versions of the Lord's Prayer. Twenty-three hymns were provided, ranging from compilations by John Macleod to contemporary hymns by Brian Wren, John Bell and Graham Maule. It aimed to be global in its selection of words and music, and achieved that goal. Reflecting on the theological perspectives of music in worship, Douglas Galbraith has written:

> It is music capable of directing our thoughts through and beyond our belonging together to our being one in Christ; music which has a numinous or transcendent quality at the same time as recognizing our need for each other; music which – after, within or in spite of the human contribution that has been made – mediates the divine.[62]

The fourth edition of the *Church Hymnary* aimed to fulfil that too.

In May 2014, a report was published entitled *The Setting of Presbyterian Worship*. It sought to inform discussion on how theology shapes not only the style of worship but also the place of worship. It gave a brief historical

---

59 *Church Hymnary*, fourth edition, Norwich: Canterbury Press, 2005, p. vii.

60 Bell, 'Scottish Hymnody', pp. 273–6.

61 Graham D. S. Deans, '*Race Shall Thy Works Praise unto Race': The Development of Metrical Psalmody in Scotland*, The Hymn Society of Great Britain and Ireland, Occasional paper 5, np, 2012, p. 31.

62 Douglas Galbraith, 'Assist our Song: Theological Perspectives on Worship and its Music', in James C. Stewart (ed.), *A Usable Past? Belief, Worship and Song in Reformation Context*, Edinburgh: Church Service Society, 2013, pp. 58–83, p. 74.

overview of church architecture and the styles found in Scotland since the Reformation, particularly noting the influence of Gothic architecture since the nineteenth century. It wryly observed:

> In 1965, at the World's Fair in New York, there was an exhibition of what was then envisioned to be the shape of cities of the future. The only recognisable building in the exhibit was the church as it was designed in a Gothic cathedral style, showing that the architects and visionaries had only one conception of what a church might always look like![63]

It set out fourteen principles of note for church buildings for the twenty-first century. One of these included the questioning of using pews rather than chairs, the importance of aesthetics – colour, shape, smell, sense of space; visibility and audibility, good and appropriate art to assist in worship and not simply to fill gaps; and that buildings should be related to the world about them. It noted:

> The Church needs to be contemporary. We are not returning to the past, though we can learn from it. Nor are we building, or creating, a space merely for the present. The Church building will be, and must be, related to the surroundings of the moment, and with an eye to the future for we are a people who have chosen not to settle down. We are instead people of faith.[64]

Sacramental reflections

One of the results of the Ecumenical Movement has been a sharing of 'international' scholarly resources, with less particular denominational emphasis. This may account for the fact that there seems to have been no major systematic works on sacramental theology emanating from Church of Scotland theologians in the last few years. There have been, however, a few practical guides and coaches for celebration of the sacraments, and there has been a significant rethink of baptismal practice.[65]

Although the implications of the Special Commission on Baptism, chaired by T. F. Torrance, was that baptism is an action of God's free grace, in 1963 the General Assembly passed Act XVII stipulating the conditions for infant baptism. Baptism may be administered to a child:

> whose parents, one or both, have themselves been baptized, are in full communion with the Church, and undertake the Christian upbringing of the child;

---

63 The Church of Scotland Mission and Discipleship Council, *The Setting of Presbyterian Worship*, Committee on Church Art and Architecture, May 2014, p. 13.

64 *The Setting of Presbyterian Worship*, p. 17.

65 For an overall view, see Mark Macleod, 'Recent Sacramental Developments in the Kirk', *Theology in Scotland* 22 (2015), pp. 29–60.

whose parents, one or both, having been baptized but not in full communion, are such that the Kirk Session is satisfied that he or she is an
adherent permanently connected with the congregation and supporting
the work and worship of the Church and will undertake the Christian
upbringing of the child;
whose parents, one or both, have themselves been baptized, profess the
Christian faith, undertake to ensure that such child grows up in the life
and worship and express the desire to seek admission to full membership
of the Church. In such cases the Kirk Session shall appoint the Elder of
the District in which the parent resides, or some other person, to shepherd
them into full communion and to exercise pastoral care of the child concerned.
who, being of unknown parentage, or otherwise separated from his or
her parents, is in the view of the Kirk Session under Christian care and
guardianship.[66]

The work of the Special Commission had been undertaken in the 1950s
at a time when infant baptism was the norm and church membership
was still relatively strong. A challenge to the first of these was made in
many articles and essays by David F. Wright, Professor of Patristic and
Reformed Christianity at Edinburgh, and an elder at Holyrood Abbey
Church, Edinburgh.[67] Though at times Wright appears to have been stuck
in the Cullman–Aland debate on infant baptism of the 1950s and 1960s,
he nevertheless called into question the assumption that infant baptism
was normative. He suggested that in infant baptism, parents and sponsors
should confess their own faith and not speak on behalf of the child:

All trace of vicarious renunciation and profession of faith by sponsors,
as though by some form of ventriloquism, must be abandoned. This
means, secondly, that the faith that is called for is that of the parents,
godparents or other sponsors and of the church community as a whole
... Thirdly, indiscriminate administration and all unnecessary haste must
be avoided.[68]

The normativity of infant baptism had also been called into question by the
1982 WCC publication *Baptism, Eucharist and Ministry*, which emphasised two equivalent alternatives of Christian initiation – believers' baptism;
and infant baptism followed by catechesis with a rite such as confirmation.

---

66 Report of the Special Commission on Baptism, May 1962, p. 22. See also Paul Nimmo,
'Baptismal Theology and Practice in the Church of Scotland', in Forrester and Gay (eds),
Worship and Liturgy in Context, pp. 92–106, p. 99.

67 David F. Wright, *Infant Baptism in Historical Perspective: Collected Studies*, Bletchley:
Paternoster Press, 2007.

68 David F. Wright, *What has Infant Baptism done to Baptism? An Enquiry at the End of
Christendom*, Bletchley: Paternoster Press, 2005, p. 80

Some studies have also questioned whether the theology of Torrance is in continuity with or a break from reformed tradition.[69] However, change in practice in the Church of Scotland was demanded by pastoral and mission concerns, since membership numbers have continued to decline and some parents seeking baptism for their child did not meet the requirements of the 1963 Act.

In 1999, a report to the General Assembly linked infant baptism to mission and evangelism. In 2000, the General Assembly introduced legislation that particularly favoured the baptism of adult believers, and in 2001 the Panel on Worship published a booklet entitled *Christian Baptism*, which gave an outline and explanation of the services in *Common Order*, with information for those preparing for baptism.[70] The booklet explained that baptism is a sign that an adult or a child has been chosen by Christ as one of his disciples. It is also the seal of entry into the one, holy, catholic and apostolic Church.[71] Sections explained who qualified for baptism and explained what takes place in the service. Practical matters such as dress, godparents, videos and documents and papers was also covered.

A new report on baptism, prepared by the Panel on Doctrine on Baptism, was presented to the General Assembly in 2003, which urged a change in requirements for infant baptism as well as the recognition of the growth in adult baptisms.[72] Drawing on ecumenical discussions, it noted:

> Among the most significant recent developments the following may be identified: the placing of baptism within a wider context of Christian initiation. *BEM* encouraged the view that there was perhaps no huge difference between two dominant patterns: infant baptism followed by Christian nurture leading to profession of faith in admission to communion (confirmation) and infant blessing/thanksgiving followed by Christian nurture leading to baptism on profession of faith. Post-*BEM*

---

69 John A. Scott, 'Recovering the Meaning of Baptism in Westminster Calvinism in Critical Dialogue with Thomas F. Torrance', PhD thesis, University of Edinburgh, 2015; Ruth H. B. Morrison, 'A Study of the Special Commission on Baptism (1953–63) and Developments in Baptismal doctrine and practice in the Church of Scotland since 1963', PhD thesis, University of Glasgow, 2016.

There has also been a question over Torrance's 'break' with Barth and the Reformed tradition. It is clear to me that it was Barth who broke with the Reformed tradition, taking inspiration from Anabaptists, and Torrance was correcting or making consistent a 'Barthian' approach to baptism. See further, Bryan D. Spinks, 'Karl Barth's Teaching on Baptism: Its Development, Antecedents and the Liturgical Factor', *Ecclesia Orans* 14 (1997), pp. 261–88.

70 Macleod, 'Recent Sacramental Developments', p. 50, with reference to an unpublished paper by John L. McPake.

71 Panel on Worship, *Christian Baptism*, Glasgow: Mackay & Inglis, 2001, p. 3.

72 Panel on Doctrine, *Report*, May 2003. John L. McPake was convener, Norma Stewart, vice-convener, and Douglas Galbraith, Secretary. For a discussion of the report, see W. John Carswell, 'Becoming Christian: Redeeming the Secular through the *Ordo* of Baptism', PhD thesis, University of Glasgow, 2017.

reflection has emphasized lifelong discipleship with a journey to as well as from faith as a still wider framework for the event of baptism;[73]

The Panel proposed that provision be made for another family member rather than a parent (but with the parent's consent) to act in the baptism of a child.

In an appendix, the report also drew the conclusion:

Christian Baptism signifies the event whereby the gracious love of God toward us, embodied in the action of Jesus Christ, is met by the response of faith. The response of faith is itself the gift of God (Ephesians 2:8), and signifies the beginning of our life within the community of the church of Jesus Christ. It is a response to the spiritual transformation that Christ has accomplished on our behalf, and it offers to us the possibility of an ethical transformation within the wider community of the church, and within the community of creation. As such, we are called to the cele-bration of baptism in all its richness and fullness, in the name of the Father and of the Son and of the Holy Spirit.[74]

The General Assembly requested services that enabled parents who were not themselves members of the Church to celebrate the gift of a child, whether by birth or adoption. In response, under the title of *Common Order*, in 2006 *A Welcome to a Child* was published, with four orders for thanksgiving and blessing.[75]

Beginning with a Faith and Order report, *One Baptism: Towards Mutual Recognition of Christian Initiation* (first outlined at Faverges, 2001, revised and published in 2006 and in final form as a study text in 2011), the WCC set out a theology that would encourage churches to recognise the 'equivalent alternatives' and see baptism as a unifying rite.[76] As part of an ongoing ecumenical initiative, in 2007, the Roman Catholic Church in Scotland and the Church of Scotland published a study booklet on baptism in both the Churches. In 2010, both published a *Liturgy for the Reaffirmation of Baptismal Vows*, for use in ecumenical settings. It took

---

73 Panel on Doctrine, *Report*, May 2003, p. 5.

74 Panel on Doctrine, *Report*, May 2003, p. 17.

75 Church of Scotland Office for Worship and Doctrine, *A Welcome to a Child*, Edin-burgh: Saint Andrew Press, 2006. The pastoral situation has a parallel in the Church of England, where those 'less churched' who seek baptism should be regarded as a mission opportunity. Sandra Millar, *Life Events: Mission and Ministry at Baptisms, Weddings and Funerals*, London: Church House Publishing, 2018; Sarah Lawrence, *A Rite on the Edge: The Language of Baptism and Christening in the Church of England*, London: SCM Press, 2019. For the idea of baptism as a Kenotic act of the vulnerable God, see Sarah Kathleen Johnson, 'Poured Out: A Kenotic Approach to Initiating Children at a Distance from the Church', *Studia Liturgica* 49 (2020), pp. 175–94.

76 World Council of Churches, *One Baptism: Towards Mutual Recognition*, A Study Text, Geneva: WCC, 2011.

the form of a Liturgy of the Word, the reaffirmation of baptism using the Apostles' Creed in interrogative form, the symbolic pouring of water, prayers and a commitment to the Christian life.[77]

On Holy Communion, in 1997 the Committee on Ecumenical Affairs published a study booklet, *Holy Communion: Why Can't We Share?* It explained why, although the Orders of Service in the Church of Scotland and the Roman Catholic Church were very similar, the Catholic Church did not practice inter-communion. It included the text of the second order of the Communion from *Common Order* and the Roman Mass and included explanations and questions for discussion.

In attempting to encourage more frequent celebrations of Communion, the Working Group on the Place and Practice of Holy Communion in 2010 published *Celebrating Holy Communion*, which included a CD. The Introduction by Peter Donald explained that 'celebrating' and 'Holy Communion' are not always in the same sentence in the minds of the membership of the Church of Scotland. Many believe it a very solemn occasion, but it is also a time of celebrating: 'the Sacrament of the Lord's Supper draws us, by the grace of our Lord Jesus Christ, into a feasting where our sinful past must be laid aside and the life of the reign of God fully anticipated.'[78] It was a study guide, and each section included questions for further discussion. It was a commentary/explanation of the *Common Order* service. The footnotes reveal that the Working Party had drawn on a variety of academic and theological sources across an ecumenical spectrum, though John Colwell's *Promise and Presence* was an important work.[79] The study noted:

> it has become clear that Christians in our tradition are more likely to be attracted to reductionism in some mode or other, i.e. seeing the Lord's Supper as more a human act than an occasion for God's close encounter; *Common Order*, in line with all the historic Reformed standards, would resist this. We believe in Holy Communion.[80]

The epiclesis was commended on grounds that the recovery of this from the Eastern Churches was valuable because it guarded against an impoverishment of the doctrine of the Trinity.[81] Yet in spite of the repeated encouragement for more frequent Communion, many parishes still limit Holy Communion to two or four times a year.

---

77 The Joint Commission on Doctrine of the Church of Scotland and the Roman Catholic Church in Scotland, *Liturgy for the Reaffirmation of Baptismal Vows*, np, 2010.

78 The Working Group on the Place and Practice of Holy Communion, *Celebrating Holy Communion*, Edinburgh: Saint Andrew Press, 2010, p. 1.

79 John Colwell, *Promise and Presence: An Exploration in Sacramental Theology*, Eugene, OR: Wipf & Stock, 2010.

80 *Celebrating Holy Communion*, p. 63.

81 *Celebrating Holy Communion*, p. 71.

A concern for inclusivity led to the admission of children to Communion in the Church of Scotland. This was first proposed in 1982, and was rejected, but finally passed the General Assembly in 1991.

Devolution of liturgical services: some snapshots

In 2015, I attended a few services in Edinburgh, Glasgow, Paisley Abbey, Iona and Stornoway. The following are summaries of the orders of service and personal comments and observations, which give some idea of how a standard pattern is adapted.

6 September 2015
Greyfriars Kirk Edinburgh, 11am service (Fifteenth after Pentecost)

Celebration of the Edinburgh Riding of the Marches. The choir wore grey 'monks' robes; the minister wore a cassock and a grey stole with ornamentation. During the procession, the clerk or beadle processed the Bible to the pulpit. The choir sang a Latin Introit. A call to worship was followed by Hymn 125, 'Lord of all being, throned afar'. After a welcome and blessing of the Edinburgh Riding Marches came the call to prayer with prayers of approach, confession and pardon, led by the associate minister, ending with a sixfold Kyrie in English sung by the choir (tune 648 CH4) and the Collect of the Day prayed by all. A mini homily was given on the care of space (connected with the Riding of the Marches) and then Hymn 238. After the Epistle, the choir sang an anthem, then came the Gospel, Hymn 348 and the sermon. A contemporary creed was recited, followed by the offering with Hymn 813, 'All praise and thanks to God'. Then came prayers of thanksgiving, intercession and commemoration and the Lord's Prayer. Hymn 103 and the Benediction concluded this very traditional Liturgy of the Word.

Mayfield Salisbury Parish Church, Edinburgh, 7pm service

Listed as Fourteenth Sunday after Trinity, the service was conducted by the Revd Scott McKenna. It was a reflective, meditative communion service, with minister, assistant minister and organist. A Call to Worship was followed by Hymn 189, 'Be still, for the presence of the Lord'. Then came a mindfulness 'body scan', with conscious breathing and a meditation, 'God is my Light', which was a taped recording from the Psalm Project.[82] Then a

---

82 https://worship.calvin.edu/resources/resource-library/the-psalm-project-reworking-genevan-psalms-for-a-new-generation/, accessed 18.3.19.

Lectio Divina and a time for reflection led by the assistant minister. Hymn 484 led into the Lord's Supper, which was from *Common Order*. Hymn 269 and Benediction concluded this communion service.

This was a pioneering meditative Eucharist, using mindfulness practices and drawing on the Christian mystical tradition, and was a weekly Communion, a place where new people found a home in the church, enabling them to join the larger congregation in the morning services.

13 September 2015
St Giles' Cathedral, Edinburgh, 10am Morning Service

Listed as the Fifteenth Sunday after Trinity, this is a weekly communion service. There were green paramounts on the pillars. The Holy Table was square, with two lighted candles. There was a procession with a kilted male carrying the processional cross. The choir was robed in off-white, lined with red. Three ministers took part, two wearing cassocks and one a black gown. Two wore green stoles, but the senior minister wore a white stole. There was a short Introit before the entrance procession. The communion ordinary was sung to a mass setting by Victoria. The Kyries were sung after the confession and before the declaration of pardon. The intercessions had complex vocabulary and at times were rather florid. The Gloria in

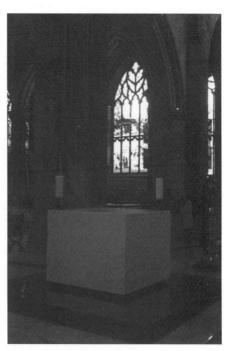

10.1 The Holy Table, St Giles', Edinburgh

excelsis was sung as an offertory. Communion was around the table, the congregation forming a huge circle in the nave. The plate had large rectangular chunks of bread, four or six pieces, and there were four large silver cups and a flagon. The communicants passed it to each other. The peace was exchanged after Communion. The recessional had no processional cross, but lay people or elders processed out with the remaining elements.

Canongate Kirk, Edinburgh, 11:15am Parish Worship
(Canongate has monthly Communion)

As already noted in the previous chapter, Canongate has used a set printed liturgy for some decades, which is periodically revised. The Order used was the ninth edition of 2011. The assistant minister presided. The Order followed the printed text other than for the intercessions, where the minister prayed his own, and he gave a Celtic-style blessing rather than the one in the printed order. The minister took most of the service from the clergy stall on the liturgical south side and read all the lessons from a raised ambo.

Thursday 17 September 2015
Iona Abbey, 9pm Communion

10.2 Thursday Evening Communion, Iona Abbey

The celebrant was a woman minister and wore ordinary lay clothes. There were about 150 people and the Abbey was candlelit. There was a table between the choir stalls. The liturgy was selected from the *Iona Service Book*. There was a dramatic reading from Exodus on manna, and the homily was on manna. Communion was passed on plates and chalices, with wholemeal bread and fermented wine. Provision was made in the south aisle for grape juice and gluten free bread. This was a very moving service.

20 September 2015
Stornoway High Church of Scotland, Isle of Lewis, 11am

10.3 Stornoway High Church, Small Sanctuary (Gaelic Service)

The English and Gaelic services are held at the same time, in adjacent sanctuaries. Built in 1909, the main sanctuary had been for the Gaelic service and the small sanctuary for the English speakers. Now the situation is reversed, and the small number who attend the Gaelic service use the small sanctuary. Because of the vote in the Church of Scotland General Assembly to admit gay ministers, many of the Gaelic-speakers left to join the Free Church of Scotland.

The Gaelic service had seventeen people, nine women and eight men. The minister wore a suit and a clerical collar. No organ or other musical accompaniment. The minister sat in the central raised pulpit. He gave a call to worship and read the first psalm. The precentor then intoned the psalm with the congregation participating. All were seated, but all stood for the Long Prayer. All were seated for the readings from Isaiah, a Psalm and a Gospel reading. Then came another metrical Psalm, sermon, metrical Psalm and Benediction. The sermon lasted some forty minutes. The deep structure of this service was apparently untouched by the nineteenth-century liturgical revivals, or *Common Order*. Here, the 'older species', as in the early nineteenth century, was still alive, though in decline.

The English service at 11am was led by the minister, Dr Wayne Pearce, who had left the Associated Presbyterian Church to join the Church of Scotland. The main sanctuary has an organ and two TV screens on the wall – these latter being installed before his arrival, but he feels duty bound to use them – for the words of praise music. He has removed a front pew, and opened up the 'Elders Box' so that the communion table is visible to the congregation. The removal of the pew allows space for marriages and to place the coffin at funerals. Since his arrival, Dr Pearce has introduced the congregational recitation of the Apostles' Creed and the Lord's Prayer. Communion Seasons are still observed, with two annual celebrations, in February and August. He has, however, introduced four evening Communions. The communion seasons are celebrated over four days, no longer five – the Monday observance has gone. He has introduced music from *Mission Praise* and *Sing Praise*, the words to which are projected on the screens. The outline for the English language service was: musical prelude, call to worship, hymn, prayer and Lord's Prayer, children's address, hymn, reading, psalm, sermon, prayer, 'Sing Scripture 35' (a Free Church of Scotland Psalm and hymn book) and Benediction.

11 October 2015
St Cuthbert's, Edinburgh, 11am

The Sunday was listed as the Nineteenth Sunday after Trinity. The holy table is marble and had two lit candles. The choir was robed and the ministers were wearing cassocks, bands and green stoles. The retired minister of Canongate Kirk, Charles Robertson, is an honorary assistant and wore his scarlet cassock, with black gown and scarf. The service was of the typical order of a 'dry' Communion, but Communion is celebrated weekly and a communion service was celebrated immediately after the Morning Service, in a side chapel. There was a large loaf of bread and two chalices with port wine. *Common Order* seemed to be the text used. Like Mayfield and St Giles', St Cuthbert's had a votive candle-stand.

Paisley Abbey, 11am Morning Service with the sacrament of Holy Baptism; 4pm Choral Evensong

Paisley Abbey was damaged by the collapse of the tower c.1553, and at the Reformation the nave was walled off and served as the parish church. Between 1858 and 1862, the north porch of the Abbey and the walls of the north transept were restored, and between 1890 and 1907, the north transept and crossing were re-roofed and re-joined to the nave. The organ was first built in 1972. It has an excellent choir and organist and serves a similar role to the cathedrals. There was a paschal candle by the font and a marble altar with two lit candles.

The Morning Service took the traditional form of Ante-Communion, with the Kyries after the confession and before the absolution. There was an antiphonal psalm sung by a cantor and congregation and the service also included the Benedictus and anthem to settings by Byrd. The baptism followed the intercessions and a hymn, and included the congregational recitation of the Lord's Prayer.

The Choral Evensong was Anglican and the service alternates with Compline. The choir was robed in cassocks and surplices and but for the minister's vesture – cassock, preaching bands and green stole – the setting and service was just as a Church of England cathedral choral evensong, with a choir of thirty and twenty-five people in the adjacent stalls. The intercessions referred to Mary, Elizabeth and St Mirin.

25 October 2015
Ednam Parish Church, 9:30am

Ednam is linked with Kelso North Church and normally has a weekly Sunday service at 9:30am. The Morning Service consisted of a Call to Worship, hymn, scripture sentences, prayers of adoration, confession and Lord's Prayer, a hymn, three lessons read by a lay woman, a hymn, sermon, Psalm 15 (metrical), prayers of thanksgiving and intercession (lay-led), the offering and dedication (lay-led) and a final hymn and Benediction. A cross adorned the shelf of the east window behind the holy table, flanked by two vases with twirling branches. According to the website, Communion is celebrated four times a year and at Easter in both churches.

Some expressions of postmodern worship

Noting that the cultural era often referred to as postmodern brings to the present generation the full range of fast-changing and radical influences, Paul Roberts believed that the various services that alt.worship (or Emerging worship, or Fresh Expressions worship) engenders offer the Church examples of Christianity enculturated to current technological society, or 'multi-media' society.

On the first visit to a service, the main impression is visual. Screens and hanging fabrics, containing a multiplicity of colours and static images continuously dominate the perceptions. There are other things: the type of music, often electronic, whose textures and range seem curiously attuned to the context of worship, smells, the postures adopted by the other worshippers, perhaps also their dress-style and hair. As the mental picture begins to fill up with detail, there is a growing appreciation that considerable technological complexity is sitting alongside simplicity and directness. The rituals – perhaps walking through patterns, tying a knot, or having one's hands or feet anointed – are introduced with simple, non-fussy directions. The emphasis is on allowing people to do what will help, liberate, and encourage their worship rather than on the orchestration of a great event. The singing is normally simple, direct, chant-like. The structure of the event is not enormously complicated. When something is rather obscure, its purpose is to invite further reflection, perhaps teasing the worshippers to look deeper beyond the surface meaning. There is the occasional ritual joke. In many services, the steady, BPM-adjusted rhythm means that it would be possible on one level to participate merely by dancing. For many of those who stay, they have never before had an experience of Christian worship like it. It is as though they have come to a new place which they instantly recognize as home.[83]

The Late Late Service was a Glasgow enterprise with Doug Gay and Andrew Thornton and represented a Church of Scotland approach to alt. worship. Music was recorded on the Sticky Music label and the words of many of the services are still available on Andrew Thornton's website as the booklet *Words from . . . the Late, Late Service*.[84] Of these services, two have been selected for description here.

Celebrating the Feast (A Quiet Service) began with 'Holy Space', had a reading from Isaiah 55:1–2, followed by a responsorial confession. Readings from John 2:1–11 and Luke 14:12–23 were listed, though it is unclear when they were read or how. 'A Ritual of Reflection' involved stations with visual objects, some for tasting, and also visual images, with quiet instrumental music. This was to last 15–20 minutes. An invitation to the Feast focused on four areas where food was set up and included meditation lasting 15 minutes. Prayers of intercession was followed by the song 'Our God in Heaven' and a rubric, 'We Share the Gifts'.

The Communion Service of 1995 seems to be designed to follow the postmodern equivalent of a Word service. It opens with a confession of sin, a prayer for new life (followed by bells), an extended explanation for the sharing of peace, and a Eucharistic Prayer of the classical shape, with all reading the epiclesis displayed on the overhead screen. Bells were rung at the end. A rubrical instruction for serving Communion followed.

Doug Gay authored a further collection with the Church of England alt. worship exponent, Jonny Baker, in *Alternative Worship: Resources from and for the Emerging Church*. This provided a host of resources, with a variety of styles. A call to worship began:

Relax your body . . .
Open your mind . . .
Engage your spirit . . .

---

83 Paul Roberts, 'Liturgy and Mission in Postmodern Culture: Some Reflections Arising from "Alternative" Services and Communities', 1995, http://seaspray.trinity-bris.ac.uk/~robertsp/papers/lambeth.html.

84 *The Late, Late Service*, printed by The Late Late Service, Glasgow, 1993. My thanks to Andrew Thornton for providing me with a copy.

This is the house of God
Prepare to worship.[85]

A prose piece entitled 'Bethlehem' reads:

Bethlehem is a place in our heads,
Some part of us assumes we could find our way through its dark streets,
After all we've known them since we were children
And Bethlehem's sleep was deep and dreamless.

Or so we claim (as if we knew).
It's understandable that we claim too much
Because Bethlehem is a kind of toytown
A place built of Duplo and fuzzy felt;
It is small and easily patronized, a little child of a place,
It could no more host the Millennium than the Olympics.

Bethlehem is a place in our heads,
Like Christmas it is intimately and uneasily linked to our sense of home.
And at Christmas some part of us needs to go there.
We need to go there because somehow in the history of our planet,
This obscure Middle Eastern town
Has become a symbol of the human home.

That is why all over the world tonight,
In Sydney and Delhi, in Lima and Lagos and London,
People have built little Bethlehem in their churches and houses.

We bring Bethlehem home, because we sense that Bethlehem
Stands for home, and not just simple sentimental home,
But an improvisation of home,
It stands for home in the face of homelessness,
And home in the face of God.[86]

More recently, possibly reflecting a rise in Scottish nationalism evidenced in the large number who voted for independence in the 2014 Referendum, two volumes by David D. Ogston, published posthumously, have appeared under the title *Scots Worship*. Ogston was a broadcaster, writer and poet, as well as being a Church of Scotland minister. The two collections – *Lent, Holy Week and Easter* (2013) and *Advent, Christmas and Epiphany* (2014) – include reflections, meditations, prayers, liturgy and 'other imaginative worship', and as a genre have much in common with some of the Wild Goose publications and the *Alternative Worship* resources of Baker and

---

85 Jonny Baker and Doug Gay, with Jenny Brown, *Alternative Worship: Resources from and for the Emerging Church*, Grand Rapids, MI: Baker Books, 2003, p. 34.
86 Baker and Gay, *Alternative Worship*, pp. 35–6.

Gay. What makes them distinctive is that some of the material is written in a Scots dialect. A litany on the incidents in the life of Jesus in the 2013 collection includes the following lines:

Christ o the whang o lowss tows Christ o the double-heidit maik
Christ o the bruckle breid
Christ o the tassie
Christ o the gairden caa'd Gethsemane.[87]

In the first 'A Scots Communion Service (1)' in the same collection, a responsive service is provided, with call to confession, a twofold Kyrie and declaration of pardon, followed by the Institution narrative and a Eucharistic Prayer. The latter begins:

M: Lift up yer hairts.
R: We lift them up until the Lord.
M: Lat's aa gie thanks tae God.
R: Richt an gweed it is.
M: Richt and gweed aagate an athhot devaul. Holy Lord, Father o aa micht, God Ivverlaistin, it faa's tull's tae gie You thanks an praise an cry You glorious, Maister and Makar o aa things, King o Heiven. Noo may the kirk abeen in glorie an the kirk on the yird tak up the timeless sang wi a single vyce:
Holy, holy, holy Lord God o Hosts,
Heiven an earth are foo o your glorie:
Glorie be tae you, Lord abeen.
Blissit is he that comes i the name o the Lord!
Hosanna in the hichts![88]

Themes from the 2014 collection include 'If on a Winter's Night: A Christmas Eve dialogue', 'The Isaiah Dream: Meditation for Christmas Eve' and 'The Storyteller: The shepherds go to the manger'. Five communion liturgies were provided, with titles such as 'God Our Sunrise: A Communion liturgy for Epiphany', 'Let Us Build a House', 'The Triumph-Song of Earth and Heaven' and 'Forge, Plate, Field and Grape'. One communion liturgy was in Scots dialect, 'A Doric Holy Communion'. The Eucharistic Prayer was prefaced with the Institution narrative, but the words were picked up again as an introduction to the epiclesis:

[Christ is deed . . . Christ will come again]
Till that day dawns (we ken nae fan: it could be the morn,
or a thoosan eers)

---

87 David D. Ogston (ed. Johnston McKay), *Scots Worship: Lent, Holy Week and Easter*, Edinburgh: Saint Andrew Press, 2013, p. 59.
88 Ogston, *Scots Worship. Lent, Holy Week and Easter*, p. 44.

We dae faat He said: we brake the Bried
An we tak the Cup. We dae weel tae be here.
Bless tae us, Lord, this Breid,
Bless tae us, Lord, Lord, this Cup.
Lat them be till us the Communion o the bodie
An bleid o the Christ: lat them be health an haleness
Till aa that are here.
Sae lat it be.[89]

This brief reference to the Institution is slightly reminiscent of the ancient anaphora of Addai and Maru, as well as one of two Syrian Orthodox anaphoras, the former acknowledged as valid by the Roman Catholic Church. What is perhaps more important is that Ogston, regardless of Scots or English, experimented with the pattern of the Eucharistic Prayer in a bid to make it contemporary, and added his own poetic genius to make his compositions attractive. It would be interesting to know whether the Scots forms have been found useful.

Resources have also been published by the Revd Lezley J. Stewart, former associate minister of Greyfriars, Edinburgh, and currently at the Church of Scotland central office in George Street, Edinburgh. *When Two or Three are Gathered* is a collection of 'creative' prayers and liturgies for group worship; *Celebrating Life in Death* provides resources for funerals; and *Let Everyone Find Their Voice: Worship Resources Inspired by the Psalms* is due out in 2020.[90]

Some parishes, such as St Andrew's and St George's West, Edinburgh, have a Sunday morning All-Age Worship, catering for families. Finlay MacDonald has noted that some congregations have also adopted Messy Church services.[91] Developed in the Church of England, this offers a weekly or monthly Sunday afternoon session for younger people and parents, with play, arts and crafts, along with Bible teaching and songs, and popular foods such as pizza.[92]

The Church Service Society continues to provide resources for the Church of Scotland. The Preface of the first edition of the *Euchologion* in 1867 noted that it was not the intention of a private group to introduce a liturgy into the Kirk, but since the Church of Scotland is part of the Church

---

89 David D. Ogston (ed. Johnston McKay), *Scots Worship: Advent, Christmas and Epiphany*, Edinburgh: Saint Andrew Press, 2014, p. 102.

90 Lezley J. Stewart, *When Two or Three are Gathered: Themes Resources for Group Worship*, Edinburgh: Saint Andrew Press, 2014; *Celebrating Life in Death: Resources for Funerals, Thanksgiving and Remembering*, Edinburgh: Saint Andrew Press, 2016; *Let Everyone Find Their Voice: Worship Resources Inspired by the Psalms*, Edinburgh: Saint Andrew Press, 2020.

91 MacDonald, *From Reform to Renewal*, p. 203.

92 Lucy Moore, *Messy Church: Fresh Ideas for Building a Christ-Centred Community*, Abingdon: Bible Reading Fellowship, 2006. For examples in the Church of Scotland, see David McCarthy, *Seeing Afresh: Learning from Fresh Expressions of the Church*, Edinburgh: Saint Andrew Press, 2019.

catholic, each minister has the liberty to use whatever in the recorded devotions of that Church he finds most suitable to the congregation's needs. It continues to do this through its journal, workshops and its newsletter, *Versicle*.[93]

Worship in the other Presbyterian Churches

The smaller Presbyterian bodies[94] declined to enter the various unions and have tended to cling to the traditions they practised at the time of their regrouping. The United Free Church of Scotland, being those members of that Church who declined to unite with the Church of Scotland in 1929, continued to allow hymns and musical instruments in worship, as well as inheriting the 1928 *Book of Common Order*. The United Free Church was part of the Church Hymnary Trust, and was involved with *Church Hymnary Third Edition* and *Church Hymnary Fourth Edition*, but has since withdrawn from the Trust. The Principal Clerk, Martin Keane writes:

> It is fair to say there has not been a wide adoption of CH4 in the United Free Church with only a handful of congregations adopting it. Most congregations had previously opted for the 'Mission Praise' or 'Songs of fellowship' hymn books. At the time of writing many were moving to using projection software to dispense with hymn books completely. . . . As a broad evangelical Church our worship will vary from traditional organ and choir to those of Praise bands and everything in between. The General Assembly has not laid down any specific form or style but each individual congregation has that responsibility with the Minister answerable to Presbytery for the conduct of worship.[95]

The most notable recent change has been that the Free Church of Scotland took the decision to allow musical accompaniment and the singing of hymns and songs other than metrical psalms. Although the pre-1900 Free Church had been party to the *Church Hymnary*, and allowed organs, more conservative congregations kept to metrical psalmody led by a precentor. The post-1900 Free Church, by an Act passed in 1905, repealed the earlier legislation and restored worship to the form and style at the Disruption.[96]

---

93 Its journal *Church Service Society Annual* gave way in the 1970s to *Liturgical Review* (the first two were called *Liturgical Studies*), and that in turn has been replaced by *The Record*. The articles in these are all available on the Society's website.

94 Membership numbers given are: Free Church of Scotland, 10,000; United Free Church of Scotland, 2,466; Free Church of Scotland (Continuing), 1,000; Free Presbyterian Church of Scotland, 1,200; Reformed Presbyterian Church of Scotland, 250; Associated Presbyterian Church of Scotland, 250–300.

95 Email to the author, 26 November 2019.

96 Maurice Grant, 'The Heirs of the Disruption in Crisis and Recovery 1893–1920', in Clement Graham (ed.), *Crown Him Lord of All: Essays on the Life and Witness of the Free Church of Scotland*, Edinburgh: The Knox Press, 1993, pp. 1–36, p. 26.

A problem had arisen in the Leith congregation, which used instrumental music, contrary to the 1905 Act. One of the senior elders and also General Secretary of the Free Church, John Hay Thorburn, defended his parish, arguing that the Church was being dictated to by Highland cultural traditions rather than Scripture.[97] Thorburn eventually left the Free Church and wrote a pamphlet claiming the Free Church of Scotland was now a Celtic sect.[98] In 1910, the denomination published *The Scottish Psalmody*, with 190 tunes. *Scottish Psalmody* was published in 1927, with ten added tunes, but deleting sixty from the 1910 edition. In mid-century, other tunes were added. Another psalter was published in 1977 and *Sing Psalms* in 2003, where a more contemporary style of English was employed. This was available as a 'staff', or split-page edition, following the nineteenth-century invention of Hatley.[99]

In November 2010, a special plenary assembly took place to debate the issue of hymns and musical instruments in worship, and the motion to allow both in Free Church services was passed by a narrow margin. The Free Church website offers the following as the normal Free Church sequence for Sunday worship:

Praise
Prayer
Bible Reading
Praise
Sermon
Prayer
Praise
Intimations
Benediction.[100]

The same website gave the following for the order of the Lord's Supper:

Fencing of the Table
Praise – usually Psalm 116, while the elements of bread and wine are placed on the Table by the elders
Praise – usually Psalm 116, while the communicants go forward and sit at the table
Bible Reading – the words of institution in 1 Corinthians 11:23–29
Prayer
Address to the communicants at the Table

---

97 Grant, 'The Heirs', pp. 27–8.

98 John Hay Thorburn, *The Church of 1843 versus a new Celtic Free Church*, 1908. I have not been able to consult this pamphlet.

99 See Chapter 5.

100 www.fpchurch.org.uk/about-us/how-we-worship/order-of-service/, accessed 3.06.2015.

Partaking of the bread and wine
Address to the communicants at the table
Praise – usually Psalm 103, while the communicants leave the table and
    resume their places in the congregation
Address to all (this is not always done)
Prayer
Praise
[Intimations]
Benediction.

In 2015, I attended two very different services of the Free Church, the first
more traditional and typical of the islands, and one in Edinburgh that had
introduced hymns, choruses and a praise band.

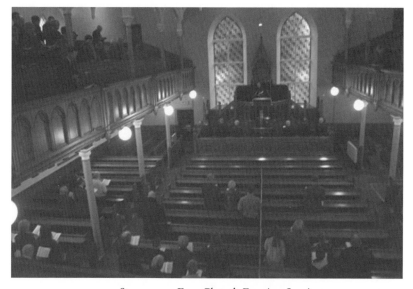

10.4 Stornoway Free Church Evening Service

On 20 September, I attended the Free Church at Stornoway, Isle of Lewis,
evening worship at 6:30pm. The minister and elders entered. The congregation sat for prayer and stood for singing. An introduction included
announcements. Psalm 96 was read by the minister, followed by the opening Long Prayer. Part of it (recorded) was as follows:

We pray Lord that there will be a largeness of heart and that there will be
an expansive vision within us so that we will see beyond just where we
are here in ourselves and that we will be able to behold something of your
handiwork throughout this world.
    We pray that we might be accorded a sense of the greatness of God,

something of the glory of God. We pray Lord that there will be a desire within our hearts to glorify God and enjoy him all the days of our life.

We pray O Lord that in such a busy world that we live in that we will be given, that we will make time to be with you because that is so important, and that so often we feel that we don't have time. Help us to realize and help us to understand that the most important thing that we can do is to spend time with you because it is through this that we become most effective, because we will, when coming from our audience with the King, like Moses, hopefully, something of the radiance of the Lord will be upon us and so we pray that we will make time for the quiet time in the midst of a very, very busy world.

O Lord and God we pray that as we gather together this evening that we will hear what the Lord will speak. We give thanks that he speaks peace to his people and he warns us not to return again to foolishness of sin. We ask Lord that you will forgive us for our foolishness; because we have to confess our sin collectively and individually, we do so even now in the quietness of our own hearts and we ask Lord that you will be merciful to us, and whether we understand our sin, whether we understand the effects of the nature of sin that we get a greater glimpse of your glory and of the holiness that belongs to you and that it will have a powerful bearing even on the way we conduct ourselves in this world. O Lord be merciful to us.

We pray to bless each of us and every one of us tonight according to our own particular needs where we are. Bless us in all the experiences that we go through, help us Lord in our relationships one with another, help us Lord in all the practical difficulties and challenges that we so often face. Help us Lord with all the things we can't do. Help us Lord in our Christian life in the things that we feel are too much for us when we so often feel overcome and afraid and weak.

O Lord give us that grace and strength. We pray we may have a spirit of contentment as we journey through life even as we were reflecting this morning. Help us Lord not to be absorbed and taken up with all the things this world offers. Although there are many blessings and many good things, may we seek above all the good part, like Mary did, that will not be taken from us.

Help us to focus upon you so that our pleasure will be in you rather than in anything else. We pray you to bless our homes and families, Lord, and all whom we love.

We pray for those who have left home, and again we think of all our young folk who have gone off to the cities and the different places throughout the world. We commit them to your care and ask that you watch over them. We pray Lord for those who have lost loved ones, whose hearts . . .

The very able precentor led the a capella psalmody – Psalm 71:14–18. The reading was from Galatians 6. Psalm 22:22–27 followed. Then the sermon was preached, followed by a brief prayer centred on the cross of

Christ. Psalm 73, verses 23–26, was sung, and the service concluded with the Grace. There was a good-sized congregation in the main worship space as well as in the balconies.

On 18 October, I attended the 5:30 pm evening service at St Columba's Free Church, Edinburgh. There were two overhead screens, which displayed all the songs, hymns and psalms. There was a praise band and two female vocalists. The minister wore a jacket but no tie. There was a new song, 'My worth is not in what I own', by Getty. The opening prayer was very lengthy and had a faux pas. Noting that we tend to see the sins of others rather than our own, the minister said, ' . . . yes, we see the sins of others and Lord we wallow in them'; there was a pause, and then, 'No Lord, we don't wallow in them, we . . .'. There was a short reading from St Matthew and then Psalm 51:1–4, 9–13, sung a cappella. H. Bonar's hymn, 'I heard the Voice of Jesus say', was sung to a rousing upbeat performance of 'Kingsfold' by the band. The theme of the sermon was sex, which may account for the attendance of so many young adults. The post-sermon prayer was a summary of the sermon in the guise of prayer. Psalm 119 second part, a capella, preceded the Dismissal.

10.5 Communion Service, London City Presbyterian (Free Church of Scotland)

Bulletins from London City Presbyterian Church, which is Free Church of Scotland, and the Free Church of Scotland at St Andrews provided by Miss Jenny Smith give an outline order of service. The former has for the morning service a Call to Worship, a hymn, a psalm (metrical) during which the offering was taken, some Bible readings, another psalm, the sermon, a hymn and the Benediction. The bulletin from St Andrews has a similar outline, but included a congregational confession of sins and the Lord's Prayer.[101]

---

101 My thanks to Jenny Smith for providing copies of these bulletins.

A contribution to the theology and practice of the Lord's Supper in the Free Church of Scotland was made by Malcolm Maclean in a book of that title in 2009, in which he considered the sacrament from the viewpoints of biblical interpretation, historical understanding and current concerns. The survey of the New Testament was somewhat selective, the tradition of Highland Communion Seasons seeming to influence the New Testament evidence. He surveyed the teachings of the Catholic Church and the Reformation Churches in the sixteenth century and sided with Calvin against Zwingli and other contenders. A very good survey of the Highland Communion Seasons from the seventeenth through to the early twentieth century was presented. He drew on more recent works on sacramental theology to critique the practice and recommended some changes. He gave a typical outline of the Supper as:

Opening Praise
Prayer
Reading of Scripture
Praise
Sermon
Prayer
Praise, while all communicants come to the area of the church
    functioning as a table
Reading of 1 Corinthians 11:25ff. as warrant for the service
Short prayer in which the bread and wine are consecrated to God's
    service and asking his blessing on them
Short address to the communicants
Communicants are given bread, then the wine
Short address to the communicants
Praise
Benediction.[102]

Maclean stressed the importance of the breaking of the bread and defended the common cup and alcoholic wine, noting that at Corinth, Paul did not suggest changing to grape juice as a remedy for their wrong behaviour.[103] The book offers a prayer suitable for use when non-Christians may be present. He also argued for children to be admitted to Communion on occasions, according to circumstance, and for more frequent celebration of the Communion, noting that the New Testament evidence supports a weekly celebration.

Following the 2010 decision to allow musical instruments and hymns in worship, one congregation and four ministers resigned and seceded from the Free Church of Scotland. Even before the General Assembly had met,

---

102 Malcolm Maclean, *The Lord's Supper*, Fearne: Mentor Press, Christian Focus Publications, 2009, pp. 172–3.
103 Maclean, *The Lord's Supper*, p. 179.

the convener of the Psalmody Committee, Donald MacDonald, resigned from the Free Church, and other ministers, including Kenneth Stewart of Glasgow and David Karoon of Arran, followed.[104] The ministers joined one of the smaller churches that see singing only psalmody and a cappella as a mark of pure worship. Some short pamphlets have appeared that defend the use of psalms only in worship, and the unlawfulness of instrumental music in 'pure' worship. The Revd John W. Keddie, when still a minister in the Free Church, but who subsequently joined the Free Church of Scotland (Continuing), lamented that, 'Patterns of worship are changing with baffling rapidity. Songs and hymns entirely of man's devising and composition have proliferated.'[105] He maintained that, 'churches holding to the authority and sufficiency of the Bible as God's Word written, should apply the principle that "what Scripture does not prescribe, it forbids"'.[106] This argument seems to have resulted in some smaller Presbyterian groups elevating this as a mark of a true church. This was already apparent in a small collection of conference papers entitled *The Worship of God* in 1998. David Silversides of the Reformed Presbyterian Church contributed a paper on the Westminster *Directory*, where the *Directory* together with the 'Westminster Standards' appear to be the hermeneutic for interpreting Scripture. In a second paper he defended the use of singing only psalmody and without musical accompaniment in worship, suggesting that the organ or piano 'could prove a Trojan horse which will bring confusion and even disaster to your church'. He opined:

> The Westminster Assembly along with the Scottish Church used poetic gifts to provide us with a good and accurate rendering of the Psalms. This was a legitimate use of poetic gift. Isaac Watts did not use his poetic gift correctly when he tried to replace the Biblical Psalter with his own compositions.[107]

Silversides contributed a short essay to a collection by Kenneth Stewart, which had a Preface by Donald MacDonald, both of whom had seceded in 2010 over the changes in music. Stewart seceded from the Free Church of Scotland to join the Reformed Presbyterian Church. In the Introduction Stewart wrote:

---

104 See the Revd Donald Macdonald's resignation letter 31 August 2011 in www.hebrides-news.com/rev-donald-macdonald-resignation-31811.html and www.bbc.com/news/uk-scotland-glasgow-west-12480877, accessed 19.11.2019; *The Scotsman* 27 May 2012, www.scotsman.com/news-2-15012/churches-in-discord-over-hymn-singing-1-2320714, accessed 19.11.2019.

105 John W. Keddie, *Sing the Lord's Song: Biblical Psalms in Worship*, Pittsburgh, PA: Crown & Covenant Publications, 1994/2003, p. 9.

106 Keddie, *Sing the Lord's Song*, p. 48.

107 Malcolm H. Watts and David Silversides (eds), *The Worship of God*, Edinburgh: Marpet Press, 1998, pp. 52 and 70.

The only way to go forward is to go back. The answer to the widespread confusion and apostasy lies in the recovery of truths once embraced – and, indeed, sworn to – but now largely abandoned and forgotten, it is the conviction of all who contribute to this booklet that the recovery of earnest, intelligent, and spiritual unaccompanied singing of Psalms in the praise of the church is a major part of the repentance and renewal so badly needed in the church today.[108]

Reformation Scotland is a Trust which has produced several pamphlets, including *Reformed Worship*. This sets out an 'updated' (modern language) version of the Westminster *Directory* for Sunday Morning Worship. It raises the question of whether, if in English services the minister will pray in modern English (or Scottish dialect), this also implies the possibility of reading contemporary translations of the Bible, since the smaller groups tend to use only the Authorized Version.

The Free Church of Scotland (Continuing) seceded from the Free Church of Scotland in 2000 over the controversy whether Professor Donald MacLeod should have been investigated by the Free Church General Assembly. Having separated, its stance was towards a more fundamentalist approach to the Westminster Confession. This Church sings only psalms, without musical instruments. The website for Knock and Point Free Church of Scotland (Continuing) explains that it continues the Communion Season tradition, observed on the fourth Sunday of April and October. Spread over Thursday to Monday, the theme of each of the days is humiliation, self-examination, preparation, celebration and thanksgiving. The website further explained:

> The Sabbath morning is a lengthy and deeply solemn service of worship. First the minister preaches, usually with a focus on the work of Christ and His achievement of salvation. . . . Then the minister 'fences' the table, by identifying who should come forward, and then proceeds to give that invitation. At the Table, he gives an address to direct our thoughts to the Lord, and to communion with Him, and follows the Biblical pattern of 1 Corinthians 11 in the administration of the sacrament.[109]

John Morrison of the Free Church of Scotland (Continuing) wrote a pamphlet entitled *The Lord's Supper*. In the Introduction he asserted that the sacrament is more than a memorial. The Westminster and other Reformed Confessions are cited to illustrate that the tradition has always understood the Supper to have a richer meaning than just a mere remembrance. Like Maclean, he stresses the importance of the action of breaking the bread.

---

108 Kenneth Stewart (ed.), *Songs of the Spirit: The Place of Psalms in the Worship of God*, Glasgow: Reformation Scotland, 2014, p. 16.

109 www.knockfreechurch.org.uk/a-scottish-communion-season/, accessed September 2015.

Although he considered the concepts of transubstantiation, consubstantiation and Calvin's ideas, he is critical of them all. He summarised:

> The purpose of the Lord's Supper then is to remember the Lord's death until He returns on the Last Day, and the spiritual edification of His people, strengthening their faith, building them up in holiness of life, enabling them to loathe and die unto sin, being more devoted and obedient to the Lord, and to renew their love for and enjoy fellowship with one another, it is therefore beneficial in a threefold sense – in relation to God, to Christ as Saviour, and to the brethren. It also points ahead to Christ's second coming, not only in remembering what He has done, but looking forward to His return and subsequent to that the gathering of His people to be forever with Him, and the end of the world.[110]

The Free Presbyterian Church of Scotland continued the practice of lining out, or 'reading the line' of the psalms in Sunday Worship in English, well into the last decades of the twentieth century, though according to Norman Campbell, it is now retained only for the psalmody (116 and 103) at the bi-annual communion celebrations.[111] It sings only unaccompanied psalmody, as evidenced by some of the contributions to Stewart's *Songs of the Spirit* and as announced on its website.

The Reformed Presbyterian Church and the Associated Presbyterian Church both continue the tradition of the Westminster *Directory*, and sing only accompanied psalmody.

Concluding observations

Whereas the Church of Scotland continues to evolve its forms of worship, and in a postmodern age provides for and allows a mixed economy of styles, the smaller bodies have limited changes to hymns, instrumental music, or no change at all, and appear to be attempting to stop the clock as they imagine it was 1644. In a postmodern age this has ecclesial parallels – those wishing to reinstate the so-called Tridentine Mass (in fact, the Missal of 1962) or preserve the services of the Church of England's 1662 Book of Common Prayer. Variety, and treasures new and old, thrive in current postmodernity, but whether the conservative rites or liturgical coelacanths can survive as we move into the ecclesial experiences of the 'Anthropocene age' is another matter. They possibly qualify as liturgical endangered species, and certainly represent a quaint survival. However, when such adherence to a nostalgic worship tradition is regarded as a mark of the true Church, this does raise serious theological questions.

---

110 John Morrison, *The Lord's Supper*, Free Church of Scotland (Continuing), Portmahomack, 2011, p. 11.

111 Norman Campbell, *Reading the Line: An English-language lined-out Psalmody tradition in Presbyterian Scotland*, Stornoway: Stornoway Gazette, 2005.

11

Some Final Thoughts and Reflections

In this study I have opted to use the older metaphor of organic growth and evolution/devolution in liturgy to delineate the developments in worship in the Scottish Presbyterian Churches from 1843 to present practice. Every year many new species are discovered – new in the sense that they have existed for epochs, but undiscovered by scientists until now. The new finds are exciting but thus far have not drastically altered the prevailing narrative of evolution of the universe and life on Earth. It is quite probable that there may well be more collections of Scottish sermons that contain Sunday prayers, such as those of William Logie, or, while printing was affordable, more congregational books, such as that prepared by David Watson, stored in cupboards awaiting rediscovery. There must also be many cyclostyled services lying in folders that were used in the 1970s and 1980s. Such discoveries will deepen the narrative, but it is unlikely that they will drastically alter it.

In the previous chapter, reference was made to the Anthropocene age, which is a proposed new geological term for the human-driven changes to the structure and functioning of the Earth. Most rational people believe that global warming and drastic climate change are real, and happening faster than formerly anticipated. Related to both this, and also to the tension between profitability and ecological necessity, there are rapid changes happening in culture and society. In the face of considerable decline in church life, the Church itself – and its worship – is discerning what mutations might need to take place to adapt to the inhospitable global and cultural climates. Some of the questions this raises are addressed at a practical level by Doug Gay in *Reforming the Kirk*. He argues that the Church of Scotland itself needs devolution and a radical appraisal of how it handles planting churches, administration and the training of ministers. He also raises the question of whether there is a place for a 'national' Church anymore. In his conclusion he notes, 'There will also be a need for further work on liturgical renewal, and I hope to write more on that in the future.'[1]

Though much diminished, the Church of Scotland is still able to play a role in the nation's social changes, as reflected in a service on 21 September

---

1 Doug Gay, *Reforming the Kirk: The Future of the Church of Scotland*, Edinburgh: Saint Andrew Press, 2017, p. 172.

2014 in St Giles' Cathedral, Edinburgh.[2] Following the referendum on independence from the United Kingdom, when the remain vote was won by a small majority, healing of divisions was needed. Finlay Macdonald wrote:

> On the Sunday after the referendum the Moderator, John Chalmers, preached at a 'Service Reflecting Shared Values and Common Purpose' in St. Giles' Cathedral. This was attended by politicians, ecumenical representatives and civic leaders and broadcast worldwide. In a powerful symbolic act, leaders from five parties represented in Parliament came forward, each holding a lighted taper, and together lit a single candle.[3]

In fulfilling this role, a printed order of service was used, and the service included symbolism – hallmarks of worship today. This national role is further illustrated by the prayers that were composed and circulated by the Revd Lezley Stewart and by the Moderator, the Right Revd Colin Sinclair, in response to the 2020 coronavirus pandemic.[4]

Gay has taken his earlier comments on worship a little further in his 2019 address to the Church Service Society.[5] One of the principal concerns he highlights is the apparent misunderstanding of worship by many of those who lead it – a deficit of understanding about to whom worship is addressed and what the various component parts of it are. He urges the Kirk to learn from the charismatic evangelical churches, which is happening in the Church of Scotland and, since 2010, in some Free Church of Scotland congregations. He urges continuing the ecumenical agenda with more dialogue between minister and congregation: 'Technology – service sheets and screens – mean that we don't have to create a people's book, and we don't have to fix our language for all time.' He encourages a continued move towards more regular Communion – monthly, and then weekly. He also stresses that liturgical renewal is a vital part of the *missio Dei*. Uniformity is not the aim, but rather helping people to do better within the styles of worship they favour. Lastly, but importantly, Gay notes that *Common Order* is now twenty-five years old. Though a good book, it is dated:

> We need new resources to accompany joining the church. We need a simpler Communion liturgy and a refreshment of the language of some of

---

2 Available on YouTube, www.youtube.com/watch?v=XeWxZTlaZ-c, accessed 8.12.19. My thanks to St Giles' Edinburgh for sending me a copy of the printed service.

3 Finlay Macdonald, *From Reform to Renewal: Scotland's Kirk Century by Century*, Edinburgh: Saint Andrew Press, 2017, pp. 209–10.

4 Several prayers were published, some ecumenical, and some were translated into Gaelic. The Revd Dr John McPake helped to edit some of them. My thanks to Douglas Galbraith for the information. Some of these are available at www.churchofscotland.org.uk/news-and-events, accessed 14.4.20.

5 Doug Gay, 'Renewing the Church's Worship', *The Record* 54 (2019), pp. 1–17.

the prayers, we need a revision of Common Order by 2024, and CH4 by 2025; the days are over for a book designed to last for 30–40 years. Both would be online resources with print-on-demand copies available, always assuming copyright issues can be overcome.[6]

The Church Service Society also organised a consultation on learning lessons from the theatre. This was not about bringing the stage into worship but about exploring the similarities and asking what might be learnt from theatre. Theatre appeals to the senses – so how can Presbyterian worship appeal more to the senses? It also connects with people mentally and physically, and parallels a spirituality of the whole being, mind and body. It could be that the communion services pioneered by the Revd Dr Scott McKenna, drawing on the Christian mystical as well as mindfulness practices, may have something to teach the wider church.

In an increasingly digital world, a pioneer of online worship with podcasts has been the Very Revd Albert Bogle of Bo'ness, with 'Sanctuary First'. The website explains:

> We seek to be a resource for the wider Christian church and a fresh way to engage with Christianity for those who don't see themselves as part of any church community.
>
> It doesn't matter if you love church and never miss a Sunday, or if you're totally disengaged from it. It doesn't matter if you can't stand church, or if you've never been and are interested to find out more. Everybody is welcome to join in, to learn more about God, Jesus, and the Holy Spirit. Whoever you are, wherever you've come from, we hope you can find a little sanctuary here.
>
> We publish prayers and readings in our Daily Worship which you can access here on the site, through our app, on social media, or by signing up to our email list.
>
> We also regularly produce short films, podcasts, blog posts, live-streamed music and spoken word events, worship leading/personal reflection resources, and training workshops.[7]

There is every reason to expect the Church of Scotland to continue a process of evolution in worship as it seeks to minister in a changing society and culture. Whether these changes will have any impact on the smaller Presbyterian bodies remains to be seen, but while those bodies regard their forms of worship as given for all time, and integral to their identity, it is likely that they will remain in a petrified state. However, to 'fossilise' liturgy is akin to attempting to stop evolution (and time!). Here the words of Dr Robert Lee are still pertinent:

---

6 In the Typescript, p. 12. I am grateful to Douglas Galbraith for furnishing me with a copy. I am unable to find this in the published version in *The Record*.

7 www.sanctuaryfirst.org.uk/about, accessed 11.05.2020.

We cannot make *yesterday to-day*, however we may cherish its memory or value its lessons. It is gone, dead and buried, and we inherit only the legacy it has bequeathed to us . . . Change is the order of the universe, the normal condition of all things mundane and human. Man may modify, he cannot prevent or arrest it; he may use it for his own benefit, but he can no more abrogate this than any other of the laws of nature. The chariot of Divine Providence still moves on in its glorious course, but it crushes those who stand in its way.[8]

---

8 Robert Lee, *The Reform of the Church of Scotland in Worship, Government and Doctrine*. Part 1, Worship, Edinburgh: Edmonston and Douglas, 1864, p. 3

Appendix
The Chapel Royal in Scotland

IAIN R. TORRANCE

The relationship between the Sovereign and the Church of Scotland is completely different from that established in the Church of England. In England, the Sovereign is Supreme Governor of the Church of England, has a formal say in the appointment of bishops and has retained a number of 'royal peculiars' within which worship is conducted outside the authority of the local diocesan bishop. For example, there are royal peculiars at St George's Chapel, Windsor; at Westminster Abbey; at the Chapel Royal within St James's Palace; at The Queen's Chapel of The Savoy; at St Peter ad Vincula in the Tower of London. Some royal peculiars are served by a team of chaplains and a dean appointed by the Queen, while in others services are conducted by chaplains to the Queen in a rota.

Holy Table of the Royal Chapel, Stirling Castle

With the possible exception of the Chapel of the Order of the Thistle, there are no royal peculiars in Scotland. Historically, the court of the King of

Scots moved between several royal palaces (Stirling, Linlithgow, Falkland, Holyroodhouse) and a chaplain and musicians would have moved with the King. The Chapel Royal at Stirling Castle was founded by Pope Alexander VI at the request of James IV and was also endowed as a school for church music. The intention was always that the Chapel Royal should set a standard for choral music and liturgy. It was there that James VI was baptised.

After the succession of James VI to the throne of England in 1603, the practice of maintaining an ecclesiastical household in Scotland fell into desuetude, though a series of Chaplains to The King were appointed by James VI, Charles I and Charles II and the appointment of chaplains remained a royal instrument for liturgical reform.

James VII expelled the reformed congregation which had met for weekly worship in the abbey church at Holyrood and intended that it should become the chapel for his newly created Order of the Thistle. The expelled congregation was housed in the Kirk of the Canongate (built 1688–91), but, deeply suspicious of Catholicism, an Edinburgh mob sacked the abbey church on 11 December 1688, leaving the Order of the Thistle without a home.

Though St Giles' Cathedral in Edinburgh displays an enormous coat of arms of George II dated 1736, the visit of George IV to Edinburgh in 1822 was the first visit by a reigning monarch since the coronation of Charles II at Scone Abbey on 1 January 1651.

The estate and original castle at Balmoral were bought by Prince Albert, the husband of Queen Victoria, in 1852, and remains part of the private property of the royal family and is not part of the Crown Estate. Balmoral became a favourite place for Queen Victoria and her descendants, who always worshipped in the small village church at Crathie, which is less than a mile from the castle. Queen Victoria, to the scandalisation of some of the English bishops, regularly received Communion in Crathie Kirk, as have her descendants. To this day, Queen Elizabeth spends August and September every year at Balmoral. Though Supreme Governor of the established Church of England, when the Queen crosses the border she becomes simply a loyal member of the national Church of Scotland. Crathie Kirk is not a Chapel Royal nor a royal peculiar, though by her choice, once she has come to know him, the Queen appoints the minister of Crathie a Domestic Chaplain.

Crathie Kirk has a number of royal memorials (there is a bust of Queen Victoria and another of King George VI). The Queen enters the church by the south door and sits in the royal pew, but in a way perhaps impossible in England, she is a regular member of the congregation. Worship at Crathie, led by the much-trusted present minister (the Revd Kenneth MacKenzie), is reverent, welcoming and suffers from no artificial formality. The local worshipping community is used to the presence of their Queen and they love her. Scripture is usually read by local elders from a modern translation and the structure of the most recent edition of *Common Order* is followed at communion services. During the summer it is not unusual for visiting choirs to sing an anthem. The composer Paul Mealor has been a regular visitor. Harvest thanksgiving is celebrated. Despite the fact that the Sovereign (and very often the Prince of Wales) are present, this is the characteristic domestic worship of a Scottish country parish. During the months of July and August, the Queen invites visiting preachers to be her guests at Balmoral for the weekend. A list of possible preachers is discussed by the Dean of the Chapel Royal with the minister, whose responsibility it is to send a list for the approval of the Queen. A result of this practice is that the Queen has a remarkably good first-hand knowledge of the Church of Scotland.

The Palace of Holyroodhouse lies within the parish of the Kirk of the Canongate. The Kirk has a royal pew and if she is in Edinburgh over a weekend and not otherwise engaged, the Queen worships there and the minister (currently Neil Gardner) has been appointed another Domestic Chaplain. Other members of the royal family use the Palace of Holyroodhouse on various occasions during the year and their natural place of worship is the Kirk of the Canongate.

Crathie Kirk and the Kirk of the Canongate illustrate successful co-operation between parish churches (not royal foundations or royal peculiars) and the domestic worship of the royal household. They are relationships built on trust, courtesy and respect from both sides.

There are occasional 'National Services' in Scotland, sometimes, but by no means always, held in Edinburgh. Examples might be the Silver, Golden and Diamond Jubilees of Queen Elizabeth. Another was the service to remember the entry of the United Kingdom and the Commonwealth into the First World War. To accommodate a realisation that, though such an event takes place in a particular building (which is not a royal peculiar as might be the case in England), other agencies, denominations and faiths also have a legitimate stake in it, there is a growing sense that these are 'Chapel Royal' rather than local events.

There are ten 'Chaplains-in-Ordinary' to the Queen in Scotland, one of whom is Dean of the Chapel Royal. These are honorary posts and the chaplains assist at various state occasions; over the years they form a relationship of trust with the Queen and other members of the royal family.

In 1905, with a very generous intent, Ronald Ruthven, the eleventh Earl of Leven and tenth Earl of Melville, planned to restore the ruined abbey church at Holyroodhouse as the chapel of the Order of the Thistle. It turned out that the walls of the abbey were too unsound to bear the weight of a new roof and the project stalled. The Earl died in 1906 and the project was continued in 1909 by his son, the twelfth Earl of Leven and his three brothers, who, with the permission of the minister and kirk session of St Giles', built and endowed a new chapel against the southern wall of the cathedral, with its own entrance from the east.

The chapel was designed by Robert Lorimer and is a tiny masterpiece of the arts and crafts movement, with elaborate carvings and a marble floor. The Dean is appointed by the Queen and is not necessarily the minister of St Giles', making the chapel closer to a royal peculiar than any other ecclesial foundation in Scotland. The green service book compiled for the opening of the chapel on 9 July 1911 (with minor adjustments) is still used on each St Andrew's Day.

Two of those prayers follow:

For the Queen's Majesty
Almighty and Everlasting God, Who art the Fountain of unfading light, the Source of abiding goodness, the Consecrator of Kings, and the Dispenser of all honours and dignities, we beseech Thine ineffable mercy for Thy servant, Her Most Sacred Majesty, Queen Elizabeth, that, as Thou hast raised her to the height of royal dignity and power, so Thou wouldest adorn her with wisdom and all other spiritual gifts: and that, since it is by Thy Grace that she reigns, so also she may through Thy mercy, live a happy life, in such wise that, being established on the foundation of faith, hope, and charity, and gladdened by the increase, prosperity, and safety of the people under her sway, she may in this transitory life govern her kingdom and Commonwealth in Thy faith and fear, and hereafter may attain by Thy mercy unto eternal and infinite joy, through Thy Son, Jesus Christ our Lord. Amen.

For the Church
O God, Who art the unchangeable Power and the Everlasting Might, look favourably upon Thy whole Church, that wonderful and sacred Mystery, and by the tranquil operation of Thy perpetual Providence, carry on the work of our salvation, that all the world may see and feel that those things which had fallen down are being raised up, and those things that had grown old are being made new, and that all things are returning unto perfection through Him by Whom Thou madest us and all things, Jesus Christ our Lord. Amen.

Bibliography

A New Directory for the Public Worship of God, fourth edition, Edinburgh: Mac-Niven & Wallace, 1900.

A Road to Roam: A Way of Celebrating Sacred Space, Glasgow: Wild Goose Resource Group, 2006.

A Statement of the Proceedings of the Presbytery of Glasgow, Relative to the Use of an Organ in St. Andrew's Church, in the Public Worship of God, Philadelphia, PA: Anderson, 1821.

A Wee Worship Book, Glasgow: Wild Goose Publications, 1999.

A Wee Worship Book, Glasgow: Wild Goose Publications, 2015.

Acts of the General Assembly of the Church of Scotland 1865 and 1876.

Adamson, Robert M., *The Christian Doctrine of the Lord's Supper*, Edinburgh: T&T Clark, 1905.

Adamson, T. N., 'How to make something of an Iron Church', in *Transactions of the Aberdeen Ecclesiological Society* III (1894), pp. 14–18.

Almond, Hely H., 'Church Music and Choirs', in The Scottish Church Society, *The Divine Life in the Church*, Second Series, vol. 2, Edinburgh: J. Gardner Hitt, 1895, pp. 206–12.

An Order of Divine Service for Children, issued by the Church Service Society, Edinburgh: Blackwood, 1886.

Anderson, James, *The Minister's Directory*, Edinburgh: William P. Nimmo, 1856.

Andrews, William (ed.), *Bygone Church Life in Scotland*, London: William Andrews & Co., 1899.

Anon, *Narrative of Messrs, Moody and Sankey's Labors in Scotland and Ireland, also in Manchester, Sheffield and Birmingham, England*, New York: Anson D. F. Randolph & Co., 1875.

Architectural Drawings of St. Giles' Cathedral, Edinburgh, Scotland's Places, https://scotlandsplaces.gov.uk/record/nrs/RHP6512/architectural-drawings-st-giles-cathedral-edinburgh/nrs, accessed 9.10.2017.

Arnott, David, *Prayers for Public Worship with Baptismal and Communion Services used in St. Giles' Cathedral (High Kirk) Edinburgh*, Edinburgh: William Oliphant & Co., 1877.

Bailie, William Desmond, 'The Rites of Baptism and Admission of Catechumens ('Confirmation') according to the Liturgy and History of the Church of Scotland', PhD thesis, Queen's University Belfast, 1959.

Baillie, Donald M., *The Theology of the Sacraments and Other Papers*, London: Faber & Faber, 1957.

Baillie, John, *Baptism and Conversion*, London: Oxford University Press, 1964.

Baird, John Wilson, 'Second Thoughts on the Book of Common Order', *Church Service Society Annual* 19 (1949), pp. 3–10.

Baker, Jonny and Gay, Doug with Brown, Jenny, *Alternative Worship: Resources from and for the Emerging Church*, Grand Rapids, MI: Baker Books, 2003.

Bannerman, D. D., *The Worship of the Presbyterian Church, with Special Reference to the Question of Liturgies*, Edinburgh: Andrew Elliot, 1884.

Bannerman, D. D., *Difficulties About Baptism*, Edinburgh: Oliphant, Anderson & Ferrier, 1898.

Bannerman, James, *The Church of Christ*, 1869, reprint, Banner of Truth Trust, np, 1960, vol. 1.

Baptie, David, *Musical Scotland: Past and Present*, Paisley: J. & R. Parlane, 1894.

Barkley, John H., 'The Eucharistic Rite in the Liturgy of the Church of Scotland', unpublished thesis submitted for the degree of DD, University of Dublin, 1949.

Barkley, John M., 'The Revision, 1963– 1973', in John M. Barkley (ed.), *Handbook to the Church Hymnary Third Edition*, Oxford: Oxford University Press, 1979, pp. 55–67.

Beckett, David (ed.), *Organs in Greyfriars*, 1990.

Begg, James, *A Treatise on the Use of Organs and Other Instruments of Music in the Worship of God*, Glasgow: D. Niven & Co., 1808.

Begg, James, *Anarchy in Worship, or Recent Innovations contrasted with the Constitution of the Presbyterian Church and the Vows of her Office-Bearers*, Edinburgh: Lyon & Gemmell, 1875, reprint in Begg, James, *Select Works of James Begg on Worship*, Puritan Reprints, np (CPSIA self-publishing), 2007.

Begg, James, *The Use of Organs and other Instruments of Music in Christian Worship Indefensible*, Glasgow: McPhon, 1866. Reprint in Begg, James, *Select Works of James Begg on Worship*, Puritan Reprints (CPSIA), 2017.

Bell, John and Maule, Graham, *When Grief is Raw: Songs for Times of Sorrow and Bereavement*, Glasgow: Wild Goose Publications, 1997.

Bell, John L., 'Scottish Hymnody: An Ecumenical and Personal Perspective', in Duncan B. Forrester and Doug Gay (eds), *Worship and Liturgy in Context: Studies and Case Studies in Theology and Practice*, London: SCM Press, 2009, pp. 259–78.

Bell, John L., *The Singing Thing: A Case for Congregational Song*, Glasgow: Wild Goose Publications, 2000.

Benson, *The English Hymn: Its Development and Use of Worship*, New York: George H. Doran Company, 1915.

Billy Graham Song Book: All-Scotland Crusade 1955, compiled by Cliff Barrows, Pickering & Inglis, Glasgow, 1955.

Bonar, Andrew A., *Memoir and Remains of the Rev. Robert Murray M'Cheyne, Minister of S. Peter's Church, Dundee*, Edinburgh: William Oliphant & Co., 1878.

Boyd, A. K. H., 'The New Hymnology of the Scottish Kirk', *Blackwood's Edinburgh Magazine* May 1889, pp. 657–67.

Boyd, A. K. H., *St. Andrews and Elsewhere*, London: Longmans, Green & Co., 1894.

Boyd, A. K. H., The New Liturgies of the Scottish Kirk', *Blackwood's Edinburgh Magazine* 148 (1890), pp. 659–75.

Boyd, A. K. H., *A Scotch Communion Sunday. To which are added certain Discourses from a University City. By the author of 'The Recreations of a Country Parson'*, London: Henry King & Co., 1873.

Breadalbane, Anne (Anne Mary MacLeod), *Memories of the Manse*, Troy, NY: Nims, 1885.

Brooks, Chris, *The Gothic Revival*, London: Phaidon Press, 1999.

Brown, Callum G., *The People in the Pews: Religion and Society in Scotland since 1780*, Glasgow: The Economic and Social History Society of Scotland, 1993.

Brown, David (ed.), *Duncan, Pulpit and Communion Table*, Inverness: Free Church of Scotland Publications, 1969.

Brown, Stewart J., 'The Ten Years' Conflict and the Disruption of 1843', in Stewart J. Brown and Michael Fry (eds), *Scotland in the Age of the Disruption*, Edinburgh: Edinburgh University Press, 1993, pp. 1–27.

Brown, Stewart J., '"A Solemn Purification by Fire": Responses to the Great War in the Scottish Presbyterian Churches, 1914–19', *Journal of Ecclesiastical History* 45 (1994), pp. 82–104.

Brown, Thomas, *Annals of the Disruption; with extracts from the Narratives of Ministers who left the Scottish Establishment in 1843*, Edinburgh: McNiven & Wallace, 1893.

Brownlie, John, *The Hymns and Hymn Writers of the Church Hymnary*, London and Edinburgh: Henry Frowde, 1911.

Brunton, Alexander, *Forms for Public Worship in the Church of Scotland*, Edinburgh: Myles Macphail, 1848.

Bürki, Bruno, 'Reformed Worship in Continental Europe since the Seventeenth Century', in L. Vischer (ed.), *Christian Worship in Reformed Churches Past and Present*, Grand Rapids, MI: Eerdmans, 2003, pp. 32–65.

Bürki, Bruno, 'The Celebration of the Eucharist in *Common Order* (1994) and in Continental Reformed liturgies', in Spinks and Torrance, *To Glorify God*, pp. 227–39.

Burnet, George B., *The Holy Communion in the Reformed Church of Scotland 1560–1960*, Edinburgh: Oliver & Boyd, 1960.

Caie, Norman Macleod, 'The Jubilee of the Church Organ in Scotland' August 1913, reprinted in *Life and Work*, 12 July 2013, www.lifeandwork.org/features/looking-back-scotland-s-first-church-organ, accessed 28.03.2018.

Cairns, David H., *In Remembrance of Me*, London: Geoffrey Bles, 1967.

Cairns, David, Pitt-Watson, Ian, Whyte, James A. and Honeyman, T. B., *Worship Now: A Collection of Services and Prayers for Public Worship*, Edinburgh: Saint Andrew Press, 1972.

Cairns, John, *Memoir of John Brown DD*, Edinburgh: Edmonston & Douglas, 1860.

Calderwood, W. L. and Woodside, David, *The Life of Henry Calderwood, LL.D., FRSE*, London: Hodder & Stoughton, 1900.

Cameron, Hugh, *Prayers for Use in Public Worship*, Edinburgh: Alexander Brunton, 1921.

Cameron, Nigel M. de S. (ed.), *Dictionary of Scottish Church History and Theology*, Edinburgh: T&T Clark, 1993.

Campbell, Murdoch, *Wells of Joy: Gaelic Religious Poems with Translations by Kenneth MacDonald and Notes by David Campbell*, Kilkerran: Covenanters Press, 2013.

Campbell, Norman, *Reading the Line: An English-language lined-out Psalmody Tradition in Presbyterian Scotland*, Stornoway: Stornoway Gazette, 2005.

Candlish, James S., *The Christian Sacraments*, Edinburgh: T&T Clark, 1879.

Candlish, Robert S., *The Organ Question: Statements by Dr. Ritchie, and Dr. Porteous, For and Against the Use of the Organ in Public Worship in the Proceedings of the Presbytery of Glasgow, 1807–8*, Toronto: Lovell & Gibson, 1859.

Cardale, J., *Readings upon the Liturgy and other Divine Offices of the Church*, 2 vols, London: Barclay, 1874–5.

Carrick, J. C., *Cameron Lees: Queen Victoria's Soul-Friend*, Selkirk: George Lewis & Co., 1914.

Carruthers, Annette, *The Arts and Crafts Movement in Scotland: A History*, New Haven, CT and London: Yale University Press, 2013.

Carstairs, Andrew, *The Scottish Communion Service: With the Public Services for the Fast Day, Saturday and Monday before and after Communion*, Edinburgh: John Anderson, 1829.

Carswell, W. John, 'Becoming Christian: Redeeming the Secular through the *Ordo* of Baptism', PhD thesis, University of Glasgow, 2017.

Chambers, William, *Historical Sketch of St. Giles' Cathedral Edinburgh*, Edinburgh: W. & R. Chambers, 1890.

Charleson, John, 'Rationale and Symbolism of Christian Churches', in *Transactions of the Glasgow Ecclesiological Society 1895*, pp. 39–52.

Charleson, John, *Why I Left the Church of Scotland*, Glasgow: William Hodge & Co., 1901.

Children's Services for Church and Sabbath School, Edinburgh: McNiven & Wallace, 1901.

Church Hymnary, fourth edition, Norwich: Canterbury Press, 2005.

Church of Scotland Office for Worship and Doctrine, *A Welcome to a Child*, Edinburgh: Saint Andrew Press, 2006.

Church of Scotland, *God's Will for Church and Nation. Reprinted from the Reports of the Commission for the Interpretation of God's Will in the Present Crisis as Presented to the General Assembly of the Church of Scotland during the War Years*, London: SCM Press, 1946.

Church of Scotland, *Report of Committee Anent Innovations in Public Worship*, Edinburgh: William Blackwood, 1864.

Church Service Society Minutes 1865–1899. This is a manuscript transcription of the original Minutes.

Clark, Neville and Ronald C. D. Jasper (eds), *Initiation and Eucharist*, London: SPCK, 1972.

Coffey, John, 'Democracy and popular religion: Moody and Sankey's mission to Britain, 1873–1875', in Eugenio F. Biagini, *Citizenship and Community: Liberals, Radicals and Collective Identities in the British Isles, 1865–1931*, Cambridge: Cambridge University Press, 1996, pp. 93–119.

Colvin, Sidney (ed.), *Letters and Miscellanies of Robert Louis Stevenson*, New York: Charles Scribner & Sons, 1900.

Colwell, John, *Promise and Presence: An Exploration in Sacramental Theology*, Eugene, OR: Wipf & Stock, 2010.

Committee on Public Worship and Aids to Devotion, 1. George T. Wright; *Choir Unions*; 2. Millar Patrick, *The Story of the Scottish Psalm Tunes*; 3. W. W. D. Gardiner, *On the Improvement of Public Worship*; 4. Millar Patrick, *The Order of Holy Communion*; 5. Millar Patrick, *The Scottish Collects: From the Scottish Metrical Psalter of 1595*; 6. (no author), *A Course of Reading for the Church Organist*; 7. Thomas Marjoribanks and John Wilson Baird, *A Year's Praise*; 8. G.

Wauchope Stewart and G. T. Wright, *Musical Services*; 9. Alexander Smart, *The Choir Master and His Choir*; 10. Alexander Chisholm, *A Primer of Psalmody*; 11. Thomas Majoribanks, *The Christian Year*; 12. Oswald Milligan, *The Scottish Communion Office and its Historical Background*, Edinburgh, nd (1930s).

Committee on Public Worship and Aids to Devotion of the General Assembly of the Church of Scotland, *The Divine Service*, Oxford: Oxford University Press, 1973.

Common Order, Edinburgh: St Andrew Press, 1994, 1996.

Connor, Steven, *Postmodern Culture: An Introduction to Theories of the Contemporary*, second edition, Oxford: Blackwell, 1997.

Cooper, James, 'Ecclesiology in (of) Scotland', in *Transactions of the Aberdeen Ecclesiological Society* 2 (1895), pp. 31–48.

Cooper, James, 'A Minister's Thoughts in Regard to the Arrangement and Furnishing of a Scottish Parish Church', in *Transactions of the Edinburgh Architectural Association* 4 (1908), pp. 29–40.

Cooper, James, *General Assembly Prayers 1917*, Glasgow: James Maclehose & Sons, 1917.

Cooper, James, *Reliques of Ancient Scottish Devotion*, Edinburgh and London: T. N. Foulis, 1913.

Cooper, James, *The Divine Liturgy: The Order at the Holy Table. East Church of St. Nicholas*, Aberdeen, 1892.

Cooper, James, 'The Order of Divine Service on Week-days, Morning and Evening in the Parish Church of St. Nicholas, Aberdeen'. Typescript 1900, on permanent loan to the Kirk of St Nicholas from the Library of Christ's College, Aberdeen.

Cooper, James, *The Revival of Church Principles in the Church of Scotland. A paper read at a meeting of the North Test Valley Clerical Society, held at Ashe Rectory*, Oxford: Mowbray, 1897.

Cooper, James, *The Revival of Church Principles in the Church of Scotland*, Oxford: Mowbray, 1894.

Cormack, Peter, *Arts and Crafts: Stained Glass*, New Haven, CT: Yale University Press, 2015.

Cotton, John, *The Way of the Churches of Christ in New England*, London 1645, reprint Weston Rhyn: Quinta Press, 2006.

Coulter, David, 'Garrisoning the Nation's Soul: Calvinism, Douglas Haig and Scottish Presbyterian Chaplaincy on the Western Front', in Michael Snape and Edward Madigan (eds), *The Clergy in Khaki: New Perspectives on British Army Chaplaincy in the First World War*, Farnham: Ashgate, 2013, pp. 75–93.

Cumming, John, *The Liturgy of the Church of Scotland, or John Knox's Book of Common Order*, London: J. Leslie, 1840.

Davie, Grace, *Religion in Britain: A Persistent Paradox*, Oxford: Blackwell, 2015.

Deans, Graham D. S., *'Race Shall Thy works Praise unto Race': The Development of Metrical Psalmody in Scotland*, The Hymn Society of Great Britain and Ireland, Occasional Paper 5, np, 2012.

Dewar, Daniel, *Elements of Systematic Divinity*, vol. 3, Glasgow: Thomas Murray & Son, 1866.

Dewar, Daniel, *The Communion Services of the Church of Scotland*, Glasgow and London: W. R. M'Phun, 1859.

Dick, John, *Lectures on Theology*, published under the superintendence of his son, Applegate & Co., Cincinnati, 1858.

Dickson, Nicholas, in *The Kirk and Its Worthies*, Edinburgh: T. N. Foulis, 1914.

Directory and Forms for Public Worship, Edinburgh: McNiven & Wallace, 1909.

Directory of Scottish Architects 1660–1980, www.scottisharchitects.org.uk, accessed 18.09.2017.

Dixon, Hugh, 'The Churches of Frederick Pilkington', *Liturgical Review* 2 (1972), pp. 8–15.

Dods, Marcus, *The Lord's Supper Explained to Young Communicants*, Glasgow: J. N. Mackinlay, 1884.

Donnelly, Mark, *Sixties Britain*, Harlow: Pearson Education, 2005.

Donnelly, Michael, *Scotland's Stained Glass: Making the Colours Sing*, Edinburgh: Historic Scotland, 1997.

Douglas, Fiona Carol, 'Ritual and Remembrance: The Church of Scotland and National Services of Thanksgiving and Remembrance after Four Wars in the Twentieth Century', PhD thesis, University of Edinburgh, 1996.

Dow, John, 'Richard Davidson: Churchman', in Harold W. Vaughan (ed.), *The Living Church*, Toronto: The United Church Publishing House, 1949, pp. 1–26.

Drummond, Andrew L. and Bulloch, James, *The Church in Victorian Scotland 1843–1874*, Edinburgh: Saint Andrew Press, 1975.

Duncan, Andrew, *The Scottish Sanctuary as It Was and as It Is, or, Recent Changes in the Public Worship of the Presbyterian Churches in Scotland*, Edinburgh: Andrew Elliot, 1882.

Dunlop, A. Ian, *The Kirks of Edinburgh 1560–1984*, Edinburgh: Scottish Record Society, 1989.

Edinburgh Evening Courant, 28 December 1865.

Edwall, P., Hayman, E. and William Maxwell (eds), *Ways of Worship: The Report of a Theological Commission of Faith and Order*, London: SCM Press, 1951.

Euchologion or Book of Prayers, Being Forms of Worship Issued by the Church Service Society, Edinburgh: Blackwood, 1867 and subsequent editions.

Farmer, Henry, *A History of Music in Scotland*, London: Hinrichsen, 1947.

Fawcett, Richard (ed.), *Glasgow's Great Glass Experiment: The Munich Glass of Glasgow Cathedral*, Edinburgh: Historic Scotland, 2003.

Fenwick, John and Spinks, Bryan, *Worship in Transition: The Liturgical Movement in the Twentieth Century*, Edinburgh: T&T Clark, 1995.

Ferguson, James, *Prayers for Common Worship*, London: Allenson & Co., 1936.

Ferguson, Ronald, *Chasing the Wild Goose: The Story of the Iona Community*, second edition, Glasgow: Wild Goose Publications, 1998.

Ferguson, Ronald, *George MacLeod: Founder of the Iona Community*, second edition, Glasgow: Wild Goose Publications, 2001.

Fisher, Michael, *'Gothic For Ever': A. W. N. Pugin, Lord Shrewsbury, and the Rebuilding of Catholic England*, Reading: Spire Books Ltd, 2012.

Fisher, R. H., *The Outside of the Inside: Reminiscences of the Rev. R. H. Fisher D.D.*, London: Hodder & Stoughton, 1919.

Forbes, Rebecca F., 'A Highland Sacrament', in *Celtic Monthly* vol. 1. 1893, pp. 61–2.

Forrester, Duncan, 'Worship since 1929', in Duncan B. Forrester and Douglas M. Murray (eds), *Studies in the History of Worship in Scotland*, second edition, Edinburgh: T&T Clark, 1996.

Forsyth, Alexander C., 'The Apostolate of the Laity: A Re-Discovery of Holistic Post-War Missiology in Scotland, with reference to the Ministry of Tom Allan', PhD thesis, University of Edinburgh, 2014.

Franklin, Foster, 'Phases of Order in Church of Scotland Worship', *Church Service Society Annual* 31 (1961), pp. 3–12.

Franklin, R. W., *Nineteenth-century Churches: The History of a New Catholicism in Württemberg, England, and France*, New York and London: Garland Publishing, 1987.

Fraser, A. P. W., 'Praise: The Melody of Religion', in Clement Graham (ed.), *Crown Him Lord of All: Essays on the Life and Witness of the Free Church of Scotland*, Edinburgh: The Knox Press, 1993.

Fraser, Robert W., *The Kirk and the Manse*, Edinburgh: A. Fullarton & Co., 1866.

Free Church of Scotland, *Report of the Committee Appointed to Consider Generally the Legislation of the Church on the Subject of Innovations in Worship*, Edinburgh: Thomas Constable, 1864.

Frost, Thomas, 'Church Music', in William Andrews, *Bygone Church Life in Scotland*, London: William Andrews & Co., 1899, pp. 98–107.

Fyfe, J. G. with J. D. Mackie (eds), *Scottish Diaries and Memoirs 1746–1843*, Stirling: Eneas Mackay, 1942.

Galbraith, Douglas, 'Assist our Song: Theological perspectives on worship and its music', in James C. Stewart (ed.), *A Usable Past? Belief, Worship and Song in Reformation Context*, Edinburgh: Church Service Society, 2013, pp. 58–83.

Garrigan, Kristine Ottesen, *Ruskin on Architecture: His Thought and Influence*, Madison, WI: The University of Wisconsin Press, 1973.

Gay, Doug, 'Renewing the Church's Worship', *The Record* 54 (2019), pp. 1–17.

Geike, Sir Archibald, *Scottish Reminiscences*, Glasgow: James Maclehose, 1904.

Gibson, James, *The Public Worship of God: Its Authority and Modes, Hymns and Hymn Books*, London: James Nisbet, 1869.

Gomme, Andor and David Walker, *Architecture of Glasgow*, London: Lund Humphries, 1968.

Graham, Liz, 'The Evolution and Impact of the Worship of the Iona Community 1938–1998', dissertation for the BD Hons, University of Edinburgh, 1998.

Grant, Maurice, 'The Heirs of the Disruption in Crisis and Recovery 1893–1920', in Clement Graham (ed.), *Crown Him Lord of All: Essays on the Life and Witness of the Free Church of Scotland*, Edinburgh: The Knox Press, 1993, pp. 1–36.

Gray, Arthur Herbert, *As Tommy Sees Us*, London: Edward Arnold, 1919.

Green, Simon, 'William Leiper's Churches', *Architectural Heritage: The Journal of the Architectural Heritage Society of Scotland* 12 (2001), pp. 38–51.

Grierson, James, *A Doctrinal and Practical Treatise on the Lord's Supper*, Edinburgh: John Johnston, 1839.

Grounds and Methods of Admission to Sealing Ordinances, Perth: Andrew Elliot, 1882.

Guthrie, Arthur, *Robertson of Irvine: Poet Preacher*, New York: Thomas Nelson & Sons, 1890.

Hall, Michael, *George Frederick Bodley and the Later Gothic Revival in Britain and America*, New Haven, CT: Yale University Press, 2014.

Hamilton, David S. M., *Through the Waters: Baptism and the Christian Life*, Edinburgh: T&T Clark, 1990.

Harding, Thomas and Bruce Harding, *Patterns of Worship in the United Church of Canada 1925–1987*, Toronto: Evensong Publications, 1996.

Harvie, Christopher, *No Gods and Precious few Heroes: Scotland 1914–1980*, London: Edward Arnold, 1981.

Hen, Yitzhak, 'Key Themes in the Study of Medieval Liturgy', in Alcuin Reid, *T & T Clark Companion to Liturgy*, London: Bloomsbury T&T Clark, 2016, pp. 73–92.

Hewat, Kirkwood (ed.), *M'Cheyne From the Pew: Being Extracts from the Diary of William Lamb*, Stirling: Drummond's Tract Depot, nd.

Hill, Alexander (ed.), *Lectures in Divinity by the late George Hill, D.D.*, New York: Robert Carter, 1847.

Hill, Ninian, *The Scottish Communion Service: A Sermon*, Edinburgh and London: William Blackwood & Sons, 1931.

Hill, Rosemary, *God's Architect: Pugin and the Building of Romantic Britain*, London: Penguin Books, 2008.

Hislop, D. H., *Our Heritage in Public Worship*, Edinburgh: T&T Clark, 1935.

Howell, A. R., 'The Restoration of Paisley Abbey', *Church Service Society Annual* 1 (1928–9), pp. 56–66.

'A Scottish Communion Season', *Knock and Point Free Church of Scotland (Continuing)*, www.knockfreechurch.org.uk/a-scottish-communion-season/, accessed September 2015.

'Order of Service', *Free Presbyterian Church of Scotland*, www.fpchurch.org.uk/about-us/how-we-worship/order-of-service/, accessed 4.12.2019.

Hughes, Kenneth Grant, 'Holy Communion in the Church of Scotland in the Nineteenth Century', PhD thesis, University of Glasgow, 1987.

Hume, John R., *Scotland's Best Churches*, Edinburgh: Edinburgh University Press, 2005.

Huyser-Honig, Joan, 'The Psalm Project: Reworking Genevan Psalms for a New Generation', *Calvin Institute of Christian Worship*, https://worship.calvin.edu/resources/resource-library/the-psalm-project-reworking-genevan-psalms-for-a-new-generation/, accessed 06.05.2020.

Inglis, C. G., 'St. Bride's Parish Church', *Liturgical Studies* [=*Liturgical Review*] 1 (1971), pp. 45–8.

Iona Community Worship Book, np and nd, but inscribed by the purchaser July 1984.

Jaffray, John, *Remarks on the Innovations in the Public Worship of God, Proposed by the Free Presbytery of Hamilton; with an Appendix, containing the Translations and Paraphrases Sanctioned for use of Private Families by the General Assembly, 1751*, Edinburgh: Bell & Bradfute, 1854.

Jasper, Ronald C. D. (ed.), *The Daily Office*, London: SPCK and Epworth Press, 1968.

Jasper, Ronald C. D. (ed.), *The Renewal of Worship*, Oxford: Oxford University Press, 1965.

Jasper, Ronald C. D., *Holy Week Services*, London: SPCK and Epworth Press, 1971.

Johnson, Cuthbert, *Prosper Gueranger (1805–1875): A Liturgical Theologian. An Introduction to his Liturgical Writings and Work*, Rome: Analecta Liturgica 9, Pontificio Ateneo S. Anselmo, 1984.

Johnson, Sarah Kathleen, 'Poured Out: A Kenotic Approach to Initiating Children at a Distance from the Church', *Studia Liturgica* 49 (2020), pp. 175–94.

Johnston, Christopher N., *Life of Andrew Wallace Williamson*, Edinburgh, 1929.

Joseph, James R., 'Sarum Use and Disuse: A Study in Social and Liturgical History', unpublished MA thesis, University of Dayton, OH, 2016.

Kay, James F., 'The New Rites of Baptism: A Dogmatic Assessment', in Spinks and Torrance, *To Glorify God*, pp. 201–12.

Keddie, John W., *Sing the Lord's Song: Biblical Psalms in Worship*, Pittsburgh, PA: Crown & Covenant Publications, 1994/2003.

Keir, Thomas H., 'The Church Hymnary: Third Edition', in *Liturgical Review* 3 (1973) pp. 26–33.

Kelly, Tom Davidson, 'The Manna of Ecclesiology: Contributions by Members of the Church Service Society in the Development of Scottish Ecclesiology from 1863', *The Record* 42 (2006–7), pp. 3–32.

Kelly, Tom Davidson, 'The pre-Disruption ecclesiology of Thomas Smyth Muir of Leith (1 Jan 1803–10 Oct 1888)'. Unfinished notes.

Kelly, Tom Davidson, 'What happened to the Sancta Sanctis?', *The Record* 27 (1994), pp. 30–2.

Kelly, Tom Davidson, *Living Stones: The Daughter Churches of Govan Parish 1730–1919*, Glasgow: The Friends of Govan Old, 2007.

Kennedy, John, 'The Introduction of Instrumental Music into the Worship of the Free Church Unscriptural. Unconstitutional, and Inexpedient, 1883', *John Kennedy of Dingwall*, www.nesherchristianresources.org/JBS/kennedy/Introduction_of_Instrumental_Music.html, accessed 14.02.2020.

Kerr, John, *The Renascence of Worship: The Origin, Aims, and Achievements of the Church Service Society*, Edinburgh: J. Gardner Hitt, 1910.

Kirkpatrick, Roger S., *The Ministry of Dr. John Macleod in the Parish of Govan*, Edinburgh: William Blackwood, 1915.

Lamb, John, 'Aids to Public Worship in Scotland 1800–1850', in *Records of the Scottish Church History Society* 13 (1959), pp. 171–85.

Lawrence, Sarah, *A Rite on the Edge: The Language of Baptism and Christening in the Church of England*, London: SCM Press, 2019.

Leaver, Robin, *A Communion Sunday in Scotland ca.1780*, Lanham, MD: Scarecrow Press, 2010.

Lee, Robert, *Prayers for Public Worship, with Extracts from the Psalter and other Parts of Scripture*, Edinburgh: John Menzies, 1858 (Facsimile reprint, Delhi 2015).

Lee, Robert, *A Presbyterian Prayer-Book and Psalm-Book*, Edinburgh: John Greenhill, 1863.

Lee, Robert, *The Order of Public Worship and Administration of the Sacraments as used in the Church if Greyfriars, Edinburgh* (1864/1873); 1873 edition, Thomas & Archibald Constable, Edinburgh.

Lee, Robert, *The Reform of the Church of Scotland in Worship, Government and Doctrine*, Part 1: Worship, Edinburgh: Edmonston and Douglas, 1864.

Lees, James Cameron, *St. Giles', Edinburgh: Church, College, and Cathedral, from the Earliest Times to the Present Day*, Edinburgh and London: W. & R. Chambers, 1889.

Levison, Frederick, *Christian and Jew: The Life of Leon Levison 1881–1936*, Edinburgh: The Pentland Press, 1989.

Levison, N., *Passiontide, or The Last Days of the Earthly Life of the Master*, Edinburgh: T&T Clark, 1927.

Liston, William, *The Service of the House of God, according to the Practice of the Church of Scotland*, Glasgow: Robert Forester, 1843.

Logie, William, *Sermons and Services of the Church*, Edinburgh: William Oliphant & Sons, 1857.

Louden, R. Stuart, 'The Lee Lecture for 1968', *in Church Service Society Annual* 39 (1969), pp. 27–37.

Lovejoy, Arthur, *Essays in the History of Ideas*, New York: Capricorn, 1960, pp. 234–5.

Lyons, David, *Postmodernity*, second edition, Minneapolis, MN: University of Minnesota Press, 2005.

Macaulay, James, *The Gothic Revival 1745–1845*, Glasgow and London: Blackie, 1975.

Macdonald, Donald, 'Rev Donald Macdonald's resignation letter 31/8/11', *Hebrides News*, www.hebrides-news.com/rev-donald-macdonald-resignation-31811.html and www.bbc.com/news/uk-scotland-glasgow-west-12480877; accessed 19 November 2019.

Macdonald, Finlay, *From Reform to Renewal: Scotland's Kirk Century by Century*, Edinburgh: Saint Andrew Press, 2017.

Macewen, Alexander R., *Life and Letters of John Cairns DD, LLD*, London: Hodder & Stoughton, 1895.

Macfarlane, John C., *An Outline History of Govan Old Parish Church*, Kirk Session, Glasgow: Outram, 1965.

Maclean, Malcolm, *The Lord's Supper*, Fearne: Mentor Press, Christian Focus Publications, 2009.

Maclean, Norman, *The Life of James Cameron Lees*, Glasgow: Maclehose, Jackson & Co., 1922.

Macleod, Norman, *Reminiscences of a Highland Parish*, third edition, London: Strahan & Co., 1871.

MacLeod, George, *We Shall Re-Build*, Philadelphia, PA: Kirkridge, 1945.

Macleod, John, *The Gospel of the Holy Communion*, Glasgow: The Scottish Church Society, 1927.

Macleod, Mark, 'Recent Sacramental Developments in the Kirk', *Theology in Scotland* 22 (2015), pp. 29–60.

Macleod, W. H., 'Church Music and Choirs', in The Scottish Church Society, *The Divine Life in the Church*, Second Series, vol. 2, Edinburgh: J. Gardner Hitt, 1895, pp. 220–6.

MacNab, W. Hunter, 'Leiper's Obituary', *RIBA Journal* 26 August 1916, p. 303.

Marshall, Rosalind K., *St. Giles: The Dramatic Story of a Great Church and Its People*, Edinburgh: Saint Andrew Press, 2009.

Mast, Gregg Alan, *The Eucharistic Service of the Catholic Apostolic Church and Its Influence on Reformed Liturgical Renewals of the Nineteenth Century*, Lanham, MD: Scarecrow Press, 1989.

Maxwell, Jack Martin, *Worship and Reformed Theology: The Liturgical Lessons of Mercersburg*, Pittsburgh, PA: Pickwick Press, 1976.

Maxwell, William D., *An Outline of Christian Worship*, Oxford: Oxford University Press, 1952.

Maxwell, W. D., 'The Book of Common Order of the Church of Scotland, 1940', in W. J. Kooiman and J. M. van Veen (eds), *Pro Regno Pro Sanctuario* (Festschrift for G. van Der Leeuw), Nijkerk: G. F. Callenbach N.V., 1950, pp. 323–31.

McArthur, Allan, *The Christian Year and Lectionary Reform*, London: SCM Press, 1958.

McCarthy, David, *Seeing Afresh: Learning from Fresh Expressions of the Church*, Edinburgh: Saint Andrew Press, 2019.

McCraw, Ian, *Victorian Dundee at Worship*, Dundee: Abertay Historical Society, 2002.

McCrie, Charles Greig, *The Public Worship of the Church of Scotland Historically Treated*, Edinburgh, 1892.

McEwan, John, *Instrumental Music: A Consideration of the arguments for and against its introduction into the worship of the Free Church of Scotland. With a Preparatory note by the Rev. George Smeaton DD, New College, Edinburgh*, Edinburgh: James Gemmell, 1883.

McGilchrist, Iain, *The Master and His Emissary: The Divided Brain and the Making of the Western World*, New Haven, CT: Yale University Press, 2009.

McKinstry, Sam, 'The Architecture of Govan Old Parish Church', 11 March 1992, www.govanold.org.uk/reports/1992_archiotecture.html, accessed 11.09.2017.

McKinstry, Sam, *Rowand Anderson: The Premier Architect of Scotland*, Edinburgh: Edinburgh University Press, 1991.

McLeod, Hugh, *The Religious Crisis of the 1960s*, Oxford: Oxford University Press, 2007.

McMillan, William, 'Euchologion: The Book of Common Order', *Church Service Society Annual* 9 (1936-7), pp. 24-33.

Meikle, William, *Illustrated Guide to St. Giles's Cathedral, Edinburgh, and the Chapel of the Thistle*, Edinburgh: H. & J. Pillans & Wilson, 1919.

Millar, Sandra, *Life Events: Mission and Ministry at Baptisms, Weddings and Funerals*, London: Church House Publishing, 2018.

Miller, Colin F., *Prayers for Parish Worship*, Oxford: Oxford University Press, 1948.

Milligan, Oswald B., *Holy Communion*, The Church of Scotland Committee on Youth, Edinburgh: William Blackwood & Sons, nd.

Milligan, Oswald B., *The Ministry of Worship*, London: Oxford University Press, 1941.

Milligan, Oswald B., *The Practice of Prayer*, Edinburgh: Church of Scotland Committee on Publications, 1938.

Milligan, Oswald, *The Scottish Communion Office and Its Historical Background*, Edinburgh: The Church of Scotland Committee on Publications, nd (*c*.1939).

Milligan, William, *The Ascension and Heavenly Priesthood of Our Lord*, Greenwood, SC: Attic, 1977.

Milligan, William, *The Scottish Church Society*, Edinburgh: J. Gardner Hitt, 1893.

Moffatt, James and Millar Patrick, *Handbook to the Church Hymnary, With Supplement*, London and Edinburgh: Oxford University Press, 1929.

Moffatt, James and Millar Patrick, *Handbook to the Church Hymnary, Revised Edition with Supplement*, London: Geoffrey Cumberlege/Oxford University Press, 1935.

Moore, Lucy, *Messy Church: Fresh Ideas for Building a Christ-Centred Community*, Abingdon: Bible Reading Fellowship, 2006.

Morris, Jeremy, *The High Church Revival in the Church of England: Arguments and Identities*, Leiden: Brill, 2016.

Morrison, John, *The Lord's Supper, Free Church of Scotland (Continuing)*, Portmahomack, 2011.

Morrison, Ruth H. B., 'A Study of the Special Commission on Baptism (1953–63) and Developments in Baptismal doctrine and practice in the Church of Scotland since 1963', PhD thesis, University of Glasgow, 2016.

Morton, Andrew, *The Church Circle*, Edinburgh: Andrew Elliot, 1871.

Morton, T. Ralph, *The Iona Community Story*, London: Lutterworth Press, 1957.

Muir, Thomas S., *A Ramble from Edinburgh to Durham*, Edinburgh: Edinburgh Printing Company, 1843.

Muir, Thomas S., *Descriptive Notices of Some of the Ancient Parochial and Collegiate Churches of Scotland*, London: John Henry Parker, 1848.

Muller, Richard A. and Ronald S. Ward, *Scripture and Worship*, Phillipsburg, NJ: P&R Publishing Company, 2007.

Munro, Donald, 'The Rise and Progress of Evangelical Religion in the Northern Highlands. IV. The Communion Seasons', in *The Monthly Record of the Free Church of Scotland*, November 1918, pp. 178–9.

Murray, Douglas, 'From Disruption to Union', in Forrester and Murray, *Studies in the History of Worship in the Church of Scotland*, pp. 65–95.

Murray, Douglas M., *Rebuilding the Kirk: Presbyterian Reunion in Scotland 1909–1929*, Edinburgh: Scottish Academic Press, 2000.

Murray, Douglas, '"Scoto-Catholicism and Roman Catholicism": John Charleson's conversion of 1901', in *Scottish Church History Society Records* 24 (1992), pp. 305–19.

Murray, Douglas, 'The Barnhill Case, 1901–1904: The Limits of Ritual in the Kirk', in *Records of the Scottish Church History Society* 12 (1986), pp. 259–76.

Murray, Douglas, 'The Scottish Church Society, 1892–1914: A Study of the High Church Movement in the Church of Scotland', PhD thesis, University of Cambridge, 1975.

Murray, Iain H., *Diary of Kenneth A. MacRae*, Edinburgh: Banner of Truth Trust, 1980.

Neale, John Mason, *Hierologus, or the Church Tourists*, London: James Burns, 1843.

Nisbet, J. M., 'Church Music and Choirs', in The Scottish Church Society, *The Divine Life in the Church*, Second Series, vol. 2, Edinburgh: J. Gardner Hitt, 1895, pp. 213–19.

Northern Chronicle, 25 July 1894, p. 6.

O'Neill, John, 'New Testament', in David F. Wright and Gary D. Badcock (eds), *Disruption to Diversity: Edinburgh Divinity 1846–1996*, Edinburgh: T&T Clark, 1996, pp. 73–97.

Ogston, David D. (edited by Johnston McKay), *Scots Worship: Advent, Christmas and Epiphany*, Edinburgh: Saint Andrew Press, 2014.

Ogston, David D. (edited by Johnston McKay), *Scots Worship: Lent, Holy Week and Easter*, Edinburgh: Saint Andrew Press, 2013.

One Hundred Years of Witness, Glasgow: Free Presbyterian Publications, 1993.

Ordinal and Service Book for use in Courts of the Church, Edinburgh: The Church of Scotland Committee on Publications, nd (1931).

Ordinal and Service Book of the Use of Presbyteries, Edinburgh: The Church of Scotland Committee on Publications, nd.

Orr, J. F. G., 'Saint Margaret's Parish Church, Barnhill, Broughty Ferry', in *Transactions of the Scottish Ecclesiological Society* 4 (1913–15), pp. 259–66.

Panel on Doctrine, *Report* May 2003.

Panel on Worship, *Christian Baptism*, Glasgow: Mackay & Inglis, 2001.

Patrick, Millar, 'The Church Worship Association of the United Free Church', in *Church Service Society Annual* 3 (1930–1), pp. 79–82.

Patrick, Millar, *The Order of Holy Communion*, Edinburgh: The Church of Scotland Committee on Publications, second edition, 1933.

Prayers for Divine Service in Church and Home, Edinburgh: William Blackwood & Sons, 1923.

Prayers for Social and Family Worship, Edinburgh: William Blackwood & Sons, 1859.

Prayers for the Christian Year, London: Oxford University Press, 1935.

Prayers for the Christian Year, London: Oxford University Press, 1954.

Presbyterian Forms of Service, Edinburgh: Robert R. Sutherland, 1891.

Presbyterian Forms of Service, Edinburgh; McNiven & Wallace, 1894.

Presbytery of Edinburgh, *Report of Special Committee on Worship and Fellowship*, May 1965.

Primmer, J. Boyd, *Life of Jacob Primmer, Minister of the Church of Scotland*, Edinburgh: William Bishop, 1916.

Purves, David, *The Sacraments of the New Testament*, Edinburgh and London: Oliphant, Anderson & Ferrier, 1904.

Queen Victoria, *More Leaves from the Journal of A life in the Highlands: From 1862 to 1882*, London: Smith, Elder & Co, 1884.

Ralston, Andrew G., *Lauchlan MacLean Watt: Preacher, Poet and Piping Padre*, Glasgow: Society of Friends of Glasgow Cathedral, 2018.

Ramsay, E. B., *Reminiscences of Scottish Life and Character*, twentieth edition, Edinburgh: Edmonston & Douglas, 1871.

Rankin, James, *A Handbook of the Church of Scotland*, Edinburgh: William Blackwood & Sons, 1888.

Reformed Book of Common Order, Edinburgh: Brunswick Impression, 1977.

Remarks on the Innovations in the Public worship of God, Proposed by the Free Presbytery of Hamilton, Edinburgh: Bell & Bradfute, 1854.

Report of Committee Anent Innovations in Public Worship, Edinburgh: William Blackwood & Sons, 1864.

'Report of Special Committee Appointed to Reconsider the Volume "Prayers for Divine service, 1923"', in *Reports to the General Assembly*, May 1925, Edinburgh: Blackwood, 1925.

Report of the Committee appointed to Consider Generally the Legislation of the Church on the Subject of Innovations in Worship, Free Church of Scotland, May 1864, Edinburgh: Thomas Constable, 1864.

Report of the Committee on Aids to Devotion', in *Reports on the Schemes of the Church of Scotland with Legislative Acts Passed by the General Assembly, 1916,* Edinburgh: William Blackwood & Sons, 1916.

Report of the Special Commission on Baptism, May 1962.

Report on Instrumental Music in Public Worship May 1883, Acts of the General Assembly of the Free Church of Scotland, vol. 37, 1883.

Reports of the General Assembly 1936, Edinburgh: Blackwood, 1936.

Reports of the Schemes of the Church of Scotland with the Legislative Acts Passed by the General Assembly 1923, Edinburgh: Blackwood, 1923.

Reports to the General Assembly, Edinburgh, 1990.

Reports to the General Assembly of the Church of Scotland, Edinburgh: Pillars & Wilson, 1987.

Reports to the General Assembly, Edinburgh, 1955.

Review in *Liturgical Review* 9 (1979), pp. 72–5.

Rickman, Thomas, *An Attempt to Discriminate the Style of Architecture in England, from the Conquest to the Reformation*, London: Longman, Hurst, Rees, Orme & Co., 1825.

Roberts, Paul, 'Liturgy and Mission in Postmodern Culture: some reflections arising from "Alternative" services and communities', 1995, http://seaspray.trinity-bris.ac.uk/~robertsp/papers/lambeth.html.

Robertson, A. K., 'The Place of Dr Robert Lee in the Development in the Public Worship of the Church of Scotland 1840–1940', in *Church Service Society Annual* 28 (1958), pp. 31–46.

Robertson, Alastair Kenneth, 'The Revival of Church Worship in the Church of Scotland from Dr. Robert Lee (1804–67) to Dr. H. J. Wotherspoon (1850–1930)', PhD thesis, University of Edinburgh, 1956.

Robertson, Charles, '*Common Order*: An Introduction', in Spinks and Torrance, *To Glorify God*, p. 11.

Robertson, Harry, *The Scotch Minister's Assistant, or a Collection of Forms, for Celebrating the Ordinances of Marriage, Baptism, and the LORD'S SUPPER, according to the Usage of the Church of Scotland, with Suitable Devotions for Church and Family Worship*, Edinburgh: Young & Imray, 1802.

Robertson, Joseph, 'Sketch of the History of Architecture in Scotland, Ecclesiastical and Secular, previous to the Union with England 1701', *Archaeological Journal* 13 (1856), pp. 228–44.

Ruskin, John, *The Seven Lamps of Architecture*, Orpington: George Allen, 1889.

Ruskin, John, *The Stones of Venice*, Volume the Third, xxxix, New York: John Wiley & Sons, 1887.

Russell, James, *Reminiscences of Yarrow*, Selkirk: George Lewis & Son, 1894.

Sanders, John, 'Ecclesiology in Scotland', in Christopher Webster and John Elliott (eds), *'A Church as it Should Be': The Cambridge Camden Society and Its Influence*, Stamford: Shaun Tyas, 2000, pp. 295–316.

Sands, The Hon. Lord, *Life of Andrew Wallace Williamson*, Edinburgh: William Blackwood & Sons, 1929.

Sankey, Ira D., *My Life and the Story of the Gospel Hymns, and of Sacred Songs and Solos*, Philadelphia, PA: P. W. Ziegler Co., 1906.

Saunders, J. Clark, 'George Sprott and the Revival of Worship in Scotland. Part I: Sprott's Theological Principles', *Liturgical Review* 7 (1977), pp. 45–54; Part II: 'Sprott's Liturgical Work', *Liturgical Review* 8 (1978), pp. 11–22.

Schaff, Philip, revised by David S. Schaff, *The Creeds of Christendom with a History and Critical Notes*, Grand Rapids, MI: Baker Books, 1998 reprint, vol. 3.

Schenk, H. G., *The Mind of the European Romantics: An Essay in Cultural History*, London: Constable, 1966.

Schmidt, Leigh Eric, *Holy Fairs, Scotland and the Making of American Revivalism*, second edition, Grand Rapids, MI: Eerdmans, 2001.

Scott, John A., 'Recovering the Meaning of Baptism in Westminster Calvinism in Critical Dialogue with Thomas F. Torrance', PhD thesis, University of Edinburgh, 2015.

Service, John, *Prayers for Public Worship*, London: Macmillan & Co., 1885.

Shanks, Norman, 'The Worship of the Iona Community and its Global Impact', in Duncan B. Forrester and Doug Gay (eds), *Worship and Liturgy in Context. Studies and Case Studies in Theology and Practice*, London: SCM Press, 2009, pp. 230–45.

Shanks, Norman, *Iona: God's Energy. The Vision and Spirituality of the Iona Community*, Glasgow: Wild Goose Publications, 2009.

Shirley, 'Dr. Robert Lee of Edinburgh: A Sketch by Shirley', *in Fraser's Magazine*, New Series vol. 1, London: Longmans, Green & Co., 1870, pp. 86–106.

Simpson, Robert Stephenson, *Ideas in Corporate Worship*, Edinburgh: T&T Clark, 1927.

Sjölinder, Rolf, *Presbyterian Reunion in Scotland 1907–1921*, Uppsala: Almqvist & Wieksells Boktryckeri AB, 1962.

Smith, James Cromarty, *This Do: A Christian's Bounden Duty*, Coatbridge: Alex Pettigrew, 1908 and 1911.

Spinks, Bryan D., '"Freely by His Grace": Baptismal Doctrine and the Reform of the Baptismal Liturgy in the Church of Scotland, 1953–1994', in Nathan Mitchell and John F. Baldovin (eds), *Rule of Prayer, Rule of Faith: Essays in Honor of Aidan Kavanagh, OSB*, Collegeville, NJ: Liturgical Press, 1996, pp. 218–42.

Spinks, Bryan D., 'Ecclesiology and Soteriology Shaping Eschatology: The Funeral Rites in Perspective', in Spinks and Torrance, *To Glorify God*, pp. 187–99.

Spinks, Bryan D., 'Karl Barth's Teaching on Baptism: Its Development, Antecedents and the Liturgical Factor', *Ecclesia Orans* 14 (1997), pp. 261–88.

Spinks, Bryan D., 'The Ascension and Vicarious Humanity of Christ: The Christology and Soteriology Behind the Church of Scotland's Anamnesis and Epiklesis', in J. Neil Alexander (ed.), *Time and Community*, Washington DC: The Pastoral Press, 1990, pp. 185–201.

Spinks, Bryan D., 'The Origins of the Antipathy to Set Liturgical Forms in the English-Speaking Reformed Tradition', in Lukas Vischer (ed.), *Christian Worship in Reformed Churches Past and Present*, Grand Rapids, MI: Eerdmans, 2003, pp. 66–82.

Spinks, Bryan D., *Freedom or Order? The Eucharistic Liturgy in English Congregationalism 1645–1980*, Allison Park, PA: Pickwick Publications, 1984.

Spinks, Bryan D., *The Rise and Fall of the Incomparable Liturgy: The Book of Common Prayer, 1559–1906*, London: SPCK, 2017.

Spinks, Bryan D., *The Worship Mall: Liturgical Initiatives and Responses in a Postmodern Global World*, London: SPCK, 2010; Church House Publishing USA edition, 2011.

Spinks, Bryan D., *Two Faces of Elizabethan Anglican Theology: Sacraments and Salvation in the Thought of William Perkins and Richard Hooker*, Lanham, MD: Scarecrow Press, 1999.

Spinks, Bryan D. and Iain R. Torrance (eds), *To Glory God: Essays on Modern Reformed Liturgy*, Edinburgh: T & T Clark, 1999.

Sprott, G. W., *The Worship, Rites, and Ceremonies of the Church of Scotland*, Edinburgh: Blackwoods, 1863.

Sprott, G. W., *The Worship and Offices of the Church of Scotland*, Edinburgh: William Blackwood and Sons, 1882.

Stamp, Gavin, 'The Victorian Kirk: Presbyterian Architecture in Nineteenth-Century Scotland', in Chris Brooks and Andrew Saint (eds), *The Victorian Church: Archi-*

tecture and Society, Manchester and New York: Manchester University Press, 1995, pp. 98–117.

Stamp, Gavin, *Gothic for the Steam Age: An Illustrated Biography of George Gilbert Scott*, London: Aurum Press, 2015.

Stevenson, Kenneth W., 'The Catholic Apostolic Eucharist', PhD thesis, University of Southampton, 1973.

Stevenson, Kenneth, 'The New Marriage Rites: Their Place in the Tradition', in Spinks and Torrance, *To Glorify God*, pp. 173–86.

Stewart, David A., revised Alan Buchan, *Organs in Scotland: A Revised List*, Edinburgh: The Edinburgh Society of Organists, 2018.

Stewart, James C., 'Cooper as Liturgiologist', *The Record* 29 (1995), pp. 17–29.

Stewart, Kenneth (ed.), *Songs of the Spirit: The Place of Psalms in the Worship of God*, Glasgow: Reformation Scotland, 2014.

Stewart, Lezley J., *When Two or Three are Gathered: Themes Resources for Group Worship*, Edinburgh: Saint Andrew Press, 2014.

Stewart, Lezley J., *Celebrating Life in Death: Resources for Funerals, Thanksgiving and Remembering*, Edinburgh: Saint Andrew Press, 2016.

Stewart, Lezley J., *Let Everyone Find Their Voice: Worship Resources Inspired by the Psalms*, Edinburgh: Saint Andrew Press, 2020.

Storrar, William, 'From *Braveheart* to Faint-Heart: Worship and Culture in Post-Modern Scotland', in Spinks and Torrance (eds), *To Glorify God*, pp. 69–84.

Story, Robert H., *Life and Remains of Robert Lee, DD*, 2 volumes, London: Hurst & Blackett, 1870.

Struthers, Gavin, *A History of the Rise, Progress and Principles of the Relief Church*, Glasgow: A. Fullerton & Co., 1843.

Subordinate Standards of the United Presbyterian Church, Edinburgh: United Presbyterian College Buildings, 1880.

Tait, J. H., 'Letter to the Parishioners of Aberlady, November 1866', copy in the Church Service Society archives.

The Abbey Services of the Iona Community, The Iona Community, Glasgow (nd, but which John Harvey dates as 1956: email 7 January 2019).

The Bailie (newspaper), No. 1480, Glasgow, 27 February 1901.

The Biblical Doctrine of Baptism, Edinburgh: Saint Andrew Press, 1958.

The Book of Common Order (1979), Edinburgh: Saint Andrew Press, 1979.

The Book of Common Order of 1940 Examined, Inverness-shire: The National Church Association, 1955.

The Book of Common Order of the United Church of Canada, Toronto: The United Church Publishing House, 1932.

The Builder 1863, http://archiseek.com/2010/1863-free-west-church-greenock-scotland/, accessed 18.09.2017.

The Building News, 20 January 1882.

The Church Hymnary, Revised Edition, London: Oxford University Press/Humphrey Milford, 1927.

The Church Hymnary, Third Edition, London: Oxford University Press, 1973.

The Church Hymnary: Authorized for Use in Public, Worship by the Church of Scotland, the United Free Church of Scotland, the Presbyterian Church in Ireland, the Presbyterian Church of Australia, the Presbyterian Church of New Zealand, Edinburgh: Henry Frowde, 1902.

The Church of Scotland, 'Service of Unity and Common Purpose, St Giles Cathedral, September 21 2014', YouTube, www.youtube.com/watch?v=XeWxZTlaZ-c, accessed 06.05.2020.

The Church of Scotland Mission and Discipleship Council, *The Setting of Presbyterian Worship*, Committee on Church Art and Architecture, May 2014.

The Courage to Say No: Twenty-three Songs for Lent and Easter, Glasgow: Wild Goose Publications, 2004.

The Daily Review (Edinburgh), 1 March 1866 and 2 May 1866.

The General Assembly's Panel on Worship, *Prayers for Contemporary Worship*, Edinburgh: Quorum Press, 1977.

The Iona Community Worship Book, Glasgow: Wild Goose Publications, 1991 revised edition.

The Iona Community: Personal Impressions of the Early Years, Edinburgh: Saint Andrew Press, 1977.

The Joint Commission on Doctrine of the Church of Scotland and the Roman Catholic Church in Scotland, *Liturgy for the Reaffirmation of Baptismal Vows*, np, 2010.

The Late Late Service, printed by The Late Late Service, Glasgow, 1993.

The Manual of the Guild of S. Margaret of Scotland. The Parish of S. Nicholas, Aberdeen, Aberdeen: W. Jolly & Sons, 1893.

The Order of Divine Service and Sundry Other Services as used with the Canongate Kirk (the Kirk of Holyroodhouse) and Edinburgh Castle, third edition, Edinburgh: Oliver & Boyd, 1957.

The Panel on Worship, *Worshipping Together*, Edinburgh: Saint Andrew Press, 1991.

The Piper O'Dundee, 5 March, 7 May 1887; 4 July, 11 July, 25 July, 22 August, 26 September, 17 October, 31 October, 27 November, 19 December 1888; 20 February, 22 May, 27 November 1889.

The Record of the Free Church of Scotland, 1 October 1863, pp. 350–3.

The Scotsman, 22 November 1918.

The Scotsman, 15 March 1867.

The Scotsman, 27 May 2012, www.scotsman.com/news-2-15012/churches-in-discord-over-hymn-singing-1-2320714, accessed 19.11.2019.

The Second Prayer Book of King Edward the Sixth (1552). With Historical Introduction and Notes by the Rev. H. J. Wotherspoon, M.A., of St. Oswald's, Edinburgh; and The Liturgy of Compromise, used in the English Congregation at Frankfort. From an Unpublished MS. Edited by the Rev. G. W. Sprott, London: Blackwood & Sons, 1905.

The St. Andrews University Psalter, St Andrews: W.C. Henderson & Sons (University Press), 1928.

The United Presbyterian Magazine, August 1884.

The Working Group on the Place and Practice of Holy Communion, *Celebrating Holy Communion*, Edinburgh: Saint Andrew Press, 2010.

Thirty Years of Broughton Place Church, Edinburgh: Howie & Seath, 1914.

Thomson, Alexander, 'An Inquiry as to the Appropriateness of the Gothic Style for the Proposed Buildings for the University of Glasgow, with some Remarks upon Mr. Scott's Design', in *Proceedings of the Glasgow Architectural Society*, 1865–6.

Thomson, D. M., *The Corstorphine Hierloom: A History of the Old Parish Church of Corstorphine*, Edinburgh: J. Blackie, 1846.

Thomson, Peter D., *'Common Order', The Record* 27 (1994), pp. 27–29.

Thornton, Cecil T., 'The St Giles Book of Common Order 1884–1926', Church Service Society Annual 24 (1954), pp. 35–40.

Thurian, Max (ed.), *Churches Respond to BEM: Official Responses to the "Baptism, Eucharist and Ministry" Text*, vol. 1, Geneva: World Council of Churches, 1986.

Thurian, Max (ed.), *Churches Respond to BEM: Official Responses to the "Baptism, Eucharist and Ministry" Text*, vol. 4, Geneva: World Council of Churches, 1987.

Thurian, Max and Geoffrey Wainwright (eds), *Baptism and Eucharist: Ecumenical Convergence in Celebration*, Geneva: World Council of Churches, 1983.

Todd, A. Stewart, *'Common Order', The Record* 27 (1994), pp. 22–6.

Todd, A. Stewart, 'The Ordering of Eucharistic Worship', *Liturgical Review* 7 (1977), pp. 11–19.

Together in Worship, Edinburgh: Saint Andrew Press, 1969.

Torrance, Iain, 'Fear of being Left Out and Confidence in being Included: The Liturgical Celebration of Ecclesial Boundaries. A Comment on the Baptismal Liturgies of the *Book of Common Worship* (1993) and *Common Order* (1994)', in Spinks and Torrance, *To Glorify God*, pp. 159–72.

Torrance, T. F., *Interim Report of the Special Commission on Baptism: Reports to the General Assembly 1959*, Edinburgh, 1959.

Torrance, T. F., 'The One Baptism Common to Christ and His Church', in Torrance, *Theology in Reconciliation*, pp. 82–105.

Torrance, T. F., 'The Paschal Mystery of Christ and the Eucharist', in *Theology in Reconciliation*, pp. 106–38.

Torrance, T. F., *Theology in Reconciliation: Essays Towards Evangelical and Catholic Unity in East and West*, London: Geoffrey Chapman, 1975.

Transactions of the Aberdeen Ecclesiological Society 11 (1896).

Transactions of the Glasgow Ecclesiological Society 1 1894 (1895).

Transactions of the Scottish Ecclesiological Society 1 (1904).

Transactions of the Scottish Ecclesiological Society 2, Part 1, 1906–7 (1907).

United Free Church of Scotland, *Book of Common Order*, London: Oxford University Press, 1928.

University of Glasgow. Class of Church History. Office for the Annual Visit to Glasgow Cathedral, Glasgow: Robert Maclehose & Co., 1909.

University of St. Andrews Chapel Service Book, St Andrews: W. C. Henderson & Son (University Press), 1931.

'Use of "Euchologion"', Church Service Society archives, nd.

Veitch, James, *Statement Concerning Innovations as now attempted in the Church of Scotland*, Edinburgh: Blackwood, 1866.

Warr, Charles Laing, *The Glimmering Landscape*, London: Hodder & Stoughton, 1960.

Warr, Charles Laing, *The Presbyterian Tradition: A Scottish Layman's Handbook*, London: Maclehose & Co., 1933.

Watson, David, *Common Prayer and Praise*, at the University Press, Glasgow: Robert Maclehose & Co, 1902.

Watt, L. MacLean, *The Communion Table*, London: Hodder & Stoughton, 1903.

Watt, L. MacLean, *The Minister's Manual*, London: Allenson & Co, 1934.

Watt, L. MacLean, *By Still Waters*, Edinburgh: Blackwood & Sons, 1904.

Watt, L. MacLean, *Prayers for Public Worship*, London: Hodder & Stoughton, 1924.

Watts, Malcolm H. and David Silversides (eds), *The Worship of God*, Edinburgh: Marpet Press, 1998.

Webster, Christopher and John Elliott (eds), *'A Church as it Should Be': The Cambridge Camden Society and its Influence*, Stamford: Shaun Tyas, 2000.

Whatley, Christopher A. (ed.), *The Diary of John Sturrock, Millwright, Dundee 1864–65*, East Linton: Tuckwell Press, 1996.

Whitson, William, *Sunday Morning: A Guide to the Christian Celebration*, Coatbridge, 1974.

Wild Goose Prints No.1, Glasgow: Wild Goose Publications, 1989.

Wilkins, Francis, *Singing the Gospel along Scotland's North-East Coast, 1859–2009*, Abingdon: Routledge, 2018.

Williamson, Andrew Wallace, *Ideals of Ministry*, Edinburgh: William Blackwood & Son, 1901.

Williamson, Colin R., 'General Assembly Prayers 1917', *The Record* 29 (1995), pp. 30–2.

Williamson, Elizabeth, Anne Riches and Malcolm Higgs, *Glasgow*, London: Penguin Books, 1990.

Winter, J. M., *The Great War and the British People*, London: Macmillan, 1986.

With the Colours: For God, King and Country, Edinburgh: Thomas & Archibald Constable, 1918.

Woolf, Virginia, 'Mr. Bennett and Mrs. Brown', a paper read to the Heretics, Cambridge, 1 May 1924, London: Hogarth Press, 1924.

Woolfenden, Graham, '"Everyday will I bless you, and praise your name forever and ever": Daily Prayer in *Common Order* and the *Book of Common Worship*', in Spinks and Torrance, *To Glorify God*, pp. 213–25.

Working Party on Worship. Draft Report to Assembly (as appendix to Committee's report), typescript, dated 15 December 1971.

World Council of Churches, 'Worship and the Oneness of Christ's Church'. Text in *Studia Liturgica* 2 (1963), pp. 243–55.

World Council of Churches, *One Baptism: Towards Mutual Recognition*, A Study Text, Geneva: World Council of Churches, 2011.

Worship Now Book II, compiled by Duncan D. Forrester, David S. M. Hamilton, Alan Main and James A. Whyte, Edinburgh: Saint Andrew Press, 1989.

Wotherspoon H. J. and J. M. Kirkpatrick, *A Manual of Church Doctrine according to the Church of Scotland*, London: Hodder & Stoughton, 1919.

Wotherspoon, H. J., *James Cooper: A Memoir*, London: Longmans, Green & Co., 1926.

Wotherspoon, H. J., *Kyrie Eleison: A Manual of Private Prayer*, Philadelphia, PA: The Westminster Press, 1905.

Wotherspoon, H. J., *Religious Values in the Sacraments*, Edinburgh: T & T Clark, 1928.

Wotherspoon, H. J., *The Divine Service: A Eucharistic Office According to the Forms of the Primitive Church*, London: Hodder & Stoughton, 1919.

Wright, David F., *Infant Baptism in Historical Perspective: Collected Studies*, Bletchley: Paternoster Press, 2007.

Wright, David F., *What has Infant Baptism done to Baptism? An Enquiry at the End of Christendom*, Bletchley: Paternoster Press, 2005.

Wright, Ronald Selby, *The Kirk in the Canongate: A Short History from 1128 to the Present Day*, Edinburgh: Oliver & Boyd, 1956.

Wright, Ronald Selby, 'Peace and Safety', *Church Service Society Annual* 25 (1955), pp. 9–21.

Yancey, Hogan L., 'The Development of the Theology of William Milligan (1821–1893)', PhD thesis, University of Edinburgh, 1970.

Young, William, 'Funerals in a rural parish', *The Record* 14 (1986) pp. 2–8.

Index